MENTAL HEALTH
AND
CONSTRUCTIVE BEHAVIOR

Wadsworth Publishing Company, Inc.
Belmont, California

MENTAL HEALTH AND CONSTRUCTIVE BEHAVIOR

E. Paul Torrance

University of Minnesota

To Pansy, my wonderful wife,
who helps me to respond more construc-
tively to stress

Preface

In this book the author presents the concept of healthy personality development and mental functioning as responding constructively to stress rather than merely adapting or adjusting to stress. He has tried to give *mental functioning* and *stress* their rightful place in the study of personality development and mental health. Generally, authors of textbooks and teachers of courses in this field have proclaimed at the outset that emphasis will be placed on the *emotional aspects* of personality development and mental health, although other aspects will not be ignored. Rarely is the concept of stress and the accumulated knowledge concerning man's ways of responding to stress even mentioned in such books or courses. The author believes that *mental functioning* and *stress* are key concepts in a consideration of the problems of personality development and mental health and that a comprehension of the accumulated knowledge concerning them is essential in the work of teachers, counselors, school administrators, school psychologists, nurses, and others who are concerned about these problems.

In every chapter of this book, the author has tried to recognize and deal with the importance of the emotional aspects of personality development and mental health, but the focus is always on healthy mental functioning in coping with life's stresses. The plot always deals with the ways by which the emotional factors disturb or facilitate the mental operations or the ways by which mental functioning affects emotional well-being and personality development.

In describing existing theories and research, the author has tried to penetrate and reconcile many apparent conflicts in them. Old ideas have been reinterpreted in the light of recent research, especially that concerning psychological stress and some of the newer understandings of the human mind and its functioning.

The author has attempted to cast existing knowledge concerning personality development and mental hygiene into a simple yet practical and potent conceptual framework. This framework should enable the reader to organize his present knowledge, the information presented in this book, and his day-to-day experiences. The material presented is intended to help the reader *to learn better how to learn* about problems of personality development and mental health. Throughout the text, the reader is asked to do specific things that will help him to learn more about these problems and to apply research information and theory to these problems. Professional training in education, psychology, and social work can be effective only when individuals develop skills in applying new information to professional problems.

The author presents mental health as a matter of responding constructively to stress, and personality development as a matter of developing skills and resources for dealing constructively with life stresses. The effects of stress on personality development and mental health are determined by three variables: the duration of the stress, the intensity of the stress, and the state of the organism. Stressful conditions lead to a variety of effects, both desirable and undesirable, depending upon these three interacting variables. On the basis of existing research evidence, experience, and observation, the author proposes a set of general guides to understanding human behavior, especially mental functioning, and to assisting individuals and groups to achieve their highest potential.

This book brings to bear on problems of personality development and mental hygiene much recent and not very well-known research concerning breakdown, stress, behavior in emergency and extreme conditions, and intellectual functioning, especially creative thinking and decision making. The author has conducted six years of research in human behavior in emergency and extreme conditions and in ways of helping individuals behave more effectively and sensibly under such conditions, and another six years of research in thinking, especially creative thinking. Examples in this book come from a variety of human experiences—families, schools, hospitals, playgrounds, businesses, industry, military groups, and the like. The author has been a high school teacher, principal, and counselor; a college teacher and counselor; and a scientist who lived close to United States Air Force survival training for six years. Many illustrations are drawn from the experiences of members of classes in personality development and mental hygiene. These students have developed a number of new ideas for solving recurrent problems affecting personality development and mental health in the fields of education, school administration, counseling and guidance, coaching, recreational leadership, special education, nursing and nursing education, industrial consulting, social work, and religion.

Practically everything that one does to try to improve personality and mental health in any situation is influenced at every step by his concept of the meaning of mental health. Part One, thus, deals with mental health as constructive response to stress. The first chapter considers criteria of mental health. The author attempts to synthesize a variety of ideas, which he hopes will help the reader clarify his concepts sufficiently so that he can cope constructively with problems in this field more effectively. In the second chapter, he expands upon the idea that personality development occurs in response to stressors both internal and external and that the effects therefrom are mediated by the three variables: the intensity of the stress, the duration of the stress, and the state of the organism. In the next two chapters, the author attempts to summarize what is known about how the first two variables affect constructive behavior and bring about breakdown.

The remainder of the book deals with the third set of variables, the state of the organism or a person's resources for coping constructively with stress. Part Two deals with personality resources for responding to stress. A description is given of the processes through which personality development goes awry, and of the most common warning signs that something is going wrong.

Part Three deals with group resources for responding to stress. In this section, the author applies many of the ideas developed in Part One to the problems of groups in coping with stress and maintaining healthy functioning. Groups are viewed as organisms. The characteristics of healthy groups are identified, as are the warning signs that development and functioning have gone wrong.

Part Four deals with mental operations and their role in coping constructively with stress. This section discusses one of the most useful conceptualizations of mental abilities and mental functioning thus far advanced, J. P. Guilford's "structure of intellect." Each of Guilford's mental operations (cognition, memory, convergent production, divergent production, and evaluation) is examined, and some suggestions are made for developing and freeing these operations to make possible constructive behavior.

E. Paul Torrance

Contents

Contents

Mental Health:
Constructive
Response to
Stress

1

Meaning of
Mental
Health

1

A society's concept of the meaning of mental health and personality adjustment determines in a large measure its child-rearing procedures, its educational practices, and most of its institutions. A classroom teacher's concept of the meaning of mental health strongly influences his relationships with his students, his disciplinary procedures, his evaluation procedures, and the content of the curriculum. Similarly, the activities of school administrators, counselors, psychologists, social workers, probation and police workers, ministers, physicians and psychiatrists, nurses, and others are determined in a large measure by their concepts of mental health.

What is mental health? Which is more useful in guiding professional behavior—a list of detailed criteria, a single criterion, a set of interrelated criteria, or an organized theoretical formulation? In this chapter, we shall examine several concepts of mental health and personality adjustment. First, we shall examine some of our society's concepts. Next, we shall take a look at some of the efforts of professional groups to formulate a useful set of criteria of mental health and try to understand the difficulties with which they have struggled.

SOCIETY'S CONCEPTS

If the child-rearing procedures, educational practices, and institutions of a society are guided by a society's concepts of "mental health," it is to be expected that these concepts will be reflected in the ideas of school children. In fact, the stories written by children portray these concepts most eloquently. Several thousand children in several countries were asked to write imaginative stories about animals and persons with some divergent characteristic, such as the flying monkey, the lion that won't roar, the boy who wants to be a nurse, and the girl who wants to be an engineer. Let us examine some of the most common themes of the stories written by children in the United States.

CONFORMITY

By far the most frequent theme of children in schools in the United States is that of conformity. To be considered mentally healthy, one must conform to the behavioral norms of the society. The following story by a fifth grade girl illustrates this theme:

> Far into the jungle of Africa lived a flying monkey named Pepper. Pepper was a well-educated monkey and very cute. . . . Pepper was unusual too. He was not like all of the other flying monkeys. You see, Pepper didn't eat bananas like everybody else. He wanted to be different. He ate peppers!
>
> No one ever went out of the jungle so Pepper, being different, decided to go to America! . . . When the people saw him, they began to laugh and then others began to scream. Then out of nowhere a man from a zoo came and took Pepper by surprise. . . .
>
> Now Pepper was sad. He didn't like the cage they put him in. He made a vow that if he ever got out he would never be different again and ten minutes later he saw some bent bars big enough to fly through. All of a sudden he flew out and in two days was back in the jungle. He kept his promise too. He was never different again. He was a good little flying monkey.

About two thirds of the stories about flying monkeys tell similar tales of conformity or of destruction. Some cultures and subcultures, however, are more indulgent of divergency than others. Stories written by gifted children in special classes are far more hopeful in outlook than those of gifted children in regular classes. In about 70 per cent of the stories of pupils in classes for high-achieving children, the flying monkey is in some way able to persist in his flying. The stories written by children in a small Oklahoma town composed of Indians, whites, and a few Negroes also reflect this tolerance of divergency. In 74 per cent of their stories, the flying monkey succeeds. The story which follows reflects some interesting aspects of this tolerance:

> Once upon a time there was a monkey named Jocko. He was not an ordinary monkey. So one day when he was flying he met up with a crow. The crow spoke but Jocko couldn't so he just grumbled. When he grumbled he scared the crow away. When he met a flying worn out shoe he knew the flying country was just ahead of him so he gained altitude and boy did he fly! When he got to the flying country, he saw flying castles, shoes, houses, cows, pigs, horses. "Boy is this strange!" he said to himself. "I thought I was the only flying monkey on earth but I'm not." He looked around and there it was. Just what he was

4

looking for, a beautiful flying princess and I mean it. And after they got married, they lived happily ever after.

It is interesting to note that the subculture from which this story came has produced such individuals as the humorist-philosopher Will Rogers and the ballerina Maria Tallchief. Stories obtained from several groups in New Mexico reflect even greater tolerance of divergency than those obtained from Oklahoma. Although there are many other factors to be considered, this tolerance of divergency may explain in part the fact that New Mexico has 116 mental hospital residents per 100,000 population while New York State has 589 per 100,000 and the District of Columbia has 866 per 100,000 (Joint Commission on Mental Illness and Health, 1961).

The effects of a society's concepts of conformity are so penetrating that they are manifested in professional behavior, as well as in the imaginative stories of children. Perhaps the most common offenders are personality tests as currently used in education, industry, and psychiatry. It is well known that conformity is factored into most such instruments.

Whyte's (1956) *The Organization Man* includes a long critique of personality tests. For example, Whyte gives the "ideal executive" profile of Sears, Roebuck on the Allport-Vernon-Lindzey *Study of Values*. The highest point on the profile is Economic and the lowest is Aesthetic, with Theoretical, Social, and Political all just above the fiftieth percentile compared with norm groups. It is interesting to compare this profile with those of MacKinnon's (1960) highly effective persons. In every field studied by MacKinnon and his associates, the high points on the profiles were Aesthetic and Theoretical. Whyte (1956, p. 219) also reported that not one of the corporation presidents he tested had a profile that fell completely within the usual "acceptable" range.

The conformity factor in personality tests is reflected in Whyte's now classical advice for cheating on personality tests in order to get a job. He counsels test-takers to observe two rules:

1. When asked for word associations or comments about the world, give the most conventional, run-of-the-mill, pedestrian answer possible.

2. When in doubt about the most beneficial answer to any question repeat to yourself:
   I love my father and my mother, but my father a little bit more.
   I like things pretty much the way they are.
   I never worry much about anything.
   I don't care for books or music much.
   I love my wife and children.
   I don't let them get in the way of company work. (Whyte, 1956, p. 217)

THE WELL-ROUNDED PERSONALITY

Another concept of mental health seared into the minds of children is that of "the well-rounded personality." Many children intuitively recognize the fallacy of this concept but see the pressures of society for the well-rounded personality to be quite relentless. The pressures are seen as most severe when some skill highly valued by society has not been adequately developed. For example, verbal skills are highly valued in our society. Consider the following story by a sixth grade girl:

> Whack! Whack! They were after him again—the Ladies Duck Aid Society, with their hair up in pin curls and their screaming, fat ducklings swimming and holding onto their skirts. They never failed. Alas! It was getting too much for little Glob-Blob. Everyday there would be quacking and screaming of ducklings while poor Glob-Blob would run as fast as he could to get away from the vicious ducks.
>
> The reason for this was because poor Glob-Blob could not quack. So every day the Ladies Duck Aid Society would chase Glob-Blob, for they said it was for the good of the ducks, and it was not only right but they were doing a good turn.
>
> It was lucky for Glob-Blob that the ducks were fat and flabby, for if they were limber, I will not mention what would happen. But one day, these lazy ducks did reduce, and when chasing Glob-Blob dealt him a good many hard blows. And the next day, poor Glob-Blob was at last doomed. The vicious quackers had come and the chase was on. Glob-Blob was failing. It is a shame so noble a duck should be doomed, but "That's life," said Glob-Blob to himself as, slowly but surely, failing, he dropped to the ground. The quackers, very pleased with themselves, sat down for a chat.
>
> But I shall always remember Glob-Blob and his death. So I shall let him finish his journey, where there will be no more quackers and chasers, and where at last he may have passionless peace forever.

The case of Kenneth, an intelligent and imaginative thirteen-year-old, is similar to that of Glob-Blob. Kenneth is very enthusiastic about many aspects of science, has accumulated an extensive store of knowledge about electricity, and at home carries out many complicated experiments. At school he is listless and bored; he daydreams and makes poor grades. Since he does not have a B-plus average, he is not eligible to participate in science clubs. The principal wants Kenneth to go out for football, a sport for which Kenneth has no enthusiasm. His teachers recognize that he is intelligent and feel that "the only way to handle a boy like Kenneth is to be rough with him, humiliate and shame him, and break his spirit."

The Kenneths and the Glob-Blobs must consider their well-intentioned counselors, teachers, principals, and parents as "quackers and chasers." They might contribute far more to society and be far happier and more successful by capitalizing upon their unique strengths rather than spending fruitless energy trying hopelessly to compensate for some divergent characteristic. They would, of course, find it necessary to achieve the basic skills in order to succeed in their chosen areas of specialization.

EQUATION OF DIVERGENCY WITH MENTAL ILLNESS AND DELINQUENCY

By the time children reach the third grade, most of them have been taught to equate divergency with mental illness or delinquency. Ideas that are different are labeled as "crazy," "silly," or "naughty." The widespread existence of this concept is reflected in their stories. Flying monkeys are frequently thought to be crazy or to be devils or under the spell of witches. Lions that won't roar and cats that won't scratch are thought to be sick. One of the stories that follows illustrates how parents may reinforce the "crazy" concept. The other painfully shows how both parents and professionals fail in understanding divergency.

> Once there was a little monkey who was always doing what his mother told him not to do. One day when he was playing outdoors with his sister he said to her, "I can do something that you will never be able to do. I can fly."
>
> The little sister said that he could not fly, so he said, "I will prove it to you." He went to the end of the branch and began to fly. First he gave a leap and off he went. His little sister was so surprised that she ran as fast as she could go to tell the mother monkey. At first, mother monkey did not believe that a monkey could fly. She told the little monkey to go and play and not to bother her.
>
> The sister finally convinced her mother to come and look. At first she sat and looked for a while. Then she told the little flying monkey to come back here, but he said that he would not come back.
>
> So that night when father monkey came home she told him all about it. And he went and got the little monkey and said for him not to fly anymore or the other animals will think he was crazy and out of his head.

The following story of the cat that doesn't scratch illustrates another aspect of our treatment of divergency:

> Once there was a cat that could not scratch. A lady came and the cat followed her so she took the cat home with her. The cat meowed and meowed, so the lady gave him some milk and he spilt the milk all over himself. So the lady put the cat in the tub and gave him a bath, but the cat did not scratch her. The lady did not understand so she took the cat to the cat hospital. The veterinarian did not understand so she let the cat go and that is the end of the cat that would not scratch and the lady and the doctor that did not understand the cat.

Many highly creative children feel that their parents and teachers do not understand them. Teachers admit that they do not know these children as well as they know highly intelligent (IQ) pupils (Torrance, 1959a). For some creative individuals only a school counselor or a remedial or special teacher may be able to provide understanding.

MASCULINITY AND FEMININITY

Most societies have rather rigid concepts of masculinity and femininity (Mead, 1935). Individuals whose behavior does not conform to these concepts are considered mentally ill or delinquent. Overemphasis or misplaced emphasis of a society on sex roles may create problems of adjustment for many individuals, especially highly talented ones who seek to fulfill their potentialities. Evidence of the effects of this concept of mental health on the mental functioning of children and adults may be seen on every hand.

The social consequences of failure to achieve the behavioral norms associated with sex roles are well understood by children by the time they reach the fourth grade, if not before. Such an understanding is reflected in the following story:

> Our story begins in the Belgian Congo where we come upon a den of lions. The mother has just had babies. The father was very proud and wanted to make them kings of the jungle. When they were still young, they had a contest to see who could roar the loudest.
> First, Tarzan tried and first a cough and then a choke and then a little roar. More of a purr, really though. Next was Leo, Jr., a fine example of his father. He cleared his throat, then a deep breath and a gigantic roar for his age. Third and last Ollie, a little tyke and not much of a lion. He tried and tried but all he could do is purr.
> Father was proud of Leo and fairly proud of Tarzan. But Ollie was a flop in his eyes.

Even when parents know and accept intellectually the fact that there is nothing unhealthy about a boy's responsiveness to beauty or a girl's curiosity about the physical and biological world, such behavior still disturbs parents and teachers. Discomfort is reflected in the following excerpt from a mother's account of her son's responsiveness to color:

> . . . He wanted a purple shirt and I didn't even know they made them, but he saved up his allowance for three weeks and bought himself one. He is very blond and, of course, he looks very well in it . . . Perhaps because Mike is a boy I can't get used to the idea that he should be concerned about color which seems almost a feminine quality. Yet, I know we are each one, male and female . . .

The story of Ollie and his brothers also illustrates the difficulty generated whenever we use a single criterion of adjustment, or overemphasize any single value or talent—whether it be masculinity, creativity, athletic skill, artistic achievement, or whatever.

Several concepts of the mentally healthy person may be inferred from the imaginative stories of children. From the most frequent themes which have been identified, we can construct what is perhaps the most pervasive picture of the mentally healthy person in our society. First, he must conform to the behavioral norms of his society. He must be well rounded and must work hard to correct any irregularities in development. If some aspect of development has lagged, he must neglect all else and achieve the expected standard. If some function or skill has been developed to an unusually high level, he must deliberately neglect further development along this line or suppress it. Individuals whose behavior is "different" are usually labeled as mentally ill (crazy, wild, etc.) or delinquent (naughty, bad, etc.). Regardless of natural inclinations and talents, the mentally healthy person according to this dominant position must conform to his society's concepts of masculinity or femininity.

CONCEPTS OF PROFESSIONAL
MENTAL HEALTH WORKERS

Now that we have examined some of the most common concepts of our society about what constitutes healthy personality, let us turn to the efforts of professional mental health writers and researchers to develop useful concepts on the basis of experience, research, and theory. Some workers have drawn up detailed lists of criteria. Others have proposed simple, one-sentence definitions of mental health. Still others have rejected both of these extremes and have offered sets of interrelated criteria or some kind of unified but complex theory. Let us examine samples from each of these approaches.

LISTS OF CRITERIA

One of the most comprehensive of the detailed lists of criteria of "good adjustment" was compiled by Tyson (1951). In his list of specific criteria he includes characteristics cited by various authorities as descriptive of the well-adjusted person. While some people might reject a few of these criteria, most will accept them readily as valued characteristics of the healthy person. His list, which follows, would make a good guide for some ambitious developer of an omnibus inventory of adjustment:

1. Adaptability—acceptance of changes both in himself and in his environment.
2. Capacity for affection—ability to love others and to accept love and support from others.

9

3. Relative freedom from fear, anxiety, and tension.
4. Appropriate behavior for one's age, sex, status, or role and for the time and place.
5. Ability to determine issues on which one may yield and those on which one should stand firm.
6. Balanced life—varied activity, multiple interests in life.
7. Code acceptance with adequate emancipation from group or culture.
8. Confidential or intimate relationship with some person.
9. Cooperation—balance between enjoyment of working alone and working cooperatively.
10. Acceptance of honest criticism without sacrificing independence of thinking.
11. Ability to profit from experience.
12. Tolerance of frustration—acceptance of facts of success with joy and graceful acceptance of failure; ability to meet failure with humor, constructive ideas, and fighting spirit rather than with fear, rage, hopelessness, or suspicion.
13. Goals that are in harmony with socially approved aims; ability to delay immediate satisfaction for long-term values.
14. Ability to live within limits of reasonable health requirements.
15. Ability to maintain sense of humor.
16. Balance between independence and dependence.
17. Self-insight (realistic self-concept).
18. Permanent loyalties with mutual satisfaction.
19. Selection of mate on basis of reason, not fantasy.
20. Moderation—no overemphasis on any aspect of life.
21. Objectivity in new situations, decisions, evaluation of failures.
22. Orderly existence in sleeping, eating, working, etc.
23. Primary attention to the present.
24. Healthy outlook on life—satisfying philosophy of life.
25. Persistence—continued adaptive action in spite of obstacles.
26. Acceptance of reality.
27. Postponement of rewards—willingness to wait for future pleasures.
28. Satisfaction—energy, zest, and spontaneity.
29. Self-control—reasonable intellectual control of emotions.
30. Self-respect or self-esteem.
31. View of sex expression as normal phase of life.
32. Social adjustment—even-temper, alertness, social consideration.
33. Tolerance—effort to get along with and understand others.
34. Social awareness—creative use of leisure time by contributing to school, family, and community.
35. Vocational adjustment.

Interesting and stimulating though this list may be, it cannot be very useful in guiding behavior in actual situations. Although the human mind is capable of memorizing such a list, it is not capable of manipulating such a large number of variables. A mind confronted by so many details adapts by organizing them and generalizing from them.

SIMPLIFIED DEFINITIONS

Next let us evaluate some of the attempts to simplify all criteria into one-sentence definitions of "good adjustment." Robert Hoppock (1957) has argued for the following definition of the "well-adjusted" person:

> If a man is healthy, he earns enough for necessities, is not often unemployed, is satisfied with his work and in his human relations in general, he is well-adjusted (p. 232).

Most teachers, counselors, and school administrators, for many reasons, reject this definition as a guide for their professional conduct. They point out fallacies in the assumption behind each aspect of the definition. They point to people who are not healthy but who are, by their values, well adjusted. They know of people who have not been able to earn enough for necessities but whom they considered mentally healthy and well adjusted. They know of well-adjusted people who are not satisfied with their work and with their interpersonal relations in general. In fact, many insist that they know people whom they would consider seriously maladjusted if they were satisfied with their work and their interpersonal relations. Others point out important values and goals not included in the definition. Without knowing the identity of the author, they identify it as a job-centered definition. In the final analysis, they admit that they would like to have for all people the characteristics described in the definition. Yet, they insist that a person may be well adjusted and lack one or more of these characteristics and that the possession of all of these characteristics does not make one well adjusted. They argue that many of the most eminent contributors to human progress have lacked one or more of these characteristics.

J. L. Moreno once suggested another definition: "If a man can live on the outside and 'get by,' he is mentally healthy." When confronted with the statement, most teachers, counselors, school administrators, ministers, and other professional workers are enraged at the suggestion of such a mental health goal. Just as the discussion becomes heated, someone interjects, "But wouldn't we be much better off, if we could achieve this for everybody? We could dispense with our mental hospitals, jails, prisons, and other correctional institutions. We could release great financial resources for education, aid to handicapped persons, and the like. The gain in talent utilization would be tremendous!" On and on the argument goes! Finally, everyone

11

admits that we fall far short of the goal of helping individuals "live on the outside and get by," but insists that we strive for higher goals.

In fairness to Moreno, it should be added that he later qualified the statement to say: "If a man can live *creatively and productively* on the outside and 'get by,' he is well adjusted." Adding "creatively and productively," of course, changed the goal greatly. Moreno used this definition as a part of his attempt to show the futility of accepting any kind of absolute definition or goal of mental health and to emphasize the importance of constructive behavior in response to changing conditions rather than passive adaptation.

SCHEMATA OR MULTIPLE CRITERIA

When faced with any overwhelming mass of data, a person naturally formulates oversimplifications. Teachers tell children that the North Pole is "cold" and that the equator is "hot." The truth is far more complex. Just so, the phenomenon of mental health or good adjustment is too complex to be represented by any simple definition. Professional workers have sought to avoid this difficulty by developing various schemata or interrelated concepts to express more accurately a meaning of mental health that will be useful in guiding professional and personal behavior. Such schemata reduce the long list of criteria, such as Tyson's, to some manageable number, usually six or seven. Furthermore, these variables are organized into some schema that makes easier their manipulation. Let us examine briefly some of them.

Scott (1958) has presented a schema that consists of a compilation of the research definitions of mental illness. He includes the following:

1. Exposure to psychiatric treatment.
2. Social maladjustment (lack of adherence to social norms).
3. Psychiatric diagnosis (resulting from psychiatric screening).
4. Subjective unhappiness.
5. Objective psychological symptoms.
6. Failure of positive adaptations.

Almost everyone has pointed out many defects in each of these criteria. In general, however, researchers have not offered these as absolute criteria and have only argued the relative usefulness of such criteria in the absence of more satisfactory ones. They represent the practical compromises which investigators have been forced to make in order to make progress in evaluating the possible consequences of various social conditions, educational practices, and the like.

Tindall (1955) has proposed a set of related measures of adjustment, having the following seven facets:

1. Maintaining an integrated personality, coordinating needs and goal-seeking behavior.
2. Conforming to social standards, harmony with standards of cultural groups.
3. Adapting to reality conditions, ability to take present hardship conditions to progress toward long-range goals.
4. Maintaining consistency, predictable behavior, hope of adjustment.
5. Maturing with age, personality and mental growth concomitant with physical growth.
6. Maintaining an optimal emotional tone, neither constricted nor overwhelmed by emotions.
7. Contributing optimally to society through increasing efficiency, reaching beyond self-centered goals.

The reader might like to compare Tindall's list with Tyson's 35 criteria. Can all of Tyson's criteria be classified under the seven categories proposed by Tindall?

Wile (1940) argues that concepts of abnormality vary according to one's frame of reference. Individuals, families, states, nations, and societies vary in their frames of reference. A person may be quite healthy according to one frame of reference and mentally ill according to another. There are also economic, aesthetic, social, and religious frames of reference. As science grows, frames of reference also change. Statistical frames of reference may also be applied. Here we may think of the normal as being the mean, the mode, or the median. According to such concepts, an intelligence quotient of 70 is, of course, as abnormal as one of 130. The criterion of desirability then has to be introduced.

One of the most thorough studies of concepts of mental health was undertaken by the Joint Commission on Mental Illness and Health under the leadership of Marie Jahoda (1958). In Jahoda's report to the Joint Commission, she rejects as unsuitable such conceptualizations of mental health as the following:

1. The absence of mental disease.
2. Normality.
3. Various states of well-being.

Absence of mental disease is rejected because there is low agreement among specialists in the field; evaluation often depends on accepted social conventions. A number of critics have attacked the report on this score, maintaining that many mental health workers wish that they could achieve absence of mental illness for all of their clients. Jahoda argues that the criterion of normality both as a statistical concept and as the way people should behave is of little or no use. Concerning the rejection of "various states of well-being" as a criterion, she points out that misfortune and deprivation are not always of one's making, and to be happy under unpleasant conditions cannot be regarded as a criterion of mental health.

Jahoda proposes as a substitute for these three common but unsuitable concepts the following six approaches:

1. Attitudes of an individual toward his own self.
2. Growth, development, or self-actualization.
3. Integration.
4. Autonomy.
5. Perception of reality.
6. Environmental mastery.

ATTITUDES OF AN INDIVIDUAL TOWARD HIS OWN SELF. Many personality theorists have emphasized the importance of self-acceptance, self-confidence, and self-reliance (independence from others and initiative from within). In this approach, Jahoda includes such dimensions of the self-concept as the following:

1. Accessibility to consciousness (self-objectification, being one's self, self-awareness, etc.).
2. Correctness (ability to see the self realistically and objectively).
3. Feeling about the self (acceptance of self, including imperfections).
4. Sense of identity (sentiment of self-regard, clarity of self-image).

GROWTH, DEVELOPMENT, OR SELF-ACTUALIZATION. The idea that man strives to realize his own potentialities is an old one. It figures prominently in the theories of Carl Rogers, Erich Fromm, Abraham Maslow, Gordon Allport, and others. Jahoda identifies the following aspects, which have been emphasized by these and other authors:

1. Self-concept.
2. Motivational processes.
3. Investment in living (achievements of the self-actualizing person as demonstrated in a high degree of differentiation, or maximum of development, of his basic equipment).

INTEGRATION. The report shows that integration as a criterion of mental health is treated with emphasis on one of the following:

1. A balance of psychic forces in the individual.
2. A unifying outlook on life, emphasizing cognitive aspects of integration.
3. Resistance to stress.

AUTONOMY. Autonomy as a criterion of mental health usually refers to the relationship between an individual and his environment with regard to decision making. Expositions of this criterion emphasize two aspects:

1. Regulation of behavior from within.
2. Independent behavior.

PERCEPTION OF REALITY. Perception of reality is considered mentally healthy when what the individual sees corresponds to what is actually there. Two aspects of reality perception are emphasized by Jahoda:

1. Perception free from need distortion.
2. Empathy or social sensitivity.

ENVIRONMENTAL MASTERY. One of the most frequently selected criteria of mental health is success in mastering one's environment. The following aspects of environmental mastery are identified in the Jahoda report:

1. The ability to love.
2. Adequacy in love, work, and play.
3. Adequacy in interpersonal relations.
4. Efficiency in meeting situational requirements.
5. Capacity for adaptation and adjustment.
6. Efficiency in problem solving.

A number of personality theorists have singled out some one of these aspects and made it the center of an entire conceptualization of personality development and mental hygiene. For example, Sullivan (1953) has made adequacy in interpersonal relations central in his theory. Psychoanalysts have focused much of their attention on ability to love and adequacy in love, work, and play. Hartmann (1951) has made the process of adaptation and adjustment the center of his theory.

The reader may want to examine some of the major theories of personality and compile a list of the characteristics of the healthy personality according to each theory. The following theorists have presented important ideas: S. Freud (1914), E. Fromm (1955), K. Goldstein (1940), A. H. Maslow (1954), C. R. Rogers (1951), and H. S. Sullivan (1953). For a comparative study of personality theories, it is best to use a general textbook such as Hall and Lindzey's *Theories of Personality* (1957) or Bischof's *Interpreting Personality Theories* (1964).

SUMMARY

A basic reason why it is so difficult to find satisfactory criteria of mental health is that "mental health" is only a minimum condition for the growth and effective functioning of the mind. Thus, professional people are reluctant to accept such limited criteria as those discussed in this chapter. For most educators, personality adjustment is too modest an ideal. As Bruner (1961) points out, "Competence in the use of one's powers for the development of individually defined and socially relevant excellence is much more to the point" (p. 59).

Nevertheless, mental health *is* a minimum condition for the growth and functioning of the mind. Mental illness "so preoccupies the person with the need to fend off realities with which he cannot cope that it leaves him without either the nerve or the zest to learn" (Bruner, 1961, p. 59). The concept of mental health that pervades this book is a painfully obvious yet somewhat unusual one. To the author, "mental health" means just what the words say—namely, the healthy, complete functioning of the mind. This cannot be interpreted as a "survival" concept of mental health. The emphasis is upon potential and involves functioning fully and completely in harmony with all of one's powers and ideals. The title of the book, *Constructive Behavior,* is intended to communicate the concept that mental health involves responding constructively to stress and change rather than adjusting to stress and change.

Some readers may argue that an individual may use effective mental functioning for ends which call seriously into question his mental health and cite such examples as the careful planning of a murder, a swindle, or leadership of a destructive adolescent gang. Such activities, however, are not "constructive" or in any way characteristic of an individual functioning completely in harmony with his powers and ideals.

Many forces both within the individual and in his external environment interfere with the full functioning of one's mental powers. The author has chosen to consider these forces under the label of "stress," since whatever interferes with a person's mental functioning is to him stressful. Thus, achieving sound mental health requires that one respond constructively to the stresses of his world in terms of his potentialities. His potentialities are resources which, in turn, enable him to cope successfully and constructively with whatever stresses he encounters in living. In the chapters which follow, an attempt will be made to show how this simple, yet neglected, concept of personality development and mental health can become a powerful resource in helping man rise to a higher level of dignity, achievement, and mental functioning.

Personality
Development and
Stress

2

Few modern men live quiet, uneventful lives. Almost all men have problems in living and must respond constantly to change and to stress. Certainly, teachers, counselors, administrators, and other school personnel spend much of their time in helping other people learn to cope with present stresses or the predicted, common stresses to be encountered. Although few people "break down" under stress, many choose unacceptable and unconstructive ways of coping with their stresses—truancy, disobedience, cheating, stealing, sexual misconduct, and the like. Others become overanxious and ineffective, failing to learn and develop mentally, blocking or blowing up on examinations, developing psychosomatic symptoms, or suffering anxiety about family relations, peer relations, and masturbation or other tabooed practices.

To help the reader understand how he can help other individuals master life stresses, a conceptual framework will first be presented. We will consider such questions as "What constitutes stress?" "How does adaptation to stress take place?" "When and how does this process go wrong?" We will then turn to a more detailed examination of the techniques used in coping with stress.

WHAT IS STRESS?

There has been so much difficulty in scientific circles concerning a satisfactory definition of stress that the term is used here in relation to mental health only with reservation. The author has embraced its use because he believes the concept of stress and recent research concerning stress provide a promising approach for examining, understanding, and coping with problems of personality development and mental health. No attempt will be made to resolve the issue of whether stress is best conceived in terms of experiential (within the individual) or stimulus (external) dimensions. It seems obvious that we must deal with both dimensions if we are to understand stress in relation to personality development and mental health.

If "survival" were the ultimate criterion of mental health, we would define as stressful those conditions that might cause death: water and food deprivation, extreme heat and cold, torture, disease, prolonged activity without rest, sleep deprivation, and the like. The psychological effects of such conditions include shock, mental confusion, inefficiency, recklessness, apathy, fatigue, exhaustion, hallucinations, thoughts of suicide, fear of insanity, and the like. All of these involve some kind of mental malfunctioning. When mental health is defined as healthy mental functioning (rather than survival), all of the conditions that have been cited here would still be relevant. Mental functioning, however, may "go wrong" as a result of conditions which constitute little or no threat to life. Such conditions would include interpersonal irritations, failure to achieve ambitions, and the like.

Almost all of the conditions listed above, if not too severe or prolonged, might call forth such responses as overcompensation, heroism, increased speed and efficiency, planning, mutual support, and similar positive behaviors that may prevent death or breakdown. In such cases, the mental abilities are functioning at an even higher level than usual, perhaps more nearly at their potential.

A person whose profession is to help other people may be expected to contribute to the prevention of such breakdowns as mental illness, delinquency, and crime, and to help individuals to succeed in their living, studies, and career aspirations. In thinking of such goals, we might define as stressful those conditions which commonly cause breakdowns or failures in living, studies, and career aspirations. We are dealing with conditions that interfere with the full functioning of the mental abilities. If the mental abilities continue to function properly, the individual will be able to cope with these problems to the best of his capacity. The conditions that have been found by research to contribute to the kinds of breakdowns and failures just mentioned include such things as these:

> Conflictual, hostile family conditions; broken home; crowded living conditions; poverty.
>
> Hostile and delinquent neighborhood; high-class, competitive neighborhood.
>
> Deprivation of love in family and among peers, lack of friends, peer rejection.
>
> Failure in studies, athletics, friendships, dating.
>
> Intense motivation or pressure to succeed, unfair or too stiff competition, no chance to succeed.

Deficient basic skills for learning—reading, arithmetic, spelling.
Physical handicaps and developmental abnormalities.
Excessive outside activities.
Uncertain or inconsistent discipline.
Physiological growth processes and new requirements of maturation.
Unstable environment.

In general, those things are stressful which usually result in failure, fear, distraction, discomfort, and rapid or inconsistent pacing and speed. Any threat to a fundamental need is stressful. Every new venture into the unknown, though enjoyable and beneficial, creates some apprehension and anxiety. In fact, any stimulus or force that changes an organism in some significant way for better or worse may be regarded as stressful. Yet stress is not always noxious. Usually, it is some stress that triggers the creative thinking process and keeps it going until a solution is achieved and communicated. Stress may cause individuals to rise to new heights of performance and achievement.

HOW ADAPTATION TO LIFE STRESSES OCCURS

At least at a general level, all stresses appear to have essentially similar effects and elicit essentially similar processes of adaptation. We can learn a great deal about stress and mental health from survival psychology. Almost all of the extreme effects found in survival situations have been found in almost every type of extreme condition. For example, hallucinations have resulted from solitary confinement and other isolation conditions. Likewise, hallucinations have resulted from food deprivation and from water deprivation when there were plenty of other people around. Hallucinations occur in men exposed to extreme weather conditions, sea survival, desert survival, even when there is companionship, food, and water. Furthermore, hallucinations occur when there is constant danger from the enemy, even when weather conditions are favorable and when there is companionship, food, and water. Much the same could be said of each of the other effects of severe stress listed above.

Observation of the commonalities in stress behavior may lead to the most useful concepts concerning guidance for the mastery of stress. At first researchers, including the author, considered it necessary to study the effects of each type of condition (cold, isolation, pain, etc.) separately. It was only as they progressed with their research, interviewing men who had survived under extremely diverse conditions, studying accounts of survival under even more diverse conditions, observing behavior under a variety of stressful conditions, and experiencing themselves a variety of stressful conditions,

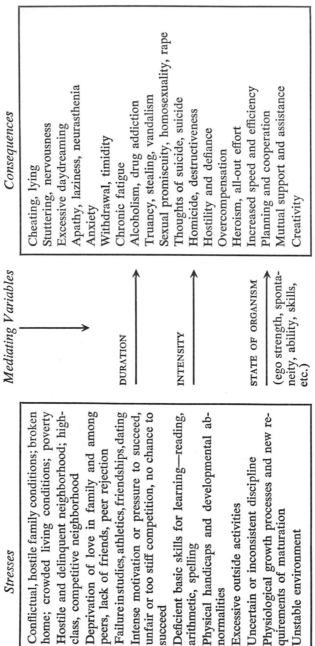

Figure 2–1. Typical Stresses Encountered and the Mediation of Their Effects

Stresses

Conflictual, hostile family conditions; broken home; crowded living conditions; poverty
Hostile and delinquent neighborhood; high-class, competitive neighborhood
Deprivation of love in family and among peers, lack of friends, peer rejection
Failure in studies, athletics, friendships, dating
Intense motivation or pressure to succeed, unfair or too stiff competition, no chance to succeed
Deficient basic skills for learning—reading, arithmetic, spelling
Physical handicaps and developmental abnormalities
Excessive outside activities
Uncertain or inconsistent discipline
Physiological growth processes and new requirements of maturation
Unstable environment

Mediating Variables

DURATION

INTENSITY

STATE OF ORGANISM
(ego strength, spontaneity, ability, skills, etc.)

Consequences

Cheating, lying
Stuttering, nervousness
Excessive daydreaming
Apathy, laziness, neurasthenia
Anxiety
Withdrawal, timidity
Chronic fatigue
Alcoholism, drug addiction
Truancy, stealing, vandalism
Sexual promiscuity, homosexuality, rape
Thoughts of suicide, suicide
Homicide, destructiveness
Hostility and defiance
Overcompensation
Heroism, all-out effort
Increased speed and efficiency
Planning and cooperation
Mutual support and assistance
Creativity

that commonalities began to emerge. Condition by condition, adaptation processes were charted along dimensions of time, space, intensity, sequence, and capacity of the organism.

Behavior under stress can be conceived of as a process through which specific stresses produce an array of effects that are mediated by the duration and intensity of the stress and the state of the organism. This conceptualization is presented schematically in Figure 2–1. In the "stresses" box are listed the specific conditions that may result in breakdown or interfere seriously with success in living, studies, career progress, and the like. Included are those stresses to which students are commonly subjected and which have figured most prominently in breakdown and failure. The "consequences" box includes a variety of the more common negative and positive effects. Any specific stress depending upon the mediating variables and their interaction may result in any of the effects. For example, failure in studies may result in cheating, lying, excessive daydreaming, apathy, alcoholism, and even suicide. The state of the organism (ego strength, spontaneity, ability, physical strengths, etc.), however, might be such that there would be overcompensation and all-out effort that would eventually result in distinguished performance and outstanding success.

Since any of the stresses *can produce* any of the effects and since any of the effects *can be produced* by any of the stresses, it is highly important that educators and other mental health workers learn to think in terms of possibilities. In creating conditions conducive to healthy personality development and mental functioning, they should learn to recognize the deficiencies and problems in present situations and to ask questions that will result in solutions. The answers may not be available readily. Consequently, it will be necessary to make many guesses.

One should also think in terms of probabilities. Certain specific conditions tend to produce certain specific effects with better than chance expectations. Research has been able to explain, predict, and control a small proportion of human behavior. As knowledge increases of the properties of the stressful conditions, duration, intensity, and the characteristics of the individual, we should be able to explain a much greater proportion of human behavior.

ADAPTATION AND DURATION OF STRESS

As research on adaptation under survival conditions continued, the data always appeared to conform quite closely to the process described by Selye (1950, 1956) for physiological adaptation and the theories of J. G. Miller (1957) and Karl Menninger (1956) for psychological adaptation. The process of mastery of stress may be represented by the curve shown in Figure 2–2.

21

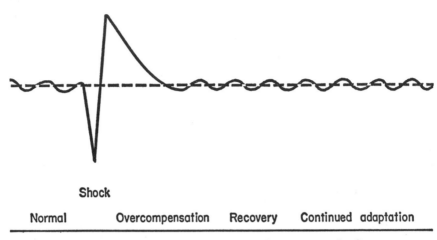

Shock

Normal   Overcompensation Recovery Continued adaptation

Figure 2–2. Theoretical Curve of Performance under Stress over Time in Case of Mastery of Stress

Let us examine the case of a college student who suddenly encounters academic failure. When the stress (failure) is suddenly encountered, there is first shock or resistance to accepting the seriousness of the situation. The student may wonder if some mistake has been made, blame the teacher or some other condition, or reason that he "just slipped up" or that "the test was no good." In successful adaptation, this is followed by rapid overcompensation and maximum effort. With recovery there is a leveling off of performance as control is gained.

If the stress is continued, fatigue occurs and ultimately there will be collapse or breakdown, the process represented by Figure 2–3. This fits in with the often stated conclusion that every man (dog, rat, sheep, goat) has a "breaking point." Before the breaking point is reached, a variety of effects may be shown. There may be mental confusion, inefficiency, recklessness, apathy, fatigue, hostility, and the like. There may be positive attempts to adapt, such as increased speed, planning, appeal for help, and the like. In fact, such adaptive actions may occur almost until the break occurs. The break may even seem sudden. Prior to the break, the signs of approaching breakdown may have been denied or ignored. Usually after the break has occurred, the warning signs can be recalled.

Let us see how this would work in the case of a college student failing in his course work. After the first shock and acceptance of the seriousness of the situation, he puts forth maximum effort. At first he succeeds, but the course becomes increasingly more difficult. He is then pushed to use more

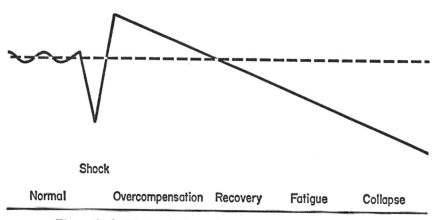

Figure 2–3. *Theoretical Curve of Performance under Continued Stress with Ultimate Collapse*

expensive coping devices. Positively, he may increase his speed of working, plan better, obtain expert help, work with another student, or exercise greater ingenuity and creativity. If the work is too difficult for him to master, this expensive output of energy eventually takes its toll and there is a breakdown of some type. It may result in withdrawal from school, delinquency, thoughts of suicide, or even psychosis. Negatively, he may react by cheating and deceit, excessive daydreaming, apathy, withdrawal, hostility and defiance, or any of the other effects listed in Figure 2–1.

Two special cases of adaptation over time deserve recognition. The first is represented in Figure 2–4. In this case, the shock or resistance to recognizing the seriousness of the stress was prolonged. The attempt to rise to the occasion was also inadequate, and the result was collapse. This behavior is typical of the individual who is unable to "go all out" in order to meet the requirements of the situation. Some individuals consistently fail because they never find anything worth their best efforts. Others keep thinking that they can "get by" with less than their best. On one occasion, the author observed a crew working at a simple problem of spanning a wide ditch with a "bridge" for about an hour until every man became almost exhausted. If they had at the beginning exerted themselves they could have accomplished the job within five minutes with relatively little expenditure of energy. As a result of unsuccessful attempts using their less expensive energies, they became so fatigued that they became incapable of the maximum effort. Thus, with extreme expenditure of energy, they failed to do

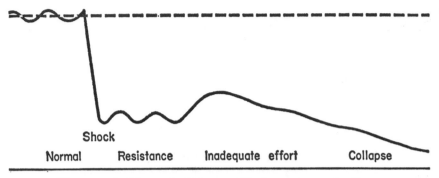

Figure 2–4. Theoretical Curve of Performance under Stress over Time with Prolonged Shock of Resistance and Inadequate Overcompensation

something which they could have done with little energy IF they had "gone all out" for a few minutes.

A failing student may reason, "This doesn't mean anything. The teacher will be easier next time." Or, he may say, "This was just an accident and I slipped up this time. I really know the subject." Rationalizing his performance, he fails to recognize the seriousness of his situation and does not adapt. He may wait too long and even the maximum effort may be inadequate; or he may put forth just a little more effort but not enough, not fully accepting the requirements of the situation.

A second case is represented in Figure 2–5. In this case, there is no recovery from shock or no recognition of the seriousness of the situation. The individual thus fails to overcompensate and collapse follows. This description might fit either the individual who faints when confronted with situations beyond his capacity or the one who responds with apathy. He may be so shocked, surprised, and hurt by the failure that he panics, becoming apathetic and unable to take any organized action. Or he may feel that no effort is worth while. Thus, breakdown of some type is evident—withdrawal from school, delinquency, or hostility.

ADAPTATION AND INTENSITY OF STRESS

A number of studies (Harris, Mackie, and Wilson, 1956; J. G. Miller, 1953) indicate that mild stress tends to result in improved performance,

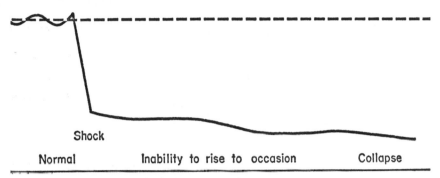

Figure 2–5. Theoretical Curve of Performance under Stress over Time with Prolonged Shock or Resistance and Inability to Rise to the Occasion

increased activity, more learning, and the like, and that extremely intense stress results in deterioration of performance and breakdown. The experiences of survivors likewise appear to conform to this principle and can theoretically be represented graphically by the curve shown in Figure 2–6.

This generalization was borne out in an experiment conducted at the USAF Survival Training School (Torrance, 1959a). A test was made of the relative effectiveness of varying degrees of pressure exerted by instructors in indoctrinating aircrewmen concerning an emergency meat ration called pemmican. Many men react unfavorably to this food, but previous research had indicated that this unfavorable reaction was primarily psychological. The subjects of this study, 427 aircrewmen from 43 small training groups, were randomly assigned to one control and six experimental groups. Subjects were issued eight of the pemmican bars for use during a nine-day simulated survival experience. Criteria of acceptance were obtained at the end of the training along with measures of how much pressure the men felt their instructors had tried to exert. The criteria included liking or dislike of the food, the number of bars of the food eaten, sickness attributed to the food, and willingness to use the food in possible emergency or extreme conditions.

When the seven groups (six experimental and one control) were arranged in order of instructor pressure (as perceived by trainees), it was found that pressure up to a point was accompanied by increased acceptability (and apparently constructive behavior). Once this point was reached, however, additional perceived pressure was accompanied by decreased acceptance (and apparently a reduction in constructive behavior). The men perceived least pressure in the following methods:

1. The instructors gave information about the food in a very straightforward manner.
2. The instructors tried deliberately to avoid any exercise of pressure or influence.
3. The instructors gave psychological information about food acceptability.

The most effective method ranked fifth in instructor pressure; instructors told the men that food indoctrination was an integral part of their training and that they would be evaluated on their use of food, both the pemmican ration and foods found on the land. In devising the methods, the experimenters had thought that this one would be perceived as the most coercive. The men, however, saw two other methods as more coercive: one in which the instructor attempted to set a good example by eating the pemmican himself and one in which psychological information about the acceptability of the food was given each man individually. These two "high-pressure" methods were least successful. For example, about 30 per cent of the men in the group given individual explanations reported that the food made them sick, while only seven per cent of the men in the group

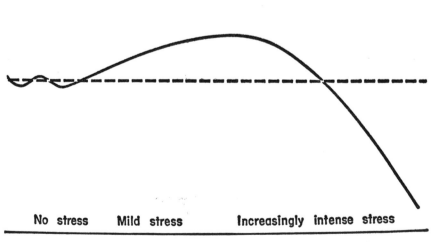

No stress   Mild stress   Increasingly intense stress

Figure 2–6. Theoretical Curve of Typical Performance under Conditions of Increasingly Intense Stress

given evaluation were sick. The mean number of bars of pemmican eaten by men in the former condition was 5.57 compared to 7.79 in the latter condition. The "highest-pressure" method was the most erratic in its effects while the evaluative produced the most uniform effects.

Although the behavior of most individuals appears to conform to the process represented by the curve in Figure 2–6, almost everyone can recall outstanding exceptions. One exception is the behavior of the man who catches all of the balls or makes all of the baskets in the practice game but misses them in the real game. This kind of behavior is represented by Figure 2–7.

In the case of the scholastic failure, we could expect something like the following. If the teacher is very lax and creates a completely relaxed atmosphere, very little learning may be expected—except, of course, among the self-starters who are themselves highly motivated. If some reasonable standard is expected and required, learning will increase with the increasing stringency of the standard up to a point. If the standard is too high, students will be overwhelmed and become so frustrated that only the most able or the most determined will learn. This special case would be represented by the student who solves his problems satisfactorily at home or in the classroom everyday, when he is not "playing for keeps." On an examination, however, he tends to block or panic and is unable to solve the simplest problems. This, however, is likely to be a fairly rare exception. The student who solves his problems at home or in the classroom is likely to perform best on an examination.

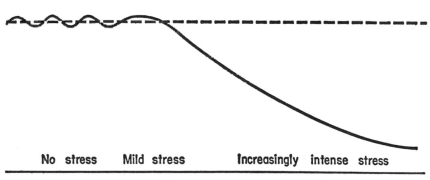

No stress   Mild stress   Increasingly intense stress

Figure 2–7. Theoretical Curve of Unsuccessful Perform-ance under Conditions of Increasingly Intense Stress

BRIEF INTENSE STRESS VERSUS
MODERATE PROLONGED STRESS

Educators are concerned primarily about two types of stress. There is greatest concern about the traumatic experience, a brief but intense stress or sudden emergency. The other concern is the mild or moderate but prolonged stress. Recent research indicates that these two types of stress require different types of defenses.

Research by S. W. Davis and his colleagues (1956) in combat in Korea has given new support to the conclusion that mild but prolonged stress is more damaging and requires a longer time for recovery than brief but intense stress. They studied the reactions of two groups of combat infantrymen. One group was engaged in intense combat for a period of eighteen hours; casualty rates were high and the conditions were intensely stressful. The second group was engaged in less intense combat, being in a blocking position behind the main line of resistance./For most of the subjects, the short period of intense combat resulted in a high degree of adrenal responsiveness, increased protein destruction, and a shift in the balance of body salts. The prolonged, less intense combat resulted in a low degree of adrenal responsiveness, normal protein destruction, and a shift in the balance of body salts opposite to that observed in men under short, intense combat. The time taken to recover to normal physiological levels after brief, intense combat was about six days; after more prolonged and less intense combat, recovery took about thirteen days.

It should not be inferred from these and other similar findings that brief traumatic experiences are not damaging. Proper therapy following a traumatic experience, however, might have a better prediction for success than therapy following mild but prolonged stress. In school counseling, there has probably been undue neglect of individuals exposed to chronically stressful conditions in the home, neighborhood, and school. It is probably such conditions that take the greatest toll in personality breakdown—mental illness, delinquency, and criminality.

The recent work of Funkenstein, King, and Drolette (1957) gives new support to the contention that early childhood experiences play a relatively stronger role in determining behavior in sudden emergencies while later experiences play a relatively stronger role in adaptation to stress over time. These investigators conducted a series of experiments on a group of Harvard undergraduates. Their attention was focused on the way these students reacted to certain new and difficult stress-inducing situations. Each student's emotional and physiological reactions were studied, with emphasis on two phases of the stress reactions—the acute emergency reaction, and the ability or failure to master stress over a period of two years. The experimenters conducted rather extensive interviews and psychological tests and collected much sociological data concerning each subject. Two types of stressful situations were used: a stressful problem situation and the sonic-confuser situation. The problem situation involved computational problems; the stresses involved included frustration of ongoing behavior, criticism, razzing, and time pressure. The sonic-confuser situation has been used by many investigators and involves the study of a person's speech by allowing him to hear by earphones his own voice with a slight time delay. Subjects were asked to read a story once aloud and then to repeat it from memory. Time pressure and electric shock were stresses added during the repetition of the story from memory. The sonic-confuser situation was presented twice during the first year and three times during the second year. It was found that the following kinds of variables are related significantly to reactions in the acute emergency phase but not the ability to master stress over time:

> Perception of parents
> Internal concept of self
> Fantasies (Thematic Apperception Test)
> Social attitudes
> Social stratification

On the other hand, the following kinds of variables are related significantly to ability to master stress over time but not to reactions during the acute emergency phase:

> Interpersonal relations
> Assessment of reality
> Integration of personality

Most scholars associate the first set of variables with early childhood experiences and the second with experiences during later stages of development. Apparently it takes a great deal of overlearning to offset the effects of early childhood experiences in reacting to sudden, intense emergencies.

ADAPTATION AND THE STATE OF THE ORGANISM

Both Davis (1956) and Funkenstein et al. (1957) found enormous individual differences among their subjects in ability to cope with stress in both the acute emergency phase and in adaptation over time. A variety of factors may enter into an individual's capacity for coping with a specific stress. He may possess outstanding skills for mastering the particular stress. Or he may lack such special abilities. Deficiencies might include such things as poor hearing, poor vision, or poor mechanical aptitude. He may lack appropriate training and/or experience for dealing with the stress.

Early childhood conditions, such as parental overprotection, may predispose him to vulnerability to stress by depriving him of experience in meeting frustration and failure. Thus state of the organism or capacity for coping with stress may be plotted in numerous ways.

Ego strength, a variable that might represent the executive capacities of the personality in managing internal tensions arising from other parts of the personality, can be used for illustrative purposes. Figures 2–8 and 2–9 represent performance under stressful and nonstressful conditions for varying degrees of ego strength.

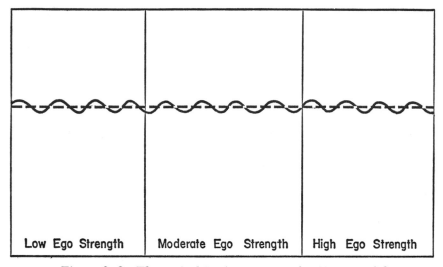

| Low Ego Strength | Moderate Ego Strength | High Ego Strength |

Figure 2–8. Theoretical Performance under Nonstressful Conditions and Varying Ego Strength Showing Low Variability

As shown in Figure 2–8, under nonstressful conditions, there may be no real difference for the three degrees of ego strength. Variability of performance may be very low. If stress is applied, however, the individual with low ego strength would tend to be overwhelmed and show a sharp decrease in performance. The individual with high ego strength, on the other hand, would improve in performance.

The above phenomena have been observed repeatedly in experiments. A sample of groups would be subjected to some type of training or treatment intended to improve performance. No such treatment would be administered to a similar sample of controls. Under relatively relaxed conditions and with easy tests or problems, there was no real difference between the experimentals and controls. As difficulty or stress increased, however, the difference became greater.

IQ or mental age is a variable that affects performance of students. If standards are low and tests are easy, students with low IQ's perform about as well as those with high IQ's. As standards are raised and the tests are made more difficult, the differences according to IQ tend to increase. Of course, the tests could be made so extremely difficult that there would again be no difference. All would tend to do no better than chance on the tests. Most teachers, in fact, recognize that a moderately difficult test differentiates more highly the better students from the poorer ones than does an extremely easy or difficult test.

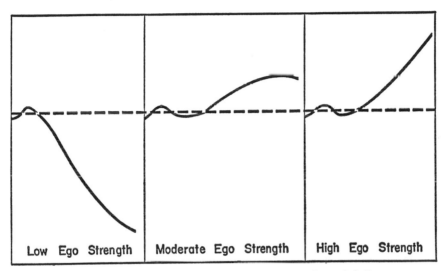

Figure 2–9. *Theoretical Performance under Stressful Conditions and Varying Ego Strength Showing High Variability*

FAILURE TO ADAPT TO STRESS

The experimental work of Pavlov (1928), Liddell (1954, 1956), Gantt (1957), and others has demonstrated that adaptation fails when the requirements of the situations are more than the organism can cope with. The discriminations required may be beyond the capacity of the organism. For example, Pavlov's dogs did not collapse as long as they could discriminate between the circles and ellipses. They broke down only when the discriminations required were beyond their capacity. The amount of data the organism is required to process may also be beyond the capacity of the organism. Thus, breakdown of some type may be expected to occur if there are discrepancies between abilities and goals. The counselor meets this problem in trying to help students who make curricular or vocational choices beyond their capacity to master successfully.

What actually went wrong in the adaptation attempts of the animals in the Pavlov, Gantt, and Liddell experiments and what goes wrong in all adaptation when stress is experienced is that there is some degree of loss of anchor in reality (contact with the environment) or lack of structure. In the final analysis, it is this loss of anchor or lack of structure which causes stress and makes it difficult or impossible for the individual to cope with the situation. Thus, the problem of adaptation becomes one of evolving or supplying a structure or anchor.

Any of several sets of circumstances may make it difficult for an individual to structure the situation, to establish anchors or guides, or to cope with the situation after structure has occurred. The situation may be unfamiliar to the individual or require rapid shifts in customary activities. The individual may not know what to do, and even if he knows what must be done, he may not know what he can expect of others. The situation may constitute a dangerous threat to his central values, blinding him to the realities that would furnish anchors. Loss of structure may be occasioned by the instability of the situation. There may be too many cues or too few. The changes may be too rapid to process adequately, or the requirements may overwhelm the individual because he has inadequate skills for coping with them.

SUMMARY

At the outset of this chapter the concept was presented that personality development and breakdown, mental development and mental illness, occur in a person's process of trying to cope constructively with the stresses, internal and external, that press upon him. An overview was given of some of the most common stressful conditions and some of the most common consequences of these conditions. Any stressful condition may lead to any of a great variety of possible consequences and any of these possible consequences may be caused by any of the conditions. What the consequences of any given condition will be depends upon the duration and intensity of the stress and the personality and mental resources of the individual, the state of the organism.

This latter concept brought about a realization of the need for mental health workers to develop their abilities to think in terms of possibles. In order to guide the reader in thinking of possibles and explaining an increasingly larger proportion of human behavior, an attempt was made to formulate some generalizations, along with some of the major exceptions, concerning each of the three types of mediating variables posited. With increasing intensity of stress, there is increasing effectiveness of performance up to a point at which there is loss of anchor in reality or lack of structure. The resulting disorganization brings about sharp decrease in performance or collapse. With the onset of a new stress or a sharp increase in intensity, there is a temporary shock effect or sharp drop in performance. Then comes a period of overcompensation after which there is recovery and settling down to normal performance. Of course, if the stress continues unabated, fatigue and collapse finally occur. All of these processes, however, may be speeded or retarded by the state of the organism—the personal resources of the individual.

Response to
Intense
Stress

3

TRADITIONAL ROLE OF TRAUMATIC EXPERIENCES

The literature on personality development, personality adjustment, clinical psychology, and mental health has traditionally placed great importance upon the role of intensely stressful or traumatic experiences. There has been a misguided tendency to try to trace the origin of all serious maladjustment and breakdown to some early traumatic experience—an emotional shock that involves at least a temporary loss of anchor in reality or disorganization of customary control. It is a shock because the resources of the individual are inadequate for coping with the situation. The individual's integrity or life is threatened. He sees little chance of maintaining his safety. He is overwhelmed by his tensions. The traditional concept holds that such experiences leave psychological wounds that weaken forever the individual's ability to cope with stress. The events associated with the traumatic experience become conditioned stimuli. The association is strengthened by reinforcement and is forever ready to spring to the fore to cause trouble in coping with stress, if not breakdown.

What results is sometimes referred to as a traumatic neurosis, an inappropriate symptom pattern of overreaction in a situation in which the individual fears for his survival. Once a traumatic neurosis has been developed, any threat to the individual's existence leads him to lose confidence in himself. He feels incapable of coping with the demands made upon him. The symptom pattern may include defensive rituals, autonomic disturbances, sensory-motor deviations, and loss of consciousness or violent vocal expressions. The development of a traumatic neurosis may be regarded as one of the organism's ways of protecting itself. Certain psychological and physiological symptoms are developed to ward off injuries.

34

Freud assigned great prominence to the psychic trauma inflicted in childhood, scarring the personality for life. The gun-shy dog and the spoiled race horse are classical examples, as is the case of the child who had an unpleasant experience the first day of school and forever hates school. There is the widespread, but erroneous, notion that all mental breakdowns are precipitated, if not caused, by a single traumatic experience.

Animal experimentation (Gantt, 1957; Liddell, 1954, 1956; Pavlov, 1928; Wolf, 1943; and others) has sought to solve some of the puzzling phenomena surrounding traumatic experiences. For example, the enduring effects of early trauma are dramatically illustrated in A. Wolf's (1943) experiments with rats. From the same litter of rats, the experimenter taped the eyes of one third, taped the ears of a second third, and permitted the other third to live as normally hearing and seeing rats. In time, the blinded and deafened rats learned to adapt as blind and deaf rats respectively. Then, the tapes were removed and in time, all of the rats learned to adapt as hearing and seeing rats. Under ordinary circumstances, it was not possible to differentiate between the three groups of rats. Whenever stress was exerted on these rats, however, the group whose eyes had been taped at birth behaved like blind rats and those whose ears had been taped behaved like deaf rats, both groups reverting to their early, overlearned, practiced modes of adaptation.

KINDS OF TRAUMATIC EXPERIENCES

A survey of the literature in developmental and abnormal psychology reveals that the following kinds of human experiences are likely to be traumatic:

1. Death of mother or father, both for children and adults.
2. Vivid frights, near drownings, near motor accidents, etc.
3. Accidents of various kinds.
4. Operations, both children and adults (especially the removal of some part which alters the self-concepts, such as an amputation or hysterectomy).
5. Sudden separation, divorce.
6. Sudden or severe deprivations (food, water, shelter, love, etc.).
7. Dog bite, attack by other animal.
8. Fire, trapped in fire and rescued, seeing someone burn to death.
9. Scenes of violence.
10. Riots.
11. Brutality in home, school, or neighborhood.
12. Oral trauma (infections of mouth).
13. Seduction (either homosexual or heterosexual).

35

14. Sexual assault.
15. Witnessing the primal scene, as in Lindner's *Rebel Without a Cause* (1944).

The reader should *not* infer from this that *any* of these kinds of experiences are *always or usually* traumatic. However, if any of them or similar experiences are badly handled or if previous development has been inadequate to cope with the situation, the effect can be damaging. Sometimes the families, friends, teachers, and others who deal with individuals who have had such experiences stifle all discussion about them. They assume that discussion of such experiences is painful and caution one another to avoid topics of discussion that might call forth associations of the painful experience. Frequently, however, such well-meant consideration does not help the sufferer. Usually it is better to talk about the experience and thereby get rid of the feelings of fear associated therewith. If the relationships (parent-child, teacher-pupil, friend-friend) are good, the damage may be only slight and only temporary.

WHAT MAKES INTENSE STRESS TRAUMATIC?

Liddell (1956) has identified four characteristics of experiences which make them traumatic: loneliness (lack of social contact), monotony, confusion, and overstimulation. A common factor in all of them is a loss of anchor in reality or lack of structure. Thus, intensity of stress may be regarded as a function of the degree to which an event or situation involves loneliness, monotony, confusion, and overstimulation and of the extent to which these produce loss of contact with the environment and lack of structure.

LONELINESS. Liddell observed that social contact is necessary in the newborn and that very young sheep or goats deprived of such contacts may be disabled for life or actually die. Psychiatrists have observed similar responses in man. New evidence has come from recent research on the effects of social isolation and reduced sensory stimulation (Bexton, Heron, Scott, 1954; Lilly, 1956; Kubzansky, 1961).

Bexton, Heron, and Scott (Heron, 1961) had as their subjects twenty-nine paid volunteer college students whose performance they compared with that of an equivalent control group. The experimental subjects, wearing translucent goggles, cuffs, and gloves, were told to lie on comfortable beds in lighted cubicles. Auditory stimuli were reduced by partial sound-proofing of the cubicles, U-shaped foam rubber pillows for the subjects' heads, and the masking hum of the fan and air-conditioner motor, which fed into earphones in the pillows. As far as possible, the subjects were prevented from finding out the time. They were fed and went to the toilet on request. Only 18 of the 29 subjects remained in the experiment long enough to complete the testing schedule. The tests included measures of intellectual functioning, susceptibility to propaganda, perceptual functioning, and physiological functioning. After two or three days in the experimental situation, subjects upon leaving had difficulty in focusing. Objects appeared fuzzy and did not stand out from their backgrounds; the environment seemed two-dimensional; and colors appeared to be more saturated than usual. The investigators also found drops in visual motor coordination as measured by such tasks as the Wechsler Digit Symbol Test, handwriting specimens, and the copying of prose paragraphs. Performance on the Thurstone-Gottschaldt Embedded Figures Test declined. All subjects reported having hallucinations, the onset being from 20 minutes to about 70 hours after entering the situation. The experimental subjects also showed greater susceptibility to propaganda about telepathy, clairvoyance, ghosts, poltergeists, and psychical research than did the controls. All of these effects indicate loss of anchors in reality, the major characteristic of traumatic experiences.

Rene Spitz's famous study (1945) of mothering in an orphanage has demonstrated the damaging effects of loneliness or lack of stimulation on the development of the infant. The experimental conditions involved the removal of the mother and failure to provide an adequate substitute except for sheer physical care. Such conditions of maternal deprivation and reduced stimulation produced serious and permanent damage. The infants did not grow normally, in spite of adequate physical care. Although the study has aroused much debate, the evidence does seem to indicate that such deprivations during infancy are accompanied by a pattern of retarded development, listlessness, and dwindling energy, which frequently ends in mental illness or death. Glaser and Eisenberg (1956) later reviewed 73 relevant studies conducted prior to 1956 and concluded that the combined evidence showed that where separation from the mother took place during the first year of life, a general depression and retardation of growth took place. Separation at later stages seems to be less severe in its effects.

Liddell's well-controlled experiments with twin goats illustrate a number of interesting facets. In one experiment, Liddell (1956) shocked twin goats, one with the mother and one alone. After 20 signals, the kids were left undisturbed for 45 minutes with lights on. At ten-minute intervals, tests were made by loud clapping of the hands. At first, both animals were lying on the floor with head pressed against it. The kid which had been shocked in the presence of the mother perked up his ears immediately. There was no response from the other kid for 45 minutes. In a similar experiment, the kids and the mother were put to pasture for three years following the shock. Retesting after three years showed that the effects had been enduring.

An individual derives many of the anchors that help him maintain his hold on reality from others. So much of his self-concept has been developed through a social comparison process that without the presence of other human beings, he lacks a guide to behavior. Thus an aircrewman performs heroically and without conscious fear while helping his buddies evacuate a burning aircraft, but is seized by loneliness and panic when he realizes that he is the only member of the crew left on the aircraft.

MONOTONY. Having been reared in the southeastern part of the United States, the author had always thought that the "battle-fatigue look" on people during long, hot spells was due only to the heat. During his first winter in Kansas, however, he noted the same look of fatigue during long, unchanging periods of cold weather. In a protracted period in an air conditioned apartment, he experienced the same feeling of fatigue in unchanging moderate conditions. Then, he began to observe the effects of other monotonous conditions. There were the same toxic effects seen in intense fatigue. The common element was the sameness which had the effect of robbing the victims of gauges for comparison.

Another type of monotony is to be found in regularly recurring dangers or alarms. Liddell points out that the inflexible repetition of alarms when long continued cannot be tolerated by man or animal. He maintains that the stress increases as the interval of waiting between signals increases. It might be said that this increase simply adds to the uncertainty, unpredictability, and loss of anchors.

CONFUSION. Almost by definition confusion is an unstructured condition in which stable anchors are difficult to fasten onto. There is unpredictability, instability, and disorganization. Liddell finds that even the white rat, gentled from birth, becomes panicky and vicious when confusion replaces routine in its laboratory tests.

OVERSTIMULATION. When anyone attempts tasks which are too difficult for him, he is headed for trouble, especially if he continues to persist toward an impossible goal. The animal, child, or adult, goaded to performance beyond his capacity, soon suffers damaging effects. The overstimulation may be in terms of demands for speed, accuracy, or complexity beyond one's capacity.

Thinking of loneliness, monotony, confusion, and overstimulation may be more helpful in identifying and understanding traumatic experiences than a long list of specific kinds of experiences. An effort has been made to show that in loneliness, confusion, and overstimulation there are rather severe losses of contacts with the environment or losses of anchors in reality. In extreme cases, there are sudden and rather complete losses of accustomed guides for behavior. Any one or all of these characteristics may be present in each of the kinds of experiences already listed as likely to be traumatic. For example, the loss by death of a mother or father is more likely to be traumatic if it results in loneliness and if there are no other social contacts to replace the loss. Loss of a father or mother may also be more traumatic if it is accompanied by confusion or overstimulation either from the event or from other events occurring at the time. The loss of a parent requires that one restructure some part of his life, establish new contacts with the environment, find new anchors in reality. If there is confusion and overstimulation, there is little opportunity to make these adaptations and begin responding constructively.

Thus, traditional concepts concerning intensity of stress and traumatic experiences appear, in the light of recent research on the psychology of stress, to contain considerable error. Intensely stressful experiences do not always produce traumatic effects and even when the effects are traumatic the damage is not necessarily permanent. Indeed, previous experiences of a mildly stressful nature and appropriate kinds of training appear to have a kind of immunizing effect in many situations involving even rather extreme kinds of stress. Furthermore, as will be shown in the next chapter, brief intensely stressful experiences may be less damaging and lasting than prolonged mildly stressful ones.

RESEARCH AND THEORY CONCERNING PANIC

One of the most dramatic effects of intense stress is panic. Some of the recent research and theory concerning panic behavior should enhance our understanding of intense stress. Thus, an attempt will be made to review briefly some of this work.

CONCEPTS OF PANIC

The term "panic" has been used in many different ways, some limiting its application to excited behavior in crowds and others reserving the term for use in rare instances of terror and paralysis. Generally, however, the term is used to refer to any highly emotional behavior which is excited by an immediate severe threat, and which results in increasing the danger for the self and others rather than in reducing it (definition suggested by Committee on Disaster Studies of the National Research Council).

The meaning of panic has been further delineated by Quarantelli (1954) as a result of his analyses of a number of disaster situations. In the following excerpt he summarizes his concept of the nature of panic:

> Panic can be defined as an acute fear reaction marked by a loss of self-control which is followed by nonsocial and nonrational flight behavior. Covertly there is an acute fear reaction, i.e., an intense impulse to run from an impending danger. Panic participants are seized by a fear of a specific object defined as involving an immediate and extreme

physical threat . . . panic is marked by loss of self-control. Two other prominent features are nonrational thought and nonsocial behavior . . . Such behavior arises from a definition of possible entrapment, a perception of collective powerlessness, and a feeling of individual isolation in a crisis (1954, pp. 272–75).

TYPES OF PANIC

Meerloo's (1950) use of the term "panic" is in harmony with the foregoing concepts and further delineates its meaning. He uses "panic" to refer to both individual and group behavior, not only fear and flight but fury, riot, and untamed aggression. He states (1950, p. 11) that panic exists when a dangerous occurrence causes a spontaneous, disorganizing reaction in the individual or in the group. Meerloo identifies and describes the following types of panic:

1. *Latent panic:* Suppressed feelings and fears with increased susceptibility to suggestion from the outside.

2. *Anticipatory panic:* Precocious mobilization of defenses with increases in taboos, magic actions, and continued anticipation of danger.

3. *Inner panic:* A sudden overwhelming of the individual by fear and anxiety with accompanying confusion and loss of direction or immobilization.

4. *Solo panic:* Uncoordinated flight to rid self of imaginary danger; accompanied by dazed amnesic state.

5. *Frozen panic:* Sudden immobility or "sham-death" usually in reaction to sudden and tremendous danger.

6. *Silent panic:* Communicationless utter despair.

The last-mentioned type of panic probably deserves further discussion since it appears to be of real importance in survival situations and since it has received practically no attention by psychologists during recent years. Meerloo (1950, p. 37) gives an interesting illustration of silent panic which occurred in a London bomb shelter in the spring of 1943. The shelter was very crowded and there was a bomb explosion nearby. The lights went out and somebody stumbled on the stairs; there was a sudden upheaval of tremendous fear but no yelling or crying. When first aid reached the scene, 200 of the 600 people were dead. Post mortems revealed no significant anatomical changes in the victims.

Apparently a similar phenomenon occurs frequently among castaways at sea. Bombard (1954ab) describes a similar panic among the victims of a shipwreck, which first interested him in survival research. As he puts it, people are literally "scared to death." He maintains that about 90 per cent of those who die as castaways on the sea do so within about two days. Since death from food and water deprivation is not likely to occur within this short a period, Bombard believes that these individuals are overcome by their fears of the unknown and die of fright. As Meerloo points out, Walter C. Cannon explains that in such cases a severe drop in blood pressure causes death, while others explain that death is caused by asphyxiation, the necessary oxygen supply to the brain having been cut off by the sudden cataleptic rigidity of muscles and breathing. Further investigation may reveal that silent panic is a much more frequent cause of death than we now recognize. Many survivors of emergencies have described incidents of passing out when seized by panic.

PRECONDITIONERS OF PANIC

A wide variety of preconditioners have been mentioned by writers and by survivors. These include such diverse conditions as lack of structure or loss of anchor, breakdowns in communications, resistance to accepting the reality of the situation or self-deception, the presence of crowd conditions, the state of the weather, deficiency in the organism of specific nutrients, psychological isolation, mental contagion, fatigue, suggestion and heightened imitation, social unrest, hunger, the shattering of group solidarity or group bonds, the presence of predisposed personalities, lack or loss of leadership, emotional tension, lack of personal and collective discipline, suddenness, errors, competition, hatred, and the like. Some of these categories are interrelated or overlapping, of course.

LACK OF STRUCTURE. It has already been seen from the earlier discussion of isolation and reduced stimulation that the stable organism apparently requires some anchor in reality. This anchor is lost, at least temporarily, when the existing structure is destroyed as a result of lack of information, breakdowns in communication, the sudden onslaught of some change or some threat, and the like. If the missing information can be obtained, if communication can be restored, panic can be averted or arrested and constructive behavior resumed.

Hudson (1954) has studied the effects of various kinds of unstructured stimuli on both human beings and animals and has found that lack of structure generates anxiety in both. In several studies, Hudson presented some sound pattern designed to lead to an interpretation of threat, generally involving both confusion and overstimulation. Some of his other experiments involved the presentation of ambiguous stimuli which were difficult to organize meaningfully. A third set of experiments involved strange combinations of familiar stimuli. For example, in one experiment students engaged in other work were presented with the sound of a bench saw running in the adjoining shop. This was a common occurrence except for the fact that the lights were out, a fact that could be observed through the half-glazed door. The shop was frequently dark, but the unusual combination of the darkened shop and the running saw produced anxiety bordering on alarm.

As a result of these studies, Hudson has proposed that anxiety is a primitive reaction and is not to be understood in terms of threat to self, values, and the like, but in terms of lack of structure or anchors in reality. He points out that the chief contribution of prior experience with threatening situations and training is the production of a more stable cognitive structure. In other words, the prior experience or the training enables a person to establish contacts with the environment, structure situations, and know what to do.

S. L. A. Marshall (1947) has written of panic in combat situations. On seven occasions during World War II, he investigated the cause of panic along the battle line. In every case, he found that the panic could be traced back to someone's failing to tell others what he was doing. Precipitate motion in the wrong direction was the open invitation to disaster in all seven cases. A typical incident is that of a sergeant who was hit through an artery during combat and ran immediately to the first aid station without telling the members of his own squad what he was doing. His own squad took after him and then the line broke. Others saw them in flight and they too ran. Someone said that the order had been given to withdraw and others picked up the word and sent it along the line.

It is a well-known strategy in combat operations, POW camps, political campaigns, and athletic contests to keep the enemy in constant suspense and to prevent his structuring the situation. Without structure the enemy will at least be delayed, if not prevented, from knowing what to do and will be unable to take constructive action.

SELF-DECEPTION AND ACCEPTANCE OF REALITY. Self-deception and resistance to accepting reality are logical consequences of lack of structure of the situation and threats to existence found in emergencies and extreme conditions. Hutschnecker has discussed this phenomenon in the following terms:

> It is always painful to awaken from self-deception to reality. If the reality turns out to be a trap with no hope of escape, it is frightening. Fear becomes panic when the original problem has been driven into the unconscious where we bury the things we cannot face (1951, p. 18).

The extremes to which an individual will go in order to resist accepting the reality of danger is illustrated in the following example given by Wolfenstein:

> . . . While such interpretations are plausible in terms of past experience, people may also cling to them in the face of conflicting

present evidence because they fear to acknowledge a more devastating reality. Thus a householder who has heard flood warnings may still try to assure himself that the water he sees on the floor was spilled by the children. Here denial tendencies support the mistaken and circumscribed idea of what is happening (1957, p. 52).

Meerloo (1950, p. 14) points out that Pavlov demonstrated how panic could be aroused artificially. By conditioning animals to certain stimuli and then suddenly stopping or changing the expected stimuli, he threw the animals into a general state of anxiety. This experience is similar to that of survivors who contend that they experienced no panic as long as they were face to face with danger. Their overwhelming fear came when expected dangerous events did not occur and there were periods of waiting. Errors in the execution of plans in a dangerous situation may also produce panic.

Strong "sets" or expectations plus breakdowns in communications or lack of structure may also trigger panic action such as bailing out of an aircraft when there is no emergency. Such an incident occurred in the case of a B-26 gunner over Korea. The gunner felt the aircraft going through some uneven motions and asked what was happening. The pilot was too busy to reply immediately, so the gunner bailed out before the pilot could reply. It was not until after the landing that the pilot and navigator discovered that the gunner had bailed out.

The possibly confusing considerations that have been introduced here may be clarified to some extent by the conclusion that the more an individual or a group knows about the natural and social phenomena involved the more likely will they be to differentiate actual from imagined danger and the more readily will they recognize actual danger as a crisis.

OTHER PRECONDITIONERS. Being in a crowd and being left alone have both been cited as preconditioners of panic. Apparently either a crowd or the lack of social interaction may destroy anchors or bases of comparison. For example, one study (Torrance, 1951) found that college students who have the most unrealistic self-concepts come either from extremely large or extremely small high schools. Apparently the moderate-sized school provides a large enough range for comparison, and the number of classmates is not so great that one is unable to place himself in comparison with others. In many cases, grossly inaccurate self-concepts cause entering college students to behave in ways which might well be called panic.

Wolfenstein (1957) has developed some interesting theories, primarily on the basis of a psychoanalytic orientation, concerning isolation and panic. Pointing out that one of our earliest childhood fears is that of being abandoned, she maintains that one of the most traumatic events of an emergency or extreme condition comes from the temporary feeling of having been wholly forsaken. She maintains that the presence of other people in moments of anticipated danger reduces fear. She attempts to show, however, that in crowds there is a competition for life. She maintains that there is a tendency to see the situation as one in which life cannot be granted to all and a basic fantasy to the effect that the death of one may assure the life of another. This tendency, according to Wolfenstein, gives rise to images of a violent struggle for life in a crowd where each would kill the others in order to survive. Thus, we have the basis for the panic reactions we find in crowds.

Poor social relations and competition may also be preconditioners of panic. The role of competition in panic has been neatly shown in laboratory experiments by Mintz (1951). These experiments involved the creation of miniature social situations in which cooperation was required for success. The basic task required the subjects to take cones out of a bottle. Only one cone could be taken out at a time and the bottle neck was easily blocked by too many cones arriving at the same time. Thus, the cones came out only if subjects cooperated with each other. Under some conditions, the experiment was presented as a measure of ability to cooperate. In others, it was presented as a contest in which one could win or lose small sums of money.

Mintz reported that in most cases serious "traffic jams" resulted when individual rewards and fines were offered, resulting in the retrieval of few or no cones. No similar disturbance occurred when the task was presented as a cooperative one. This experiment is presented as an analogy of what happens in panic-producing situations where cooperative behavior is needed for success and is rewarding to individuals as long as everybody cooperates. One good example in real life is a theater fire in which evacuation is orderly as long as everyone cooperates. Once the chain of cooperation is broken, however, it is no longer rewarding to individuals and panic and disaster result.

SUMMARY

Traditionally, intense stress and traumatic experiences have been offered as explanations of much personality maladjustment and mental breakdown. In such experiences, the shock is so great that the individual loses his anchors in reality or customary control and is unable to respond constructively to the demands of the situation. The problem has been studied largely through animal experimentation and disaster situations. The evidence seems to indicate that intensely stressful situations are not always traumatic and that the effects of traumatic experiences are not necessarily long-lasting.

Some of the major characteristics of experiences which make them traumatic are intense loneliness, monotony, confusion, and overstimulati all of which involve loss of structure or anchors in reality. The results intense stress are often referred to as panic which may take any one several different forms: latent panic, anticipatory panic, inner panic, solo panic, frozen panic, and silent panic. Various types of situations lacking structure are preconditions of panic. Various types of self-deception, resist-ance to the acceptance of realistic dangers, lack of social interaction, and the like also make individuals and groups susceptible to panic.

Response to
Prolonged
Stress

4

Some of the general theories of stress which have been developed in other fields seem to be very useful in solving problems related to personality and mental functioning and bringing about constructive behavior. Notable advances in the study of stress behavior have been made possible by the theories and research of Hans Selye (1950, 1956) concerning physiological adaptation to stress. The fields of medicine, psychiatry, and military operations have profited greatly from these advances. Research in psychology, sociology, and education related to stressful conditions would probably advance more rapidly if further studies were designed to test Selye's general theory of stress. Much of the existing confusion would soon disappear, if this were done. Educational practice could be greatly improved by an application of some of the ideas provided by Selye's contributions.

GENERAL THEORIES OF STRESS

Selye has maintained, against considerable opposition, that the human organism makes a nonspecific response to all types of stress and has called this the "general adaptation syndrome" (G.A.S.). According to him, the syndrome evolves in time through three stages: the alarm reaction, the stage of resistance, and the stage of exhaustion. The syndrome is called "general" because it is produced only by agents which have a general effect upon large portions of the body, "adaptation" because it stimulates defense and thereby helps the attainment and maintenance of a stage of accustomization, and "syndrome" because its individual manifestations are coordinated and even partly dependent upon each other.

J. G. Miller (1957) has extended Selye's concept as follows: "Living systems respond to continuously increasing stress first by a lag in response, then by an overcompensatory response, and finally by catastrophic collapse of the system." Miller also maintains that systems which survive employ the least expensive defenses against stress first and the more expensive ones later. Karl Menninger (1956, 1963) has also reinterpreted Selye's concept in terms of psychological behavior. Menninger (1963) has also emphasized the fact that in all instances physiological reactions are accompanied by psychological reactions and psychological reactions to stress are always accompanied by physical reactions.

Those who have studied disasters such as floods, tornadoes, and explosions have developed a set of concepts not greatly different from those employed by Selye, Miller, and Menninger. Killian has summarized the process of adaptation in disasters as follows:

> Initially the individual tends to interpret perceptual cues related to disaster in terms of his apperceptive mass, deciding what has happened on the basis of what he thinks might happen in the situation. Personally disorganized behavior, particularly panic, is not typically modal but occurs under special conditions. . . . Structuring activity, often the appearance of disorganized personal behavior, is typically a modal response in all zones early in the post-impact period. . . . Much initial behavior, both adaptive and maladaptive, is of a nonrational reflexive nature. The disaster syndrome, usually characterized by a state of "apathy" or "shock," affects a large number of persons (1954, p. 69).

Killian's description of the process of adaptation becomes clearer if seen in the light of a specific set of experiences of a junior high school teacher. During his first week of teaching, one of this teacher's pupils had an epileptic seizure. The teacher had not been forewarned that this pupil was subject to seizures. The pupil was new in the school, so other pupils were unaware of this fact also. Interpreting events in terms of the "apperceptive mass," the teacher at first thought that the pupil was "putting on some kind of act" for the amusement of his classmates. A number of the other pupils burst into uproarious laughter. The teacher immediately began trying to restore order, berating both the epileptic boy and his classmates. The teacher's admonitions had no effect on the boy. By now, the teacher realized that the boy had lost all control and was endangering himself. Responding irrationally to his first impulse, he tried to restrain the boy. It appeared to the other pupils that the teacher was fighting with the boy. Some of them were shocked and silent. Others were uproarious, making the teacher intensely angry. The teacher began yelling and flailing at these disorderly students. Thus, most of the teacher's behavior was nonrational and maladaptive. (Another teacher, in a similar situation, sensed that the student was having a seizure of some type and dispatched one student to find the school nurse. This act had the communicating effect of restoring order among other pupils. Constructive behavior was then possible. This teacher's response may also have been nonrational but was certainly adaptive.) After the seizure had subsided and its cause communicated, the entire class and the teacher behaved as though in a state of shock. There was perfect quiet. The teacher tried to summon some appropriate response but finally resorted to some very mechanical and routine task. Obtaining little or no response, he assigned students the task of rereading the day's assignment in the text. Very quietly and apathetically they busied themselves with this task for the remainder of the period. On the following day, the teacher was able to place the event in perspective for the class and whenever seizures occurred in the future both the teacher and the pupils behaved constructively.

Meerloo (1950) maintains that there are two factors that can be distinguished in the process of adaptation to any kind of stimulus. The first is a *mechanical* factor, an initial automatic adaptive behavior through trial and error. If the adaptive response has been practiced and overlearned, it may be performed automatically and the person involved may be unable later to recall his behavior. If the adaptive response has not been practiced and overlearned, a person is likely to respond in terms of early-learned childhood responses, usually of a trial-and-error type. The second factor is *purposeful* behavior with a search for a greater margin of safety and less expenditure of adaptive energy. This involves problem-solving behavior. If the stimulus is strange, unexpected, and dangerous, it will probably require what is commonly referred to as "creative problem-solving," especially if there is no single best or correct response.

What Meerloo proposes is a set of polar tendencies, a hasty mechanical adaptation as opposed to a delayed aim-conscious adaptation. Automatic control, according to this conceptualization, requires three general conditions. The first is *self-regulation,* requiring some mechanism for sensing problems, recognizing errors, and setting in motion a change of action. The second is *evaluation,* wherein some type of measuring device is brought into play to provide a guide for behavior according to some standard. Too many of these regulating and evaluating devices or standards, however, can delay constructive behavior and lead to breakdown. The third is *rapidity.* Measurement and regulation must be fast enough to restore constructive behavior before disaster results. Cannon (1939) also held that every complex organization, such as the human being, must have more or less effective self-righting mechanisms to maintain its functions and prevent disorganized behavior under stress. He also thought that an understanding of these self-righting mechanisms might offer clues for improving those adaptations which functioned inefficiently and unsatisfactorily.

If theories of instruction are examined in the light of these concepts, it would be hypothesized that teaching by authoritative identification is likely to result in the solution of problems by mechanical adaptation while discovery methods are more likely to lead to the solution of problems by delayed aim-conscious adaptation. In methods of authoritative identification, pupils are taught responses by repetition and some authority corrects their errors and prescribes the correct response. In methods of discovery, pupils are taught skills for detecting and correcting their own errors. Teaching by authoritative identification may lead to adequate behavior when situations are predictable but not in unpredictable ones. In unpredictable situations, teaching by methods of discovery is more likely to produce constructive behavior.

The Applezweigs (1954) maintain that behavior under stress may be made considerably more meaningful within the framework of a motivational theory. They define psychological stress as a conflict of motives. An understanding of behavior in a stress situation would require knowledge concerning the nature of both the stressor and the stressee. To implement their motivational theory of stress, they have developed an inventory which provides scores according to the following need scheme:

1. Escape from present pain or fear.
2. Avoidance of future pain or discomfort.
3. Social approval, or belongingness.
4. Self-realization, or creativity.

In many respects, this scheme fits quite neatly the problem of motivation in education and helps to describe the adaptations students make. Educators usually strive to activate the second of the above needs, avoidance of future pain or discomfort. This motivation, however, may at times be in conflict with the student's need to escape from the present inconveniences and fears involved in education. This need can be counteracted somewhat by the fact that he must learn certain things even to avoid present pain and fear. Social approval may either implement motivation for learning and thinking or be in conflict with it depending upon the prevailing norm of his group or what he perceives this norm to be. Similarly, the need for self-realization or creativity can be marshalled to support motivation for learning and thinking or it can be permitted to languish from lack of stimulation.

MECHANISMS OF REACTING TO STRESS

From the various lines of thought already cited, it seems clear that there is a recognition that the mechanisms required to adapt to stress over time are quite different from those called into action in sudden emergencies and unexpected stress. The work of Funkenstein, King, and Drolette (1957), discussed in Chapter 2, makes these differences clearer. Now, let us examine what is involved in adapting to stress over time, according to the Selye, Miller, and similar models.

LAG IN PERFORMANCE

What goes on during the lag in performance which occurs when an emergency arises, or when stress is markedly increased? Quite obviously, this lag may be a period of structuring, restructuring, and preparation for rising to the occasion. If this is the case and if the structuring is accomplished expeditiously, the delay is valuable. If it represents a resistance to accepting the realities of the situation and if it lasts too long, this lag is extremely dangerous. Even the accounts of survivors who have lived to tell their stories reflect the high frequency of this dangerous resistance. Moseley's (1957) analysis of aircraft accidents reflects the tendency to resist accepting the seriousness of the danger. A large proportion of fatalities occurred from bailouts which had been delayed too long. Llano (1955), in his analysis of a large number of sea-survival experiences, found that pilots were often reluctant to admit their inability to "make it back" and waited too long to send out a proper distress signal or make adequate preparations for ditching.

Students of disasters also see resistance to acceptance of reality as a major difficulty in getting people to take proper adaptive action in floods and other disasters. Fritz and Williams (1957) insist that, even with reliable knowledge about an imminent danger, a large population is not willing to heed a warning. They blame this unwillingness on lack of experience with disaster, the delusion of personal invulnerability, inability to adopt a new frame of reference so as to expect unusual events, dependency upon protecting authorities, seizing upon reassuring communications, and denying or disregarding communications predicting disaster. Even when the disaster strikes, the recognition of danger is frequently delayed, according to Fritz and Williams. People reinterpret the danger signals by associating them with some familiar or normal event. For example, the roar produced by high winds in the vortex of a tornado is often interpreted as the sound of a train passing nearby. A combat aircrew may interpret enemy flak as a hail storm. In fact, precisely the same phenomena have been described so repeatedly and so uniformly that it seems quite certain that we can accept this resistance to accepting the seriousness of a danger as one of the effects which must be dealt with through research and training.

Let us examine the words of several survivors as they describe this phenomenon in their experiences in surviving some emergency or extreme condition:

> I saw the truth but I did not want to see it . . . Yet I could not reconcile myself to the obvious (Tchernavin, 1934, p. 45).

50

I myself felt that I must be dreaming. When I compared notes afterwards with my comrades, I found that they had thought the same (Lias, 1954, p. 19).

Their [British] seamen hesitate to admit that a ship is sinking until it has departed from beneath their feet. Rather than admit they will cling, at imminent peril to their lives, to a riddled steel sieve and propose to conduct it home to port (Whyte, A. P. L., 1942, p. 179).

"This can't be happening to me." It was as if I were standing over at one side of the room. . . . It was like watching a movie . . . (Greene, 1953, p. 179).

SHOCK

Shock may occur concomitantly with lag in adaptation; it may occur immediately after the all-out action or overcompensatory response; or, it may occur long afterwards. Shock reactions are, apparently, defenses that the organism uses to protect itself and make life more bearable. In fact, Spiegel (1955) describes the kind of paralysis involved in shock reactions as resembling the playing possum seen in animals. When animals are exposed to fear or threat, they frequently play dead, apparently to fool their enemies. The person paralyzed after an emergency is frozen to the spot and cannot do anything.

Shock has been described in a variety of settings. It has been observed in an entire population, as in the case of France during World War II:

"No," she replied, "they are not France. You have seen people who are paralyzed. They don't yet realize what has happened to them . . . It's very complicated. It's like the moment after an accident. You know that something bad has happened, but you still don't feel it." (Brooks, 1942, p. 43).

Spiegel offers the following psychological description of the shock reaction:

The critical, appraising part of the personality is unable, under these circumstances, to determine accurately what is taking place. In catastrophic events of great tempo one of the most damaging things noticed by the individual after the event is that he was unable to do anything effective, because he didn't know clearly what was happening. This is frequently true of combat events, of airplane crashes, of automobile accidents, of railway accidents and so forth. Everything happens too fast . . . So the personality becomes flooded with fear . . . The physiologic reactions are excessive . . . The trembling, the sweating, the internal turmoil is of such a degree that the ego functions of awareness, judging, planning and self-control are beaten down . . . by the sheer raw pressure of the emotion (1955, p. 47).

It is usually the length of the delay in taking adaptive action that makes shock dangerous. There are times when the situation is such that it is safe to rely upon normal processes of recuperation to operate. Unfortunately, there are also times when the situation demands that individuals "snap out of it" in order to take adaptive action to preserve life, and especially to respond constructively.

A number of procedures for speeding recovery from shock have been reported by survivors. A majority of these have involved some type of countershock. Braddon (1955) described an incident in the Southwest Pacific during World War II that illustrates the power of countershock. A man felt too weak from wounds and shock to clamber out of a canal until wild pigs and dogs came along eating the dead. Then, in horror, the man leaped out of the canal and ran for miles.

Men who have experienced prolonged stress have also offered a number of suggestions concerning how shock or the prolonged effects of shock may be avoided. One of the most frequent, of course, is training through which men obtain realistic ideas of what to expect. Many have emphasized the fact that training which reinforces feelings of invulnerability is no help. Many also feel that reasonable expectations should be held of personnel in emergency and extreme conditions. There is some evidence that individuals respond more favorably to realistic expectations than they do to unachievable ones.

Some of these conclusions are especially relevant to problems of mental health in school situations. For example, a teacher, principal, or nurse may have to take some unusual action to get a child to recognize the seriousness of his situation. Teachers would do well to acquaint pupils with expectations and requirements. Similarly, principals and supervisors might be wise to make it clear to teachers what is expected of them at the very outset of their relationship, at the time they are hired, if possible.

OVERCOMPENSATORY RESPONSE

Of critical importance in crises, emergencies, and extreme conditions is the ability to summon the overcompensatory response, to "go all out." This response requires ability to mobilize aggressive energy. Some individuals characteristically tend to meet frustration nonaggressively while others meet it aggressively. These tendencies seem to be caused by early experiences of the individual. Of both theoretical and practical importance is the problem of what can be done to reinforce early aggressive learning and increase the probability that the overcompensatory response will be elicited when needed.

Another aspect of the overcompensatory response might be conceptualized in terms of risk. The individual, to survive, apparently employs the most economical mechanisms possible, but there may come a time when he must risk the more expensive ones. Many people fail to take adaptive action because they are afraid to exert themselves and thus deplete their energy.

This is true of the prisoner of war who clings to the safety of the camp instead of attempting to escape or of the pilot who clings to his aircraft instead of ditching or bailing out. Risk taking, however, is fraught with new and often unavoidable tensions and is frequently avoided. Again, this is a problem of much theoretical and practical import. The relationship of early life experiences to risk-taking tendencies will be discussed in later chapters.

MAINTAINING ADAPTATION

In many emergencies and extreme situations more than the "big push"—the overcompensatory response—is necessary for survival or adequate adjustment. Some stresses last a long time. Even when the danger has passed, however, there are chances of collapse. A woman who aided airmen escaping from Europe during World War II stated her hypothesis about this kind of behavior quite simply to one of the airmen she assisted:

> But I look at the young men who arrive like that, and I believe that the thing the doctor calls a chill is a symptom of mental strain, nothing physical. It is because the young man has been wanting so much to cross the mountains for so long. He crosses them and something that was taut inside him begins to sag. The doctor says it is a chill, but doctors are still groping in the dark (G. Millar, 1953, p. 423).

Taking a cue from this common-sense explanation of the phenomenon, we might hypothesize that there are two types of defense open to the individual who must endure a tremendous amount of tension in order to maintain adaptive action. One is to adopt some kind of insulating defense, such as pretending that "it doesn't matter—nothing matters." Another is to devise some technique for relieving tension. Some people display violent outbursts, but survivors report unusual ways of relieving tension, as illustrated in the following statement by Llano from his study of sea survivors:

> Several men stated that they drank [water] to relieve tension or to take their minds off the seriousness of the situation. After an especially severe shark attack which left the survivor's raft awash, the individual expressed himself as "terribly depressed." While in this mood he drank all his water supply, which he credits with reviving his spirits (1955, p. 49).

Activity of all kinds, of course, is known to be a good antidote in maintaining adaptation and constructive behavior during periods of lull. Experienced members of scientific expeditions who become accustomed to living under extreme conditions plan definitely for activities.

Men in dangerous situations seem to dread those long periods in which all is going monotonously smoothly; they long for some trouble, for something to make them struggle. Nansen describes this great misery in the following terms:

> . . . This inactive, lifeless monotony, without any change, wrings one's very soul. No struggle, no possibility of struggle! All is so still and dead, so stiff and shrunken . . . What would I not give for a single day of struggle—for even a moment of danger! (1897, p. 423).

High morale may also serve as a protective mechanism that helps to sustain continued adaptive action. Its role is described by Kardiner and Spiegel as follows:

> High morale is a protection for the soldier. Morale may apply to abstract and remote levels like democracy, freeing the world from Nazism, and the like; but it also applies to concrete and immediate levels, to such matters as cigarettes, dirty socks, theft of equipment, and the attentions given the group by the rear echelons (1947, p. 37).

In maintaining adaptation over a period of time, people can expect to be aided by some apparently automatic and certainly nondeliberate processes. The processes of adaptation to cold and heat stress have been well documented by the careful investigations of the Climate Efficiency Sub-Committee of the Royal Naval Personnel Research Committee. For example, in a study on cold acclimatization and finger numbness, Macworth (1953) found that men adapt physiologically when their hands are repeatedly exposed to moderately severe levels of windchill. An important practical effect of this finding was that manual work becomes more feasible under moderately severe windchill conditions with this increased acclimatization. Fingers do not become numb as rapidly and sensory feedback is better. The adaptation effect, however, was not great enough to prevent the development of frostbite. In Macworth's study both the experimental and control subjects started the tests before cold exposure with equal tactile sensitivity as measured by the vibration test technique. The experimental (exposed or acclimatized) men arrived for the test with fingers considerably warmer by an average of 3.6° C. Studies have also shown that Eskimos working outdoors are able to maintain normal finger skin temperature for a longer period after the start of cold exposure than are Eskimos who usually work indoors.

EXHAUSTION AND COLLAPSE

As stress continues unabated or reaches high intensity, the dangers of exhaustion must be guarded against. Much of the scientific discussion of this topic has been conceptualized under the term "overloading." Such conceptualizations generally hold that the organism has a certain amount of "adaptation energy" and that energy used to combat one type of stress is less available for reacting to other stimulation. This theory has not yet been elaborated through laboratory research, but many of the behaviors reported by survivors fit into this theoretical framework. For example, it may explain why there are apparent shifts in the priorities of various primitive needs during survival situations and why only one of these needs at a time seems to be able really to come to the forefront in emergencies. Survivors have reported that they were unaware of pain from very severe injuries, or of hunger and thirst after three or four days of food and water deprivation, or of fatigue after days of exertion. It also probably explains why almost all survivors report an almost total lack of sexual desire during stressful experiences. Other more pressing needs are apparently absorbing all of the available "adaptive energy."

Exposure to an overwhelming stress (such as prolonged starvation, worry, fatigue, or cold) can break down the body's protective mechanisms, no matter what their nature. There are, of course, factors that can shorten or prolong this process. Among those which hasten exhaustion, Shils and Janowitz (1949) list the following: disruption of primary group life, breaks in communications, loss of leadership, depletion of personnel, and ascendancy of preoccupation with physical survival.

A number of other ideas have been advanced by both survivors and scientists concerning rebound from exhaustion and the factors which enable an individual to continue adaptation long beyond what he considered possible. Many have hypothesized the existence of a tendency to assume some of the characteristics of the wild beast or of primitive man under conditions of severe stress. Many see this tendency as a positive factor in survival and perceive it as being associated with heightened sensory capacity—hearing, sight, smell, speed. Others see it as a type of regression dangerous to survival. Nansen (1897), Deane-Drummond (1955), and many of the men interviewed by the author describe the tendency as a factor that emerges automatically and comes to the rescue of the individual. Langhof (1935), Cohen (1953), and others have described a dangerous regressive tendency that corresponds to loss of dignity and return to primitivization. This sometimes involves a fading out of what is referred to as the "veneer of civilization"—polite manners regarding eating, speech, and toilet; refinements in dress and grooming; etc. Primitivization may have adaptation and survival value because more energy is made available for the action necessary in coping with the demands of the stress. If these lapses reflect or result in losses of self-esteem, however, the opposite may result.

Creativity and invention are constructive forces that have perhaps been given too little attention in the study of problems of personality development and mental health. Men who have survived extreme conditions describe creative and imaginative behaviors that not only solved immediate problems for them but apparently gave them renewed energy for continued adaptation. One aircrewman who survived many extreme situations in escaping from behind enemy lines in Korea described how he was incapacitated by injuries and other physical symptoms until he suddenly conceived of an idea for escaping. His physical symptoms disappeared or at least were

55

no longer noticed. Ward Millar's (1955) account of his experiences in evading and escaping from Korea is filled with many examples of inventiveness. He treated infected wounds by applying in powder form his halazone tablets for purifying water. On another occasion he had overslept at a critical point in his escape attempt and, to prevent a recurrence, he invented a natural alarm clock. Before going to sleep the next day, he drank a large quantity of water and was awakened at just the right time to continue his travels, which brought him to safety.

Even creative activities such as writing poetry seem to be useful in situations involving prolonged stress. Nansen occasionally became quite despondent while experiencing prolonged stress during some of his explorations. He usually recognized that he was becoming depressed, accepted his right to become depressed not only with the mercilessness of the extreme weather conditions but with the tedium and the repeated failures. He apparently found relief through both art and poetry. His books are beautifully illustrated with his drawings, paintings, and photographs (Nansen, 1897). The following is an expression through poetry of some of his feelings during one period of despondency:

> I laugh at the scurvy; no sanatorium better than ours.
>
> I laugh at the ice; we are living as it were in an impregnable castle.
>
> I laugh at the cold; it is nothing.
>
> But I do not laugh at the winds; they are everything; they bend to no man's will . . . (Nansen, 1897, p. 412).

DIFFERENCES BETWEEN IMMEDIATE MASTERY AND MASTERY OVER TIME

Before examining a few of the educational implications of the information about prolonged stress, an effort will be made to summarize what is known about the differences between immediate mastery of stress in the acute emergency phase and ability to master stress over time. Some of the leading theories have already been cited. In general, students in this area have concluded that man's primitive, automatic, early-learned reactions are operative in the immediate mastery of emergencies, while purposeful, deliberate actions are likely to come into operation during adaptation over time. There have been few experimental studies involving prolonged stress or adaptation over time. A rare exception is the experiment by Davis and his associates described in Chapter 2.

The finding of Davis and his colleagues that a man recovers rather quickly from severe stress of short duration and that the more harmful effects result from prolonged exposure seems to help explain a number of observed phenomena. For example, Graybiel (1957) uses it to help explain the results of a long-range study of naval aviators. He found that only seven of the 1,056 aviators studied died of disease during the 12-year period of the study, a death rate less than half that of men of comparable age in the general population. He also found from a larger sample that in every age group fewer pilots died of heart disease than nonpilots among Navy officers. Graybiel believes that these findings can be explained in part by the fact that on the average the Navy pilot flies less than one hour a day. When the stress is intensive, the period is usually followed by rest and recuperation, which provides an opportunity to recover.

Research in complex, natural situations such as those studied by Davis and Taylor and by Graybiel is difficult to evaluate. More recently Funkenstein, King, and Drolette (1957) have demonstrated that problems of the same nature can be studied in the laboratory. Although they did not attempt to study sustained or chronic stress reactions, they did study both acute emergency reactions and the ability to handle stress as time passes. In the laboratory, they interpreted the immediate reactions of their subjects (college students) during the initial stress situation as representing their "habitual acute emergency reactions." The subjects' over-all reactions to the stress situations, described in Chapter 2, were interpreted as representing ability to handle stress over time.

Another feature of adaptation over time was also brought out by the studies of Funkenstein and his associates. Some subjects handled the acute stress in such a manner that its effects were dissipated or reduced. Thus, its effects did not become chronic. Such a reaction is analogous to the mastery of stresses in daily life. When the individual fails in the mastery of stress, reactions to an acute stress begin to take on the characteristics of prolonged stress. In other words, the person is unable to "turn off the emotion" and the effects begin to accumulate until they become overwhelming and breakdown results.

On the basis of the work described in Chapter 2, Funkenstein and his associates have hypothesized that acute emergency reactions, representing basic personality disposition, are predictive in healthy subjects of the qualitative content of the psychosis or psychosomatic illness, should one develop. Proneness to develop such illnesses is related to the other aspect of adaptation to stress, the ability to handle stress in a time continuum. In terms of personality development, one's habitual method of reacting is determined or altered by his early life experiences. Adaptation over time is more likely to be affected by later experiences.

SOME EDUCATIONAL APPLICATIONS OF KNOWLEDGE ABOUT PROLONGED STRESS

If nothing else, knowledge concerning the consequences of prolonged stress should alert educators to its seriousness. This means that teachers, counselors, administrators, and other school personnel should be able to recognize the signs of fatigue and the warnings of impending breakdown.

FATIGUE

If teachers want to make use of the technical knowledge concerning fatigue, they will probably find quite practical the three psychological criteria of fatigue discovered by Bartlett (1940, 1943). Bartlett has sought to observe behavior under very rigorous conditions rather than to rely upon organic changes. His three psychological criteria of fatigue may be regarded as three stages in the psychological process of becoming fatigued. First, there are gross variations of timing with a lack of knowledge on the part of the individual of these timing irregularities. As the process continues, these irregularities spread to all phases of the activity. In this connection, Bartlett also states that there is some evidence that mental fatigue shows the same characteristic of growing irregularity of successive steps within the performance required. The second criterion is a splitting up or disintegration of the visual field or "field of display," as Bartlett calls it, with the consequence that the right actions are done at the wrong time and others are omitted altogether. Third, there are localized discomforts, aches and pains, and the like. Psychologically, Bartlett describes this stage as a progressive widening of the field from which selection is made, with a consequent loss of direction. When this stage has been reached, Bartlett states, all that the person can do is rest.

Bartlett's three criteria describe the process by which the individual loses anchor with reality or contact with the environment. Even in the first stage, he is unaware that his timing is irregular. Then there is a splitting up or disintegration of the field of display and finally there is a loss of direction. If we look at continued exercise itself as a stress, we find essentially the same process of adaptation as we find in response to other stresses. This way of looking at fatigue phenomena would fit into other research findings concerning it. For example, we might say that increased motivation postpones or prevents the onset of fatigue because, in a way, the increased motivation itself helps to maintain the anchor.

Putting the signs of fatigue into plain language, classroom teachers and other school personnel should be sensitized to the following as signs of fatigue:

1. Diminished initiative, keenness, and enthusiasm—a "so what" or "let it drift" attitude.
2. Tendency to shun others and sit alone.
3. Quarrelsomeness.
4. Tendency to criticize others.
5. Restlessness.

6. Increased use of props, such as tobacco and alcohol.
7. Drowsiness.
8. Mechanical quality of movement.
9. Loss of weight.
10. Loss of confidence.
11. Recklessness and boldness calculated to restore confidence.
12. Carelessness about safety, even about death.

School personnel should also be sensitive to these signs in themselves and in their colleagues.

Teachers, parents, and professional mental health workers should also be sensitive to some of the subtler effects of fatigue, such as unawareness of dangers, deterioration of skills, loss of perspective, forgetfulness, hallucinations (in advanced stages), increased susceptibility to persuasion, and inhibition of formerly strong drives. Sensitivity to such signs should be useful in preventing the shock experienced by teachers and parents when some child who has long been a model of behavior and high achievement suddenly breaks down, becoming ill, starting to do failing work, or resorting to misbehavior or violence. Such a child may have been "doing his best" for too long.

Adapting to intense stress after intense stress may also take on the characteristics of adaptation to prolonged stress. Teachers and parents, who are responsible for the introducing of children to new experiences and for guiding them in new experiences that children themselves initiate, especially need to be aware of the dangers inherent in a prolonged series of new experiences. Lois Murphy (1962), for example, points out that strangeness shock occurs at varying levels at all ages. It is repeatedly found in even the early days of infancy in the simplest form, a change in the stimulus situation. Her photographs record the frown on the face of the four-week-old baby who, after being nursed at the breast for the first weeks, was offered a bottle. The child's first months in school are also filled with such simple examples of strangeness shock. Most schools confront children in the fourth and seventh grades with too many such experiences within too short a period, making for discontinuities in development and in adjustment. Along with the introduction of strange experiences there should be periods that permit the assimilation of these new experiences. Otherwise, children show the debilitating effects of prolonged stress.

Motivation, excitement, interest, activity, and the like may prevent certain types of fatigue, but rest and relaxation are also necessary. Periods of intense effort should be followed by periods of rest or play. It should not be assumed that these periods of relaxation following periods of intense effort are wasted. For example, many inventors and scientific discoverers report that their great ideas occurred while they were in the bath tub, in church, or sitting under an apple tree. Most of the recent plans for the deliberate development of new ideas and inventions (Allen, 1962; Osborn, 1963; W. J. J. Gordon, 1961) include periods of relaxation following tension and vigorous conscious effort. Many modern inventors report that most of their ideas occur during temporary periods of relaxation after a period of vigorous thought. Teachers and school administrators should plan for periods of rest and should teach children to make productive use of them. Periods of all-out effort should also be planned and children challenged to test their limits from time to time.

SOCIAL ISOLATION

Another type of prolonged stress experienced by many children is that of isolation. When any youngster is for any reason excluded from his group, he suffers continuing emotional stress. He needs assistance in discovering the causes of his isolation and the remedy. Otherwise, there will be considerable damage to personality development and mental health. The specific characteristics of the child obviously will influence the kind of assistance that needs to be given. Kaluger and Martin (1960) have offered the following suggestions for helping the gifted child avoid prolonged loneliness, and these can probably be adapted for many others as well: *

1. Help the child learn how to join a group.
2. Help him develop the art of small talk.
3. Let him share room responsibilities with others.
4. Teach him to serve on a committee as well as to head one.
5. Assemble gifted children for social and cultural activities.
6. Avoid making the gifted child room representative; he is not "representative."
7. Let him learn to live under decisions made by average people.
8. Assign him to such school tasks as librarian, cashier, and hall guard; these duties will enable him to know many boys and girls.
9. Do not always choose him to do errands; other children also need experience.
10. Allow him to give his classmates help with homework in return for help in games and sports.
11. Foster in him a concern for slower learners.
12. Rebuke him when necessary, particularly if he is doing other work when he should be listening.
13. Give him some tasks that others have done with ease but that are sure to be difficult for him.
14. Suggest that he seek help from others.
15. Make your pattern of discipline apply to all but expand your curriculum plans to include learning tasks of varying degrees of difficulty.

* Reprinted from *Elementary School Journal* by permission of The University of Chicago Press. © 1960 by The University of Chicago.

16. Assign the gifted child a slow reader as a reading pal.
17. Explore the ideas of a book review or story review when the child may open up the treasury of his reading to his classmates.
18. Now and then make him responsible for an active game or mixer for the class.

OTHER RESULTS OF PROLONGED STRESS

Although many examples of behavior under conditions of prolonged stress will be examined in this book, it might be well to examine a few more special types to broaden our concept of the applicability of the principles related to adaptation to prolonged stress. The isolation of the gifted child is one type. The mentally retarded child may find it difficult to cope with stress. The blind, the deaf, and other children with special handicaps are under prolonged stress. If for no other reason, the blind child can be regarded as functioning under sustained stress because his blindness has deprived him of some of the most important anchors in reality. Through their senses people maintain their contacts with the environment, and vision provides them with one of their most important contacts with the environment, especially distant contact. Vision and hearing are the two senses of distant contact. Of the two, vision is the more stable. What is heard is gone forever. Therefore, there is a tendency to be less certain of what one hears than of what one sees. Loss of any one of the senses places a greater load on the other senses in maintaining contact with the environment. Certain adaptations take place within limits, just as in Macworth's experiment on adaptation to cold. Actually, however, there is never any complete letup in the stress produced by blindness. It is possible, however, to let up in the demands upon the blind person, especially in areas where visual contact with the environment is important. The blind child can compensate in many ways for his lack of visual contact with his environment but he has to learn ways of relieving some of the constant threat that results. As will be shown in later chapters, many of the strategies for doing this are essentially the same as the strategies for adapting and responding constructively to prolonged stress.

Another type of prolonged stress exists for many people who are forever being urged "to do their best" by their parents, friends, teachers, doctors, dentists, ministers, priests, rabbis, the press, radio, television, and other media. Day and night they are urged to improve themselves in some way—their health, their minds, their manners, psyches, eating habits, muscles and posture, even their love-making. All of these things are of course improvable, but constant pressures to improve in all of these ways can be overwhelming. The overambitious person, the person who wants to be thought well of by everyone, the person who tries to be "well rounded" —all are likely to be caught in a never-ending, unreasoning effort that may lead to fatigue, exhaustion, and collapse.

SUMMARY

Now that some of the accumulated knowledge concerning adaptation to stress over time in this chapter and to intense stress has been reviewed, what are the implications? What does it all add up to? Is such knowledge important in education and other everyday enterprises?

If we assume that one of the school's functions is to equip individuals to cope with the common, predictable stresses of the culture, there can be no doubt. Such information is necessary in determining what to teach, how to teach it, and how to evaluate the outcomes. The nature of the existing knowledge, however, is more likely to be useful in responding constructively through what has been described in this chapter as delayed aim-conscious behavior. This does not mean that the knowledge included in these two chapters cannot be translated into the more mechanical, practiced, and overlearned actions. It means that it is not possible to predict and prepare for all future emergencies in specific, precise ways.

From existing knowledge, it seems clear that behavior usually changes under stress, that it becomes more variable under stress, that individuals resist accepting the seriousness of a danger, thus delaying adequate adaptive action and making overcompensation necessary. Research and experiential data provide many clues about reducing this delay in adaptation and constructive behavior, minimizing the effects of shock, insuring rapid rebound, maintaining sustained adaptation and constructive behavior over a long period of time, and facilitating adaptation in groups.

In general, the evidence indicates that performance tends to improve with increasing stress up to a point at which constructive behavior becomes impossible and disorganized behavior results. An event or situation may be considered stressful to the extent that it causes a person to lose contact with the environment, anchors in reality, or guides to behavior. Lack of social contacts, monotony, confusion, and overstimulation all help to destroy guides to behavior in the environment. It also seems rather clear that a person responds to continuously increasing stress or sudden pressure first by a lag in response, then by overcompensatory response, and finally by collapse, if the stress is unabated. The evidence also indicates that in sudden emergencies a person relies largely upon early-learned and overlearned behaviors. In adaptation to stress over time, later-learned behaviors play a more important role than in coping with sudden or new emergencies. These later-learned behaviors also tend to be more important than early-learned behaviors in coping with stress over time and learning to behave constructively.

Personality Resources and Response to Stress

2

Psychosexual
Development as
Coping with Stress

5

In the next three chapters, an attempt will be made to come to grips with some of the problems related to the third set of variables which mediate the effects of stress, the "state of the organism." Included in this set of variables are the physical, mental, emotional, and spiritual resources of the individual. These resources emerge as the organism copes with the demands of the environment, internal and external. Personality growth and maturity are achieved as the person learns to respond constructively with these stresses.

WAYS OF VIEWING PERSONALITY RESOURCES

There are many ways of viewing the process by which personality develops in order to cope constructively with the ever increasing demands and stresses encountered by the members of any society. In a book of this scope, it is possible to do little more than list personality theories and perhaps present the major concept behind each of them. Two theories will be presented in some detail, and several others will be mentioned. In this chapter, the psychoanalytic theory of the stages of development of inter-personal relations is reinterpreted.

The developmental approach to personality has been chosen on the rationale that almost all individuals in our society encounter at various stages of life certain common, predictable stresses. Some of these stresses arise from man's humanness and will be found in all cultures. Others spring from the demands of the particular culture, while still others are idio-syncratic and are unique to certain subgroups, families, or individuals. In order to cope successfully with the common, predictable stresses, the indi-vidual must develop certain skills or take certain adaptive actions. If this does not happen, the course of healthy personality development is disrupted.

PSYCHOANALYTIC CONCEPTS OF HEALTHY PERSONALITY

The basic psychoanalytic concept that seems most useful in characterizing healthy personality or the personality's resources for coping with stress is "ego strength." This term is used to represent the executive capacities of the personality in coping with external threats and managing internal tensions arising from other parts of the personality (id and superego). Thus, whatever makes for ego strength should contribute to the individual's capacity for coping with stress.

According to psychoanalytic theory (Jourard, 1958, pp. 8–9), ego strength depends upon a number of things. First, the individual must achieve genital primacy. This means that sexuality is not blocked by feelings of guilt, anxiety, and the like. Use of energy is orderly and economical and there is alternation between sexual tension and satisfying sexual release. Pregenital strivings are sublimated and/or gratified, providing the energy necessary for socially valued activities and achievement. The Oedipus or Electra complex (the child's rivalry with the parent of the same sex for the love of the parent of the opposite sex) must be outgrown. The individual is able to give up his incestuous claims on the parent of the opposite sex, "make peace" with the parent of the same sex, and seek a love partner on the lover's own merits. He is able to overcome his mixed feelings toward both parents and feels a friendly affection for them. The ego is free from its struggle with the id and the superego, and rational thinking and action are possible. In other words, the ego is stronger than the id and the superego. The healthy person can feel both pleasure and pain more fully, since he does not have to repress his feelings and impulses. Finally, he has the capacity to do productive work, unhampered by needs to compensate for feelings of inferiority and irrational guilt. In other words, he can live fully and completely in harmony with his potentialities and interests.

MEASURING EGO STRENGTH

A number of instruments have been devised for assessing a person's ego strength but thus far each seems to measure somewhat different characteristics (Barron, 1953; Zander, Thomas, and Natsoulas, 1957; Cassel, 1958, 1959). Zander, Thomas, and Natsoulas have reported one of the few attempts to validate measures of ego strength against criteria of stress behavior. In devising their instruments, they tried from the outset to make operational the concept of ego strength. In developing one of their measures, they used spontaneously given self-descriptions. Scoring was accomplished with the use of a detailed guide, with plus values for the following indicators and minus values for their opposites:

1. Indications that ability exists to control emotional tension.
2. Indications of flexibility in control of tension.
3. Indications of felt obligations and standards to guide behavior.
4. Indications of low levels of tension.
5. Indications of executive abilities of the ego by self-reflections on the over-all ability of the ego.
6. Evidence of participation in specific areas of activity.
7. Evidence of existence of or pursuit of goals.
8. Evidence of motivation or energy for activity.

Zander, Thomas, and Natsoulas (1957) also developed two measures of ego strength with simple true-false scoring. One of these is called a multidimensional scale because several dimensions or clusters appear to exist in it. The second is called a unidimensional scale and forms a Guttman scale with a coefficient of the reproducibility of .91. The items in this scale are given below in order of the most to the least difficult:

1. I am one who never gets excited when things go wrong.
   (Correct response is true.)
2. Every now and then I lose my temper when things go wrong.
   (Correct response is false.)
3. I have very definite, established goals in life which I intend to pursue at all costs.
   (Correct response is true.)
4. Often I find myself doing and saying things that turn out to be things that shouldn't have been done or said.
   (Correct response is false.)
5. Every now and then I can't seem to make up my mind about things.
   (Correct response is false.)
6. Sometimes I don't care whether I get anywhere in life or not.
   (Correct response is false.)
7. There are odd moments every now and then when I suspect that I might go to pieces.
   (Correct response is false.)

In studies involving the quite realistic stress situations of Air Force survival field training, Zander, Thomas, and Natsoulas (1957) obtained quite encouraging evidences of the construct of ego strength. The ego strength measures were given to 459 male Air Force personnel just before they were exposed to a four-day simulated survival experience. Considerable effort, stamina, and will to persist against difficulties were required of the subjects. They were deprived of most comforts and conveniences, many going without sleep or food for long periods of time. Immediately after the survival exercise, the subjects went on an 18-hour exercise to test their ability to escape capture under specific survival conditions. During and after the exercise the subjects completed questionnaires and records designed to provide measures of survival-relevant behavior. Observations of behavior were also obtained by trained observers during the simulated survival experience. Subjects high in ego strength compared with those low in ego strength were found more often to be men who evaded capture in the 18-hour exercise, experienced less difficulty and disturbance during the simulated survival experience, indicated greater motivation to persist and survive, and refrained from attributing blame to themselves when actually captured in the 18-hour problem.

Another assessment procedure designed to give measurements of the relative strengths of impulses, ego, and supergo is the IES Test developed by Dombrose and Slobin (1958). In the test tasks that constitute this procedure, the ego, or cognitive, processes are assessed as they interact with the other processes of the personality (id and superego). One of the test tasks (Picture Title Test) consists of 12 drawings of activities and objects which may be classified as impulse and superego categories. Subjects are instructed to make up an appropriate title for each picture. An ego score is awarded when the emotional and orienting factors of the picture are integrated by the title. This score is balanced against impulse, superego, and defensive scores obtained in a similar manner. The Picture Story Completion Test consists of 13 sets of cartoons. In each set, two or three cartoons begin a story and the subject has to complete the story from three choices (impulse, ego, and superego). The Photo-Analysis Test makes use of nine men's photographs. Two questions are asked about the behavior and feelings of the men pictured and three plausible responses are provided for each question. In each case, the three responses represent impulse, ego, and superego behaviors or feelings. The Arrow-Dot Test is a perceptual-motor task involving the solution of 23 simple graphic problems. The subject is asked to take the shortest possible line from the point of an arrow to a dot, between which are a variety of solid lines defined as barriers. Dashed lines and gapped bars are not mentioned in the instructions and present the subject with opportunities for self-limitation. Responses are scored in terms of impulse, ego, and superego, depending upon whether the subject goes directly to the goal regardless of barriers, uses the most direct legitimate path, or is deterred unnecessarily by nonexistent barriers.

The IES Test represents an even more involving attempt to define operationally the ego strength construct. It brings into play the intellectual abilities. Unfortunately, this instrument has not yet been tested in terms of stress criteria.

EGO STRENGTH AS A MEDIATOR OF STRESS

Without regard to specific measures of ego strength but with regard to the construct, let us review how ego strength may be expected to mediate stress. Let us use three degrees of ego strength: low, moderate, and high. Under relatively nonstressful conditions, little variability is found in the way ego strength operates. If stress is applied, however, the individual with low ego strength becomes overwhelmed and shows a marked decrease in performance. The individual with moderate ego strength shows an increase in performance up to a point at which a decrement sets in. The individual with high ego strength, on the other hand, continues to show an increase beyond this point. Ultimately, however, he too shows a decrement in performance if the intensity and/or duration is great enough. This is an example of the repeated finding that, under stress, variability of performance becomes greater than under relatively nonstressful situations. In other words, some individuals perform better than usual under stress while others do more poorly.

DEVELOPMENT OF EGO STRENGTH THROUGH PSYCHOSEXUAL STAGES

The development of ego strength may be seen as accomplished through the psychosexual stages of development. At each stage of psychosexual development, the individual encounters new demands or stresses. Some of these are largely biological in nature while others are largely cultural or social. The onset of some of these stages is occasioned by biological changes and of others, by events in the family situation, such as the arrival of a brother or sister.

Let us now examine each of the psychosexual stages of development, looking into the nature of the events that usher in the stage, typical causes of difficulty, and some of the milder and more severe consequences of failure to cope adequately with the stresses involved.

ORAL STAGE OF DEVELOPMENT

The first stage of development, the oral, emerges from the infant's struggle for survival. Its first aspect is the *oral erotic* or *pleasure* phase. Later, there is the *oral sadistic* or *aggressive* stage.

ORAL EROTIC. The first oral satisfactions, or relief of anxiety or tension, are derived from sucking. Later, these satisfactions come from drinking, eating, smoking, kissing, talking, laughing, and the like. The early efforts to cope with the demands of survival and to reduce anxiety meet with varying degrees of success, depending upon the actions of the mother or other persons involved in the feeding. In this struggle, the oral erotic stage may become fixated. Freud (1925) has defined fixation as "a particularly close attachment of the instinct to its object." The strength of a fixation is generally measured in terms of its resistance to change, either by extinction or by retraining. Measures have been developed to study the roles of such influences as amount of reinforcement of a particular behavior, strength of the drive at the time of learning, the amount of reward, the interval between the instrumental act and goal response, punishment, effect of previous extinctions, strength of drive at time of extinction, and the like (Sears, 1944). All of these influences have been found through experimental research to affect resistance to change of fixated behavior.

In the case of oral erotic fixations, the resistant behaviors occur as a result of one of the following four conditions (Fenichel, 1945):

1. Excessive frustration in nursing, thumb sucking, or the like.
2. Excessive satisfaction in these oral activities.
3. Inconsistent satisfaction in oral gratification.
4. Simultaneous anxiety reduction and oral activity.

If for any of these reasons the oral erotic striving becomes fixated, the individual continues to seek anxiety reduction through oral erotic activities. In other words, striving for oral satisfaction becomes a dominating force in the individual's personality. One of the milder consequences is the development of what many psychoanalytically oriented students of personality refer to as the "three G's syndrome" (gullibility, garrilousness, and gregariousness). Symbolically, at least, the gullible individual seeks satisfaction by taking in (believing) whatever he is told. Through garrilousness and gregariousness, he engages in such oral erotic activities as talking, laughing, smoking, eating, and drinking.

If the fixation is severe, it is thought that the consequences may include such difficulties as alcoholism, peptic ulcer, asthma, depression, overeating and obesity, sexual promiscuity and oral perversions, and certain types of schizophrenia, chiefly the stuporous types (Fenichel, 1945). These become the individual's modes of coping with stress or his attempt to relieve anxiety. These methods of coping are especially likely to emerge or re-emerge, if the person experiences prolonged or severe stress and if he has earlier experienced success with oral erotic ways of coping with his anxieties.

ORAL SADISTIC. Fixation at the oral sadistic or aggressive stage results from excessive satisfaction, frustration, or inconsistent satisfaction in biting, chewing, and the like. Or, it may result from anxiety reduction from biting, chewing, or other orally aggressive behavior. It appears, of course, only after the eruption of teeth.

The milder consequences are thought to include sarcasm, malicious gossip, argumentation, nagging, or other oral sadistic trends. The more severe consequences are thought (Fenichel, 1945) to include: pathological sadism, pathological aggressiveness and hostility toward women, vampirism among women, manic-depressive disorders, and addiction. Again, these pathological behaviors may be viewed as the individual's attempt to cope with frustration resulting from stress. Such behaviors have become dominant as a result of early fixation stemming from one of the causes just cited. Fenichel (1945) has summarized a large amount of evidence, primarily clinical, in support of the possible consequences listed above.

ANAL STAGE OF DEVELOPMENT

As in the case of the oral stage of development, the anal stage has both an erotic and a sadistic or aggressive aspect. Both types of disturbance arise over difficulties in toilet and cleanliness training. Earlier, the infant has been free to evacuate at any time when the tension in the bladder or colon becomes too great. This is the expulsive stage. Later, pressures are exerted, first through encouragement and later through sterner methods, to cause him to withhold his urine and feces until the appropriate time and place. This is when the retention phase begins. As soon as the sphincter muscles are mature, the child is capable of retaining or expelling largely at will, and it is thought that he uses this as a weapon against his parents. If he sees them as a source of frustration, he will defecate in revenge; if he sees them as rewarding, he will defecate at the right time and place. If the training is too rigid or severe, he may retain the feces too long and become constipated. Thus, fixations at this stage may result from excessively strict, indulgent, inconsistent, conflictual, or premature toilet and cleanliness training.

Recent investigators such as Lois Murphy (1957b) have pointed out that individual differences in patterns of growth and in maturation occur and that these mediate the effects of the stresses inherent in toilet training. These individual differences help to determine the dominance or priority of various coping mechanisms. For example, a child may reduce the stressfulness of toilet training if his vocalization and linguistic development progresses rapidly and creatively enough to permit him to talk about his bodily experiences at the time the culture calls attention to them. Such a child may integrate the toilet and cleanliness training more satisfactorily than the child who cannot communicate how he feels.

ANAL EROTIC (RETENTION). During the process of toilet and cleanliness training many attitudes concerning cleanliness, orderliness, punctuality, submissiveness, and defiance are developed. As English and Pearson (1955) insist, the main problem is one of autonomy versus shame and guilt.

One characteristic way of resolving this conflict is the anal erotic or retention route. Associated with the fixation of this mode of coping with stress is the petulant, parsimonious, and pedantic personality (frequently referred to as the "three P's"). Such personalities become withholding in all areas of their life and are cold, inhibited, and unable to give affection. The quest for satisfaction through retention generalizes to include affection, money, time, ideas, and other possessions. The obstinacy and orderliness may be seen as attempts to hold onto what one has and to ward off danger by maintaining tight control. Many students, however, are not convinced that such ways of coping become generalized to such a great extent as this. Certainly much remains to be learned about the ways in which such generalizations take place. An interesting beginning is to be found in the work of Williams (1941), who showed experimentally that when two rather similar habits are learned there is a transfer of strength from one to another and both habits become more resistant to extinction than either would be separately.

Apparently when a person who has learned anal erotic ways of coping is subjected to a sufficiently stressful situation, the predisposition is for the breakdown to be in the direction of the compulsive-obsessive neurosis. In the symptoms of this neurosis, he expresses symbolically his forbidden tendencies and/or his defenses against them. A common compulsive symptom consists of washing one's hands constantly, a need associated with high anxiety about dirt in general. The patient, however, is not aware of the meaning of such behavior in terms of his repressed "dirty" impulses. Ritualistic activities, arranging and rearranging belongings, putting on clothing in a particular order, and the like are other symptoms. Such a person spends much of his time and energy unproductively but he is unable to control these irrational tendencies. If the stress is lightened, the symptoms may fade out, at least temporarily.

ANAL SADISTIC (EXPULSION). Some of the milder consequences attributed to fixation of the anal expulsive type and found in a variety of clinical studies (Fenichel, 1945) include aggressive temper outbursts, masculine striving, conflicts about eating, and playing of practical jokes. Some of the more severe consequences are violent rages, cruelty, destructiveness, sadism, and paranoia. Thus, the tendency to meet the stresses experienced in cleanliness and toilet training by aggressive, uncontrolled, punishing behavior persists and finds expression in adult forms.

PHALLIC STAGE OF DEVELOPMENT

During the third stage of psychosexual development, the phallic stage, there are four commonly experienced areas of disturbance. In the experience of most children, one of the earliest of these is masturbation. Later, depending upon parental reactions and the family structure, fears of castration develop along with penis envy, Oedipus and Electra complexes, and sibling rivalry.

MASTURBATION. As the child's curiosity about his own body increases, usually between six and twelve months, it is quite natural for him to manipulate his genital organs. Parents, however, find this disturbing and try to prevent its occurrence. An immediate reaction is to scold or otherwise punish the child. If the child becomes aware of its pleasure-producing effect, the practice may recur and be accompanied by even more severe punishment in the form of shaming, spanking, isolation, or threats of castration. Fixation may occur as a result of excessive pleasure or reduction of anxiety. Masturbation is likely to recur during adolescence, apparently as a means of reducing sexual tension at first. Then, it may become associated with the reduction of nonsexual tension. In some groups, it may also occur as a status mechanism associated with proving that one is a "man." It may, of course, persist into adulthood, or recur for various reasons. The frequency of masturbation in adolescence and adulthood is reflected in the finding of Kinsey and his associates (1948, 1953) that 92 per cent of American males and approximately 50 per cent of American females have practiced masturbation at some time.

There is fairly general agreement among psychoanalytically oriented students, as well as psychologists and psychiatrists of other orientations, that the stimulation of one's own genitals for sexual pleasure is normal in childhood, in adolescence under present cultural conditions, and in adulthood as a substitute when no sexual partner is available. Furthermore, some psychoanalysts (Fenichel, 1945, p. 75) report that persons whose sexual activities are blocked by external circumstances and who absolutely refuse to resort to masturbation as a way out show some unconscious fear or guilt feeling as the source of the inhibition. Some regard this, as well as the absence of masturbation during adolescence, as indicating a poor prognosis in psychotherapy.

Common consequences of disturbances concerning masturbation at all stages of development include anxiety, feelings of guilt, and fear. Among the more severe consequences found in psychoanalytic studies are the following: anxiety, hysteria, neurasthenia, enuresis, kleptomania, gambling, and addiction. There is no evidence, however, that masturbation itself causes mental illness, stuttering, stammering, impotence, frigidity, nor any of the above consequences of disturbance in this area. These are consequences from the conflicts, fears, and anxieties generated by attitudes toward the practice.

CASTRATION FEARS AND PENIS ENVY. In order to discourage masturbation or other disapproved behavior, parents or nurses may threaten to deprive the boy of his newly discovered and prized penis. Evidence has been

73

found, however, that even when no such threats have been made, boys have an unconscious fear that they will lose this possession. Such fears and anxieties may spring from the father-hostility inherent in the Oedipus complex or from the overemphasis in the society on the importance of the male. Thus, the stress may come from actual or implied threats or from fears generated by shortcomings particularly in measuring up to society's concept of masculinity. The girl may also be caught up in similar stresses. Discovering her lack of a penis, she may blame her deprivation on her mother. What follows is frequently labeled penis envy or masculinity complex.

Some of the milder consequences found in psychoanalytic studies include anxiety, feelings of inferiority, masculine strivings in the boy or masculine protest in girls, femininity in men or revenge on men in women. All of these increase the stressfulness of a child's adjustment and make the development of healthy control or mastery of the environment more difficult. If these stresses are prolonged, there may be more severe consequences in adolescent or adult personality such as exhibitionism, impotence, male and female homosexuality, sexual perversions such as fetishism and transvestism, or persecution feelings such as are found in paranoid schizophrenia.

OEDIPUS AND ELECTRA COMPLEXES. The boy's initial attachment is to the mother from her relationship in satisfying his oral needs. As the phallic phase develops, this attachment becomes more directly sexual. The father, however, is soon recognized as a rival for her favors; hostile wishes, including those of death and injury, arise. The behavior that results has been labeled the Oedipus complex after the Theban king of ancient Greece who killed his father and married his mother without knowing that they were his parents. This story emphasizes the unconscious nature of the boy's desire for union with the mother. In childhood it is manifested by desire for caresses and attention, by desire to sleep with the mother, and the like. A similar state of affairs may arise between father and daughter. The girl, according to psychoanalytic theory, feels that she has been shortchanged or betrayed by her mother, and turns her love to her father, finding in him some solace for her distressing lack of maleness. Out of this grows the girl's complex, frequently called the Electra complex after another story. Ultimately both of these complexes are resolved by identification with the parent of one's own sex and sublimated feelings toward the parent of the opposite sex. This process, however, may be greatly delayed and in some cases never accomplished.

Some of the logical consequences of the Oedipus and Electra complexes include jealousy and envy, feelings of inferiority through inability to compete successfully with the parent of the same sex, overambitiousness in an effort to win the affection of the parent of the opposite sex. Among the more severe consequences found in psychoanalytic studies (Fenichel, 1945) of inability to cope successfully with the prolonged or intense stresses which arise from this situation are impotence and frigidity in adult life, an insatiable drive for sexual relations, or schizophrenia.

SIBLING RIVALRY. The arrival of a newborn brother or sister is a tremendous threat to a child's position. It deprives him of privileges and parental attention, and in time brings about unfavorable comparisons and further deprivations. All of these undermine the child's sense of adequacy and in time act as a prolonged stressful condition. Immediate effects include such things as outright jealousy, regression to more childish behaviors, and the like. In time, increased shyness and timidity, tendencies toward daydreaming, negativism, and overcompetitiveness may result. There are also the many secondary effects that grow out of inability to cope with the stressfulness of the situation. For example, early frustrating experiences may result in excessive cruelty of one sibling to another. This in turn may result in injuries, feelings of fear and guilt, and other reactions that add to the intensity of the stress. Or, if the child is unsuccessful in competing with a sibling, he may resort to various kinds of delinquent or withdrawal behavior. For example, if the competition is in the area of school grades, such a child may cheat on examinations.

Sibling rivalry is intensified by parental conflicts, separations and divorces, favoritism shown to any one child, or inadequate attention. All of these add to the intensity and duration of the stressfulness of the situation and thereby increase the chances of fixation and disastrous effects. Many things can, of course, be done to reduce the intensity and the duration of the stressfulness attendant upon sibling rivalry. It is probably impossible, however, to expect to eliminate it.

Related to the problem of sibling rivalry is that of the effects of birth order on personality development and ability to cope with the stressful demands of life. Since the early theoretical work of Alfred Adler, a number of studies of this problem have been made. One of the most relevant and productive is a series of studies by Schachter (1959) in which reaction to stress is related to birth order. In a series of laboratory experiments, Schachter found that early-born subjects are more anxious and frightened when subjected to a standard anxiety-producing situation such as threat of electric shock than are later-born subjects. When given a choice, anxious early-born subjects choose to be together with other subjects, while equally anxious later-born subjects do not do so. Then, from several sets of independently collected data, Schachter tested his hypotheses in real-life analogues. He had hypothesized that troubled and anxious first-borns would choose social means of coping with their anxieties while later-borns would tend to seek out nonsocial means. Accordingly, he found that later-born individuals are overrepresented among chronic alcoholics and that first-borns are underrepresented among them. First-born and only children are more likely to seek help through psychotherapy and to continue in therapy over a longer period of time than are later-born individuals. Later-born fighter pilots proved to be more effective combat pilots than first-born pilots.

In attempting to interpret these findings, Schachter (1959, p. 43) points out the fact that a mother with her first child is undoubtedly more uncomfortable and more worried than she is with her later children. Thus, she probably responds to more signals, responds more quickly, and generally does a more effective job of reducing anxiety with her first child than with later ones. Thus, at an early age first-born and only children learn to rely upon the presence of another person to reduce anxiety.

GENITAL STAGE OF DEVELOPMENT

The first aspect of the genital stage of development is the establishment of the ego ideal, an identification with an admired person of one's own sex. In spite of disturbing factors that arise in many families, most boys learn to identify with their fathers and most girls learn to identify with their mothers. Through this process of identification, the child not only finds a way of coping with life stresses by identifying himself with the achievements of another but also learns techniques for coping with stress, especially those growing out of society's prescribed sex roles.

This process may be disturbed by conditions that are so intense and prolonged in their stressfulness that the individual is not able to manage them successfully. Negative relations with the parent of the same sex and failure to make peace with that parent may disturb the process. Inability to imagine oneself as an adult male or female may make identification difficult and retard or even prevent the process from taking place. A weak or inadequate parent of the same sex or the unavailability of a same-sex model may be disruptive. Such conditions are likely to occur if the father is unable to support the family, if the father is passive and the mother overly dominant, if the father is absent from the family a great deal, or if there is no male in the home. Since a child reared under such conditions is likely to have kindergarten and primary teachers who are women, his chances of finding a suitable same-sex model for identification are indeed limited.

Common consequences of disturbance in this area are immaturity, inability to assume an adult role, or delay of acceptance of adult roles. There may be effeminacy in the male or overmasculinity in the female, or there may be narcissism (self-love, sexual attraction toward oneself, or self-gratification of sexual desire). If the stressfulness of the condition is too intense or prolonged, there may be more severe consequences such as homosexuality, fear of marriage, or failure to fulfill adult roles.

The second aspect of the genital stage is finding an anaclitic love object or loved one of the opposite sex. Many factors may disturb or block this process. Fixations or unresolved problems at earlier stages of psychosexual development may interfere. Unsuccessful dating experiences, the unavailability of peers of the opposite sex, seeking this ideal outside one's social and economic status, and the like may cause difficulties and lead to conditions of intense and prolonged stress. An individual may be seeking this ideal in someone who resembles his or her own father or mother. Frustration may come through an unsuccessful attempt to find such an ideal or in disillusionment upon finding it. Stresses arise when the boy who marries a girl like his mother treats her as he has treated his mother, or when the girl who marries a man like her father reacts to him as she has reacted in the past to her father. Such behaviors are well-established, overlearned, and practiced. Thus, they are easily elicited when conditions are stressful.

METHODS OF STUDYING STAGES OF PSYCHOSEXUAL DEVELOPMENT

In the foregoing outline of the stages of psychosexual development, most of the supporting evidence comes from clinical studies, clinical practice, and other descriptive studies. Occasionally there have been experimental studies such as those cited by Sears (1944) and those of Schachter (1959), but these have been rare. Both clinical and experimental studies, however, constitute scattered and unsystematic evidence for supporting a theory of the psychosexual stages of development. One interesting systematic attempt to study and to test many of the formulations related to the psychoanalytic theory of psychosexual development is to be found in the work of Blum (1949, 1950) through a projective technique known as "The Blacky Pictures."

The Blacky Pictures consist of twelve cartoons which picture the adventures of a dog named Blacky. The cast of characters consists of Blacky, Mama, Papa, and Tippy, a sibling figure of unspecified age and sex. Each of the cartoons depicts either a stage of psychosexual development or a type of relationship within that development. Represented are oral eroticism, oral sadism, anal sadism, Oedipal intensity, masturbation guilt, castration anxiety or penis envy, positive identification, sibling rivalry, guilt feelings, positive ego ideal, and love objects (ideal and anaclitic). To male subjects, Blacky is presented as the "son"; to female subjects, Blacky is represented as the "daughter." Subjects are asked first to tell a spontaneous story about each cartoon. They are then asked a series of questions related to the psychoanalytic dimension represented by each picture. The first and main piece of research of a statistical nature (Blum, 1949) was a study of 209 college students and showed that statistically significant findings in the areas of sex differences and psychoanalytic dimensional intercorrelations were in striking agreement with postulates in psychoanalytic theory found in the writings of Freud and Fenichel.

Blum (1949) scored his 209 (119 male and 90 female) Blacky test records in the form of analogues of psychoanalytic dimensions of psychosexual development. He found a number of statistically significant differences between the responses of the two sexes and a number of statistically significant intercorrelations among the dimensions. Evidence was then sought in the writings of Freud and Fenichel to determine whether the significant test findings were consistent with psychoanalytic theory. Agreement between theory and test results was found in 14 of the 15 test areas in which the viewpoint of the theory had been stated specifically. For example, the test results showed that subjects who have adopted positive ego ideals are more likely to choose anaclitic love objects (males, $r = .61$; females, $r = .38$; combined, $r = .50$, significant at less than the .01 level of confidence). He found that theory holds that a positive ego ideal implies identification with the wholesome standards of the same-sex parent. The boy identifies with his father and the girl identifies with her mother. The transition from idealization process to choice of love object similar to the one chosen by the ideal follows naturally. Thus, in this case, Blum concluded that theoretical inference and test results are in accord with one another.

Since the original statistical study by Blum, the Blacky Pictures have been published as a projective test and have been used in clinics with individual children and in a number of descriptive and experimental studies.

SUMMARY

One of the common ways that students of human behavior have conceptualized personality development is in terms of stages of psychosexual development. Through these stages of psychosexual development a person achieves what has been described in psychoanalytic terminology as ego strength. Generally, ego strength is interpreted to include ability to control emotional tension, flexibility in the control of tension, the existence of felt obligations and standards to guide behavior, low levels of tensions, use of self-reflection, existence of or pursuit of goals, and motivation or energy for activity. Ego strength may then be regarded as a mediator of stress.

In terms of the psychosexual stages of development, the earliest learning to cope with stress occurs during the oral stage in the infant's attempt to gain satisfactions through sucking (oral erotic) and biting or chewing (oral sadistic). Learnings during the second or anal stage of development result from attempts to train the child to be clean and dry. These learnings may take either erotic (retention) or aggressive (expulsion) directions, depending upon a combination of child-rearing practices, accompanying stresses, maturation, and the like. Oral and anal ways of responding may become fixated if there is excessive frustration or deprivation, excessive satisfaction, inconsistent satisfaction, or anxiety reduction as a result of the oral or anal behavior. Such fixations may hinder the development of ego strength and capacity to cope with stress. During the third or phallic stage, some of the most commonly experienced areas of disturbance in psychosexual development are masturbation, fears of castration or penis envy, rivalry of the child with the parent of the same sex for the love of the parent of the opposite sex, and sibling rivalry. All of these disturbances may affect the course of personality development and the achievement of ego strength. In the final stage, the genital, a person finds an ego ideal, an identification with an admired person of the same sex, and an anaclitic love object, a loved one of the opposite sex.

Development of Interpersonal Skills as Coping with Stress

6

Just as the state of the organism can be considered in terms of ego strength, it can be viewed in terms of interpersonal skills. Most of the ideas that will be discussed in this chapter are those of Harry Stack Sullivan (1953, 1954). Sullivan based many of his ideas on the belief that basic needs for satisfaction and security are stressors that give rise to tensions, and that the satisfaction of these needs requires interaction with other people from the moment of birth. In the satisfaction of or the denial of needs, interpersonal relations evolve and interpersonal skills develop. If needs can be satisfied without the arousal of undue anxiety, a basis for security and good mental health is established. If attempts to satisfy needs for satisfaction and security are met with tenderness, there is no anxiety. Rarely is anyone so fortunate, however; interpersonal inadequacies and distortions in interpersonal perceptions develop.

In Sullivan's way of looking at personality development, the self-system develops out of a person's interpersonal experiences. A person is always looking for cues from others about himself and these cognitions become the anchors whereby he fashions his self-definition. Thus, one's self-concept is determined primarily by the way others define him, beginning with the appraisal of one's parents. The process of socialization introduces stressors that bring about further development of interpersonal skills. As the child grows, he experiences fear of punishment. If the authorities who carry out the socialization process are reasonable and predictable, the emerging individual has a cognitive basis for the development of sound interpersonal relations. If these authorities are irrational and unpredictable, he has no such basis for developing stable interpersonal relations. As he encounters new authorities, his self-concept is revised and new interpersonal skills develop. The first authorities are usually the child's parents or some parent substitute. Then there are adults outside the family—the kindergarten teacher, the Sunday school teacher, the playground director. Later the authority that mediates the socialization process is peer-group consensus, first one's own-sex peers and later both own-sex and opposite-sex peers. Then there are police, employers, work groups, unions, and professional groups.

The need for intimacy seems to produce tensions especially before the onset of adolescence. At this time, an intimate friend of the same sex may become of almost equal importance with oneself. With the actual onset of adolescence, there is what Sullivan calls a collision among the needs for security, intimacy, and lust. This collision is very stressful for many young people and requires much reorientation in adaptation. As a person acquires his full repertory of interpersonal relations—as a worker, spouse, parent, citizen, patriot, etc.—still further stresses occur and additional interpersonal skills are developed.

The skills a person possesses for coping with stressful conditions modify the effects that the intensity and duration of the stress will have on adaptive behavior. For example, when students are tested (subjected to a stressor), those who have the highest skills in handling the subject matter (cognitive skills) will achieve higher scores than those who have marginal skills. If standards are low and tests are easy, students with marginal cognitive skills perform about as well as those with highest skills. As standards are raised and tests are made more difficult, the differences in performance according to skills or competencies tend to increase. Of course, the tests can be made so difficult that there is no difference according to skill. No students could find any bases to guide their decisions, and all would tend to respond no better than chance on the test. Most teachers recognize that a reasonably difficult test differentiates more effectively the better prepared (more skilled) students from the poorly prepared ones.

Since many of the stresses in society grow out of interpersonal relations, interpersonal skills become key factors in coping with the daily stresses of life. It is indeed a rare person who can cut himself off from relations with others for long periods of time without undergoing serious personality deterioration and breakdown.

Sullivan (1953) makes the development of interpersonal skills central to his theory of personality development and mental health. Just as psychoanalytic theory views mental health in terms of ego strength, Sullivan views it in terms of nonparataxic interpersonal relations (behaving toward others realistically in regard to traits, feelings, and attitudes). Just as ego strength is achieved through the psychosexual stages of development, nonparataxic relations are achieved through progressive stages of cognitive development and mastery of interpersonal skills. Cognitive development, as used here and in succeeding chapters, refers to all of a person's ways of knowing and perceiving (recognizing, becoming aware of, realizing, guessing and testing, experimenting, empathizing, experimenting and discovering, inquiring and finding out, thinking, comparing and judging, categorizing and stereotyping, appraising, disparaging, dichotomizing, and the like).

Since any major disruption of the relationship between an organism and its environment brings about stress and each stage of interpersonal development is ushered in by such a disruption or discontinuity, at least in American society, concepts for coping constructively with stress are applicable. Each stage of development is accompanied by new demands that require new cognitions and interpersonal skills, and each is accompanied by increased stress and temporary lags in certain kinds of mental functioning and consequent ability to deal constructively with problems.

First, an attempt will be made to elaborate the concept of nonparataxic interpersonal relations as a cognitive process. A summary will then be given of each of the stages conceptualized by Sullivan (1953). At each stage, an effort will be made to identify the new foci of interpersonal relations, the new cognitive skills required for constructive behavior, and the nature of the discontinuity or disruption between the individual and his relationships to the environment. Typical areas of difficulty will be identified for each stage of development.

CONCEPT OF NONPARATAXIC RELATIONS

According to Sullivan's conceptualization, a person is best able to cope with stress and maintain sound mental health when his interpersonal relations are nonparataxic—in other words, when he behaves toward others realistically and adequately in terms of their actual feelings, attitudes, abilities, skills, etc. This requires a rather deep kind of perceiving or knowing (cognition). Mental functioning and capacity for behaving constructively under stress are impaired when relations with others become parataxic—that is, when a person starts behaving toward others as if they had feelings, attitudes, abilities, skills, etc., which in reality they do not possess. Distortions in cognitive processes and thus in interpersonal perception result in anxiety, fear, dread, horror, loathing, terror, and anger, which are exhausting and lead eventually to breakdown.

Involved in parataxic interpersonal relations are such phenomena as malevolence, hatred, and isolating techniques; deceitfulness; self-isolation; overcompetition and fear of competition; ostracism and stereotyping; disparagement; one-sided love affairs; loneliness; intimidation; ridicule; jealousy; and the like. In order to cope with the discomfort that arises from these, a person engages in what Sullivan calls "security operations" using "dynamisms," which are somewhat similar to defense mechanisms as commonly used in psychoanalytic and current mental health literature.

Psychologists have devised a variety of means for estimating the degree to which a person is parataxic in various aspects of his interpersonal relations. In fact, one of the most legitimate uses of personality tests in general may be to aid teachers, counselors, and others in becoming more cognizant of the feelings, attitudes, abilities, and interests of students and thus become more nonparataxic in their relations with students. In other words, information or cognitions yielded by personality tests may help teachers, counselors, and others to behave more constructively. No attempt will be made to survey all the methods by which parataxic relations may be assessed, but a few will be described as illustrations.

INTERPERSONAL CHECKLISTS

A number of interpersonal checklists have been devised for studying interpersonal relations and distortions in interpersonal perception. Perhaps the most useful and theoretically sound of these is one developed by LaForge and Suczek (1954; Leary, 1957). In one sense, the LaForge-Suczek Interpersonal Checklist provides a kind of taxonomy of interpersonal relations. A wide range of detail in scoring information is possible, ranging from a simple love-hate score to sixteen scores or even a score on each of the 134 separate items. Persons are asked to describe themselves and others important in their interpersonal world by selecting the adjectives that are appropriate. Others in their interpersonal world may be asked to describe themselves, as well as the subject. Discrepant scores indicate possible parataxic relations and sources of difficulty in coping with stress.

Adjectives were chosen along a four-point continuum under the following sixteen categories: Dominating, Proud, Rejective, Punitive, Critical, Complaining, Distrustful, Modest, Submissive, Respectful, Trustful, Cooperative, Loving, Supportive, Generous, and Advising. By combining these sixteen variables into pairs, the number of scores can be reduced to eight. The following is an illustration of the way adjectives are arranged in degree of intensity for the Dominating variable (Leary, 1957, p. 456):

1 Able to give orders
2 Forceful
  Good leader
  Likes responsibility
3 Bossy
  Dominating
  Manages others
4 Dictatorial

An example of parataxic relations is a person who has a score of 2 according to his own description, but a score of 7 or 8 when others describe him. The person perceives himself as "able to give orders" and as "forceful," but not as "bossy, dominating, manipulative, or dictatorial." Such a set of scores occurs frequently when a husband and wife describe themselves and each other. The checklist can also be used with an entire class. In discussion classes, the students may describe themselves, the teacher, and the remainder of the class (majority of the class). The functioning of the group improves when students learn that others also perceive themselves as generous, supportive, loving, cooperative, and trustful.

SCHUTZ'S FIRO TECHNIQUE

Schutz's (1958) FIRO (Fundamental Interpersonal Relations Orientation) technique may be regarded as an attempt to reduce the enormous complexity of interpersonal behavior to permit its study and improvement. The basic idea behind the FIRO tests is that human behavior can be understood in large part as the result of characteristic ways people have of dealing with other people. Schutz (1955) has demonstrated that information about these fundamental interpersonal relations orientations can be used as the basis for improving the compatibility and productivity of various kinds of groups.

Schutz maintains that every individual has three basic interpersonal needs—inclusion, control, and affection—and that these three needs constitute a sufficient set of areas of interpersonal behavior for the prediction and explanation of interpersonal behavior. One version of the test (FIRO-1) yields scores on the following scales:

1. I like groups where people get personal.
2. I like to talk about myself in a group.
3. I like to have people like me.
4. I like to get recognition for what I do.
5. I express it when I like someone better than the others.
6. I participate in group discussions.
7. I make suggestions to a group I'm in.
8. It's more efficient for a group to follow rules.
9. I like a group that follows rules strictly.
10. I don't like to seek aid in difficult situations.
11. I maintain my own opinion when others disagree.
12. I like to be a leader in a group.

The items making up the scales are presented in random order and respondents are asked to answer: Agree, Slightly Agree, Slightly Disagree, or Disagree. Scales can also be combined in such a way as to obtain relative needs for inclusion, control, and affection. Schutz sees his three types as being reasonably close to Freud's three libidinal types (narcissistic, obsessive, and erotic), Fromm's three kinds of relatedness, and Horney's moving toward, against, and away from people.

Schutz (1959) maintains that a leader can help a group to become more effective or healthy by pointing out to individuals that they and other people have basic needs, and that an understanding of these needs and of what people are trying to do may make each individual more tolerant of other people's behavior. He believes that serious interpersonal problems in a group can be handled best if the covert difficulties are brought into the open and handled directly. Serious interpersonal difficulties left concealed only smolder and then erupt at the expense of efficiency and productivity. Schutz describes one situation in which the leader of a group told one member that he did not like the way the member was acting in the group and he felt he should contribute more. After a brief but difficult and bitter exchange, the two began to tell each other their feelings about each other, and the situation improved markedly. Essentially what had happened is that the discussion had reduced the degree of the parataxic relations and they could now behave in terms of realistic perceptions. In addition, much of the hostility apparently was also dissipated.

SOCIOMETRIC PROCEDURES

A variety of other devices might also be used in studying, understanding, and reducing parataxic interpersonal relations, but only one other type of procedure will be offered to illustrate some of the possibilities. The use of what have been termed "sociometric" procedures was introduced by Moreno (1934) for just such a purpose. Elsewhere (Torrance, 1956b), the author has proposed some systematic ways of diagnosing group ills through the use of this technique. Essentially what is involved in the use of sociometric procedures is to have the members of a group to make choices and rejections on the basis of criteria that are realistic to the group (sit next to, work with, etc.). Such information is especially useful in helping group members who are isolated or rejected find greater acceptance and become more effective as group members.

Schutz (1959) has designed a set of criteria to fit the FIRO theory, but sociometric items may be designed according to many other rationales. The following are examples of some of the items used by Schutz in two studies (one involving students in a course on Creative Marketing Strategy and the other involving teams working in the Antarctic under Operation Deepfreeze of the International Geophysical Year):

> *Inclusion Items:*
> Men you most look forward to seeing at the group meetings.
> Men you find most interesting and stimulating.
> Men you least like to see at the group meetings.
> Men who most bore you, who are most dull and uninteresting.

Control Items:
Men who exert the most constructive influence in your group.
Men who are most competent and show the best grasp of the problem.
Men who are least competent and grasp the problem most poorly.
Men who exert the least constructive influence in your group.

Affection Items:
Men you like best.
Men in whom you could most easily confide and discuss personal problems.
Men you like least.
Men in whom you would be least likely to confide and discuss personal problems.

He also designed a set of items under these same three categories which were more descriptive and referred to personal characteristics of group members. These are as follows:

Inclusion Items:
Men who most need to be encouraged by the group before they will participate.
Men who are the lowest participators in group activities.
Men who try hardest to gain prominence.
Men who seem most uncomfortable when encouraged by the group to participate.

Control Items:
Men who are most bossy.
Men who are rebellious.
Men who are most indecisive.
Men who are most compliant.

Affection Items:
Men who try hardest to be close and personal.
Men who are most anxious to be liked.
Men who are most likely to reject attempts by others to be friendly.
Men who are most cold and unfriendly.

This might be a good time for the reader to design a set of items that would be applicable to some group in which he is interested (an elementary classroom, a school faculty, a football team, a band, etc.) and then work out a set of alternative ways of using the information in order to reduce the parataxic relations in the group and improve its functioning.

STAGES OF INTERPERSONAL DEVELOPMENT

The stages of interpersonal development as conceptualized by Sullivan provide a means of understanding the cognitive process by which parataxic or nonparataxic relations come into being. This particular conceptualization of development lends itself to analysis in terms of stress concepts because each stage usually begins with a crisis. In the transition from one stage to another the child seems to be regressing and teachers and parents tend to panic. At the beginning of each stage there is, at least in American culture, a high degree of parataxic relations. A child may have worked out an excellent set of strategies for coping with one set of demands. When new demands come along he is disorganized until he recognizes that his old techniques will no longer work. At first, he behaves in a very parataxic and unconstructive manner. Usually, he adapts to the new demands (though not always constructively) and develops new skills and learns to behave in a less parataxic manner.

Sullivan's theory is also useful because it incorporates concepts relative to patterns of thinking. By these mental processes a person interrelates with others. Thus mental processes become important in personality functioning.

INFANCY

The period of infancy extends from birth to about age 18 months, being concluded by the development of the capacity for communication through speech. The focus of interpersonal relations is upon feeding and other care and the person or persons doing the feeding and supplying the care. The infant's task is to learn to rely upon others to supply his needs and wishes. He struggles to develop ways of expressing needs and wishes. In this struggle he develops many of the interpersonal skills which he will continue to use throughout his life in controlling his environment. These skills are practiced and overlearned in somewhat the same way that the oral behavior in psychoanalytic theory is learned. In later life such behaviors occur spontaneously when the individual is confronted with new or stressful demands.

In this early struggle to communicate his needs and desires, the infant engages in a great deal of experimental behavior with the resources he possesses. It must take a great deal of guessing, testing, and modifying of guesses for the infant to learn how to interpret the facial expressions of others and to use his own facial expressions and tools to make known his needs and desires. His crying and other prespeech vocalizations are powerful tools for expressing his feelings, needs, and desires. His mouth is used for taking in (sucking), cutting off (biting), rejecting (spitting), and holding onto objects (mouthing or sucking) introduced by others. Various satisfaction responses occur when needs are satisfied and there is a feeling of comfort.

The capacity for empathic observation apparently has its beginning during this stage, as the infant learns to perceive the feelings of others as his own immediate feelings. There is also autistic invention, a primary unsocialized state of symbol activity through which the infant feels that he has control of his environment. Through experimentation, exploration, and manipulation he becomes acquainted with himself and his environment. It is in this way that he learns to differentiate between his own body and the rest of his environment. This is how he makes his environment more familiar and less threatening. To do this he uses his mouth, eyes, arms, and legs in reaching out, holding on, striking, feeling, rooting, and playing. In the process of exploring his own body, he may discover the pleasure of masturbation. In American society, this practice produces strong anxiety in parents who place taboos on such behavior.

Emergency reactions arise in response to situations which for the infant are new, unstructured, or lacking in known anchors to guide him. Such situations are seen as threatening by him, and reinforce his feelings of helplessness and powerlessness. He responds by crying, increased motor activity, or apathy and somnolent detachment. As the stressfulness of the situation increases, patterns of behavior arise to communicate increased need for help. These emergency reactions may take the form of increased struggle or greater dependency.

Fear is usually elicited by external events such as sudden, loud noises, sudden movements, or sudden changes in the situation. Rage is brought on by external obstacles that limit expression of needs and wants. The beginnings of anxiety come from the discomfort experienced by the infant, or by his empathic observation of a mother or mother substitute who is tense or generally uneasy.

The chief area of disturbance in interpersonal skills during the infancy period is manifested through anxiety, fear, dread, horror, loathing, and terror, usually as a result of neglect, lack of interaction, or threats to safety. The infant struggles to communicate these feelings through excessive, paralyzing, exhausting crying.

CHILDHOOD

The childhood stage usually extends from about one and one half to six years. It begins when the child achieves the capacity for communication through speech and ends when he begins to form relationships with children of his own level, who share his attitudes toward authority, activities, and the like. During childhood, the foci of interpersonal relations are upon the authority relationship with parents and associations with siblings and playmates.

The child learns during this stage to accept interference with his wishes in relative comfort, without the excessive, paralyzing crying found in infancy. He begins learning to see his own wishes in relation to those of others. He recognizes for the first time that he has the ability to stand alone to some extent. He becomes able to tolerate separation from parents and develops interest in associating with age mates and siblings. In his struggle to adapt to the new demands of these interpersonal situations, he becomes aware that he must postpone gratification of his own wishes in deference to others to attain certain satisfactions.

In this process, the child develops a number of new resources for coping with interpersonal demands. Speech and verbal communication become increasingly important tools for coping with his environment. He is now able to make meaningful sounds in making known his needs and wishes. He still relies upon certain nonverbal means of controlling his world. For example, the anus is a tool used in giving or withholding a part of himself to control the significant people in his environment. In this way, he expresses his feelings in response to the stressors he encounters.

The child's self-concept grows during this stage and is made up of the reflected appraisals of parents, siblings, playmates, and other significant persons. He maintains and increases his store of autistic inventions, which serve as tools through which thoughts, feelings, and words have a magical power of fulfilling needs and wishes. Many parents, however, work very hard to rid the child of such fantasies, frequently prematurely before his intellectual development is such that he can engage in sounder types of thinking.

Experimentation, exploration, and manipulation continue to increase throughout most of this period. The child's aggressive behavior, reaching out into the world, exhibitionism, imitation, curiosity, increased locomotion, masturbation, and parallel play are some of his ways of becoming further acquainted with himself and his world. Near the end of this period, however, there are increasing prohibitions against questioning, manipulation, and exploration. In spite of restrictions, however, most children will continue to ask questions because there are still many puzzling and disturbing elements in the interpersonal relations around them which they are, or feel they are, prevented from investigating. At any rate, a number of studies such as those of Andrews (1930) show that almost all types of imaginative and manipulative behavior diminish at about age five.

During the childhood period the process of identification becomes a tool for coping with the demands of the environment. The child uses this device in an attempt to be like some person who is important to him. This development ties in with the emergence of the concept of gender and the beginnings of the process of learning sex roles.

To such emergency reactions as fear, rage, and anxiety, the child adds during this period anger, shame, guilt, and doubt. Now, with the guidance of adults he can use these reactions in learning. *Anger* arises in the form of destructive feelings and thoughts in response to frustrating situations. *Shame* is expressed in the form of feelings of self-consciousness or embarrassment as a consequence of the child's feelings that there is something unacceptable about his behavior, thoughts, or feelings. *Guilt* is shame and anger directed at oneself. *Doubt* makes the child uncertain about what he should or should not do. All of these behaviors should be recognized as emergency reactions that require relatively expensive energies. Frequent or prolonged occurrence of these reactions, therefore, should be recognized as a signal that stress is taking too heavy a toll on the child's energies for adaptation.

Some of the typical consequences of heavy expenditures of energy include speech difficulties such as stuttering and stammering; malevolence, hatred, and isolating techniques; deceit; resentment; self-isolation; and regression to earlier modes of adaptation (fear, rage, and the like). It will be noted that most of these consequences involve in some way difficulties in communication. Sullivan (1953, p. 225) points out that by the end of childhood, the pressures toward socialization have placed a big premium on carefully sorting out that which can be agreed to by the authorities. The child discovers that he can get himself laughed at, punished, and so on for reporting fantasy or unusual ideas. Such ideas are ridiculed as being "silly" or "wild." He is beginning to learn that it is dangerous to report thoughts for which consensual validation is lacking. Suppression of thoughts naturally reduces the freedom and enthusiasm to communicate. Thus, it is not difficult to understand why so many of the disturbances of this period involve some kind of difficulty in communication.

THE JUVENILE ERA

The juvenile era extends from about age five to nine. The juvenile has a continued need for playmates of both sexes, and authority relations extend to authorities outside the home—teachers and principals at school, playground directors, Sunday school teachers, and the like. Some readers may recall the Hank Ketcham cartoon of Dennis the Menace on a soap box haranguing his compatriots at kindergarten, " . . . and she's not our MOTHER! Right? So why should we have to MIND her? Huh? Why should she blow whistles at us? Huh? . . . "

Thus, the major skills required for coping with the world during this stage are social subordination and social accommodation. It is during this period that the child begins to see authority figures (including parents) as people. Recognition of this fact is frequently shocking, especially to parents. Art Linkletter (1959) reports with amusement in *Kids Say the Darndest Things* the incident of a primary grade youngster, saying, while talking about a forthcoming school play, "We're going to have *real* people in the audience—not just mothers and fathers."

Though much of the juvenile's gratification still comes from adults, parents and teachers especially, he is just beginning to obtain gratification from his peers. He begins to explore and test the sharing activities, attitudes, values, and beliefs of his peer group. He begins to distinguish his different roles in various situations and acts out some of these roles.

In order to cope with the problems inherent in the demands of this period, the child acquires skills in competition, compromise, cooperation, stereotyping, ostracism, and disparagement. There are also further refinements in his skills of experimentation, exploration, and manipulation.

Competition is used in striving for affection and/or status with others. It involves all of the activities that go into getting to a desired goal. *Compromise* is the device through which the child gives and takes in order to maintain his own position. *Cooperation* is used in maintaining his own position by adjusting and adapting to the wishes of others. *Stereotyping* is a skill whereby people are placed into categories such as "the boys," "the girls," "the teachers," "the Jews," and the like to simplify the structure of the people in his world. *Ostracism* is the device through which some children exclude others from association with them. *Disparagement* is the skill through which the juvenile reduces the importance of individuals who may threaten his security. All of these skills, it will be seen, are used in the child's struggle to maintain his security or protect feelings of personal worth. Sullivan refers to them as "security operations."

For most children, the juvenile era provides further opportunity for refining the skills of experimentation, exploration, and manipulation. Adult disapproval of such activities, however, begins to reduce the curiosity and imagination of many children near the end of this period. If permitted to do so, juveniles experience learning as fun through cooperative play, recreation, and curiosity. It is their way of becoming more aware of themselves and their world. The author (Torrance, 1963) finds that during this period girls tend to give in to disapproval of manipulation and experimentation, and as a consequence many of their creative thinking abilities lag behind those of boys. Boys, on the other hand, increase in their manipulative behaviors during this stage with accompanying growth in their creative thinking abilities. It is well known, of course, that girls excel boys during this stage in vocabulary, reading, and the like. The typical areas of difficulty during this period are the following:

> Failure to learn social subordination.
>
> Overcompetition or fear of competition.
>
> Prolonged rejection by playmates in the ostracism or stereotyping process.
>
> Excessive ostracizing, stereotyping, and disparaging or being the victim of such on the part of others.
>
> Failure to "grow out of" this stage.

Perhaps most important of all during this stage is what Sullivan (1953, p. 243) calls "conception of orientation in living." A child is oriented to living if he can grasp the integrating needs that usually characterize one's interpersonal relations, the conditions appropriate to their satisfaction and relatively anxiety-free discharge, and the willingness to forego immediate opportunities for satisfaction or enhancement of one's own prestige for more or less remote goals. Sullivan maintains that if the juvenile's orientation in living is not well organized, his future contributions to the human race will likely be relatively unimportant or will be troublesome, *unless* he has good fortune during succeeding phases of development.

It should be noted that it is in this latter respect that Sullivan's orientation differs from Freud's. According to Sullivan, there may be interpersonal experiences at any stage of development that help to repair the damages wrought during the earlier stages. Psychoanalysts maintain that such damages are likely to be repaired at later stages of development only through depth psychotherapy such as psychoanalysis.

PREADOLESCENCE

For most individuals the period of preadolescence extends from about nine to twelve years. This period is ushered in by the development of the capacity to love another individual and ends with the first evidences of puberty. The foci of interpersonal relations are on an intimate chum of the same sex and on membership in preadolescent society. This calls for such skills as understanding of what matters to another person, social assessment, and social organization. Many remedial effects may result from the intimate relationship with a peer of the same sex and much of the damage to personality accumulated during earlier stages may be repaired.

During this stage, the child identifies himself with peers of the same sex to the exclusion of peers of the opposite sex. To boys, the only worthwhile people are boys. To girls, the only worthwhile persons are girls. Many children develop stronger loyalty to chums than to family members and the disparity may be disturbing to the family. After some difficulties at the beginning of the period, when creative activity and creative thinking abilities diminish, creative growth becomes evident.

A powerful force during this period is the love the individual develops for a peer of the same sex. This intimate relationship enables him to talk and to think about the things that really matter to him and to another person. He learns to express himself freely and truthfully. Tolerance, sympathy, generosity, optimism, and empathy flow from intimacy. Thus, the preadolescent emerges from the isolation that usually develops during the latter part of the juvenile era for many youngsters.

At about the beginning of this stage, there is a growing need for consensual validation. Many children reach a stage at which they are afraid to think until they find out what everyone else is thinking. This skill of finding out involves talking things over, comparing notes with others, and coming to a way of action. It represents an attempt to add more structure to one's world and to find anchors in reality. Unfortunately, many children are overconcerned about peer approval and conformity to the norms. In this process, some appear to sacrifice their creativity forever. Most, however, recover it after a time, if they are fortunate in establishing the intimate peer relationship and can discover ways of maintaining their individuality without sacrificing their security. Consensual validation may be regarded as one of the important security operations of this period.

Closely akin to consensual validation is the device of collaboration. It is a step forward from cooperation. Group success becomes important. There is a desire to maintain one's position in the group to derive rewards from group accomplishment.

Pressures to conformity have reduced the questioning, experimentation, and manipulativeness of most children by the time this stage has been reached. Certain refinements in the skills of experimentation, exploration, and manipulation emerge during this period. Out of the struggle to investigate his world and the accompanying disapproval and punishment, the preadolescent may show rebellion through restlessness, hostility, irritability, irresponsibility, and disobedience.

Although this period has tremendous therapeutic possibilities, it is also fraught with dangers. The intimate relationship with a peer of the same sex may be too intense or too one-sided. Teachers, recreational leaders, and others may unwittingly be the objects of "homosexual crushes." There may be disasters in timing these developmental stages. In some subcultures there may be excessive pressures to begin dating during this period. Since the child has not yet developed the skills necessary for coping with a heterosexual relationship, the result may be a disaster in timing. Failure in establishing an intimate relationship with a peer of the same sex or in gaining acceptance in adolescent society may result in a kind of loneliness and intimidation that is also tragic in its consequences.

EARLY ADOLESCENCE

For most individuals, the period referred to by Sullivan as early adolescence extends from twelve to fourteen years. It begins with the first evidence of puberty and ends with the completion of the physiological changes of adolescence. One of the foci of interpersonal relations continues to be the chum of the same sex. Although there is an interest in a "sweetheart," the early adolescent does not usually seek intimacy in this relationship with a member of the opposite sex. The chum of the same sex continues to be the confidant.

During this stage, the individual is learning the skills of becoming independent. He learns to evaluate his own limitations and powers, to anticipate the consequences of his decisions, and to evaluate critically ideals, beliefs, attitudes, and values.

To achieve success in these new stages of interpersonal relations, he requires some rather difficult skills. He needs increased sensitivity to what matters to another person, and he needs loyalty to the chum. Similarly, he needs the skills of dating and dancing and of carrying on a conversation with members of the opposite sex. In the process of developing these skills, there may be a collision of the needs for security, intimacy, and lust.

The acquisition of skills requires new types of experimentation, exploration, and manipulation—again amidst new and perhaps even stronger and more threatening sanctions. The early adolescent experiences an intense interest in becoming an adult and may actively rebel against authority, engage in fantasy, masturbate (with fantasies), and overidentify with heroes, cliques, and crowds. It is through such experimentation that he achieves a realistic perception of himself in relation to other individuals. The tragedies of misdirected experimentation during this period are too numerous and well known to recount.

Anxiety functions during this period to restrict the early adolescent's awareness so that he may continue to function productively in spite of the conflicts among his needs for security, intimacy, and lust. Otherwise, his feelings of inadequacy and insecurity in his new role would be overwhelming. He is especially besieged by feelings of guilt, shame, fear of not measuring up, and the like.

As is well known, this stage of development in the culture of the United States is a very dangerous one. It is especially unacceptable to many parents. Parents become disturbed and by their behavior throw "off course" what might otherwise be relatively smooth development. They become jealous of the attention to the chum of the same sex and to the sweetheart. As a result they ridicule, disparage, and otherwise discourage these associations.

Many very crippling attitudes are developed during this stage. One of these is the dichotimization of women as "good women" and "bad women" in boys and the dichotimization of men among girls.

Failure to develop the skills required for success may result in a failure to change the preadolescent direction of the intimacy need. Homosexual play and autosexual behavior may become established modes of adapting. There may also be a return to isolation or resort to such mental hygiene props as alcohol, delinquent behavior, unusual dress, and the like.

Although many of the difficulties of early adolescence arise in the sexual area, Sullivan warns that frequently there are difficulties far more serious than sexual ones. Many of the sexual difficulties, he maintains

(1953, p. 296), are remedied in the process of dealing with the other problems.

LATE ADOLESCENCE

The stage designated by Sullivan as late adolescence begins not with the completion of the physiological changes of sexual maturation, but with the achievement of a patterning of preferred genital activity and continues with the establishment of a "fully human or mature repertory of interpersonal relations, as permitted by available opportunity, personal and cultural" (Sullivan, 1953, p. 297). The foci of interpersonal skills include an intimate relationship with a peer of the opposite sex and the development of a full repertory of interpersonal relations (worker, spouse, parent, citizen, patriot, and the like).

In order to achieve success in these new relationships, an individual must have a realistic perception of himself as an adult and realistic perceptions of others. He must have self-respect and respect for the dignity and worth of others.

According to Sullivan, the chief difficulty is in the development *of parataxic relations with others*. It is difficult to avoid behaving toward others *as if* they have traits, feelings, or attitudes which in reality they do not possess. The development of parataxic relations is another security operation through which the individual seeks to minimize anxiety. The processes involved extend from selective inattention through all of the other classical dynamisms (universal human techniques of adaptation) to the gravest dissociation of one or more of the essential human dynamisms. These distortions result from misfortunes in development, restrictions of opportunity, and the like. Severe under- and overevaluation of self; confusion from past experiences, hurts, and slights; and retention of the interpersonal relations of earlier stages of development are just a few of the special obstacles to the achievement of nonparataxic interpersonal relations, an important aspect of mental health.

EXAMPLES OF RESEARCH ON PARATAXIC RELATIONS

A number of studies in education and mental hygiene have relevance to Sullivan's concept of parataxic interpersonal relations. Hughes (1957) describes a study which shows that about 50 per cent of the teachers in a survey thought that their principals disliked them. The principals, however, expressed very positive feelings of liking for the teachers. Zander, Cohen, and Stotland (1957) have revealed some of the misperception among members of the mental health professions (psychiatrists, psychologists, and psychiatric social workers). Duncanson (1961) has shown some of the nonparataxic relations among school board members and school superintendents.

INTERROLE ATTITUDES AMONG MENTAL HEALTH PROFESSIONS

Since the study by Zander, Cohen, and Stotland (1957) involves three of the mental health professions, it will be described briefly as an example. This study examines the nature of the interrole attitudes and behaviors of psychiatrists, clinical psychologists, and psychiatric social workers. Although many of the results of the study are presented in terms of the average or typical attitudes of one professional group toward another, the investigators show that some persons within each profession differ from the majority of their colleagues. The relationship variables studied include perceived relative power to influence, acceptance of power position, frequency of professional contacts, relative knowledge and skills, and satisfaction with providing advice for others. As is well known, the mental health professions constitute a hierarchical society. Psychiatrists occupy a superior position over clinical psychologists and psychiatric social workers and the prescribed working relations call for them to supervise members of the ancillary professions. Ancillary workers include not only psychologists and social workers, but also psychiatric nurses, occupational therapists, recreational workers, aides, and the like. These other workers are not involved in the Zander, Cohen, and Stotland study, however.

The results of the study (1957, pp. 133–41) show that the psychiatrist believes he is admired and liked by psychologists and social workers. "He is friendly toward them and willing to work with them, but he is not interested in winning their favor or good will, nor is he anxious to have their liking for him increased. He places much higher value on his own profession than he does on theirs." The responses of psychiatrists toward psychologists are somewhat different, however, than toward social workers. The psychiatrist is less comfortable with psychologists and prefers fewer contacts with them. He tends to value and respect psychologists more than social workers, however.

The typical psychologist or social worker is eager to be liked and respected by psychiatrists, tries to do whatever will make a favorable impression, and values greatly the profession of psychiatry. The typical psychologist wants to be liked and respected by social workers and tries to promote cordial relations with social workers. The typical social worker sees psychologists as intent upon winning recognition for their profession. He believes that he is equal to psychologists in ability and influence.

All of these perceptions vary somewhat according to the degree of power a person attributes to himself. A psychiatrist who attributes high power to himself thinks psychologists and social workers respect and admire him and seek to win his favor, and he is ready to associate with them. The psychiatrist who attributes low power to himself believes that psychologists and social workers dislike him, and he wants to avoid associating with them. Clinical psychologists and psychiatric social workers high in self-attributed power want few contacts with psychiatrists, have little desire to talk with them, and are unconcerned about winning their favor. Psychologists and social workers who are low in perceived power are eager for frequent contacts with psychiatrists, like to talk with them, seek to win their approval, and value psychiatry more than their own profession.

Acceptance of the power position, frequency of professional contacts, satisfactions from providing advice for others, prestige in own profession, and satisfaction with interrole relations were also found to be related to interrole attitudes. As a result of the study, Zander, Cohen, and Stotland concluded that attempts to improve role relations by such simple devices as providing more frequent contacts, or increasing one's knowledge of what each profession values and does, will be inadequate. Other more basic difficulties, they contend, may negate such laudable efforts. They place greater confidence in procedures directed toward the development and maintenance of more comfortable role relationships.

RESEARCH ON PERSON PERCEPTION

Both psychologists and sociologists have devoted considerable study in recent years to some of the fundamental problems of person perception and interpersonal behavior. Some of this interest and activity is reflected in a collection of these studies edited by Tagiuri and Petrullo (1958). All of these studies (as well as many of those which have appeared in such professional journals as *Sociometry, Journal of Abnormal and Social Psychology, Journal of Personality, Journal of Educational Psychology,* and *Psychiatry*) reveal the frequent occurrence of what Sullivan calls parataxic interpersonal relations and the damaging effects of such on personal and group effectiveness. Among the leaders in this area of research are Fritz Heider (1958), Solomon Asch (1952), Renato Tagiuri (1958), O. K. Moore (1958), Edward Jones and John Thibaut (1958), Fred E. Fiedler (1954), Theodore M. Newcomb (1956), Robert R. Blake (1958), Paul F. Secord (1958), Helen Peak (1958), and others. As Tagiuri points out in the introduction of the volume edited by him and Petrullo, little in a scientific sense is understood about how people perceive or know their human environment and how these processes are related to action. These studies do indicate, however, that such problems can be investigated by scientific methods and that man's ability to perceive others more accurately can be improved.

97

SUMMARY

Sullivan's interpersonal theory of interpersonal relations was chosen as one of the ways of looking at personality development because its conceptualization lends itself to consideration in the light of stress theory and theories of mental functioning. Basic needs for satisfaction and security may be seen as stressors that give rise to tensions, which result in the development of interpersonal skills and patterns of thinking. As a person's thinking develops and he is able to perceive accurately the attitudes, abilities, and interests of others, increasingly he is able to behave more constructively in his interaction with others in meeting his basic needs for satisfaction and security.

Several psychometric and sociometric methods were reviewed as methods of becoming more aware of nonparataxic interpersonal relations and correcting errors in thinking. The LaForge-Suczek Interpersonal Checklist, the work of Leary, Schutz's FIRO technique, and Moreno's sociometric procedures were suggested as possible ways of facilitating the development of more realistic interpersonal perceptions.

Sullivan's conceptualization of the interpersonal stages of development was offered as an example of the ways by which a person develops the cognitions and abilities needed in behaving constructively to the stresses and requirements of his environment. Each stage has different foci, requiring new interpersonal skills and ways of thinking and giving rise to new problems. In American society, discontinuities or new sets of demands tend to make each stage fairly distinct, largely because of the stressfulness of new demands for which preparation has been inadequate.

Research related to interpersonal perception has increased in recent years and has demonstrated that problems in this area can be investigated and that man's ability to perceive other people more accurately can be improved.

Other Aspects of Development as Coping with Stress

7

The two preceding chapters presented in highly condensed form two different ways of thinking about personality development, coping with stress, and responding constructively to the environment. In spite of the differences in the two approaches, the sensitive reader will see many similarities. Freud and Sullivan tried to describe essentially the same phenomena through their stages of development—the processes of becoming a person, the stages through which a person learns to cope with the stressors of his environment and to behave constructively. Freud endeavored to explain these stages of development in terms of psychosexual processes, because he believed that the understanding and control of the psychosexual processes offer the key to constructive human behavior. Sullivan tried to account for them in terms of cognitive processes and interpersonal skills because he believed that these offer the keys to constructive behavior. Other writers have chosen different approaches, and a few of these will be examined briefly in this chapter.

Although both Freud and Sullivan attempted to describe the process of becoming a person and thus the process by which a person learns to cope constructively with life stresses and to maintain mental health, they represent rather divergent points of view concerning the "fixedness" of personality. Both saw early experiences as highly important in personality formation. Freud, however, emphasized more than Sullivan the power of early experiences to fix a personality structure or characteristic ways of behaving. Sullivan maintained that personality continues to change and that experiences during any stage of the life history may change dramatically the personality structure and characteristic ways of behaving. He saw the preadolescent stage as unusually hopeful. If a child during this stage establishes a healthy, intimate relationship with a peer of the same sex, much of the damage of earlier stages may be repaired. If one is able in the later adolescent stage to establish such a relationship with a peer of the opposite sex through marriage, much may yet be done to repair earlier damage.

On the surface, the emphases of Freud and Sullivan concerning the early determination of personality would appear to be contradictory. An examination of stress research, however, suggests that each may have had in mind different types of behavior. Freud's observations may have emphasized emergency behavior or immediate reactions to stress, while Sullivan's may have emphasized adaptation to stress over time. The reader will recall Wolf's (Murphy, 1947) research with rats blinded or deafened at birth. After the tapes had been removed from their eyes or ears, as the case might be, they learned to behave over time as fully seeing or hearing rats. When subjected to sudden or intense stress, however, they reacted as blind or deaf rats. The reader will also recall the study of Funkenstein, King, and Drolette (1957) with Harvard University students. The early experiences of their subjects seemed to be most important in predicting immediate reactions to stress, while their later experiences seemed to be more closely related to ability to adapt constructively to stress over time. It may be that sudden or intense stress calls forth those primitive, early-learned, overlearned ways of behaving practiced during the early years of life. In adapting to stress over time, however, there is opportunity for such mental operations as recognition, memory, problem solving, imagination, judgment, and the like to function. Since these mental operations have continued to develop beyond the early years of life, later experiences become more important when there is enough time for these operations to function.

STAGES OF DEVELOPMENT AS USEFUL CONCEPTUALIZATIONS

Important in many theories of personality development is some conceptualization of "stages" or "phases" of development. In psychoanalytic theory, there are the oral, the anal, the phallic, and the genital stages. In interpersonal theory, there are infancy, childhood, the juvenile period, preadolescence, early adolescence, and late adolescence. Many theorists or investigators find such conceptualizations useful. Although approximate ages are given for the beginning and end of each stage, almost all proponents of stages of development are very careful to emphasize that precise limits cannot be placed on the stages, that the stages are ushered in by the onset of certain kinds of behavior or experiences (environmental demands), rather than by chronological age alone. Since most of the environmental demands are common predictable ones, the approximations usually work fairly well.

Some personality theorists find no use for a conceptualization that calls for stages of development. They maintain that personality development is continuous rather than discontinuous. It is, of course, true that even in our culture some children make the transition from one stage to another in what appears to be an orderly manner with few manifestations of disorganized behavior. In some cultures, almost all children seem to show continuity in personality development, and observers cannot identify the beginning of a new stage of development. Such cultures have few discontinuities; age groups are not segregated in the activities of the community and the school, and children are not confronted suddenly with new demands and expectations. In these cultures, mental development also seems to be more continuous than in cultures having many definite discontinuities that apparently make for identifiable "stages of development."

In relatively discontinuous cultures such as the United States, each stage of personality development seems to begin with some kind of crisis or new set of demands for which the child has not been adequately prepared. The severity of the crisis depends upon how well the child has been prepared to cope with the new demands, how much support he finds in his struggle to master new skills, the resources he has for mastering the new skills (especially his mental abilities), and how rigorously and harshly the new demands are enforced. Teachers, parents, and counselors should be cautioned not to panic if a child seems to be regressing as he moves from one stage to another. A child may learn to respond constructively to one set of demands or rules and suddenly be faced with new sets of requirements. First, there is likely to be disorganization until the child recognizes that old techniques and strategies are no longer appropriate. Finally, adaptation is made to the new requirements and eventually constructive behavior should result.

DEVELOPMENT OF CREATIVITY

Quite likely much behavior that seems puzzling can be understood, predicted, and guided more effectively when examined in terms of the new demands and stresses that confront children at each stage of development. The author's research into the development of the creative thinking abilities or imagination provides some validity for this idea. Using data from studies by Andrews (1930) of preschool children and research by the author and his associates of elementary, secondary, and university students, it is possible to construct a generalized developmental curve to represent the development of the creative thinking abilities (to be discussed in greater detail in later chapters). This generalized curve is shown in Figure 7–1.

It will be noted that beginning at age three there is an increase in imaginative thinking until a peak is reached at about age four and one half. A drop occurs at about age five and is followed by growth in the first, second, and third grades. At about age nine, near the end of the third grade or at the beginning of the fourth grade, there is a severe decrement in almost

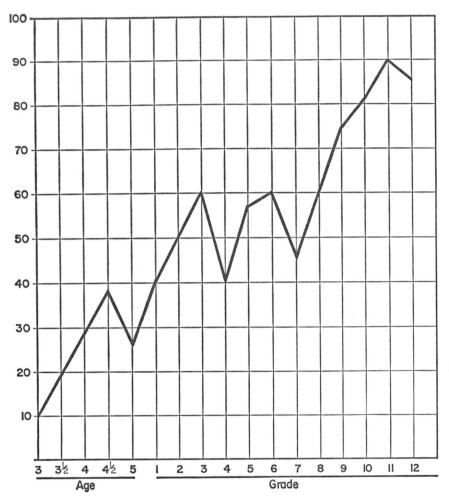

Figure 7–1. Generalized Developmental Curve of the Creative Thinking Abilities

all of the creative thinking abilities. Then comes a period of recovery, especially for girls in the fifth grade and for boys in the sixth. After this, there is another decrease in the seventh grade with recovery in the eighth grade and continued growth until a peak is reached in the eleventh grade. After this there is a leveling off or slight drop near the end of the high school period. Few groups have thus far exceeded the performance of eleventh graders. Studies of the performance of many individuals under many conditions, however, indicate that decrements continue to occur during crises throughout the life span.

It is interesting to note that each of the generalized drops occurs at ages at which the transitions from one stage to another begin. The drop at about age five occurs at the end of the childhood stage and the beginning of the juvenile stage with its demands for social accommodation, compromise, and acceptance of authorities outside the home. The second occurs at the onset of the preadolescent stage with its increased need for consensual validation. The third occurs at the onset of early adolescence with its increased anxieties that restrict many areas of awareness and demands for conformity.

The points of discontinuity in creative development correspond to peak ages for referrals to mental hygiene clinics and similar agencies. One recent study of psychiatric referrals in the Los Angeles area indicates that more children in the fourth and fifth grades are referred to psychiatric services than in any other grades. The next highest peak occurs in the seventh and eighth grades. At the Psychoeducational Clinic at the University of Minnesota, a peak age for referrals is at around age five at which time about as many girls as boys are referred. Another peak is reached at about age nine or ten, at which time the referral is much more likely to be a boy than a girl. These same peaks appear in the distribution of the correspondence which the author receives from parents about creative children who are experiencing some severe problems of adjustment or mental health. The author analyzed a sample of 100 such letters written to him. Figure 7–2

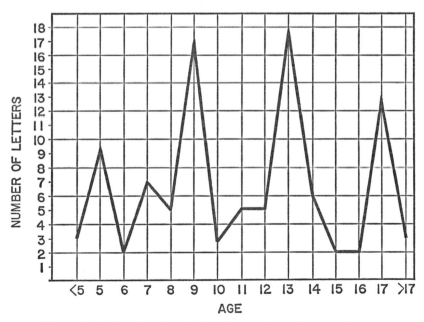

Figure 7–2. Distribution of 100 Letters from Parents Concerning Creative Children in Difficulty according to Age of Child

presents the data derived from this analysis. It will be noted that these peaks coincide with the discontinuities in the developmental curve shown in Figure 7–1, the peak periods for psychiatric referrals, and the transition stages as formulated by Sullivan. The largest number of letters came from the parents of nine-year-olds and thirteen-year-olds, the age groups that show the most severe drops in creative thinking ability and in creative activities. Five-year-olds and seventeen-year-olds seem to cause the next greatest concern.

COMPARISON WITH STAGES CONCEPTUALIZED BY GESELL INSTITUTE

It is also possible to relate the dips, spurts, and plateaus in the curves of creative growth with the cycles and stages conceptualized by the Gesell Institute on the basis of its vast array of developmental data (Ilg and Ames, 1955, p. 23). The following is a brief representation of the changes from two years on:

2 years	5 years	10 years	Smooth, consolidated
2½	5½–6	11	Breaking up
3	6½	12	Rounded—balanced
3½	7	13	Inwardized
4	8	14	Vigorous, expansive
4½	9	15	Inwardized-outwardized, troubled, "neurotic"
5	10	16	Smooth, consolidated

It could be hypothesized that the first peak occurs between four and 4½ years during the period described as "vigorous, expansive." The drop occurs between 4½ and five during that period described as "inwardized-outwardized, troubled, neurotic." Similarly, the second peak during the first part of the third grade occurs between age eight and age nine during a second period of vigor and expansiveness and is followed by a drop between nine and ten during a second period of conflict and troubled, "neurotic" behavior. The cause of the drop near the end of the sixth or beginning of the seventh grade is less obvious. One guess, however, is that it can be explained in terms of the stage between eleven and twelve described by the Gesell Institute as "breaking up." Apparently the "breakup" at this stage is more severe than at other times.

Ilg and Ames (1955, p. 23) are careful to explain that some children continue their development in a calm and smooth manner and cannot be described in terms of the stages of development shown above. So we find it with some children in regard to their creative growth. Ilg and Ames also point out that some children are so vigorous in nature that at *every* age they are out of bounds. So we find it with some of our highly creative children; they continue developing and testing their "wild" ideas in spite of the laughter and ridicule that they encounter.

STAGES OF DEVELOPMENT OF AFFECTION

Almost all clinicians and investigators of mental illness recognize the importance of the development of affect or love. Almost invariably, something has gone wrong with the development of affection in delinquents, the mentally ill, and other disturbed individuals. Many psychiatrists and psychologists have attempted to describe the process by which this development goes off course. One of the clearest conceptualizations of the stages of this kind of development has been offered by Sheviakov and Redl (1956, p. 6). Sheviakov and Redl see these stages as the essence of emotional growth and as one of the major aspects of spiritual growth. They characterize these stages roughly as follows: *

STAGE 1: SELF-CENTEREDNESS AND SELF-LOVE. Almost all investigators have characterized infancy as a period of self-centeredness or omnipotence. Each individual is in his concept the center of the universe; all else revolves around him.

STAGE 2: LOVE OF PERSONS IN IMMEDIATE ENVIRONMENT. During the second stage there is a gradual development of love for mother, first as comforter and source of pleasure, and later as an object of affection for whom small sacrifices are made. This affection, which spreads gradually to the father and to others in the immediate environment, occurs during the period which Sullivan labels as Childhood, if this period is a reasonably happy one. Otherwise, this stage may be delayed or may never occur.

STAGE 3: CLUB OR GANG STAGE. Next the child forms strong attachments to a group, club, or gang. At times, he has strong loyalties to a group of children most like himself, usually of the same sex. Various interests, social and psychological characteristics, and the like may serve as the basis of these identifications and loyalties. Ordinarily this stage occurs in the intermediate grades during what Sullivan labels Preadolescence.

STAGE 4: CLIQUES OR SETS. As the period of adolescence progresses there is usually a further broadening of affect to include contemporaries of both sexes. The loyalties are to a group usually referred to as a "clique" or

* Paraphrased from *Discipline for Today's Children and Youth* by G. V. Sheviakov and F. Redl (rev. by Sybil K. Richardson). Copyright © 1944 and 1956 by the Association for Supervision and Curriculum Development, Washington, D. C. By permission.

"set." Social problems that concern the adult have not yet gripped the adolescent. Romantic love develops during this period but is rather self-centered.

STAGE 5: ATTACHMENTS TO INDIVIDUALS AND GROUPS. Typically during the young adult years a further expansion of affect takes place. Gradually the young adult develops intense attachments to a mate, his children, his church, club, and professional or trade group. Interest may also extend to his community, state, and nation. The element of "my" family, "my" home state, and the like are still important.

STAGE 6: DEVOTION TO IDEALS. Although many individuals never reach the sixth stage, the person regarded by Sheviakov and Redl as mature in his development of affect extends his loyalties beyond himself and his immediate associates. He becomes devoted to such ideals as justice, liberty, tolerance, sympathy for the downtrodden, and other broad human values. He places these human values above personal gain, comfort, and personal loyalties. An ideal or a principle becomes more important than one's group, one's friends, even one's family.

In democratic societies, education seeks to develop affect through all six stages. In authoritarian societies, however, education substitutes for the sixth stage in the concept of a master race or privileged class. Youths in such societies are trained to discriminate against those not like themselves, racially or ideologically.

VOCATIONAL AND CAREER DEVELOPMENT

Vocational and career development may also be conceptualized in terms of the individual's efforts to cope with the changing demands and pressures of life and the process of becoming a person. To be satisfactory, such a conceptualization must include the entire life span. In general, however, scholars in the field and vocational guidance workers have not concerned themselves with the vocational and career development that takes place below the high school level. This serious deficiency in educational thinking can be remedied. Elementary schools can make conscious use of such devices as role playing, role tests, and role training. The vocational guidance program of the elementary school might include a survey of the characteristic vocational roles of the community, and some roles outside the community. Children can be assigned these roles, can enact them and discuss the discrepancies between the actor's performance and the demands of the role in terms of adequacy and enjoyment.

Such experiences prepare children to cope more adequately and constructively with the common, predictable stresses in society by broadening their vocational horizon, helping them become more aware of the world about them, helping them to understand better themselves and their world, educating them to be more effective and spontaneous as individuals, and providing a vehicle by which vocational information can be imparted to them in a meaningful, integrated, and realistic fashion.

Elizabeth Andrews, in 1930, suggested that vocational guidance should be begun in the nursery, not by forcing on the child a vocation selected by teacher or parent, but by allowing him to develop along the lines of his prevailing interests. Her contention was that we should encourage rather than inhibit children in their creative acts—their questioning, experimenting, exploring, and testing. It is not necessary that the child's creative acts conform to adult standards. English and Pearson (1955) have argued for a similar point of view. They encourage adults to find out whether or not children observe how the workaday world operates and where they can fit in. For example, parents should find out whether or not their child is observing butchers, mechanics, engineers, doctors, and lawyers and what they do, so that he can at least begin thinking about where his place is to be.

Although several writers in the vocational guidance field have presented conceptualizations of the stages of vocational and career development, one offered by Super (1957) appears fairly satisfactory for our purposes. He bases his conceptualization on the psychological life stages defined by Buehler (1933). These stages are as follows:

1. Growth stage, conception to about age 14.
2. Exploratory stage, age 15 to about 25.
3. Establishment stage, age 25 to about 45.
4. Maintenance stage, age 45 to about 65.
5. Stage of decline, beginning at about age 65.

Super discusses each of these stages except the first, cautioning that the age limits are only approximations and vary from person to person. He also points out that there are different kinds of career patterns. For men, he describes the following types of career patterns: stable, conventional, unstable, and multiple-trial. For women, he describes the stable homemaking career pattern, the conventional career pattern, the stable working career pattern, the double-track career pattern (working and homemaking), the interrupted career pattern, the unstable career pattern, and the multiple-trial career pattern.

EXPLORATORY STAGE. The exploratory stage involves the development of an understanding of the self, trying out adult roles, finding a mate, finding an occupation, and finding one's place in the community. By the time an individual in our culture reaches adolescence he has had a chance to develop to a considerable degree his self-concept and to test it in a variety of situations. He finds these opportunities first in the home and in the neighborhood. As the demands of his environment take him into the school, church, and community activities, he has other opportunities. Part-time or vacation employment, work in school clubs, participation in Boy Scouts, 4-H Club, and the like provide further tests of his self-concept and help him to measure himself against various vocational roles. Thus, the process of ascertaining and testing reality dominates vocational development during the exploratory stage. School provides opportunities for reality testing through its formal curriculum, vocational orientation courses, activities (drama, journalism, science, and farming clubs), informal exploration, and new role models. Many schools and colleges offer work programs that afford further opportunities for exploration.

During the exploratory stage the discrepancies between aspirations and abilities and achievements are worked out. The individual attempts to implement his self-concept and as a result may engage in considerable floundering and tryout. In finding his place in the world of work, he comes to grips with the problems of choosing, locating, and getting a job; modifying his self-concept and adjusting to lacks of opportunity or resources, social expectations, authority, fellow workers, and the like; meeting demands of family and home; and adapting to community pressures. He learns to cope with problems of adjustments to work requirements, technical requirements, work routine and tempo, work attitudes and values, work load, security, and waiting for advancement. There is considerable mobility during this stage; aimlessness, dissatisfaction, and various kinds of floundering may interfere with development.

ESTABLISHMENT STAGE. During the establishment stage, the worker establishes a family, a home, and a role in the community, in addition to making a place for himself in the world of work. He establishes a practice, builds a business, or develops a work history that establishes him in a trade. The self-concept has been modified and implemented. The individual's place in the world of work is becoming stabilized. According to Super, establishment in a career means the end of floundering but not the end of mobility. The stabilization process is accompanied by the achievement of seniority, family responsibilities, and emotional ties. There may, however, be various economic and social forces that disrupt the process.

In general, the advancement process moves forward with its ups and downs. The worker must cope with problems of informal relationships (knowing the right people), merit and achievement, techniques of acquiring a clientele, and the like.

MAINTENANCE STAGE. The focus of the maintenance stage is on holding one's own in the family, holding things together, keeping up appearances in the community, and seeing that the business continues to flourish or that position in a profession is maintained. Super describes it as the stage during which the individual is striving to preserve his self-concept or is being nagged by his self-concept. Rarely does the individual attempt to introduce new ideas during this period. The record of new ideas, invention, and discovery shows that most great ideas have been produced before their authors have reached 40 or 45.

Lehman's (1953) careful study of age and achievement documents the fact that few creative contributions come during what Super calls the maintenance stage. Lehman is careful to point out, however, that it is not age itself but the factors that accompany this stage of career development and age change that bring about a reduction in creative production. He lists such factors as the following:

1. A decline in physical vigor, energy, and resistance to fatigue.
2. A decline in sensory capacity and motor precision.
3. Serious illness and bodily infirmities.
4. Glandular changes.
5. Marital difficulties and sexual problems.
6. Indifference toward creativity caused by the death of a loved one.
7. Preoccupation with the practical demands of life.
8. Success, promotion, increased prestige, and responsibility with less favorable conditions for concentrated work.
9. Having achieved these goals, less striving for further achievement.
10. Contentment with what has been done.
11. Apathy because of nonrecognition and destructive criticism.
12. Negative transfer, resulting in inflexibility.
13. The better education of younger people who have lived in more stimulating environments.
14. Psychoses, alcoholism, narcotic addiction, etc.

The factors suggested by Lehman can be viewed in terms of the intensity and duration of stress and the capacity of the organism to cope with stress. Thus, all three sets of variables combine to reduce creative productivity during this and the subsequent stage.

As Super (1957) suggests, there may be considerable stress even in maintaining one's position. It is a period of fruition and self-fulfillment, however. If the worker has not established himself securely in an occupation, this period is likely to be a very frustrating one. Job insecurity, downgrading, financial setbacks, uncongenial activities and associates, and the like are common stresses. These increase difficulties in coping with home and community problems. It is the period of broken homes and divorce.

STAGE OF DECLINE. The stage of decline is characterized by decreased energy and stamina, a tapering off of productivity in one's vocation, and curtailment of social and community activities. Vocationally, as Super (1957, p. 72) points out, the individual tapers off the volume of his sales, the number of students advised, or the number and complexity of his activities. Super divides the period of decline into two substages: one decline leading to retirement and a second during retirement itself. During the first of these substages, it may be necessary for the individual to change his work. These changes tend to be in the direction from employment by others to self-employment or employment of others. The older worker is likely to be in a professional, managerial, or skilled occupation. In many cases, he moves into some kind of work where he can set his own pace. Coping with the internal and external changes of this period produces new problems of adjustment. Changes in self-concepts, changes in work roles, and changes in one's way of life may be quite stressful to many individuals. Many, however, work out very constructive adjustments to retirement and continue to be productive and creative.

Among the many outstanding examples of people who have maintained a high level of creative productivity during what is commonly the stage of decline are Benjamin Franklin and Thomas A. Edison. Franklin (Van Doren, 1938; Franklin, 1951) continued to be productive as a diplomat, inventor, and writer through his 60's, 70's, and into his 80's. He was past 80 when he participated in the Constitutional Convention in 1787. Edison is credited with 180 patents obtained after he was 60 years old, not counting his many innovations for the military services during World War I, one of his most productive periods (Dyer, Martin, Meadowcroft, 1929; Josephson, 1959). Forty-six of these came after Edison was 70 years old and include quite a diversity of products.

DEVELOPMENTAL TASKS

Another useful conceptualization in psychological and educational thinking is that of developmental tasks. Havighurst (1952), who introduced the concept into the literature defines a developmental task as "a task which arises at or about a certain period in the life of the individual, successful achievement of which leads to his happiness and to success with later tasks, while failure leads to unhappiness in the individual, disapproval by the society, and difficulty with later tasks" (p. 2). Thus, developmental tasks provide a basis for predicting the common stresses with which individuals must cope at various periods in life. Some of these developmental tasks are common to all cultures while others are closely tied to our own culture. There are also some variations in different social classes in our own culture.

One interesting aspect of the conceptualization of development in terms of tasks, as implemented by Havighurst and his associates (Havighurst, 1952; Havighurst and Orr, 1956), is that it encompasses the span from infancy through later maturity. A list of the developmental tasks given by Havighurst is presented below. A detailed description of these tasks, their biological and cultural basis, and educational implications has been presented by Havighurst (1952). *

Infancy and Early Childhood:
Learning to walk
Learning to take solid foods
Learning to talk
Learning to control the elimination of body wastes
Learning sex differences and sexual modesty
Achieving physiological stability
Forming simple concepts of social and physical reality
Learning to relate oneself emotionally to parents, siblings, and other people
Learning to distinguish right and wrong and developing a conscience

Middle Childhood:
Learning physical skills necessary for ordinary games
Building wholesome attitudes toward oneself as an organism
Learning to get along with age mates
Learning an appropriate masculine or feminine social role
Developing fundamental skills in reading, writing, and calculating
Developing concepts necessary for everyday living
Developing conscience, morality, and a scale of values
Achieving personal independence
Developing attitudes toward social groups and institutions

Adolescence:
Achieving new and more mature relations with age mates of both sexes
Achieving a masculine or feminine social role
Accepting one's physique and using the body effectively
Achieving emotional independence of parents and other adults
Achieving assurance of economic independence
Selecting and preparing for an occupation
Preparing for marriage and family life
Developing intellectual skills and concepts necessary for civic competence
Desiring and achieving socially responsible behavior
Acquiring a set of values and an ethical system as a guide to behavior

Early Adulthood:
Selecting a mate
Learning to live with a marriage partner
Starting a family
Rearing children
Managing a home

* From *Developmental Tasks and Education* by R. J. Havighurst (New York: Longmans, Green & Co., Inc., 1952). Courtesy of David McKay Company, Inc.

Getting started in an occupation
Taking on civic responsibility
Finding a congenial social group

Middle Age:
Achieving adult civic and social responsibility
Establishing and maintaining an economic standard of living
Assisting teen-age children to become responsible and happy adults
Developing adult leisure-time activities
Relating oneself to one's spouse as a person
Accepting and adjusting to the physiological changes of middle age
Adjusting to aging parents

Later Maturity:
Adjusting to decreasing physical strength and health
Adjusting to death of spouse
Adjusting to retirement and reduced income
Establishing an explicit affiliation with one's age group
Meeting social and civic obligations
Establishing satisfactory physical living arrangements

The necessity for continued adaptation and learning to cope constructively with new demands, internal and external, should be obvious from this conceptualization. Educators and other mental health workers should be able to derive many rather direct implications from this kind of formulation. The acquisition of these developmental skills, in the terms of our over-all conceptualization, constitutes a major resource for mediating the effects of life stresses.

SUMMARY

In this chapter, several additional ways of viewing the process of development have been presented. These are only a few of the ones that might have been offered as examples, and each by necessity had to be simplified. Since simplification was necessary, the reader might want to select one of these ways of looking at development and elaborate each stage of development in terms of the common, predictable stresses of our culture that come into operation with the onset of each new stage.

Some of the issues concerning theories of stages of development (discontinuities in development) and development as a continuous process were identified and discussed. Using the development of the creative thinking abilities as an example, it was shown that in the United States there are developmental discontinuities at about the kindergarten, fourth, and seventh grades and that in more continuous cultures these discontinuities in development tend not to occur. These periods of discontinuity in the United States seem to be accompanied by increases in mental health and behavior problems. Similarities or parallels were identified in the stages of development as conceptualized by Ilg and Ames.

Using Sheviakov and Redl's conceptualization, the following stages of development of affection were identified and discussed: self-centeredness and self-love, love of persons in immediate environment, club or gang stage, cliques or sets, attachments to individuals and groups, and devotion to ideals. Super's conceptualization was used in tracing vocational and career development. The following stages were identified: exploratory, establishment, maintenance, and decline. Different kinds of career patterns were also identified. Finally, Havighurst's conceptualization of developmental tasks was presented as a still further way of viewing development as coping with ever new demands for new cognitions and skills.

How

Development

Goes Wrong

8

Edward Cooney, Jr., had always given a good account of himself. He was an honor student, gentle in manner, and handsome. Thus, his parents, neighbors, and teachers were shocked at the news that he had murdered a 3½-year-old girl near his home in Philadelphia. Everyone was puzzled. What went wrong?

Perhaps the father of the murdered girl was approximating the truth when he wrote of the 15-year-old Cooney's parents, "They undoubtedly took naïve pride in his constant good behavior, neat appearance and good performance at church and school, never suspecting that this very goodness was a serious cause for worry in the light of what must have been left unaccounted for."

Whether it is murder, a disabling depression, ulcers, stealing, or a psychotic break, almost every breakdown or evidence of breakdown leaves even the closest observers puzzled. The signs of impending breakdown are not always clear and are usually the clearest *after* the break occurs. Even though there have been repeated signs of warning, their significance is clouded by many factors. Even some of the most serious signs will be mixed with signs of healthy adjustment. The more hostile, aggressive signs are least likely to escape notice, and in some respects the luckiest people are those who attempt to cope with their difficulties by engaging in open misconduct. Such behavior cannot be ignored. It can be mishandled, but, at least, available sources of assistance are frequently galvanized into action.

SOME COMMON WARNING SIGNS

We have already examined several conceptual schemes for observing predictable processes of development and deviations from healthy growth. In the psychosexual stages of development, we have seen that fixations may occur at any stage if there are excessive deprivations, excessive indulgence, inconsistency, or simultaneous reduction of anxiety and the occurrence of the behavior that becomes fixated. In the stages of interpersonal development, we saw things going wrong at all stages of development when the individual fails to master the interpersonal skills necessary to cope with the problems of that stage. We also saw how things go wrong in the development of affect, in vocational and career development, and in the learning of developmental tasks.

Although the signs of impending breakdown are not always clear, there are some fairly dependable ones which can be used by parents, teachers, and school principals to spot children who may need extra help. These signs can at least be accepted as the basis of hypotheses that something is going wrong or has gone wrong with the individual's struggle to cope constructively with life's demands.

LACK OF MENTAL, EMOTIONAL, OR SOCIAL GROWTH

Although there are many kinds of irregularities in various aspects of mental, physical, emotional, and social growth, any gross irregularity in growth might possibly be a sign that something has gone wrong. For example, if a child's intelligence quotient (IQ) continues to go down year after year, something has happened to interfere with the type of mental growth measured by this kind of test. At least, certain kinds of mental growth are not keeping pace with earlier rates. The same could be said of other types of measures of intellectual growth, such as the creative thinking abilities and the evaluative abilities. Many schools periodically measure various aspects of achievement and physical growth. Failure to show growth in any area of development is a sufficient cause for concern. It should not be concluded from this that we should press relentlessly for the well-rounded type of development discussed in Chapter 1 in connection with the case of Glob Blob, "the duck that wouldn't quack."

Perhaps the most common measure of mental growth used by schools is the intelligence test, the results of which are translated into an intelligence quotient (IQ) or a mental age. Until recently, psychologists held that IQ was constant and that fluctuations from time to time were caused by errors in measurement—defects either in the test or in the administration and/or scoring of the test performance. Well-conducted longitudinal studies, however, have shown that fluctuations in IQ have meaning in terms of mental growth and mental health (Bayley, 1955; Sontag, Baker, and Nelson, 1958; Kagan, Sontag, Baker, and Nelson, 1958). The study by Sontag, Baker, and Nelson, involving children from a few months of age to 10 years, indicated that over 60 per cent of the sample fluctuated more than 15 IQ points over this period of time.

This study, conducted at the Fels Research Institute, also showed that certain factors are associated with consistent increases or decreases in IQ over time. The researchers compared the 35 students who gained the most IQ points on retests with the 35 who lost the most and found those who gained most to be characterized by independence, mastery, and an attitude that competition was emotionally comforting. Those who showed the greatest losses in IQ were characterized by lack of parental love, dependence, and an attitude that competition was not emotionally comforting. A subgroup who seemed to go down in IQ scores relatively late in the developmental period were all girls. These girls manifested an attitude that the role of femininity was, in itself, anxiety reducing, making mental growth unnecessary for anxiety reducing. Lichter, Rapien, Seibert, and Sklansky (1962) in their study of intellectually capable students who drop out of high school also found that in general the girls in their sample had done excellent work during the elementary school years but had somehow become overwhelmed early in their high school careers. This was not true of the boys in this study.

LEARNING DIFFICULTIES

Since stress impinges on the actual thinking processes and takes up energy that might otherwise be used in learning, the appearance of severe learning difficulties may also be a sign that "something has gone wrong in personality development and mental health." Two recent studies (Harris, 1961; Lichter, Rapien, Seibert, and Sklansky, 1962) of intellectually capable students who fail to do their school work adequately contribute a great deal to our understanding of learning difficulties and reinforce the idea that learning difficulties are warning signs that stresses are becoming overwhelming to a youngster. These studies, however, were unable to take into consideration the role of faulty teaching methods, emotionally disturbed teachers, and the like as a part of the stressful condition.

Harris compared two groups of boys: (1) the learners whose causes for referral to the Illinois Institute for Juvenile Research did not include a learning difficulty, who had never repeated a grade, and whose school reports indicated that they were currently doing at least average work, and (2) the nonlearners whose causes for referral were solely or predominately learning problems and whose school reports confirmed this complaint and indicated that they were failing in at least one subject. All subjects had an IQ of at least 90 on an individually administered intelligence test, no proven or strongly suggestive organic damage, and an adequate school report and social history. A number of important differences were found between the learners and the nonlearners. A significantly greater percentage of boys from lower-middle- and lower-class families were present in the nonlearner group than in the learner group. These boys from lower-class families lacked motivation to learn for the sake of learning and received little intellectual stimulation in their families. Nonlearners were much more likely than learners to come from disorganized families—families in which there was incompatibility of the marriage or in which the mother was employed outside the home. These nonlearners were characterized by difficulties in concentrating, reading problems, and repeating of grades. Harris attributed these manifestations to a chronic feeling of insecurity as to whether the home would stay intact or come apart. In the nonlearner group, he found that the mothers of boys with low average intelligence were overambitious for their boys. He explained the boys' resistance to learning in terms of their punishing their pressuring mothers by thwarting the mothers, in order to preserve their autonomy, to avoid being measured and found either wanting or successful. The nonlearners compared with the learners more often showed extremes in the area of aggression. They were either aggressively hostile or extremely submissive. This finding was explained on the basis of the fact that extremes of rage (or anxiety over expressing rage) interfered with learning. The openly aggressive boys had higher intelligence scores than did the submissive ones, suggesting that the "energy of free aggressiveness is necessary for intellectual vigor and alertness" (p. 141).

The Lichter, Rapien, Seibert, and Sklansky (1962) report is of a treatment study of 105 intellectually capable students (60 boys and 45 girls) who were on the verge of dropping out of high school, a problem highlighted by the fact that about 46 per cent of all children in the United States fail to complete their high school education. These investigators concluded that the students wanted to leave school because they wanted to run away from a disagreeable situation without being impelled to run toward any definite and positive goal. In other words, their motivation was to reduce the stressfulness of their lives by leaving school. The learning difficulties of the boys in this investigation began in elementary school while the girls started getting into trouble in high school. After receiving counseling help in coping with mental health problems, 77 per cent of boys and 44 per cent of the girls (all on the verge of dropping out at the time counseling was initiated) were able to continue in school. The investigators concluded with a feeling of surety that almost all of their subjects had severe personality problems that interfered with their learning.

INTENSE ISOLATION OR REJECTION

If a child experiences intense or prolonged isolation or rejection, he is almost invariably having difficulty in coping with the stresses in his life. Such children can be spotted in many ways. For this purpose many teachers make use of sociometric techniques such as those described by Moreno (1934, 1956), H. H. Jennings (1948), Northway and Weld (1957), and others.

There are other more obvious signs. For example, just before writing this chapter, the author administered a battery of tests to help evaluate some of the outcomes of an experimental summer camp. The tests were administered in the camp's dining hall. One boy was having difficulty in finding a seat, so the author went to his aid. At each table where there was a vacancy, the other children asserted that the place had already been taken by someone who was getting water or the like. Recognizing this boy as one who had been somewhat obnoxious during the pretest, the author quickly found him a seat at a small table at the side of the room. Later, it was learned from the camp counselors that the boy was the most thoroughly rejected youngster in the entire camp. Children who do not join in the group's activities, do not share in the group's private jokes and idiosyncratic expressions, and the like may also be isolated or rejected.

In the two studies of youngsters showing learning difficulties, it was found that intense isolation or rejection was involved in many of the personality disturbances that interfered with learning. For example, Harris (1961, p. 23) suggests this as one of the reasons for the learning difficulties of the lower-class boy. The lower-class boy is treated less well in the school system than the middle- or upper-class boy. "He is made to feel unwanted in the classroom, in the playground, in the clubs and in other extracurricular activities . . ."

The recent animal research by the Harlows at the University of Wisconsin (Harlow, 1958, 1962; Lagemann, 1963) suggests the vital importance of intense isolation in mental health. In some of the earlier experiments with monkeys, Harlow (1958) emphasized the role of the mother or mother substitute in the process of learning to love and lay the foundations for mental health. One of the more recent findings, however, leads to the conclusion that it is as important for a youngster to form healthy relationships with others his own age as it is for him to have a good relationship with his parents. Experiments had already shown that monkeys brought up in complete isolation were unable to show affection, learn to live together, or perform sexually. Six months or more of isolation produced severely disturbed monkeys, incapable of forming social or sexual relationships. The Harlows' (1958) first step after this was to try to pinpoint the factors in mothering that insure healthy development.

In the first series of experiments (1958, 1962), some monkeys were reared with their own mothers, while others were reared with "manikin mothers," some made of wire and some made of wire and terry cloth. These manikins featured different combinations of maternal attributes—milk from a nursing bottle, a heating pad for bodily warmth, rocking motion from a built-in motor, and a soft, terry-cloth "skin." The monkeys reared with the terry-cloth mothers appeared to develop quite well until it came time for them to find mates and become parents themselves. Not one of the males, despite strong sex drives, became a father. The females resisted all advances, and only because of the patience and persistence of two experienced breeding males did four of them eventually become mothers. These four female monkeys, however, alternately ignored and abused their infants and in six months of living together never showed affection toward their young.

In the next series of experiments (Harlow, 1962; Lagemann, 1963), the Harlows set out to determine whether the dummy mothers were to blame. In the first series of experiments, the young monkeys had been in separate cages where they could see, hear, and chatter with others, but could not play together as babies usually do. In the second series of experiments the same mothering variables featured in the earlier experiment were retained. Some monkeys in each group were cut off from playmates while others were allowed to play with other young monkeys at varying intervals. The results show that regardless of mothering or lack of it, infants who have a chance to play with other little monkeys became socially normal monkeys. All the monkeys deprived of contacts with other little monkeys were unable to interact normally with other monkeys, socially or sexually. These results give new strength to the use of intense isolation and rejection as an indicator of possible serious mental health problems.

PERSISTENT AND RECURRENT DIFFICULTIES

As Redl and Wattenberg (1959) point out, much of the conduct of a child that puzzles adults comes and goes. It is the child who has a difficulty that lasts for a long time or that continues to recur with considerable frequency who needs help. Or a particular symptom such as thumb sucking may be abandoned and replaced by some other symptom or abandoned temporarily and resumed every time a stressful condition occurs.

As we have already noted, children confronted with new demands or with stressful family or school conditions will experience temporary personality disturbances. In fact, personality growth seems to come from experiences in coping with new demands and stressful conditions. Naturally, they will make mistakes in coping with these problems. The acceptance of a mistake as one's own is the first step in this growth process. The error then presents a problem and sets the thinking processes in motion. The child whose difficulties are persistent and recurrent may not recognize his error or may deny responsibility for the error. Or there may be some defect in his thinking processes, as will be discussed in the latter part of this chapter in connection with the psychopathic deviant and the schizophrenic personality.

Some personality theorists (Helson, 1948; Bonney and George, 1958) have advanced a theory of adaptation level to explain some types of persistent and recurrent difficulties in adaptation. The theory proposes (Bonney and George, 1958, p. 1) that each person through early life

119

experiences, develops a generalized level of adaptation for unexpected and inappropriate stimuli, which may be anything from a simple line drawing to a complex and stressful social situation. It is held that for each person there is a general level beyond which the unexpectedness of the stimulus results in a displeasure through anxiety and another level below which the unexpectedness or predictability of the stimulus results in displeasure or indifference through boredom. They also maintain that these levels of adaptation vary among individuals, have a predictable degree of generality within an individual from one type of stimulus to another, and are measurable. Such a theory emphasizes the importance of recognizing signs of persistent and recurrent difficulties in adaptation among young children as a possible measure for preventing mental illness.

RESISTANCE TO REMEDIAL PROCEDURES

Experienced teachers develop a varied repertory of procedures for remedying or eliminating most behavior problems. A lonely child can be teamed with other children in class activities. A child who daydreams can be offered challenging and interesting activities. A child who loses control easily can be supported by signals that he is lapsing; he can be placed near the teacher or can be joked with to drain off irritability and hostility. The child who does not respond to the usually effective repertory probably needs special help of some kind. The major areas where the teacher can help are in learning difficulties, especially reading, and disturbing behavior.

OTHER SIGNS

Redl and Wattenberg (1959, pp. 414–15) identify three other kinds of signs that indicate possible needs for special help. First, some seriously disturbed children are often compulsive in their behavior. That is, they really want to improve but simply cannot control their behavior. Second, many disturbed children have a weak realization of reality, daydream excessively, are excessively suspicious, have one-sided romances, or show rage far beyond the provocation. Among disturbed boys, a common symptom is unusual passivity or docility. This was a sign of trouble that a discerning teacher or parent might have recognized in the case of Edward Cooney, Jr., given at the beginning of the chapter. A third sign that a child may need help is the existence of a life situation known to pose a heavy psychological burden or stress on the child. For example, the presence of most of the conditions listed in the "stressors" box in Figure 2–1 in Chapter 2 should serve to alert the school to possible need for help.

Mayer and Hoover (1961) have conceptualized these danger signals in terms of stages. Although many of these danger signals have been discussed in relation to the discussions of psychosexual stages of development and the interpersonal stages of development, the Mayer and Hoover lists are somewhat more inclusive and independent of a single theory of personality and will be summarized briefly:

FROM BIRTH TO TWO YEARS: Unusually slow physical development, excessive passivity, lack of responsiveness, excessive restlessness, or constant severe difficulties in sleeping or eating.

FROM TWO TO FOUR YEARS: Frequent night terrors, constant refusal to eat anything except a few relatively unwholesome foods, refusal ever to drink out of a glass or cup, refusal to begin toilet training, marked lack of interest in other children (especially toward the end of this period), inability to let mother out of sight without panic, panic (not just shyness) when anyone other than a parent approaches.

FROM FOUR TO SIX YEARS: Inability to get along with other children (either constant fighting or anxious withdrawal), repeated and intentional cruelty to animals, constant overt destructiveness, intense frequent temper tantrums with no apparent provocation, continuing unwillingness to be separated from mother, intense fears of not one but many things encountered in everyday living, consistent day or night wetting or soiling, stuttering and other speech difficulties, frequent tics, inability to fall asleep unless a parent is present, inability or unwillingness to do anything for himself.

FROM SIX TO EIGHT YEARS: Absorption in fantasies which are treated as real; real fears about going to school (frequent anxiety attacks in the morning, vomiting, stomach-ache, etc., for which no physical cause can be found); continuous bedwetting, thumb sucking, and frequent genital manipulation in public; failure to show a beginning interest in learning; intense worry about becoming ill or fears of bodily injury; pronounced fear of elevators, crossing the street, etc.

FROM EIGHT TO ELEVEN YEARS: Constant sitting or lying around the house, continuous complaints that there is nothing to do and nobody likes him, recurrent lying and stealing (not just an occasional lapse), setting fires, panic reactions in group situations, constant contrariness, repeated running away from home or truancy from school, real difficulty in keeping up with class at school (in spite of good ability), frequent episodes of engaging in sex play with children of either sex, continuous open rejection of appropriate sex role.

FROM ELEVEN TO FOURTEEN YEARS: Inability to make friends, or intense, exclusive preoccupation with dating; excessive eating or extremely poor appetite; severe nail biting, refusal to take responsibility at home and at school; persistent failure in school after having initially done well; preoccupation with the use of obscene language; persistent general lack of interest in life; excessive fear of growing up, playing only with younger children.

121

FOURTEEN THROUGH SEVENTEEN YEARS: Constant open rebellion against all authority, inability to see need for any limits on behavior, excessive withdrawal, preoccupation with own thoughts, intense preoccupation with dating, more than an isolated episode of overt homosexuality, use of narcotics, excessive smoking or drinking, excessive crying, no interest in pursuits more demanding than television and movies in spite of normal intelligence, frequent expressed fears of being unable to amount to anything, preoccupation with schoolwork to exclusion of all else, constant need of parental approval even in minor decisions.

The foregoing lists of signs help to evaluate the seriousness of the behavior in terms of the child's age. Some behaviors that might be regarded as healthy at an early age might be cause for genuine concern at an older age. No one symptom alone should be regarded with alarm. The symptom merely warns us that there may be—though there is not necessarily—a need for professional help. The behavior must also be viewed in the context of the culture in which the child is being reared. Mayer and Hoover (1961, pp. 16–18) offer a set of questions that can be used in deciding whether a set of signs is serious enough to warrant a referral to a mental health clinic, psychiatrist, school psychologist, or other professionally trained person. They suggest the following five questions:

1. Is the child's behavior generally appropriate to the circumstances in which he finds himself?
2. Is the child's behavior generally in keeping with his age?
3. Are there real difficulties in the child's environment that may be to blame for the problem?
4. Has there been a radical change in the child's behavior?
5. How long has the symptom lasted?

SOME COMMON CAUSES

It must be remembered that a symptom of something having gone wrong may arise from any of several dissimilar sources. Trouble arises when, for some reason, the individual lacks adequate anchors to guide him and is unable to cope with the demands for adaptation.

The inability to find adequate anchors may stem from lack of experience or previous premature and unsuccessful attempts to cope with the demand. In fact, in one study (Torrance, 1956a) of the ability of aircrewmen to take in stride various stressful conditions, it was found that those least able to deal successfully with these difficulties had either postponed excessively or attempted prematurely to master the various skills expected of children in our culture (driving a car, dating, dancing, and the like).

It may at first appear ridiculous that either excessive postponement or premature attempts in learning to drive a car could be related to difficulties in coping with stress. Either may be a part of a pattern of behavior that may be indicative of personality difficulties. The boy who attempts prematurely to learn to drive may be under pressure from parents and others to become adult. If this is a part of a pattern, he is likely to be overwhelmed by pressures and by his inability to cope adequately with the demands that are thrust upon him. The boy who postpones excessively the mastery of these skills may be the victim of many other holding-back operations on the part of his parents and teachers. These, too, may place him under great stress and handicap him in coping with the various demands that are thrust upon him, in spite of his parents and teachers. He is likely to be unable to compete successfully with his peers or to be able to compete in only very limited areas, such as school grades. He may even be handicapped in this limited competition because the frustration from being unable to hold his own in adolescent society may so impair his mental functioning that he is unable to perform adequately even in areas that are open to him.

Difficulties in maintaining satisfactory anchors in reality may also arise because the individual may have no defenses available. He may have tried to kid himself into thinking that "it can't happen" to him and as a result has not thought out in advance what he would do in various emergencies. Or a situation may have in it unknowns that make it impossible for him to defend himself. Or the knowns may call for so many of the organism's more expensive energies that the experience is exhausting. This lack of preparation is illustrated in experiments showing that adaptation to stressful experiences takes place with repeated exposures. For example, Taylor, Brözek, Henschel, Mickelson, and Keys (1945) found that with successive periods of starvation, subjects reacted more favorably both physiologically and psychologically. These investigators collected metabolic, physiological, and psychomotor measurements on four men who performed hard work under rigidly controlled conditions during five successive 2½-day fasts. The total calorie deficit was about 10,000 calories and the successive fasts were separated by five- to six-weeks intervals. During the second and third days of the fasting all the men were able to maintain the blood sugar at a significantly higher level in the fifth than in the first fast. Motor speed and coordination deteriorated less during the fifth fast than during the first period. Reaction time and pattern tracing showed a statistically significant improvement, and two other psychomotor tests showed trends in the same direction. In other words, the experience of fasting had become less stressful to these men by the fifth fasting. The men knew what to expect and they could cope with the experience with less expensive energies.

In studies of the acceptability of an emergency ration (pemmican) in simulated survival situations (Torrance, 1959b), it was found that on a second exposure to the food even those men who had had prior unfavorable experiences responded more favorably than those who had had no experience in using the food. This more favorable reaction was expressed not so much in words concerning the food as in the amount of food eaten and in the small number of men who experienced illness as a result of eating the food. These and other findings indicate that even unfavorable experiences permit individuals to find the anchors that enable them to cope with stressors with increasing comfort and effectiveness.

The organism employs a number of characteristic defenses in adapting to stressors. Some of these are adopted in an attempt to find less expensive ways of adapting to life's demands. Although many of these less expensive ways of coping with stressors may be useful in emergencies, they may actually prove to be quite expensive when relied upon habitually. They prove to be more expensive because the defensive actions are not adequate to solve the problems involved and it requires a great deal of energy to keep them in operation. Some of these characteristic defenses will be identified and discussed in the section which follows.

Some individuals manifest the various signs of something having gone wrong because they have rejected or are trying to reject demands for adaptation. Delinquent behavior and neurotic behavior may both stem from this source. The delinquent's rejection of demands usually grows out of hostile interpersonal relations. The psychopathic deviate's rejection appears to arise from a dramatic unconcern for the consequences of his behavior. Many neurotics, on the other hand, may inwardly reject these demands but appear to be overconcerned about the consequences of their behavior and are thereby paralyzed in their attempts to carry out constructive action. The schizophrenic may be said to have given up hope of meeting the demands for adaptation.

PROBLEM-SOLVING WAYS OF COPING

One way of looking at the matter of how development goes wrong is in terms of deviations from the problem-solving process. Within this conceptual framework, the common signs that have been identified in this chapter are indications that a person's problem-solving thinking has gone off course. When problem-solving ways of coping with stressors are used successfully, the intellectual resources or mental operations are functioning, relatively unhampered by common sources of trouble.

Many scholars have attempted to conceptualize the problem-solving way of coping with stressors. Some have called it "the scientific method" or "scientific thinking." Others call it the "creative problem-solving process." Still others have used the terms "reflective thinking" or "critical thinking." Regardless of the labels used, there is essential agreement in the descriptions of the process. What follows is an attempt to integrate several of these descriptions (Dewey, 1933; Patrick, 1955; Burton, Kimball, and Wing, 1960).

1. RECOGNITION AND DEFINITION OF THE PROBLEM

According to Dewey (1933), thinking originates when there is a state of doubt, hesitation, perplexity, or mental difficulty. In other words, there is discomfort or tension that results in the recognition of a problem, a gap in knowledge, a deficiency of some kind. In some cases, the process becomes blocked at this point. The individual is uncomfortable and may realize vaguely that something is wrong, but he cannot figure out what is bothering him. Even worse, some "tough-skinned" individuals insulate themselves so thoroughly that they do not progress even this far in the problem-solving process. Such individuals may appear to be quite happy with their adjustment or development. Everyone around them, however, may have quite different feelings.

In successful problem-solving, the individual becomes aware of what is bothering him, he determines whether or not the problem is a real one and whether or not it needs to be solved. Then he confronts such problems as, "Where can we start?" or "Is the problem within our capacity to solve?" As this kind of thinking progresses, the individual starts finding out whatever he can about the problem and how it might be approached. Ideas may shift rapidly. Typically, it is a period of discomfort, characterized by doubt and perplexity. It leads, as Dewey states (1933, p. 12), to acts of searching, hunting, inquiring, and finding material that will resolve the doubt and dispose of the difficulty.

2. INCUBATION

Failing to solve the problem through conscious processes, a person frequently lets up for a while. Although he engages in other activities, he continues to mull over the problem. During this period, the chief idea continues to recur in different mental sets or configurations. As ideas have been "incubating," the problem becomes more clearly defined.

3. HYPOTHESIZING

Finally, out of the discomfort, the awareness of something being wrong, the searching, hunting, and inquiring, comes some relief. Some call it the period of illumination. Others call it the idea-producing or hypothesizing stage. At any rate, a number of possible solutions or promising courses of action are produced. Studies of group decision making (Torrance, 1957a) indicate that the more of these hypotheses or the broader the range of judgments considered, the more accurate are the decisions.

Frequently the importance of this stage has been underrated. Its importance, however, in education is emphasized in McDonald's (1965) concept of the teacher as hypothesis maker and in the author's research (1964), which shows that highly effective mathematics teachers are characterized by a far greater amount of hypothesis making or troubleshooting behavior than are their less effective colleagues. More will be said later concerning its role in personality development and mental health.

4. INQUIRY OR SEARCH

A number of activities may be involved in the stage of inquiry or search. Characteristically there is some kind of testing of the hypotheses advanced in the preceding stage. There is experimentation of some type, accompanied by the collection of data, relevant facts, evidence, and authoritative opinion. Various types of statistical and nonstatistical analysis may be employed. Induction, deduction, and analogy may be brought into play.

5. DECISION

Next, on the basis of testing and past experience, the hypotheses are accepted, rejected, or modified and retested. This process brings into play the evaluative abilities. A decision can now be made concerning the initial state of doubt or uncertainty, and the tension induced thereby is reduced.

6. APPLICATION

The tension is not fully relieved, however, until the decision is communicated, tested, or used. The need to communicate what one has discovered or decided appears to be a very strong one in most persons. This step in the process may bring into play the imagination and what are termed by many as the creative thinking abilities.

Especially relevant to mental health is Dewey's (1933, p. 16) warning that a person can think reflectively only if he is willing to tolerate uncertainty and suspense and to go to the trouble of searching. Many individuals find both suspense and searching disagreeable. They want to complete these processes as soon as possible. Shortly we shall see how this aversion to uncertainty throws off course the process of adaptation to stressors as reflected in delinquency, neurosis, psychosis, and the like. From these facts, the reader will recognize the importance of developing in children the ability to produce and evaluate a variety of possible solutions, to think in terms of possibles, and even to toy with the consequences of the improbable.

SOME COMMON FAILURES IN PROBLEM SOLVING

Psychopathic deviate, neurotic, and psychotic behavior may be regarded as indications of common failures in the problem-solving process. In some way, for some reason, the process has gotten off course and the individual has been unable to use his mental abilities constructively in coping with stressors. As already indicated, there is a tendency to adapt first by using the least expensive energies. The first signs of trouble may be learning difficulties. Or, almost as soon, there may develop various kinds of defense mechanisms. As long as these defenses work, the individual is able to ward off breakdown, even though much of his coping with life stresses is far less effective than it might be. Use of defense mechanisms is a minor deviation from the process outlined in the foregoing section. More severe deviations are found in psychopathic deviancy, neuroses, and psychoses.

LEARNING DISABILITIES

Some children very early develop an aversion to learning by authority. Their learning difficulties are well known and have been the subject of much investigation. Remedial programs in reading and number work are increasing. In recent years, it has become increasingly clear that many children develop a distinct preference for learning by authority to the exclusion of learning through creative problem solving. Such children gradually become crippled in their ability to cope with life stresses because they do not master problem-solving techniques. This happens even to very brilliant children, who, in some schools, are excellent "grade getters." Leah Levinger (1959) has given an example from her clinical experience. Rod, an intellectually gifted boy, came to Dr. Levinger as a worried transfer student in his sophomore year in high school. He was disturbed because he was doing less brilliantly than in the lower grades, fearful that his mental powers were slipping. In another school Rod had apparently made all A's with relative ease. In his new school, the teaching methods were different. Having been taught by apparently rather authoritative methods, he was unable to relate different aspects of grammar study to the expressive whole. He was not challenged by work on style or the finer points of analysis. He was easily confused when asked to do something that required thought and judgment. He failed to show the kind of critical thinking required in mastering modern mathematics, although mathematics had formerly been his favorite subject. Dr. Levinger found Rod in the psychological testing situation to have a truly brilliant mind, grimly focused on how well he was doing but devoid of curiosity or delight in solving problems. Rod had become so imbued with the need for the right answer that Dr. Levinger was doubtful whether, at the age of 15, he could recapture a love for questions, or develop tolerance for the unknown.

Rod was faced with a serious discontinuity in his change from one school to another. He had developed an excellent memory for facts and a capacity to give the correct answer. Now, when asked to see relationships, ask questions and inquire, use his imagination, make decisions, and solve problems, he had neither the interest nor the skills for meeting such demands. Learning experiments have repeatedly shown that when methods of teaching are changed different mental abilities are brought into play and different people become the stars. McConnell (1934) reported a carefully conducted study comparing performance in second grade arithmetic under two methods which he labeled as "authoritative identification" and "learning by discovery." Neither method proved to be uniformly superior to the other. On two of the seven achievement tests given at the end of the seven-month experiment, children learning by authoritative identification achieved at least some advantage over their peers who were learning by discovery. On the other five tests, children who learned by discovery showed some degree of superiority, though not always a statistically significant one. There were consistently higher relationships between mental age as measured by the Pintner-Cunningham Test and scores on the achievement tests under the method of authoritative identification than under the learning by discovery method. In other words, different children became the stars and the failures under different methods. With some of the current curricular changes in physics, chemistry, biology, and mathematics, investigators (Ornstein, 1961) are finding that the traditional predictors of achievement are not working as well as they worked with traditional materials and methods. The new materials and methods, which provide considerable opportunity for experimentation and inquiry, approach science as a way of thinking rather than as an accumulation of knowledge to be transmitted. Some of these methods will be discussed in detail in later chapters of this book.

COMMON DEFENSES

In each of the common defensive mechanisms, some minor deviation will be noted in the problem-solving process, as the following examples will show.

NEGATIVISM. Negativism as a defensive reaction occurs very early in the life cycle and is first employed as a technique for coping with certain demands with the individual's least expensive adaptive energies. The child's language development is limited at the age at which this mechanism is first employed (about 18 months), and it is easier for him to say "No" than to say "Yes, but . . ." or "Yes, if . . ." or to give some other explanation. The negative reaction is also aggravated by parents and others who hurry or interrupt the child, not permitting him to complete what he has started. A habit that starts in this way, however, may grow into a general stubbornness and rejection of authority. The use of this defense may even develop into a refusal to recognize the existence of a problem or an obstacle. Thus, the very first step in the problem-solving process goes wrong, since adaptive action cannot be taken until the seriousness of the situation is recognized.

DECEIT. Deceit develops as a defense in much the same way that negativism does. Children, at an age when their intellectual abilities are not yet very well developed, find it easier to conceal or deceive in coping with demands of the environment. These abilities to conceal and deceive grow to become inadequate and inappropriate behavior that becomes troublesome in later life. Deceit and concealment, which may involve refusal to recognize the realities of the situation, certainly result in a failure to explore alternatives and think of consequences.

RATIONALIZATION. Fundamentally, rationalization is little different from deceit in its dynamics. Rationalization is usually defined as a device whereby the individual justifies his beliefs or actions by giving reasons other than those which activated or motivated him. Whatever else may be involved in rationalization, certainly the reality testing and modification aspects of thinking are malfunctioning, deterred apparently by the potential discomfort entailed in accepting one's true motivations.

SUBLIMATION. Many authorities in the field of mental hygiene recognize sublimation as one of the more useful of the defense mechanisms. This mechanism is defined as a device whereby a socially approved activity is substituted for a socially disapproved one, especially in the redirection of sexual energy into nonsexual channels. Sullivan (1953, p. 153) calls it a long-circuiting of the resolution of situations and considers it a process of tremendous importance in adaptation to stressors. What happens to the problem-solving process is perhaps best characterized by Sullivan's term, "long-circuiting."

IDENTIFICATION. If sublimation involves long-circuiting, identification may be seen as short-circuiting. Defined as a mechanism of the unconscious by which the individual identifies himself with persons, groups, or other objects of his admiration to gain security or power and to become like those whom he admires, identification is another of the more useful defenses. Use of the identification mechanism may lead to difficulties in new situations or in situations where the behavior or values that have been internalized are inappropriate. In one sense, the mechanism may become a substitute for thinking or problem solving.

DISPLACEMENT. Displacement represents another short-circuiting device. Through this process there is a transfer of emotion from an appropriate set of ideas to an inappropriate set of ideas. In all probability the entire problem-solving process is short-circuited. If not, the process certainly breaks down in reasoning by analogy. Because the substitute objects of the displacement process are seldom as tension reducing as was the original object, tension remains.

COMPENSATION. Compensation is, in a sense, another type of concealment or deception and represents a failure to test or accept reality. Defined as the counterbalancing of any defect of structure or function by the putting forward of an approved characteristic to conceal the existence of an undesirable one, compensation may be a useful mechanism. To the extent that it interferes with the creative acceptance of one's limitations and prevents one from achieving his potentialities, it represents a dangerous kind of short-circuiting of the problem-solving process. Perhaps the more serious deviation is in the impoverishment of the idea-getting stage, a defect which would not be likely to arise, if there is a creative acceptance of limitations.

PROJECTION. Projection is another device of self-deception whereby a threatening impulse is projected onto someone else. The person who projects simply expresses the threatening impulse by making it appear that he is defending himself against an external danger. Such behavior is a gross short-circuiting of the problem-solving process, one which originates at the very outset and in actuality denies responsibility for a problem.

REACTION FORMATION. In reaction formation, the individual seeks to control antisocial tendencies by developing behavior patterns that are usually the exact opposite of the threatening antisocial tendencies. Usually, the expression of reaction formations is elaborate, requires considerable energy to maintain, and constitutes a prolonged stress. In one sense, the processes involved resemble somewhat the long-circuiting found in sublimation. The process is short-circuited, however, in that the hypothesis-making stage is omitted or limited by a kind of tunnel vision.

DAYDREAMING. Daydreaming is another method of short-circuiting the problem-solving process, yet may sometimes result in ideas that become springboards to successful solutions to problems thought insoluble. People seem to be more reluctant to discuss their daydreams than their dreams (Baughman and Welsh, 1962, pp. 408–409). The primary reason for the difference in reluctance seems to be that people feel more accountable for their daydreams than for their dreams. This is understandable since our society so strongly values the visibly industrious child and punishes the contemplative, reflective, thoughtful child, fearing that he is idle or engaged in something evil. Thus, children are usually made to feel guilty about daydreaming and fail to use this mechanism in as positive a manner as they might. Daydreaming may sometimes serve as a prelude to positive action and laudable ambition. It may also reduce tension, merge into creative thought or effective planning for future action, and may reduce hostility and aggression.

OTHER MECHANISMS. Other defenses, such as regression, withdrawal, attention-seeking, repression, ritual, and compulsion, represent some kind of short-circuiting of the problem-solving process.

PSYCHOPATHIC DEVIATE BEHAVIOR

Catherine Patrick (1955, p. 88) has offered a plausible explanation of the process whereby the thinking of the psychopathic deviate or delinquent goes astray. She pictures the psychopathic deviate as an individual who has experienced severe conflict, perhaps between his impulses and the demands of his environment, or perhaps among conflicting demands of his environment. Faced with such a difficult problem, the deviate is extremely uncomfortable and unhappy. Finally, when he has a hunch, all of the tension and unhappiness of the preparation and incubation stages are suddenly ended. He is elated and relieved that he has found "a solution." This "wonderful idea" gives him so much relief that he clings to it and refuses to undergo, not only the process of thinking of alternative solutions, but also the final stage of revision and verification. He cannot bear to face the possibility that his solution may possibly be inadequate. He holds onto his erroneous idea and may spend many hours elaborating it instead of revising and verifying it according to reality. He rushes out and applies his idea and consequently involves himself in trouble. Since he refuses to test his hunches against his prior experience, he does not profit very well from experience and continues to involve himself in difficulties.

NEUROSES

The neuroses represent continuing struggles to cope with chronic states of stress and may possibly be best regarded as representing the organism's attempt to maintain continued adaptation to prolonged stress. The techniques of coping and the thinking processes involved vary somewhat from one of the neuroses to another.

1. ANXIETY STATES. (a) The most common of the anxiety states is the *anxiety reaction*. In this state, anxiety is usually chronic with occasional acute anxiety or panic. In terms of thinking processes, the individual is uncomfortable and is aware of his discomfort, but usually is not aware of what is making him uncomfortable. In the panic state or acute anxiety, the individual senses impending catastrophe without being able to specify its nature. Thus, the problem-solving process is stopped at its very beginning. The problem cannot be defined and dealt with. The process is not short-circuited or long-circuited, as in the case of the defense mechanisms discussed in the preceding section. The individual continues to struggle to master the anxiety without the use of anxiety-reducing mechanisms. The

131

anxiety thus becomes a prolonged stress which will ultimately result in breakdown, if it is not reduced or relieved.

(b) *Asthenic Reaction.* A second anxiety state is the *asthenic reaction,* which involves physical and mental fatigue. The individual escapes threatening situations and painful circumstances by somatic complaints. In this state, there is an apparent refusal to think. In effect, the person has reached the ascending phase of the curve of adaptation to stress over time.

(c) *Hypochondriacal Reaction.* In the hypochondriacal reaction, the anxiety is focused on the individual's state of bodily health. The dynamics are similar to those of the asthenic reaction. He uses his symptoms to manipulate others by obtaining sympathy and support. Apparently, needs for sympathy are so overwhelming that the individual's awareness is so restricted that he cannot perceive the real problems involved.

(d) *Phobic Reactions.* Phobic reactions are unrealistic in terms of reality and reduce the individual's capacity to cope with his stresses. Phobias are thought to be acquired from early life experiences involving strong fear in the presence of some object or circumstance associated with embarrassment or shame. Here the emotional reaction shuts off awarenesses that would result in a realistic perception of the problem.

2. HYSTERIA. The *conversion reaction* is the most dramatic of the hysterias. Commonly, the individual has a severe physical symptom that has no organic basis. The symptom, though real, may take a form that is inconsistent with the actual patterning of the nervous system. Involved are reactions to stresses that the individual cannot cope with directly. Such an individual seems to have an overpowering desire to be well thought of and to maintain this view in the eyes of the others in this indirect way. The thinking processes appear to involve a type of short-circuiting similar to that involved in most of the defense mechanisms. Conversion hysterias such as paralysis of a hand or arm, blindness, and the like may give a person a socially approved escape from an unpleasant and otherwise apparently inescapable job. This type of solution tends to reduce the chances of constructive solutions to the actual problem. Various types of forgetting (amnesias), forgetting combined with flight (fugues), sleep-walking, repressed or dissociated ideas or emotions, and the like are other types of refusals to follow through the problem-solving process leading to constructive behavior.

3. OBSESSIVE-COMPULSIVE REACTIONS. The obsessive-compulsive personality recognizes that his behavior is irrational, but he does not seem to be able to control his thinking and follow through the problem-solving process. Through this type of reaction, an individual attempts to displace

certain unacceptable or threatening impulses into some other form. In obsessions, the thinking of certain ideas prevents more threatening ones from emerging. Compulsions appear to represent attempts to deal with danger by organizing things in a certain way or working so fast and furiously that the threatening impulses do not have a chance to emerge.

4. NEUROTIC DEPRESSION.   Depression is defined as an emotional state characterized by dejection, unpleasant thoughts, and foreboding. All thinking, especially evaluative thinking, is negatively slanted. Depressed individuals are unable to see themselves and their situation realistically and lack the capacity to see possible positive outcomes.

5. PSYCHOSOMATIC DISORDERS.   The psychosomatic disorders represent either defenses against anxiety or consequences of chronic stress. Certain types of disorders are thought to be associated with certain characteristic patterns of coping with life. For example, peptic ulcers are thought to be the consequence of conflicts over dependency. Victims of this disorder are described as ambitious, driving, struggling for independence, but unconsciously seeking a dependent relationship with someone. Their thinking requires excessive energy since the dependence and independence conflict must be resolved at almost every turn.

PSYCHOSES

Both organic and functional psychoses represent rather extreme failures to maintain anchors in reality and to behave constructively in response to stress. In other words, development has gone badly wrong. Contacts with the environment are lacking or extremely few, leaving the individual with few guides to adaptive or constructive behavior.

The organic psychoses all involve some kind of organic damage to or interference with mental functioning. The nature of the damage or interference affects directly the victim's thinking or problem-solving behavior. The organic psychoses may result from infectious diseases such as syphilis and encephalitis, brain tumors and head injuries, toxic and metabolic disturbances, nutritional deficiencies, endocrine disturbances, epilepsy, and aging. In the organic psychoses, guides to constructive behavior have been reduced or destroyed by physical factors and do not respond to psychological treatment. Thus, the functional psychoses are of more interest than the organic psychoses to most psychologists and educational workers.

There are three main classes of functional psychoses: the schizophrenias, the paranoid disorders, and the affective disorders. By far the largest numbers are claimed by the schizophrenias. About 25 per cent of the hospital beds utilized for any reasons in the United States are occupied by schizophrenics. Theorists (Lazarus, 1961, p. 351) have differentiated two main types: process and reactive. Process schizophrenia is a disorder of long standing, has its origins early in life, and in its nature is more like that of reaction to prolonged, continuous stress. Reactive schizophrenia is of sudden onset and partakes more of the nature of reactions to intense, sudden stress. The outlook for possible recovery is more favorable in reactive than process schizophrenia, as might be predicted from the fact that process schizophrenia is a response to prolonged stress, and reactive schizophrenia is a response to intense stress. It will be recalled that research indicates that generally people rebound more rapidly and completely from brief periods of intense stress than from prolonged moderate stress.

In one exploratory study (Hebeisen, 1960) of the thinking of partially recovered schizophrenics (including simple, catatonic, hebephrenic, and paranoid), it was found that they are extremely inflexible and paralyzed in their thinking. For example, when asked to list unusual uses of tin cans, Hebeisen's sample of schizophrenics were unable to break away from the obvious "container" response. A total of 87 per cent of their responses were container uses, compared with 40 per cent for graduate students, 33 per cent for college juniors, and 17 per cent for fourth, fifth, and sixth grade children. In other words, these partially recovered schizophrenics were afraid to depart from any but the safest and most obvious responses. Even this may be interpreted as a limited contact with the environment. Lacking guides to behavior, they refuse to produce anything but the safest and most obvious responses and have little capacity for constructive behavior.

Simple schizophrenics adapt by social withdrawal, a gradual narrowing and loss of interest, and lack of emotion and feeling. The social withdrawal robs them of social contacts and the guides that this gives for behavior. The loss of interest and lack of emotion and feeling are likely to involve reduced sensory stimulation and a monotonous kind of existence, which results in further losses of contact with the environment. *Catatonics* may react in either a stuporous or an excited manner. Hallucinations and delusions are common, indicating a rather severe estrangement from the environment and loss of anchors in reality. *Hebephrenics* react with emotional indifference and infantile behavior. *Paranoid schizophrenics* are characterized by delusions of grandeur and persecution. If the schizophrenic rather than the paranoid pattern predominates, the delusions are likely to be bizarre, irrational, and changeable, taking first one form and then another. Loss of contact with reality of a relatively extreme degree is characteristic of all four types of schizophrenia, leaving the victim with little capacity to respond constructively to stress.

Paranoid disorders involve delusional systems, usually persecutory or grandiose. The term "paranoid" is used to describe a quality of thinking, an intellectualized system of defenses characterized predominately by delusions. These systems of defense may range from the severe disturbances to a general sense of grandiosity and suspiciousness. Usually, the defense system itself seems quite logical, but it is built upon some false premise. The tightness of the defense system reduces awareness and contacts with the environment and thus the victim's capacity to cope constructively with stress.

Affective psychoses are marked by disturbances in mood or emotion, just as schizophrenias and paranoid disorders are characterized by disorders in thinking. There are two major manifestations: manic states and depressive states. Saying that affective psychoses involve disturbances in mood or emotion does not mean that thinking is not affected in the affective psychoses. The prevailing mood may restrict or seriously influence thinking. In the manic state, a person's thinking may be overly bold. In the depressive, the same person's thinking may be overly cautious, fearful, and timid. In neither case is he able to think realistically, in terms of the way things are. In some cases, a person with an affective psychosis may attempt to avoid thinking. By definition, however, affective psychoses are not thought disorders. One of the greatest dangers is that tensions will become so overwhelming that the individual thinks of suicide as the only way of reducing the discomfort. Loss of will to live and more subtle ways of suicide may also arise. All adaptive and constructive action ceases and no attempt is made to solve problems.

SUMMARY

Impending breakdowns, both major and minor, are heralded by warning signs. Many factors operate to blind a person to the warning signs concerning both himself and others with whom he is associated. There are some fairly dependable and objective signs that parents and teachers can use to detect impending breakdowns and see that children and young people receive the help that will enable them to cope constructively with life's stresses. Any indicator that a person is not behaving constructively might be regarded as a sign that the developmental process is to some degree going wrong. Some of the more important indicators are lack of mental, emotional, or social growth; learning difficulties such as failure to learn to read; intense isolation or rejection; persistent and recurrent behavioral difficulties; and resistance to remedial procedures. Other more specific indicators can be expected during each period of life, peculiar to that period. A list of some of the more common, predictable signs in the United States were prepared by a group of child-study experts and summarized in this chapter. All of these signs are in some way indicative of increasing estrangement from the environment with decreased capacity for responding constructively to change and stress.

A single indicator of something having gone wrong with the developmental process may arise from quite dissimilar sources. Involved in all causes, however, is some condition or experience that robs the individual of anchors in reality or guides to behavior. Lack of experience, premature and unsuccessful attempts to accomplish some goal, excessive postponement of attempts to master skills for adaptive and constructive behavior, unavailability of defenses and lack of preparation, and rejection of society's demands for adaptation are some of the common causes. Constructive behavior results from the application of problem-solving methods and should have as its goal functioning completely and fully in harmony with the individual's potentialities and interests. Involved in this process is a recognition of the problem, a definition of the problem, incubation, hypothesized solutions, inquiry or search, decisions, and applications.

Failures in problem solving are present when there are serious learning disabilities, resort to common defenses, delinquent and psychopathic deviate behavior, neurotic conflicts, and psychotic breakdowns. All represent varying degrees of loss of contact with the environment and decreased capacity for coping constructively with stress.

Group
Resources and
Response to
Stress

3

_____

How
Groups
Cope with Stress *

9

Just as there are healthy and unhealthy individuals, there are healthy and unhealthy groups. Groups as groups break down, just as individuals break down. Families, teams, classroom groups, school staffs, work groups, bands, school systems—all have problems in coping with stresses. The members of the group may be healthy as individuals, and each may possess outstanding abilities, training, and skills. Yet the group may have difficulty in coping with even mild stresses.

Thus, teachers, counselors, coaches, administrators, supervisors, parents, and others must be interested in the health of groups as groups. If they are to prevent group breakdowns, they must have guides for answering such questions as the following:

> What standards of achievement should be required?
> What degree of efficiency should be demanded?
> How frequently should changes be made?
> When and how should competition be used?
> What degree of independence should be permitted?
> How much effort should be elicited?
> What speed of performance should be required?
> What degree of relaxation is needed?
> How difficult should assignments and examinations be?
> How long should groups be made to work?

* Much of the material presented in this chapter has been adapted from the author's chapter entitled "A Theory of Leadership and Interpersonal Behavior" in *Leadership and Interpersonal Behavior,* edited by L. Petrullo and B. M. Bass, and used by permission of the publisher, Holt, Rinehart and Winston.

In this chapter, an attempt will be made to present a systematic description of the processes by which groups cope with stress, the forces that enable them to hold together, and the procedures whereby they can strengthen these forces. In the next chapter, an attempt will be made to apply some of these concepts to school groups of various kinds with special emphasis on the prevention of group breakdown. Most of the ideas that constitute this formulation were developed in the process of carrying out a six-year program of research concerned with adaptation to emergency and extreme conditions, a program in support of United States Air Force survival training. Looking at group behavior from this vantage point should enable the reader to see more clearly phenomena that operate daily in groups of all kinds in our society.

The author's formulation concerning group behavior under stress is in many respects similar to the formulation that has already been presented for individual behavior under stress. Thus the pattern of the presentation will be familiar. First, the crucial character of group stressors that make them different from "nonstressful" conditions will be examined. Next, an attempt will be made to sketch a model of the process of adaptation, with special emphasis on the mediation of stress through dimensions of duration and intensity of stress and group characteristics (the state of the organism). One of the conceptual schemes that has seemed most productive in studying how groups cope with stress will then be sketched. Finally, some ideas about how group behavior under stress can be improved will be presented.

CRUCIAL CHARACTER OF GROUP STRESS

As in the case of individual stress, the distinctive element in group stress is the lack of structure or loss of anchor in reality experienced as a result of the stressful condition. In the group situation, this loss of anchor in reality makes it difficult or impossible for the group to cope with the requirements of the situation, and the problem of preventing group breakdown becomes one of supplying an anchor and of supplying the expertness for coping with the demands of the situation.

Any of several sets of circumstances may make it difficult for the perceiver to structure the situation or to cope with the situation after structuring has occurred. The situation may be unfamiliar to the group and may require rapid shifts in customary activities. The group may not know what to do, and even if they know what to do, they may not know who should do what with whom. The situation may also constitute a dangerous threat to central values of the group as a group or of group members. The threat may blind the group to some important realities of the situation. Loss of structure may be occasioned by the instability of the situation or of group members or by confusion concerning the demands of the situation. There may be a lack of cues or too many cues. The changes may be too rapid to process adequately, or the requirements may overwhelm the group because the group has inadequate skills for coping with them.

Groups spontaneously, sometimes perhaps unconsciously, do many things to safeguard the means for maintaining continuity of structure under stress. It is fairly well documented (Torrance, 1958a) that groups prefer continuity in leadership from nonstressful to stressful situations. Some investigators of behavior in extreme conditions involving groups argue that the leader in a stressful situation should be the person who is best qualified to save the group, regardless of his rank, status, or usual leadership position. On this issue, the evidence seems to indicate rather clearly that the leader of a group under stressful conditions should be a regular member of the group and should be the same as the official leader under normal operating conditions. Flying personnel, for example, are extremely reluctant to accept superior technical leadership when survival is at stake in favor of their usual commander who may have few, if any, special qualifications for survival in the particular situation. Only 13 per cent would accept a highly skilled survival technician in such a role. The failure of an outside leader to recognize and use the power of the indigenous leader may have disastrous consequences where there is serious threat to the safety of the group.

Using a structured projective technique in which men wrote stories about five different pictures involving groups under stress and answered multiple-choice questions about them, the author explored this issue with 181 men experienced in stressful situations involving groups. About 84 per cent of these men indicated a clear preference for continuity in leadership.

Evidence in favor of the official leader under normal conditions as the leader under stressful conditions was found in a combat follow-up study (Torrance, 1958a) of aircrews in combat over Korea. The extent to which the regular crew commander was chosen at the end of survival training as the "best survival leader" of his crew was a consistent and effective predictor of combat effectiveness. Commanders of crews that were dissolved and not assigned to combat as crews received fewer such choices than those of combat crews. Further, commanders of the less effective combat crews received fewer choices than the commanders of the more effective ones, effectiveness determined by mission success and ratings of effectiveness.

In spite of this strong preference for continuity of leadership, even established leaders (including teachers, principals, coaches, and the like) must apparently continue to validate their leadership or power roles by providing the structure and expertness necessary for the group's survival. Thus, leaders of long and distinguished experience must demonstrate again and again their expertness. For example, Grosvenor (1920), in describing the illustrious Peary's last exploration to the North Pole, tells how Peary won a foot race with his men near the North Pole. Peary was noted for his consideration of his men and for the intense loyalty that he inspired. There are also many accounts of leaders who fail to validate their power roles and who, in effect, lose their influence over the group.

When there is no designated leader, the person who is able and willing to provide the essential structure emerges as leader. Tyhurst (1958) cites a number of episodes that illustrate the principles that seem to operate in such situations. In the Winnipeg flood a number of leaders emerged. One arose in connection with the attempts of a community to erect a dike. The men were working with tremendous energy but with little organization and effectiveness, until a hypomanic contractor came along. This man took over and started ordering heavy earth-moving equipment from all over Manitoba. Assuming a responsibility that no one else would take, he did not bother about who was going to pay for the use of the equipment, who was going to return the equipment, and the like. Shortly, the community was surrounded by a dike, which is still there. The emergent leader disappeared and no one has heard of him since.

Another example (Tyhurst, 1958) was a stock boy who emerged as a leader in a severe department store fire in Halifax that killed 13 people. The fire started on the ground floor. The boy was on the third floor and saved about two dozen people, who were milling around, by taking them out through a skylight in the roof. He had often used this skylight to escape from work. He was extremely calm and was very effective for this group. Tyhurst contends that his leadership amounts to more than his being familiar with the setting, because many people who are able to get themselves out of danger quite well do not concern themselves with others.

There may be conflicts or even failure to survive when the designated leader does not provide the essential structure and expertness (Torrance, 1954a). A leader may delegate leadership functions to someone who is able to supply the structure and expertness or to utilize the resources of the group in making decisions. In other cases, an able and popular individual spontaneously may assume command either by mutual consent or at a somewhat less conscious level. The incompetent leader may be abandoned or otherwise disposed of by the group and in rare instances may be removed by mutinous action. The sanctions against mutiny are so strong, however, that there are strong barriers to the emergence of a leader other than the designated one (Torrance, LaForge, and Mason, 1956).

When stress is severe, a leader may forget that he is leader. Things may become so confused in a school that the principal may ask, "Why doesn't the head of this school do something about this mess?" On a particularly hectic day the classroom teacher may find himself saying, "The teacher of that class ought to straighten things out!" forgetting he is the teacher. Even in combat, commanders under severe stress have been known to abdicate their power roles, expecting someone else to take over. S. L. A. Marshall (Field and Davis, 1953, p. 19), for example, tells of personal experience with General Dutch Kaiser. During one extremely violent combat episode, Kaiser came to Marshall telling him that he had been going around from group to group, asking, "Who is in command here? Who is in command?" In most cases he found no one. Marshall asked him, "General, didn't it occur to you that you were in command?" Kaiser replied, "You know, stress becomes so great that under these conditions, it never occurs to you that you are the one to give orders. I may have thought of that, but I was looking for someone to help me out, and that is why I was going around and saying, 'Who is in command?' " In spite of this apparent tendency to abdicate the power role in times of severe stress, there are of course many accounts of heroic commanders who sacrifice themselves, pushing forward to structure and restructure the situation for the group being commanded.

GROUP PROCESSES OF ADAPTATION

Group adaptation can most profitably be conceived of in much the same way as individual adaptation. This conceptualization is presented schematically in Figure 9–1. In the "stressors" box are listed some of the specific conditions that produce a loss of structure and place heavy loads upon groups. In the "consequences" box are listed the common negative and positive outcomes. Theoretically, *any* of the specific stressors may lead to *any* of the consequences or symptoms. For example, failure to attain the group's goal may result in apathy and collapse or in hostility and defiance. The same consequence may also arise from quite dissimilar sources. The ability and structure of the group, the quality of its leadership and interpersonal behavior, however, might be such that there would be an overcompensation and all-out effort, which would result in distinguished performance and heroic success. In other words, there is an interaction of the mediating variables.

Next, let us examine the course of adaptation when viewed along the dimensions of duration, intensity, and group characteristics.

DURATION OF STRESS

To the extent that we have been able to assess group performance under stress along a time continuum (Torrance, LaForge, and Mason, 1956), the data appear to conform quite closely to the process described for individual adaptation. When there is mastery of stress, this process may be represented schematically by the theoretical curve shown in Figure 9–2. In other words, when the stress is suddenly encountered, there is an initial

143

Stresses	Mediating Variables	Consequences
Failure of group mission or objectives; unrealistic goals		Panic, disorganization, lack of group-task efficiency
Attack by hostile individuals or groups	DURATION →	Apathy, lack of effort, loss of will to live
Difficult tasks; frequent repetition of events		Excessive hostility, defiance, destructiveness, lawlessness, etc.
Sudden emergencies		Exhaustion, collapse, dissolution of group
Deprivation of physical, social, emotional, cognitive, and/or aesthetic needs		Overcompensation, all-out effort, victory over superior forces
Discomfort from cold, heat fatigue, lack of sleep, etc.	INTENSITY →	Increased speed and group-task efficiency
Lack of group-task structure		Control of panic, maintenance of will to live (continue adaptation)
Presence of an incompetent, competitive, hostile, erratic, unpredictable, disloyal, or other deviate member	LEADERSHIP AND →	Excessive disharmony, interpersonal strife, "survival of fittest"
History of internal strife	INTERPERSONAL BEHAVIOR	Lack of trust, mutiny, etc.
Inadequate training for individual and group tasks		Planning, good group decisions, cooperation
Loss of a group member		Mutual support and self-sacrifice of members
		Inventiveness and creativity

Figure 9–1. Typical Group Stresses and the Mediation of Their Consequences

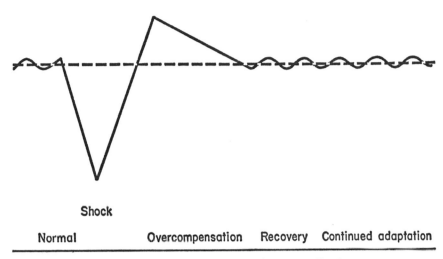

Shock

Normal   Overcompensation   Recovery   Continued adaptation

Figure 9–2. Theoretical Curve of Group Performance under Stress over Time in Case of Mastery of Stress

shock or resistance to accepting the seriousness of the situation. This lag is followed by rapid overcompensation and recovery with a leveling off of performance as control is gained.

If the stress is continued long enough, regardless of the intensity of the stress and strength of the group, fatigue occurs and ultimately there will be collapse, as represented in Figure 9–3. There may be vast differences, however, in the length of time required for different groups under different intensities of stress to reach a breaking point. Before the breaking point is reached a variety of both positive and negative effects may be manifested. There may be confusion, inefficiency, recklessness, apathy, fatigue, hostility, changes in leadership, and the like. In fact, such actions may occur almost until the break appears, and the break may seem sudden. Before the break, the signs of approaching breakdown may have been denied or ignored. Usually, after the break has occurred, the warning signs can be recalled.

Since there are interaction effects among the three classes of mediating variables, it should be recognized that there will be a number of deviations from the general rule.

INTENSITY OF STRESS

A number of laboratory studies of individual behavior (Harris, Mackie, and Wilson, 1956) indicate that mild stress tends to result in

145

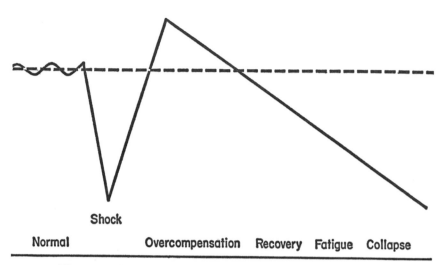

Shock

Normal   Overcompensation   Recovery   Fatigue   Collapse

Figure 9–3. Theoretical Curve of Group Performance under Continued Stress with Ultimate Collapse

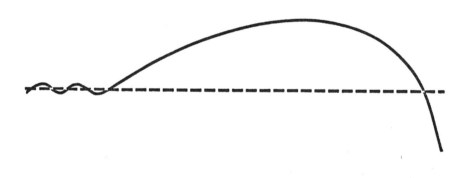

No stress   Mild stress   Increasingly intense stress

Figure 9–4. Theoretical Curve of Typical Group Perform-ance under Conditions of Increasingly Intense Stress

improved response, increased activity, and the like, and that extreme stress results in deterioration of performance. Accounts of group survival in emergencies and extreme conditions and observations of men in survival training support a similar conclusion for groups. This relationship is represented graphically by the curve shown in Figure 9–4. The performance curve rises with increasing stress up to a point and then descends.

GROUP CHARACTERISTICS

It is within the framework already sketched that group characteristics mediate the effects of stress. One useful way of studying the process of adaptation of groups through group characteristics is to think in terms of the linkages or forces that hold groups together—for example, affect, power, communication, and goals (Torrance, 1954b).

To use affect (liking-disliking) linkages as an example, theoretical functioning over time may be represented by the curve in Figure 9–5. According to this model, after a brief period of dislocation and momentary estrangement, there are manifestations and expressions of increased affect and feelings of closeness. In many groups strong interpersonal hostilities and repulsions change to strong positive affect, at least for a time. In time this increased affection returns to normalcy. If the stress continues unabated, however, there may be a deterioration of these affectional relationships. People become irritated with one another's faults and have no other objects available upon which to project feelings of aggressions resulting from frustration.

Effective leadership and healthy interpersonal relations may be expected to decrease the lag at the onset of stress and prolong the period of continued adaptation in the face of unabated stress. Two special models of ineffective leadership and unhealthy interpersonal relations might, therefore, be added to the one represented by Figure 9–6. During the overcompensatory phase, affect linkages may be strengthened, only to collapse after the first feeling of safety has been experienced. This relationship is the same as that depicted in Figure 9–4. At first, the common danger draws the individuals together. Once the first danger has been passed, however, some members feel that they no longer need the others. They may even feel angry that they have "weakened" in feeling kindly toward their fellow members. Under such conditions some groups, because of the quality of the forces that hold them together, collapse, while others rebound as shown in Figure 9–6. In this case, the group has retained its capacity to diagnose its ills and interpret the feedback (information about its own functioning).

If affect linkages are viewed in terms of sociometric structure, evidence (Torrance, 1957b) indicates that instability occurs under stress. Effective groups show greater stability in sociometric structure (pattern of inter-

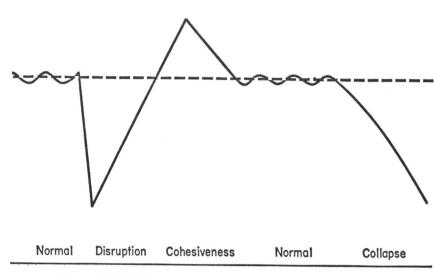

| Normal | Disruption | Cohesiveness | Normal | Collapse |

Figure 9–5. Theoretical Functioning of Affect Linkages
(Liking-Disliking) in Groups under Stress over Time

personal choices) than ineffective ones. Measures of group performance increase in variability under stress. Group members become better acquainted with one another, less aware of prestige differences, and more tolerant of disagreement. Official social structures tend to give way to informal structures under stress; and, in extreme stress, social structure tends to break down and not to be replaced.

Power, communication, and goal linkages appear to operate in much the same way as affect. When stress is first experienced, there is a tendency for power linkages to be exercised more firmly. As time goes on, the leader may, because of his inexpertness, lack of interest, or personal maladjustment, fail to validate or maintain his power and as a result lose the support of the group. Collapse is then imminent. Similarly, communication and goal linkages tend at first to become stronger and then weaken and finally collapse if the stress is prolonged. Furthermore, there is an interaction effect among the four types of linkages discussed. For example, the effects of weak affect linkages may be counteracted by strong power, communication, and/or goal linkages.

The theoretical functioning of affect linkages under increasing intensity is the same as shown in Figure 9–6. As intensity increases, affect linkages increase in strength until some theoretical limit or apex is reached. After this, there tends to be a decline in strength. Power, communication,

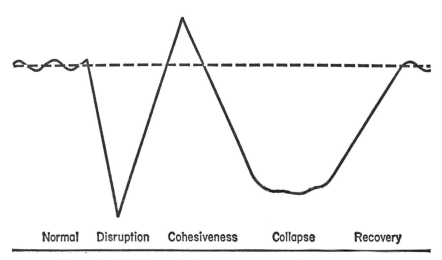

| Normal | Disruption | Cohesiveness | Collapse | Recovery |

Figure 9–6. Theoretical Functioning of Affect Linkages in Groups under Stress over Time (Comeback following Collapse)

and goal linkages appear to function in essentially the same manner. With increasing stress the leader (principal, teacher, etc.) tends to tighten up, delegate responsibility and power to subordinates, and check group members' performance more closely. As the apex is reached, however, the leader feels so threatened that he either takes away all power from others or abdicates his own power role. In some cases, he does both concurrently and this is when the group really falls apart. Under moderate stress, communication tends to become more frequent, but under intensity, communication breaks down. Under moderate stress, goals tend to become more important, more worth while. Under intense stress, group goals tend to become less important, less worth while.

Each of the leader behaviors described above has its adverse effects on the effectiveness of the group and upon the mental functioning of group members. These in turn increase the stress upon both the leader and group members. An experiment by Lee, Horwitz, and Goldman (1954) gives some idea of the implications of these dynamics for classroom learning. The subjects of this experiment were 153 male, ROTC, college freshmen who were recruited on the basis of an appeal to assist in evaluating different kinds of teaching methods. The men were formed into 30 groups of four to six persons each, and each group was set up as a miniature classroom in

149

which a teacher instructed the subjects on the construction of a number of different paper objects.

Subjects were told that midway on each of the instructions, decisions would be made about whether to repeat the instructions or go ahead without repeating. At each decision point, the subjects' desires, in their different strengths, were posted on a board in view of all subjects. In all three experimental conditions, the experimenter posted the students' desire as favoring repeating the instructions. This was made plausible by giving the instructions very rapidly so the subjects usually did vote to repeat. In all cases, the instructor's desire was posted as not favoring repetition of instructions. In all cases, the teacher went ahead without repetition. In condition A, this was a legitimate act as the students had not been led to expect that they would be given the power to decide. Thus, this implied no reduction of the students' power. In conditions B and C, this was not a legitimate act. Students had been led to expect that they would have the power to decide. In condition B, the teacher doubled the weight of his own desire and reduced the legitimate weight of the desires of the students and the Armed Forces. In condition C, the teacher in effect quadrupled the weight of his own desires, with consequent higher reduction of the legitimate weight of the desires of the students and the Armed Forces. The three conditions were run under each of two different teachers in an attempt to control for possible effects of differences in personal characteristics of teachers.

The subjects' perception of power reduction agreed very closely with what the experimenters had attempted to induce. Using a seven-point hostility rating at the conclusion of the experiment, the following means were obtained for treatments A, B, and C: 2.16, 2.72, and 3.53 (significant at the .001 level). Differences between teachers were not significant. At both the beginning and the end of the experiment the subjects were asked to give their impressions of the teacher on an adjective checklist. Differences in the direction of less favorable ratings were taken as a measure of aggression. The mean drops in ratings under treatments A, B, and C were 4.50, 12.10, and 14.54 (significant at the .01 level). The difference between teachers was not significant. It was also found that treatment A produced less attention to "irrelevant" teacher behaviors such as dropping papers on the floor. It was also found that the hostility engendered under treatments B and C interfered with learning as measured by a performance test in which subjects remade the paper objects (significant at about the .05 level). Thus, it appears that the reduction of power to make decisions in a group increases hostility, aggression, and attention to job-irrelevant behavior or minor irritations; and it interferes with learning. A variety of teaching experiments are needed to determine other implications of the conceptualization of adaptation to stress that has been offered in this section.

IMPROVING GROUP BEHAVIOR

A fundamental characteristic of a stressful situation is its demand for a level and type of activity sharply departing from the customary behavior pattern of the group. The new activity may demand the use of skills that have previously been of minor importance or completely unused. Thus the process of adjustment to the stressful situation is aided by factors that reduce the discontinuity or abrupt nature of the change, factors such as readiness of the group to perceive and accept an emergency, good communication networks, willingness to experiment with new types of organization and new types of behavior, and the presence of relevant skills in group members. Reducing the lag and prolonging adaptation depend then partly on the degree of behavioral change required and partly on the resources that the group possesses. Since the concern here is for the improvement of group behavior, an effort will be made to place some of the facts we have discovered in relation to the four linkages discussed: affect, power, communication, and goals.

POWER LINKAGES

Thus far, findings suggest that the following behaviors or conditions affect adversely the power linkages of groups under stress:

1. A history of conflict among the various echelons of power involved (Torrance, LaForge, and Mason, 1956).
2. Failure of official leaders to accept the informal leadership structure of the group (Torrance, LaForge, and Mason, 1956).
3. The breakdown of official units or subgroupings at the onset of stress, with the tendency for those most able to cope with the stress to form a unit, leaving those least able to cope with the stress in units lacking resources for meeting the demands of the situation (Torrance, LaForge, and Mason, 1956).
4. Isolation of the leader or leadership group from the remainder of the group (Torrance, LaForge, and Mason, 1956).
5. Reduction of the power of the group by the leader with an accompanying increase in hostility (Torrance, LaForge, and Mason, 1956).
6. Abdication of power roles or functions customarily assumed (Torrance, LaForge, and Mason, 1956).
7. Unwillingness of designated leader to "act outside of authority" (Torrance, 1958a).
8. Attempt by the group to function without a designated leader (Torrance, 1958a).

151

9. Changes in leadership and/or failure of leader to fulfill group's expectations (Torrance, 1958a).
10. The failure of the leader to resolve his increased feelings of loneliness and isolation (Torrance, 1958a).

A few of these findings need to be discussed in detail.

The desirability of having a designated leader in a small group under stress has been questioned frequently. A careful examination of group survival accounts of self-styled "leaderless groups" usually indicates the presence of an informal, yet rather powerful, leader. In spite of the evidence and indoctrination concerning the necessity of a leader under stress, about 17 per cent of aircrewmen subjects favored having leaderless groups. Perhaps an even larger percentage of groups tend to operate on the assumption that it is undesirable to have a leader in a small group under stress, much to their disadvantage.

The leader of a small group under stress should be a regular member of the group and should be the same as the official leader under normal conditions. Such a leader will prove to be far more influential than an outsider would be in determining the behavior of members (Torrance and Mason, 1956). The intelligent leader is able to overcome technical deficiencies by using available outsiders and group members as resource persons in making decisions, while retaining the decision-making function. From a practical standpoint, when the formally-designated leader does not function or is not present, an emergent leader may have to be used. Such a leader typically emerges on the basis of uniquely qualifying experiences, previous experience in stressful situations, expert skills important to the group, superior training, or the like.

Under stress, men generally expect a leader to behave in much the same way as he usually behaves, with the exception that he checks on things more closely (Torrance, 1958a). They believe that stress does not warrant a change in the relationship of the leader to his men and that his decisions should not be questioned. Furthermore, they believe that the leader should undergo the same hardships and dangers as his men, but that he should avoid being "just one of the boys." Although men appear to want a leader to behave as he usually does, leadership behavior actually becomes more variable under stress.

The loneliness and isolation of the leader is a common phenomenon and appears to be intensified by stress, except when a leader abdicates his power role. If the stress is prolonged and intense, the leader may be overwhelmed by the tensions aroused. He may either establish a confidential relationship with a trusted subordinate or in some way cease his coping behavior or lose his will to live. In business, industrial, educational, and athletic groups the leader may transfer, resign, or retire. A highly expert leader may be able to associate quite intimately with his men without apparent harm to his exercise of power. A leader may consciously employ the strategy of taking into his confidence some member of the group both to reinforce control and to provide psychological support for himself.

Perhaps dynamically related to the phenomenon of loneliness of the leader, and the feelings of some people that small groups under stress should function without leaders, is the tendency of leaders to abdicate power under conditions of stress. It will be recalled that this abdication tends to occur at the same time the leader reduces the power of group members to make decisions and initiate action. It is logical to interpret this kind of behavior as a sign of loss of contact with the environment and such behavior certainly results in a loss of contact, a reduction in the number of available guides to behavior, and the consequent incapacity to cope constructively with stressful conditions. As indicated earlier, abdication rarely occurs except under conditions of severe stress and apparently operates at an unconscious level. Analogues of this kind of behavior can be found in the classroom, on the athletic field, and in the principal's office. They occur in the classroom when the teacher forbids and punishes pupils' efforts to initiate their own learning activities and to structure learning situations, yet fails to give learners the structure that is necessary for success. Unless grossly incompetent, such teachers are likely to be under considerable stress of some kind.

A leader's unwillingness to "act outside of authority" may paralyze a group and cause it to delay dangerously its adaptation to stress and to incapacitate it in maintaining constructive behavior. Many outstanding examples of poor adaptation by German officers during World War II (Guerlain, 1943) occurred as a result of the German's unwillingness to do anything forbidden by rules and regulations. Many of the great performances in war, athletics, science, and business have occurred when leaders have been willing "to act outside of established procedures," often regarded as "authority." In a similar way, the author has observed that teachers and principals fail to act constructively on behalf of children because in doing so they would be "acting outside of authority" or differently from established practices, policies, or rules and regulations. Frequently the teacher or the principal will say, "I know that this is unfair to the children. I know it isn't right, but what can you do?" They will then recite a string of what have been called "killer phrases" such as: "That's beyond our responsibility." "That's not my job." "The parents will never buy it." "We've never done it before." "That's not the school's problem." "The School Board will never go for it." "I'd be the laughing stock of the school." In most cases, "acting outside of authority" does not require "taking the law in one's hand." Frequently it involves only the assumption of valid responsibilities; parents and school boards will welcome the action; and others will applaud rather than laugh. At times, however, it does involve the assumption of calculated risks.

AFFECT LINKAGES

On the basis of data now available, the following conditions appear to disturb the affect linkages in groups under stress and to interfere with the ability of groups to cope with stress:

1. Interpersonal stresses resulting from differences in values and from personality incompatibilities of members (Torrance, LaForge, and Mason, 1956).
2. Unwillingness of a member to respond to group pressures to conformity and to perform role expectations (Torrance, LaForge, Mason, 1956).
3. Discrepancy between the values of the leader and the predominant values of group members (Torrance, LaForge, Mason, 1956).
4. Failure to give mutual support and to sacrifice personal goals for group goals (Smith, 1959).

From observations of groups under stress and accounts of group survival, we have reasonably good models for the adaptation processes involved in the first two conditions listed above. First, the group exerts pressure to influence the offending member to adapt. Then the leader exerts pressure, and possibly the group rejects the offending member. Finally the group absorbs his roles so that it does not depend upon him for the performance of the functions necessary for their survival.

If the leader differs in some way from the rest of the group, the disruption of affect thus occasioned appears to become aggravated under stress. For example, difficulties in group decision making may be encountered if the leader differs too sharply in some crucial personality characteristic (such as authoritarianism) from the other members of the group. Leaders with moderate needs for conformity to the opinions and judgments of the group members (Ziller, 1953) appear to be more flexible than those with either high or low needs and to show more confidence in their group's ability to make good decisions. Groups that are highly attractive to members are also more flexible in decision making and more confident than low attraction groups.

Of special importance in coping with stress is the problem of increasing mutual support and willingness to sacrifice individual goals for group goals. When man scents danger, he appears to have a peculiarly strong desire to be with others. At the same time, evidences of unwillingness to sacrifice for the welfare of the group and of "survival-of-the-fittest" behavior are frequent and strong. In giving and receiving aid in groups under stress there is a great deal of ambivalence, and this ambivalence appears to fluctuate with the duration and intensity of the stress. Under severe stress, everyone must have support but capacity to give support is extremely limited. Those who sacrifice most for the welfare of fellow group members appear to survive longest under severe stress. There is also a tendency for those who achieve apparent safety or some satisfaction of a deprived need to refuse to sacrifice for the welfare of the group.

In general, mutual support and willingness to sacrifice for the welfare of the group increase chances of survival and reduce the discomfort of the stresses, whatever they may be. Individuals who fail to give aid to other group members suffer losses in self-esteem. Persons who lose group support through either calculated or unconscious rejection appear to be hurt psychologically, and they are less likely to survive.

Some of the factors that seem to increase willingness to sacrifice are group integrity; agreements among group members; close friendships and previous acquaintance; similarity of cultural background, religion, and group mores and norms; national pride; internal self-government; group pressures; the influence of the leader; success of the central mission of the group; and prevention of breaks in the cooperative pattern.

Actual accounts of group behavior under stress, observations of groups in realistically simulated emergencies and extreme conditions, and laboratory experiments (Smith, 1959) support the notion that unwillingness to sacrifice for the group is increased by opportunities to keep secret one's failure in this regard. Smith used an experimental apparatus adapted from Crutchfield's (1951) group squares test. Two independent variables were studied. The first was a high individualistic motivation induced by an evaluation set versus low individualistic motivation with no threat of evaluation. The second independent variable brought into play an overt situation, in which the group members knew when a fellow member failed to sacrifice his solution to help the group, versus a covert situation, in which the group members did not know when a fellow member failed to sacrifice. The subjects were 20 six-man groups that had been living together for at least five days and would continue to function as groups for about ten more days in a simulated survival situation. Each of the 20 groups was tested separately, five under each of four experimental conditions.

The subjects were seated in a circle with their backs to one another. Each subject was given the task of assembling a square with geometric pieces. As the initial pieces given each subject did not form a square, subjects had to request and exchange pieces by means of a tray carried around by the experimenter. The instructions indicated that it was easy for one or two people to form a square but difficult for everyone to have a square at the same time. By manipulating the tray, the experimenter contrived that each subject complete his square at the end of the second round. In the third and fourth rounds, each subject held his square unmodified because no one requested a piece held by him. Thereafter, the tray indicated a request for a piece that would break up each subject's square. These

Table 9–1. *Number of Subjects Who Sacrificed on Each Critical Trial in Four Experimental Conditions (N = 30 in each condition)*

CRITICAL	HIGH IN-DIVIDUALISTIC MOTIVATION OVERT	LOW IN-DIVIDUALISTIC MOTIVATION OVERT	HIGH IN-DIVIDUALISTIC MOTIVATION COVERT	LOW IN-DIVIDUALISTIC MOTIVATION COVERT
1–4	20	25	2	4
5–8	2	1	2	6
9–12	0	1	2	4
13–16	0	0	2	4
Never sacrificed	8	3	22	12

rounds were continued until each subject had given up the requested piece, or until there had been 16 critical trials.

In summary, an attempt was made to create the following four psychological conditions:

High individualistic motivation. The individual was placed in danger of losing status because of failure on an intellectual task which would become a part of his official record. At the same time, he was faced by requests for help by his fellow group members. To help them would increase the possibility that he would fail.

Low individualistic motivation. The results would be anonymous and the task was not known to measure anything, just experimental. Group members, however, were placed in conflict between their desire to do well and their desire to help their fellows.

Overt conditions. Group members knew that their decisions would be known by the group.

Covert conditions. Group members knew that their fellow group members would not know how they resolved the conflict. It was clear, however, that the experimenter would know how the conflict was resolved.

Observer reports and interviews with subjects indicated that the experimental manipulations produced the anticipated psychological conditions. In fact, some subjects experienced acute and obvious conflict. The data in Table 9–1 show when the subjects in each condition broke their squares, thus endangering their individual solutions. In Table 9–2 the data are simplified to permit a chi-square analysis. The chi square on the number of subjects in all of the covert groups who broke their squares, compared to the number in all the overt groups, was 18.81 (significant at the .01 level). The chi square comparing the high individualistic condition with the low individualistic condition was 8.00 (significant at the .01 level).

Although the experimental condition may seem superficial, it did seem to be a very powerful experience to the participants and at least suggests

Table 9–2. Number of Subjects Who Sacrificed in Four Experimental Conditions (N = 30 in each condition)

	OVERT	COVERT	TOTALS
High individualistic motivation	22	8	30
Low individualistic motivation	27	18	45
Totals	49	26	

From E. E. Smith, "Individual Versus Group Goal Conflict" *Journal of Abnormal and Social Psychology*, 1959, *58*, 136. Used by permission of the author and the American Psychological Association.

several things concerning the conditions that make for mutual support in groups. It appears that people tend to choose the attainment of their own goals in preference to attainment of a group goal more frequently when their actions are secret than when their actions are known. People also tend to choose the attainment of their own goals in preference to the group goal more frequently when there is the threat of external evaluation and a matter of official records than when there is no such threat. In the experiment, this finding held only in covert conditions, however.

COMMUNICATION LINKAGES

The following conditions appear to be most prominent in interfering with communication linkages that impair group functioning and threaten group survival:

1. Failure of a group member to inform the others about what he is doing (Marshall, 1947).
2. Failure to pool information that would provide a basis for diagnosing the seriousness of the danger and for reducing resistance to accepting its seriousness (Torrance, LaForge, and Mason, 1956).
3. Confining communication to dyads or cliques rather than communicating to the entire group (Torrance, LaForge, and Mason, 1956).
4. Failure to use group judgments in making decisions, and leadership techniques that interfere with use of group judgments (Ziller, 1957a).
5. Power differences that interfere with communication of information needed in decision making (Torrance, 1954c).
6. Unwillingness to disagree in the decision-making process (Torrance, 1957a).

The first two conditions are too obvious and too widely known to require elaboration. S. L. A. Marshall (1947) during World War II established the importance of failure to tell others what one is about in the causation of panic. Equally well known is the danger of failures to recognize and accept the seriousness of impending or present dangers and the consequent failure of the group to take adaptive action. Perhaps less well established is the tendency of groups under severe stress to break down into dyads or other subgroup formations and to confine communication to these formations. Under moderate stress, however, there appears to be a tendency for the members of a group to polarize around a leader and to respond more precisely to his communications. In time, however, these subgroup formations tend to develop and to interfere with the communication linkages.

Many of the findings concerning group decision making under stress relate rather directly to problems of maintaining communication linkages, but there is no way to relate them to the dimensions of duration and intensity. In general, leaders appear to feel a greater than usual need to seek the judgments of group members when conditions become stressful. At the same time, group members are increasingly willing to place their lives in the hands of a strong leader who promises to get them out of the predicament. In spite of the haste with which many decisions must be made during emergencies and extreme conditions, experiences of survivors indicate that even in sudden emergencies leaders can profit from the judgment and information of group members in reaching decisions.

On the matter of leadership technique (Ziller, 1957a), it appears that group members react most favorably to a group-decision situation under conditions permitting self-determination and reinforcement from the leader. Leaders using techniques of decision making in which they have no knowledge of the group's opinion prior to stating their own are more reluctant than leaders using group-centered decision-making techniques to make a decision that may involve the risk of the lives of group members.

Concerning the consequences of power differences, it was found in one experiment (Torrance, 1954c) that influence on decisions is in line with the power structure of the group and that the structure may interfere markedly with the quality of the decision. In rearranged or temporary groups, as compared with intact or permanent groups, the effects of power differences are lessened. In three-man groups with well-defined power structures the occupant of each power position tended to be assigned or assumed interaction behaviors characteristic of his position. The person with highest status appealed to solidarity, obtained suggestions and opinions, and evaluated them. The person of intermediate status tended to be freer to disagree, while the lowest-status member seemed to be afraid to disagree and tended to withdraw from the decision-making process. Permanent groups more frequently made decisions that indicated a willingness to make a personal sacrifice for a group member, while temporary groups more frequently made decisions of a more flexible, sequential type.

Disagreement during the decision-making process appears to contribute to the making of "good" decisions (Torrance, 1957a), if the disagreement is task-centered rather than person-centered. Disagreement also has possible negative effects, if there develops any "negative identification" among members of the group. The expression of disagreement tends to be inhibited by status or power differences, the permanency of the relationships of group members, leadership techniques, and negative criticism. Pooling the results of several experiments (Torrance, 1957a), it appears that the advantages which accrue from disagreement and the tolerance of disagreement stem from the fact that disagreement increases the range of judgments considered, decreases chances of misunderstanding among group members, increases the group's willingness to take calculated risks, and increases willingness to accept the group's decision.

GOAL LINKAGES

Some of the most salient factors that seem to weaken goal linkages are these:

1. The making of concessions to immediate comfort.
2. Weakening of goals and loss of will-to-survive.
3. The absence of a plan or strategy for coping with the stress.

In accounts of both individual and group survival, the making of concessions to immediate comfort looms important in weakening goal linkages. This phenomenon was particularly clear in the Blizzard Study (Torrance, LaForge, and Mason, 1956). During and immediately after the blizzard entire subgroups failed to build fires, dry footgear, and exercise other precautions against frostbite. Men lost important items of equipment, such as gloves, on their rough downhill trek and simply failed to exert themselves to pick them up. If subgroup norms had placed a value on recovering equipment instead of making such concessions to immediate comfort, this extra energy would have been expended by most individuals.

The loss-of-will-to-survive phenomenon has been an object of special study. Factors involved in the maintenance of will mentioned most frequently by survivors are these: instincts of self-preservation, determination based on some kind of unwavering decision, something to live for (family, home, democratic way of life, mission, immediate purpose, and the like), dignity and self-esteem, concern for someone or something outside self, group influences, some reason for hope, all-out efforts, religious faith, and various combinations of these. Whatever leaders can do to reinforce the above factors should strengthen goal linkages. A field experiment and a laboratory experiment concerning group factors relevant to will-to-survive (Zander, Thomas, and Natsoulas, 1957) indicated that the following factors are significant: degree of pressure from others, legitimacy of pressures from others, internalization of pressures from others, attraction of the crew, personal goals, and ego strength.

Many groups studied by the author seemed to be on the verge of collapse until someone developed a plan or strategy for coping with stress. The development of such a plan or strategy seemed to give the group new and unexpected resources for adapting to the requirements of the situation.

SUMMARY

Since groups may be viewed as organisms and may break down, just as individuals do, an attempt has been made to apply stress concepts to group functioning and breakdown. The crucial character of group stress lies in a lack of structure or loss of anchors or contacts with the environment. There may be a lack of structure both in the group itself and in the situation in which the group has to function. In either case, the lack of structure makes it difficult or impossible for members to know what to do. Most groups look to a leader to establish structure both within the group itself and for the task to be accomplished. Any single stressor may produce any one of a variety of types of breakdown or malfunctioning, just as any particular type of breakdown may result from any one of a variety of stressors. The processes, however, are essentially the same in all instances and resemble quite closely those observed in individuals. With the onset of stress there is a lag in performance, followed by all-out overcompensation, a return to normal, with fatigue and collapse occurring if there is not respite from the stressful conditions.

Groups may be thought of in terms of the forces that hold them together and give them organismic properties. These may be conceptualized in terms of affect, power, communications, and goals. In improving group behavior under stress, the strength of these forces or linkages may be examined and treated. Much of the research that has been reported may be organized according to these concepts and group functioning may be observed and analyzed in terms of them.

When
Groups
Break Down

10

Thirty-seven students are in a small room. The course is eleventh grade English. The abilities of the 37 students cover a wide range. Reading ability ranges from fifth grade to college freshman. IQ runs from 70 to 140. Most of the students ride buses, some from as far away as 26 miles.

As a group, they find it hard to work together on class projects such as the homecoming float, class play, and class meetings. They are considered difficult to handle by most of the teachers. The most experienced teacher had the most success. The English teacher had the least.

A student in English class would refuse to read orally, or read with misplaced emphasis. If the teacher were to read, the class might hum softly—at least two-thirds would. The artists would draw caricatures of the teacher and pass them around—or draw them on desks with labels. The more pressure the English teacher used, the more out of hand they became. It was utterly impossible to teach them. Most of them refused to turn in written assignments. Cliques were always fighting one another and could agree on nothing.

This is a group mental health situation familiar to me. I *was* the English teacher! *

Whatever the cause, a class that fails to learn breaks down as a group. The athletic team that fails to function—or fails to win in spite of weak opposition or in spite of the fact that they are blessed with talent—breaks down. The school faculty that fails to function and to achieve a good learning situation breaks down. Such groups cannot long survive. The teacher may be fired. The coach may be burned in effigy. The principal may be run out of the community. Whatever happens, the group has failed to function and to fulfill its purpose. Its reason for existing has vanished.

* The above account was written by a teacher enrolled in a course taught by the author.

In general, the processes of group breakdown have not been open to scientific study. Such investigation is usually perceived as too threatening in natural situations. Investigators have been reluctant to subject laboratory groups to stresses severe enough or prolonged enough to bring about breakdown. Thus, for useful concepts about group breakdown, it is necessary to go to the literature on disaster, will-to-survive, and panic. In these areas, there is a considerable literature, although scientific investigation has been rare. Physicians have long recognized the importance of will-to-live in the recovery of their patients. It is demonstrated when they say, "We have done all we can—now it is up to the patient," and summon a child, wife, or mother to the dying man's bedside to rekindle his will-to-live.

It has been shown that the processes of group breakdown can be studied scientifically using concepts of "will-to-live." In survival research, "will-to-survive" is defined as "continued adaptive behavior and successful control of tension." Breakdown or failure to survive as a group may then be considered either as a settling-in of apathy, or the arousal of panic. As a result of either reaction, the group becomes unwilling or unable to deal constructively with new demands or crises. In the classroom, the group is unable to learn, to think productively, or to make decisions. Perhaps one of the most difficult and most important jobs the classroom teacher faces is to help the individuals who compose a class to become a functioning group.

In this chapter, an effort will be made to present some concepts that have their origin in stress research but that can be used productively in understanding and preventing group breakdown generally. These concepts have been derived from studying the accounts of hundreds of groups in emergencies and extreme conditions, interviewing the surviving members of such groups, observing and studying the behavior of several hundred groups in simulated survival situations, and testing groups in stressful laboratory situations.

BEHAVIOR ANALOGOUS TO LOSS OF WILL-TO-LIVE

If our interest is in understanding and preventing the processes of group breakdown, we must investigate behaviors that may be considered as analogous to loss of will-to-survive and that would lead to breakdown or destruction. Such behaviors can then be used as signs that the group as a group is "unhealthy" and requires some type of treatment. On the basis of clues concerning the nature of loss of will-to-survive, it is possible to identify such indicators. Such indicators, of course, can be used only as a warning that something is going wrong with the group's ability to cope with its problems and that breakdown is impending unless the process is reversed.

The following four subcategories have been developed for classifying this kind of behavior: failure to take adaptive action, failure to take care of essential requirements for existence, reckless or panic-like behavior, and lack of group-esteem. Although these categories are interrelated and to some extent overlapping, they have proved useful in identifying behaviors analogous to loss of will-to-survive and breakdown.

FAILURE TO TAKE ADAPTIVE ACTION

Failure to take adaptive action when the situation changes (new demands, higher requirements, speedups, and the like) refers to general apathetic reactions. In the classroom, they may be manifested by a slowness or failure in responding to a change in the situation. Individuals may remain inactive or idle at times when action is required. They have to be prompted to get back to work after a break, to get in assignments, to continue with class exercises, and the like. They have to be "driven" to accomplish essential activities.

Scientifically, this problem has been studied primarily under the rubric of "resistance to change." A good example of investigations to develop methods of preventing nonadaptive behavior and resistance to change is an investigation by Coch and French (1948) in a factory situation. Four groups of workers were studied. These groups were roughly equivalent in terms of the efficiency ratings of the groups before the change, the degree of change involved, and the amount of "we-feeling" observed in the groups. Three procedures were used in introducing the change. The first experimental procedure involved the participation of representatives of the workers in designing the job changes. The second experimental procedure involved two groups and consisted of total participation by all members of the group in designing the job changes. In a control group the members were only informed of the change and the new method was explained.

The first experimental procedure produced an unusually good learning curve. After fourteen days, the group using this procedure had attained the set standard, its members were generally cooperative among themselves and with their supervisors, and no one quit the job. The second experimental procedure resulted in an even quicker recovery, attaining a level 14 per cent above the prescribed norm. Group members worked well with their supervisors, showed no aggression, and no one quit. The control group improved little beyond its original efficiency ratings and did not attain the prescribed standard. There was much resistance and aggression toward the standard and 17 per cent quit during the first 40 days. After two and one-half months, the control group was reassembled and the second experimental procedure (total participation) was used. The group then rapidly achieved and exceeded the standard of production.

A systematic treatment of adaptation to planned change is to be found in Lippitt, Watson, and Westley's *The Dynamics of Planned Change* (1958). Many changes are not planned or are brought about by forces far removed from the group that must cope with the change. A good source of research information about group adaptation to changes of this type is *Man and Society in Disaster* edited by Baker and Chapman (1962).

FAILURE TO TAKE CARE OF ESSENTIAL SURVIVAL NEEDS

Failure to take care of essential survival needs occurs when an individual fails to eat the food available and makes no real effort to obtain other food. This kind of behavior was found in survival training when a trainee became dehydrated because he had failed to go to the trouble of melting snow or to take other action to obtain water. It also occurs when men fail to build shelters in freezing weather. When students do not listen to instructions, do not read assignments, or do not carry out the exercises necessary to master required skills, an analogous thing occurs in the classroom. In a basketball game, such failures include these: not trying for a basket, failing to pass the ball, or failing to do anything else necessary to score. Failures in a school faculty include these: failure to provide a schedule, to make assignments, to structure learning situations, to evaluate work, to keep the building warm, and the like.

Of the various streams of research that bear on the problems of meeting the requirements for existence, disaster research provides some of the most provocative and helpful findings. From this research there has emerged considerable consensus concerning the phases of adaptive behavior necessary for group survival in disasters. The conceptualization of these stages might serve as a helpful guide in assisting groups to cope with stressful conditions. The following conceptualization has been offered by Powell and Rayner (1952) and follows quite closely those offered by other investigators in this field:

1. WARNING. Mistakenly or not, some apprehension arises from conditions out of which danger may arise. A group should use this period to think of alternative courses of action should the possible danger eventuate, to develop the necessary skills for carrying out these courses of action, and to establish a group structure suitable for coping with the predictable stresses. If some unusual event is anticipated in a classroom such as a visit by a distinguished person, a change in schedule or classrooms, or a test, behavior is more likely to be constructive than if there had been no warning.

2. THREAT. People are exposed to communications from others, or to signs of an approaching danger, indicating specific, imminent danger. The group can now narrow the range of alternatives and prepare itself more specifically to cope with the stresses. If a class knows that they will be examined on books *A* and *B* rather than possible *A, B, C, D, E,* and *F,* their

behavior is more likely to be constructive. Also, if they know the test will be a test of creative applications or multiple-choice items, their behavior is more likely to be constructive than if they had to prepare for all possible types of examination. If a basketball team knows that it is going to have to compete with a team that has a seven-foot forward who usually scores 40 points per game, their behavior is more likely to be constructive than if they had no knowledge about the nature of their competition.

3. IMPACT.   The disaster strikes, with concomitant injury, destruction, and disruption of ongoing activities. The group now relies primarily upon overlearned, automatic procedures, established sets, and the like. This is one of the major reasons for practicing fire drills and other emergency procedures in schools. Any predictable emergency to which children are likely to be exposed should be prepared for by rehearsal, practice, and overlearning.

4. INVENTORY.   The people exposed to the severe stress of disaster begin to form a preliminary picture of what has happened and of their own condition. This restructuring process is necessary in rebounding from shock. It involves reorganizing both the group and the situation or task. The football coach whose team was routed, the band director whose charges disgraced him, and the teacher whose pupils failed an examination miserably are all faced with this problem. These are good times to take stock and try to figure out what went wrong and how they might respond more constructively in the future.

5. RESCUE.   Activity turns to immediate help for survivors, first aid for the wounded, freeing trapped victims, fighting fire, and the like. It involves a focus on immediate rather than long-range plans and the establishment of priorities to insure existence and constructive behavior. First aid must be administered before the group can give its attention to long-range goals or even usual goals. In the classroom, a teacher may have to do something about injured feelings, hostility among pupils, or paralyzing fear, before he can even begin to help the class work out a plan to remedy some learning difficulty or some behavior problem.

6. REMEDY.   More deliberate and formal activities are undertaken toward relieving the stricken situation. The group and its leader diagnose the difficulty, decide on some positive course of action, and proceed deliberately toward a solution. This should be done as quickly as possible but at times cannot be hurried. This is what is needed in the case of the badly beaten football team, the panicked band, and the failing students. Here is where regular problem-solving procedures are needed. Emphasis must be placed upon decision and positive action, however.

7. RECOVERY. For an extended period, the stricken group recovers its former stability or achieves a stable adaptation to the changed conditions that the disaster has brought about. In the classroom, pupils resume their learning and move in positive, creative directions toward goals.

Failure to follow through at any one of these stages may lead to the disintegration of the group and failure to achieve its goals.

RECKLESS OR PANIC-LIKE BEHAVIOR

Reckless, erratic, or panic-like behavior in a group may occur under pressure of continued failure, fatigue, unexpected demands, and the like. In survival situations, group members may take unwarranted chances, fail to pinpoint themselves on the map at crucial points, select routes without surveying the situation, and fight blindly rather than avoid dangers by strategy or adaptation. In the classroom, students or teachers show recklessness by trying to solve problems with inadequate information, without taking stock and finding out what they know and what they do not know at crucial points; they may embark upon projects or assignments without taking a look at what is to be done.

Whether in the classroom, in a work situation, or in a natural disaster, reckless and erratic group behavior seems to occur whenever contacts with reality are weakened or lost. This loss of contact with reality may occur because the group has inadequate information about the situation (undertakes a problem without investigating what is required) or distorts the information received. The healthy group looks for evidence in the environment and accepts this evidence even if it goes against the group's desires. The unhealthy group does not seek evidence, and it rejects evidence that does not please the group. Under some social conditions, persons appear to become less concerned with testing the evidence than with seeing what they want to see. Such phenomena have been demonstrated in a number of studies. For example, Pepitone (1950) conducted an experiment in which boys were quizzed by a three-man board in order to decide which boy was to receive a valued award. When all board members were equal in power, the boys perceived the one who was most approving of them as most powerful and the one who was least approving as least powerful. When all board members were equal in their approving behaviors, the boys perceived those who were most powerful as most approving and those who were least powerful as least approving.

In one study, Mellinger (1955) found that persons who had a strong liking for certain colleagues with whom they disagreed on an important issue were more reluctant to perceive any disagreement between themselves and others than were persons who disliked the others with whom they disagreed. Mellinger (1956) also studied interpersonal trust and communi-

166

cation. He drew 244 pairs from a population of 330 professional scientists engaged in a laboratory research and compared them on their attitudes about the long-range consequences of a new research program, their attitudes of trust toward each other, their reports as to whether they had discussed the new program, and their estimates of each other's attitudes about the issue. If a scientist did not trust another scientist, he tended to hide his own attitudes about an issue so that the accuracy of the other's perception was impaired.

In each of these experiments we see at work some of the forces that produce, in Sullivan's terms, parataxic interpersonal relations. Group members lost some degree of contact with reality, losing the bases for adapting their behavior in such a way as to cope optimally with the stresses of the situation.

LACK OF GROUP-ESTEEM

Lack of self-esteem occurs in extreme situations when men sink to animal-level concerns and begin to feel unworthy of living. In survival training, this category includes failures to observe the most rudimentary principles of camp and trail discipline, "living like a pig," extreme uncleanliness, and the like. There may also be a lack of self-esteem stemming from lack of confidence in ability to take care of one's self. Another analogous sign in training occurs when a man considers some survival skill too difficult to master and does not continue efforts to master it. He may also express unworthiness, and he may feel he has been rejected by the group. In the classroom, a new skill may seem too complex. Or the teacher may continually make the pupils look foolish or stupid. Such behaviors lead to anxieties that eventually become overwhelming and cause members of the group to cease trying to learn. Lack of group-esteem occurs when members feel that the group does not deserve to exist, that they would be better off without the group, and that they are no longer attracted to the group or influenced by it.

A variety of forces have been found to influence group-esteem. Apparently various sources of influence in the group can establish goals that individual members accept as valid bases for judging their performance and the stronger these goals are imposed the more likely are they to affect group-esteem. Stotland, Thorley, Thomas, Cohen, and Zander (1957) found that failure on a task that was highly relevant to the group's future achievement resulted in lower self-evaluation than failure on a task that was not relevant to the group's achievement. Zander, Thomas, and Natsoulas (1957) found that failure where superiors made demands perceived as legitimate stimulated lower self-evaluation than where the demands were seen as nonlegitimate. Rasmussen and Zander (1954) found that failure in a group that was highly attractive to the members generated lower self-

167

evaluation than where the group was less attractive. These and other findings concerning factors that affect group-esteem can serve as guides in preventing breakdowns resulting from lack of esteem.

DANGERS IN THESE SIGNS

All four types of signs just discussed warn us that the forces being generated by the duration and intensity of the stress are beginning to become greater than the group's adaptability. The settling-in of apathy or the arousal of extreme panic reflected in these signs makes the group unable to cope with new crises, demands, changes, or the like. Extreme panic is perhaps most likely to occur when the group loses its anchors in reality and is unable to re-establish them. This loss of anchor in reality may refer to a lack of structure of the task (knowing what must be done to survive), a lack of structure of the group (knowing who must do what with whom), or both. Although both intensity and duration of the stressful condition are involved in panic, intensity and suddenness are perhaps more important. Although apathy may occur from the shock of sudden or intense stress, it is perhaps most likely to occur from the fatigue that accompanies prolonged stress. In either case, the group loses its anchor in reality, becomes overwhelmed by tensions, and ceases adaptive efforts.

BREAKS IN GROUP LINKAGES

From the foregoing it seems apparent that the critical problem involved in preventing group breakdown is to help the group maintain its structure. The problem becomes one of identifying and strengthening the forces that hold groups together and give them structure.

As already set forth in the preceding chapter, four aspects of group structure are important: affect, power, communication, and goals. If any of these aspects of structure are weak, each of the others is likely to weaken. A group may continue to function, however, if certain aspects remain strong, even though others may be weak. For example, a group, in which affect is weak (members dislike one another), may function effectively if the power, communication, and goal linkages continue to be strong. There is a danger, however, that the weakening of the affect linkages may weaken the others.

A set of questions has been developed for detecting the signs in a group's behavior that may serve as a warning that breakdown is impending. Such a list of questions might be useful to a supervisor in going into a classroom, looking for possible signs that the group has broken down insofar as the accomplishment of its purpose is concerned. It might also be useful to a coach, athletic director, school principal or superintendent, supervisor of nursing, band director, or anyone else interested in promoting the effectiveness of groups. The questions have been devised to test the strength of the four types of linkages discussed above.

AFFECT LINKAGES

Negative answers to the following questions may be regarded as possible indicators that the affect linkages of the group are weakening and need strengthening, if the group is to survive or accomplish its purpose.

Do members of the group help each other without being asked? Research indicates that the members of effective groups give one another a great deal of support, voluntarily help one another, and influence one another. If members of the group have to be told to help one another or be made to help one another it is because the power linkages are strong. Even though strong power linkages may delay breakdown, having to exercise power to coerce members into helping one another will eventually create overwhelming tension itself.

The body of research on group cohesiveness gives rather strong support to the idea that liking for one another in a group is associated with voluntary action on the part of members in behalf of the group. Back (1951) has reported an experiment in which he induced varying degrees of cohesiveness by telling the members that they would or would not like one another, would receive a prize for the best group performance, and would serve as a model of a highly productive group. His subjects were 70 pairs of college students who had not known one another previously and were of the same sex. Each subject was instructed to write a preliminary story about a set of three pictures. The pairs were then brought together and asked to discuss the story. Each subject was then asked to write a final story. Although the subjects thought that the sets of pictures were identical, there were actually small differences that led to different interpretations. Among other findings, Back reports that in the high cohesive groups the members made more attempts to reach an agreement and made more serious efforts to enter the discussion.

Do members willingly teach each other when the group is learning new skills? In almost any group, some members master new skills more readily than do others. If members like one another, they spontaneously teach one another these skills. They thereby strengthen their own mastery of these skills and speed up mastery by other members of the group. A number of classroom experiments both at the elementary level (Durrell, 1961) and at the graduate level (Torrance, 1958b) have demonstrated that students working in groups learn more than do students working alone. It should be emphasized that failure of members of a group to teach each other when the group is learning new skills does not cause breakdown but rather is symptomatic of a condition that leads to breakdown.

The study at the graduate level (Torrance, 1958b) provides insights concerning groups that failed to survive as well as the nature of the increased learning in the groups that survived. The subjects of this study were 80 graduate students including experienced teachers and administrators, enrolled in a course in personality theory and mental hygiene. Students were given the option of working alone or in groups to develop and present some original idea relevant to the course. The 58 who chose to work together were assigned to three-person groups, but groups were permitted to dissolve or rearrange themselves to the extent possible. The 22 students who chose to work alone appeared to be either afraid to expose their ideas to others or did not want to be hampered by sluggish, mediocre, or critical peers. Some stated that they were unwilling to adapt to a group's way of working in favor of their own habitual manner of working. Twelve members who originally chose to work in a group withdrew from the group activity and several others shifted from their original group to another one.

The experiences of the groups that collapsed in comparison with those of the groups that persisted are especially enlightening. They indicate that many teachers, administrators, and other educational workers are ill prepared for working together creatively and productively. The data suggest that cooperation is in part a matter of skills, a matter of not knowing how to use productively and creatively the experiences and talents within a group. In part, the difficulty arose from the attitudes of the persons involved. Some did not grasp the potentialities of the group for meeting their needs or meeting the needs of other members of the group. Some abandoned the group as soon as they had gotten an idea, either through group processes or from other sources.

The most encouraging finding of this exploratory study is that those who persisted in groups compared with those who worked alone or withdrew from groups made greater gains in information as measured by pretests and posttests, were able to generate a larger number of original ideas concerning mental health problems at the end of the course, and tended to be judged superior in the extent of which they achieved personal and professional meaningfulness of the course content. It was also interesting that those who scored highest on the pretest tended to make greater gains than those who scored lowest, a rather unusual phenomenon in pre- and posttesting. Many alternative explanations can be offered for these observed differences, but participation in a creative group provides a logical explanation of the differences. Apparently some of the groups met almost daily over coffee, at lunch, and in other contexts. In such informal situations, there was apparently much discussion of the concepts presented in class and in the textbooks. These discussions probably helped to clarify and fix in the minds of the participants the technical information, to alert them to more possibilities in ideas and problems, and to grasp the personal and professional meaningfulness of the course content. In summary, it might be said that the groups that survived consisted of members who were willing to teach one another and that as a result the members tended to show greater growth in almost all of the types of achievement assessed.

If a member of the group is ill, in trouble, or does not know what to do, are the others concerned? If the members of a group like one another, they are concerned about the welfare of the others. Groups verging on breakdown are not likely to feel concerned about one another. In one such group, a member fell down a 100-foot snow bank. The other members of the group just laughed and continued plodding along.

A long list of human tragedies chronicles the importance of mutual concern and support as a factor in group survival. One must conclude that when everyone's life is in danger very little comradeship is evident, yet the chances of survival are vastly increased if affection among members of the group persists. The following excerpts of Stewart's (1936) account of the famous Donner Party tragedy illustrate the dangers of lack of mutual support and willingness to sacrifice for the group:

> The emigrants were no longer a "company"; there were only a number of family groups each for itself, some of them ready to cooperate only when manifest good was to be gained for themselves (Stewart, 1936, p. 66).
>
> . . . Now under the stress of circumstances almost too great to be borne, the cruel individualism of the westerner had gained the upper hand, at least with many of the emigrants. These, more and more, fought wolfishly for their own families alone. An old man had been allowed to die on the trail; babies with tongues thick from thirst had been refused water (Stewart, 1936, p. 80).

Following reports of many examples of this kind of behavior among United States servicemen in POW camps in Korea, there was a general probing of the educational and child-rearing practices that might produce this kind of group behavior under stress. Among the many suggestions, Meerloo advanced the following suggestion and criticism:

> Our current scholastic practice stimulates ambition in a few children, but stifles it in others. Instead of promoting cheating by our rigid examination rules, why do we not allow children to help one another in the solution of common problems? (Meerloo, 1956, p. 271).

Deutsch (1949ab) in studies published several years earlier similarly suggested that educators might well re-examine the assumptions underlying their common usage of competitive grading systems. He found that greater group productivity results when the members or subunits are cooperative rather than competitive in their interrelationships. The intercommunication of ideas, the coordination of efforts, the friendliness and pride in one's group appear to be disrupted when group members see themselves as competing for mutually exclusive goals. Competitive conditions also produce greater expectations of hostility from others than do the cooperative conditions.

Is the joking in the group good-natured rather than vicious? People who like one another feel free to joke with or "kid" one another. This joking, however, is good-natured. Where there is little liking or disliking, there is a tendency for little joking to take place. If the predominant affect is one of disliking, the joking is likely to be vicious, disparaging, and biting. The nature of the joking among the children in a classroom, among members of a team, or among the members of a school staff may reveal much about the strength of the affect linkages of the group. Although this sign may be useful in detecting difficulty in groups of all ages, the problem is especially acute during what Sullivan calls the Juvenile Era. It is during this stage that children begin learning how to function as groups and it is also at this stage that they have such difficulties as ostracism, stereotyping, and disparagement. A classroom group beset by an excessive number of these difficulties may make learning and teaching extremely difficult and personality disturbances rampant.

Although many observers of group behavior in stressful situations have noted the nature of the joking or wit and its relevance to the health of the group, little empirical research on the issue is available. Flugel (1954), summarizing the accumulated knowledge concerning humor and laughter, concluded that there is general consensus that humor performs a useful social function. A number of investigators maintain that humor in a group serves as "a social corrective by preserving mental stability and social unity in the face of the incongruous, the unexpected, and the socially disruptive" (Flugel, 1954, p. 731).

Do group members get over disagreements easily? If the members of a group like one another, they feel free to disagree. Groups that have a great deal of tolerance for disagreement function more effectively than groups in which there is little or no disagreement. In a classroom, the children should feel free to disagree with one another and with the teacher. If all of the teaching is by authority, the latter is not likely to occur.

In a study of aircrew effectiveness in combat over Korea (Torrance, 1957a), it was found that the more effective crews, in comparison with the less effective crews and crews that broke up, were characterized by greater tolerance of disagreement. This and other studies (Torrance, 1958a) support the contention that the more effective groups are characterized by greater participation, initially wider divergence of expressed judgment, and greater acceptance of decisions. If the affect linkages of the group are weak, however, there is likely to be a lingering aftereffect of disagreement and a consequent deleterious effect on the thinking and decision making of the group.

Are the members able to disagree without losing their tempers and becoming emotional? If the members of a group dislike one another, disagreement is threatening and may be viewed as frustrating. Thus, there is likely to be loss of tempers and display of emotion rather than reasoning and judgment. If members like one another, disagreement is not so threatening and as a result there is less need for such behavior.

Loss of tempers and other emotional behavior in response to disagreement is part of the general problem of tolerance of disagreement and may be encountered in any group where disagreement is encouraged and/or permitted. In general, people do not like to have others disagree with them and are likely to see all disagreement as evidence of personal rejection. Thus, there is a need to differentiate person-centered disagreement and task-centered disagreement and to transform the former into the latter whenever possible.

Are all members included in activities? Do all members share in the peculiar language and jokes of the group? Any group that lives and works together for any considerable length of time develops expressions and jokes that communicate a great deal to members but mean little to outsiders. If the affect linkages of the group are strong everyone will be "in on" these expressions and jokes. If not, some members will not understand because they have been excluded from some of the group's activities. In a classroom, those children who are left out of such activities are likely to feel lonely and rejected and as a result be under stress and fail to learn effectively. Having such individuals in a group that must meet emergencies impairs group effectiveness.

The entire field of sociometric research documents the fact that groups containing severe isolates or rejectees are unhealthy (Moreno, 1934, 1956). It is quite likely that severe isolation or rejection impairs an individual's mental functioning, especially as it relates to group performance, since it represents an important step in the direction of loss of contact with reality. Among the many studies that document this conclusion is one by Northway and Rooks (1955) on creativity and sociometric status among nursery school children. The subjects were 30 children in nursery school and kindergarten. Each was given a standard sociometric test and the McCallum form board test of creativity. There was no statistically significant relationship between creativity and intelligence, age, or mental age. All cases very low sociometrically fell in the noncreative category of the McCallum test and all cases very high sociometrically fell in the creative category. Although there was some overlap in the sociometric scores of the creative and noncreative categories, the differences in means were statistically significant (8.39 versus 3.75, significant at the .05 level of confidence).

Do all members want to remain in the group? If an individual feels that he is not liked by the other members of the group, or if he does not like the other members of the group, he is uncomfortable. A natural reaction to discomfort is to try to escape, to get out of the group. Requests for transfers in military organizations, changes in employers, resignations in a school staff, and withdrawals from school are frequently signs of weak affect linkages. Other considerations, such as increased opportunities or salary elsewhere, may also be operating. Often, however, individuals turn down job offers far superior in salary and status to what they have because they like the people with whom they work.

Some of the research on factors related to absenteeism and turnover in group membership provide some of the scientific basis concerning this sign of poor group health. In studies by Mann and Baumgartel (1953) and Mann and Sparling (1956) of blue-collar men, it was found that low absence rates tended to be associated more with work-group characteristics, such as feelings of acceptance by the group, team spirit, and favorable evaluations of the group's performances, than with factors related to supervision, the company as a whole, opportunities for advancement, and the like. A number of studies (Libo, 1953) indicate that turnover is related to the attractiveness of the group and the liking of members for one another.

Do few accidents occur in the group? When people do not like the members of their group they are likely to be careless about following safety rules. Field studies in a variety of industrial situations have suggested this explanation for many accidents rather than the traditional explanation of accident proneness, a personality characteristic which has all but defied identification through psychometric devices. It is also likely that an unusually high incidence of accidents on the playground, in the classroom, and on the athletic field is associated with a low degree of affection among the members of the group for one another.

Himler (1951) says that it is generally agreed among safety engineers that over 80 per cent of industrial accidents are caused by personal reactions; he recommends that efforts be made to achieve a better understanding of the degree of satisfaction of basic human needs. One of the most detailed studies of situational factors affecting accidents was reported by Patterson and Willett (1951). In studying accidents in Scottish coal mines, they found that long-term fluctuations in accident rates from mine to mine showed substantial correlation (.58). Their evidence suggests that this relationship could not have been caused by mechanical conditions since there was essential similarity in official safety practices, equipment, mechanization, and the like. In an experiment following this observation, they acted upon the hypothesis that the chief long-term causal factor in a growing rate of accidents was a growing lack of cohesion in the community accentuated by long-wall face techniques in working the mines. Patterson and Willett (1951) introduced a series of community steps aimed at increasing the cohesion of the working group in a particular section of the colliery. Off the job, smokers, concerts, group trips to Glasgow and Edinburgh for football matches, and various informal parties were fostered. On the job, there was emphasis upon the interdependence of the members and the institution of a system of painting sections yellow, indicating, "I have left this section safe for the man who follows me here." In another mine, the system of painting was instituted without the devices used to develop liking for one another or group cohesiveness. In the experimental mine, there was a decrease in accidents during the first year amounting to 54 per cent of the number predicted from the past curve and the correlation among mines. There was no decrease in the mine that served as a control. While it is impossible to control many of the variables in a field study of this type, this study certainly suggests the possible usefulness of a high incidence of accidents as an indicator of weak linkages and an unhealthy group.

Do members have pride in the group? If the members of a group like one another, they tend to be proud of the accomplishments of the group. In an effective group, the members find the group attractive to them and are willing to make sacrifices for its welfare.

Here again studies of group cohesiveness document the importance of pride in the group as an indicator of strong affect linkages. Out of this research, the following are some of the factors associated with an individual's feeling of pride in his group:

1. The member is evaluated positively by others in the group (Jackson, 1953).
2. Other members are helpful rather than hindering or depriving persons (Deutsch, 1949ab).
3. Other members are seen as having interests like his own (Libo, 1953).

POWER LINKAGES

Negative answers to the questions that follow may be interpreted as possible indicators that breakdowns are occurring in the power linkages of a group. If a large number of negative answers appear, an examination should be made of the various bases of power or ability to influence (French and Raven, 1959): reward power (perception that the influencer has the ability to reward), coercive power (perception that the influencer has the ability to punish or coerce), legitimate power (perception that the attempt to influence is right and just), referent power (perception of identification with the influencer), and expert power (the perception that the influencer has some special knowledge or expertness).

Does someone take responsibility for organizing the activities of the group? Every member must know what must be done and with whom he is to do what. The official leader usually assumes responsibility for structure.

175

He may, of course, designate some individual or subgroup to do assigned tasks. The necessity for structuring is a major reason why groups without an official leader frequently break down. Everyone is reluctant to offer structure because each person lacks too many of the bases for power listed above (usually reward, coercive, and legitimate bases). If anyone does give structure, he tends to become the leader. In the classroom, it is the teacher's responsibility to organize activities or see that someone else does.

The conclusion that lack of structure in a group results in unpleasant or stressful consequences has been well documented through small-group research. In one study, Cohen, Stotland, and Wolfe (1955) tested the hypothesis that an unstructured situation is more frustrating than a structured one. These investigators assumed that people have a need for cognition that corresponds to their tendency to organize their experiences meaningfully. In this study, an ambiguous story presented to subjects generated more frustration than a structured one, as measured by the subjects' ratings of the story. People with a high need for cognition, however, experienced more discomfort from the lack of structure than did those with a low need for cognition.

A number of very subtle factors have been shown to interfere with the process of organizing the activities of a group. Ziller's (1957b) study of group size provides an excellent example of one such factor. He placed individuals and groups of from two through six members in a variety of decision-making situations. Increased size up to four resulted in improved problem-solving performance. Groups of four and five did not show this linear tendency, although groups of six performed in line with this linear trend. It was observed that dyads and triads made effective use of their manpower resources without organization. Groups of four and five tended not to organize their resources and apparently suffered as a result. Groups of six, however, tended to recognize immediately the need for organizing their activities, took steps to organize, and apparently profited as a result.

In a large group, is authority distributed among members rather than retained by the leader? Many leaders, including teachers and principals, are reluctant to relinquish any of their power to others. As a result, they permit themselves to become overwhelmed with details. If remedial action is not taken, the group eventually breaks down because essential functions cannot be performed. Failure to distribute power within a group is likely to be accompanied by a low level of structure, which is especially damaging to group functioning under stressful conditions.

Small-group experimentation suggests that breakdown results within the group when power is not distributed. Expert knowledge and original ideas do not receive consideration. In one experiment (Torrance, 1954c), it was shown that consideration of ideas is inhibited by differences in status or power among group members. In three-man groups with a clear hierarchical

176

structure, it was found that the man of lowest status was just as likely to produce the correct solution as the man with the highest status. The solution of the man with the highest status, however, was frequently the only one considered, resulting in the group's acceptance of an inferior or incorrect solution. Furthermore, this failure to consider the ideas of low-status members was more prevalent in more or less permanent groups (men who had been working together as a group and presumably would continue working together) than in temporary groups.

Is control maintained easily? In any group things may get out of control occasionally, but in healthy groups control can easily be regained. A group whose leader feels that he must hold tight reins of control often breaks down most easily. The author has studied the characteristics of fourth grade classes and the kinds of controls which their teachers exercise. Thus far, he has found two fourth grade classes that have shown continued creative growth as measured by creative thinking tests. In both of these classes, things occasionally got out of hand. Everyone is full of ideas, alert, curious, and active. In both classes, however, control was easily restored by the teacher and in some cases by a student officer. In one of these, a class of over 40 pupils, the teacher had one word which would restore perfect quiet and stillness. This word was "Freeze!" This made it a kind of game. No matter what a pupil was doing he stopped immediately, assuming the position he was in at the time. The teacher could then communicate instructions and orderly learning activities could be resumed.

Many of the definitions of power offered by social psychologists make use of the concept of control (Cartwright, 1959). Apparently both overcontrol and lack of control are detrimental to the mental health of individual members and to the healthy functioning of the group. In a sense, both result in a loss of structure or contact with reality. If there is lack of control, there is confusion and no one knows who is doing what or who has done what. If there is excessive control, there is a loss of structure insofar as members are concerned, because only the leader is responsible for maintaining the structure. Since their ideas no longer count, group members tend to stop observing, producing ideas, and making evaluations.

Can the group make decisions without undue delay? Some groups fail to survive or to accomplish their goals because they are unable to make decisions or can do so only with great delay. Careful consideration should be given to important decisions, and disagreement should be tolerated. Skills of social accommodation and compromise may be needed, however. A considerable body of knowledge on group decision making is now available to guide groups in improving their decision-making skills.

The problem most pertinent to the making of decisions without undue delay is that of determining how to resolve disagreements. The tolerance of disagreement and the ability to make decisions based on a diversity of alternatives are related to effective group decision making. Schutz (1958) sees the difficulty as one of disagreement on how the decision-making process should proceed. He cites the story of Van Gogh and Gauguin and their furious relationship as an example of an incompatibility resulting from differences in basic orientations. Van Gogh was known as a man of high sensibilities and great needs for giving and receiving love. Gauguin was a prime example of "controlled emotion, who carefully avoided a strong relationship with one woman by enjoying a rapid turnover." When Van Gogh and Gauguin lived together, their inability to work together and reach agreements became well known and their relationship had a near-homicidal outcome. Schutz (1958, p. 117) maintains that there will be difficulties in making decisions in groups where some members like highly structured groups and others prefer a relative lack of structure, where some prefer to work in teams (oversocial) and others prefer working alone.

Do group members carry out decisions, requests, and commands willingly? The teacher, coach, principal, or other leader who has to coerce individuals into carrying out decisions, requests, and commands should examine his exercise of power. Something has gone wrong. It may be that disagreement was not permitted or not encouraged and the leader thought that everyone was going along with the decision. As a matter of fact, there is a tendency for groups in which there is disagreement in the decision-making process to hold more firmly to the decisions of the group than in groups where there is no disagreement. A member of the group may not understand what the decision of the group actually is. Groups may be reluctant to carry out requests and commands, if they have not been given reasons for them, or if the ideas and solutions of members have not been considered.

Research indicates that in most groups there is a tendency for power differences to prevent consideration of the ideas of low-status members (Torrance, 1954c). There is also a tendency to consider only the ideas initially supported by the majority. Frequently minority ideas are superior to majority ideas and will be adopted unanimously, if considered. For example, Maier and Solem (1952) have shown experimentally that the quality of group thinking is improved when the leader sees that consideration is given to minority ideas. In this experiment, five-and six-man groups were given the well-known horse-trading problem: A man buys a horse for 60 dollars and sells it for 70 dollars. He buys the horse back for 80 dollars and resells it for 90 dollars. How did he come out in the trade? In some groups a person was chosen by the group members to play a leader role and in other groups a person was selected to be an observer. In neither condition did the elected person give his own opinions about the solution of the problem. The subjects recorded their answers to the problem privately both before and after the discussions. In both conditions, the discussion increased the number of correct answers, but the groups with leaders showed the most improvement. Improvement was most likely to occur when the leader saw that consideration was given to the solution of minority members.

Does the leader back up those to whom he delegates authority? The leader who is jealous of his authority and delegates it with reluctance is usually quite gleeful to find fault with the performance of the person to whom he delegates authority. Such behavior, however, is a sure way to group breakdown. Such a leader finds it extremely difficult to maintain the loyalty of any of the members of the group and his own power is weakened thereby. A leader may be displeased with the performance of the individual to whom he designates authority. He must still back this person up, however. In some cases, he may have to enforce an unwise decision made by the subordinate and tell him of his error in private. In other cases, amends may have to be made to the group and an error admitted, but in such cases, the leader must share responsibility for the error in judgment.

COMMUNICATION LINKAGES

Quite obviously a group cannot hold together when communication among members is not adequate. Negative answers to the following questions are signs that something has gone awry in these linkages.

Does the leader keep the group well briefed? Does he pass on information from interdependent groups, superiors, and the like? Although it is possible to overcommunicate—that is, give group members more information than they can use—the fault usually lies in the opposite direction. All members of a group must have enough information to do what is expected of them. In conducting research in elementary schools, the author has noted big differences from class to class and from school to school in the extent to which information about the coming of the research team has been communicated to pupils. In some classes, the visit of the research team appears on the blackboard in the plan for the day. In others, the pupils had expected that they would be engaging in their usual activities. In some cases, the effects on performance is clearly apparent. Usually, classes that have been informed appear to be "warmed up" for the activity and enter into it with vigor and enthusiasm. In other classes enthusiasm can be elicited if the experimenter finds out in advance that this "warmup" has not taken place or if the activity is regarded as more pleasant than the usual activity. In some classes, however, a quiet hostility seems to exist throughout the group and little creative thinking is elicited.

Do all members, from top to bottom, keep others informed as to what they are doing? Any enterprise can become miserably fouled up and flounder hopelessly if any member fails to inform others of his plans and activities. For example, in a school, the janitor and the engineer need to understand the aims and philosophy of the school. They need to know about deviations from the regular schedule, special activities, and the like. Otherwise, they are not equipped to meet the demands and may become overwhelmed and unable to perform their functions. Similarly, the principal, teachers, and frequently the pupils need to know about any unusual activities of the janitor or engineer. Such activities might require a change in the plans of the teachers and pupils.

There is considerable research evidence (Hare, 1962, pp. 276–85) concerning the role of group health and communication among members. Almost always, group members with one-way or limited communication experience frustration, antagonism, hostility, and decreased effectiveness. Each member is subjected to a decrease or loss of his contacts with the environment or loss of anchor in reality. An example of such a study is one by Leavitt and Mueller (1951). These investigators created an experimental situation in which there was one-way communication and the receiver of the information was given no opportunity to feed back acknowledgments, questions, or negative reactions to the sender. Accuracy and confidence were reduced for both sender and receiver (indicating a reduction in the contacts with reality). Initially, there was a feeling of hostility on the part of the receiver toward the sender but this disappeared.

Do the members of the group influence one another a great deal? Overemphasis on conformity and blocks to independent thinking decrease the effectiveness of most groups. Group members must be open to influence from one another, however. Research has demonstrated rather consistently that, in an effective group, members characteristically do a great deal of influencing of one another (Festinger, 1954; Back, 1951). In such a group, an independent or divergent thinker has a better chance of influencing the group than in other types of groups.

Do members consider one another's opinions? Are disagreements permitted? Unless the opinions of all members are considered, and unless disagreements are permitted, full communication within a group is not possible. Ultimately, such deficiencies can bring about breakdown.

GOAL LINKAGES

It is well known that having a common goal may hold a group together under stress. When individual members lose their goal orientation, the operation of the group's goal orientation and the common danger may save them. In some cases, however, it is the individual's goal orientation that must revive the group's goal orientation. The following questions may be used in assessing the strength of a group's goal orientation.

Do the members of the group know what they are trying to do and how they can achieve their goals? Unless group members have a goal and some ideas about the paths that lead to the goal, they are likely to have little contact with reality and be extremely anxious and uncomfortable. This view is strongly supported by theory and research in social psychology. It has been demonstrated in an experiment by A. R. Cohen (1953, 1959) involving telephone operators who were being evaluated by a supervisor. The goal of each operator was to obtain a good evaluation, but the paths toward the goal were not always clear. By varying the degree of structure (consistency and ambiguity), Cohen found that those subjects whose cues were inconsistent and solutions ambiguous experienced greater difficulty adjusting to the situation than did those subjects who had a clear path toward the goal. Subjects who experienced the ambiguous situation were less secure, had lower self-evaluations, were less motivated, and worked less efficiently.

Continuing Cohen's line of investigation, Raven and Rietsema (1957) varied the clarity of the goals and paths to the goals in an experiment involving undergraduate college students. One group of subjects was instructed to cut into geometric figures materials for a group in another room constructing objects from the materials. Through the use of tape recordings by which instructions were given the subjects during the experiment, the experimenters were able to produce one condition in which the group goal and path were clearly perceived by the subjects and another in which the subjects were unaware of what the group in another room was building or of the procedure being followed. The experiment yielded data that support the hypothesis of the investigators that unclarity of group goal and path have negative effects on the member's relationship with his group, as well as on his own basic individual adjustment or mental health.

Do the members of the group accept learning assignments and exercises? Do they see the reasons for this kind of learning, thinking, or practice? One test of goal orientation is the willingness of individuals to work hard to achieve their goals. If there is griping concerning the necessity for study, drill, practice, or rehearsal, it is likely that the strength of the group's goal orientation is not very great. If the pupils in a class reject learning assignments or fail to carry out exercises, it is a sign that goal linkages have broken down and that the situation has become dangerous. These questions may be applied to athletic teams, school staffs, and many other types of groups. Thus, an important role of the teacher, principal, coach, or counselor is one of clarifying goals and paths to those goals.

Do group members focus their energies on getting the job done, rather than dissipating their energies in interpersonal squabbles, griping, pursuit of personal pleasures, or the like? Almost inevitably the needs of the group collide with the needs of the individual. Such conflict may result in frustration, failure, and short-time perspective (Argyris, 1961). In groups that survive, members work out adaptations or integrate these two sets of needs over a period of time. If too much energy is dissipated in satisfying individual needs to the exclusion of group needs, the enterprise will fail.

Much of the theoretical work and research of Argyris (1957, 1961) has been concerned with the lack of congruency between the needs of healthy individuals and the demands of the formal organization. On the basis of a series of depth studies of organizations and the personalities who compose them, he maintains that employees are often placed in work situations where "they are provided minimal control over their workaday world; they are expected to be passive, dependent, and subordinate; they are expected to have a short-time perspective; they are induced to perfect and value the frequent use of a few skin-surface shallow abilities; and they are expected to produce under conditions leading to psychological failure" (Argyris, 1961, p. 331). As the frustration and failure increase in degree or are prolonged, the functioning of both the organization and the individual is impaired. Subordinates experience competition and intersubordinate hostility; they focus on the parts of the organization or the goal rather than on the wholes. Employees react to these stressors by such devices as leaving the organization; climbing the organizational ladder; defense reactions (day dreaming, aggression, ambivalence, regression); becoming apathetic and disinterested toward the organization, its makeup, and its goals; creating informal groups to sanction defense reactions, apathy, and lack of self-involvement; evolving group norms to perpetuate such behavior; and acculturating the youth to accept these norms.

Are group members really trying to accomplish something rather than being concerned only about meeting requirements? In school situations, pupils frequently become obsessed by meeting requirements and appear to forget the real goals of education. Unfortunately, meeting requirements seems to become more important the further up the educational ladder the student goes. Some graduate schools attempt to obviate this difficulty by establishing no set number of hours for the granting of degrees. Though deviations may occur, a set of expectation in terms of required courses, credits, and the like develops and the concern returns to meeting requirements. Recently one student who had withdrawn from a course which the author was teaching explained, "I decided to drop the course you teach, because I found that I had already read the textbook used in another course and thought that that course would be easier."

The consequences of clarity of goals on creative productivity is illustrated by an account of one industrial research organization with a staff of highly qualified men and an extremely poor record of patents and inventions. In frustration and disgust, the director reprimanded the group for its lack of patents and inventions. The general reaction was: "Why didn't you tell us this was what you wanted?" Shortly thereafter there was a heavy stream of patents and inventions coming from this group.

Do group members avoid short-cuts that would get them out of work or training? The search for short-cuts is essentially the same problem as the emphasis on meeting requirements. The group member who wants to get out of training *is* interested in meeting requirements rather than in making use of the training to achieve group goals.

Are members on time for scheduled activities? Tardiness and absenteeism may reflect unconscious rejection of the group goals. Being late for scheduled activities hurts group performance and reduces the value of the activity for all members. Although tardiness may seldom result in group breakdown, it may be regarded as a sign that goal linkages need strengthening.

Do group members play the game rather than complain that certain activities are unnecessary? If the goal is regarded as important, group members will be willing to "play the game with all they've got" and give it a chance to succeed. If group members hold back and wait for other members to prove that the enterprise will succeed, quite likely it will fail, and the group will break down.

Theory and research related to the concept of identification with the group and its goals help us to understand the mental health problems created by a lack of goal clarity. Festinger (1950) has pointed out that in an unclear situation, a person seeks some kind of "social reality" and may adopt the cognitive structure (knowledge) of the individual or group with which he identifies. In this case, a lack of goal structure in his group may result in such psychological discomfort that he will identify himself with some individual or group outside his own group. The lack of goal clarity in his own group is so threatening that he may even sabotage the efforts of his own group in favor of the goals of another group whose clarity of goals gives him structure and some degree of security.

APPLYING CONCEPTS

How can information about signs of impending group breakdown be used to prevent breakdown and improve performance? Although awareness of the signs may be insufficient, developing an awareness of the danger signals is frequently a necessary first step. Various kinds of feedback can be used. In some cases, a group can provide its own feedback. In others, a supervisor or an outside "expert" may provide such feedback. Research (Torrance, 1953) concerning the effectiveness of various kinds of feedback indicates that it does not matter a great deal whether the feedback is given by an outside expert, the leader of the group, or the group as a whole. The important thing is that the feedback be structured adequately so that the group's attention is focused on the important problems. It is for this reason that feedback based on a study of the questions given in the foregoing section may be useful.

The reader might find it useful to observe some group, using the list of questions given in this chapter as a guide. Or he might form some *ad hoc* groups and ask them to do some difficult and stressful task. He could then observe their performance and see how many of the signs of group breakdown he can spot. If these groups are then provided with feedback concerning their performance, they can later see how much their performance is improved thereby.

SUMMARY

Behavior analogous to "loss of will-to-survive" was taken as a model for examining the processes of group breakdown and outlining programs for avoiding such breakdowns. Failure to take adaptive action, failure to take care of essential requirements for existence, reckless or panic-like behavior, and lack of group-esteem were identified as crucial in group breakdown. Small-group research from a variety of sources was examined to gain a deeper understanding of how these four kinds of behavior contribute to group breakdown and impair a group's capacity to cope constructively with change and stress. The occurrence of these four signs warns a group that the forces being generated by the duration and intensity of the stress are becoming greater than the group's adaptability.

It was also shown how the conceptualization of different kinds of group linkages (affect, power, communication, and goal) can be used in diagnosing problems in group functioning and possibly in averting breakdown or improving performance. A set of questions was proposed by the author for making this kind of analysis. Suggestions were also made for applying this list of questions in practical operations involving groups under stress.

Mental Resources and Response to Stress

4

Introduction:
Man's Mental
Operations

11

The study of mental operations is the final stage of the conceptualization of the processes of personality development and mental hygiene. As this conceptualization began to unfold in Chapter 2, an effort was made to show how any one of the many stresses typically encountered by an individual may lead to any one of the kinds and degrees of breakdown common in our society. Emphasis was given to the fact that the degree and nature of the breakdown depends upon three kinds of interacting variables: the duration and intensity of the stress and the state of the organism (personality resources).

An attempt has been made to establish some general principles for guiding and predicting behavior and to show how each of the three variables influences behavior. In terms of intensity, it seems that moderate stress tends to improve performance but that severe stress results in disorganization, inefficiency, and even breakdown. In terms of duration of stress, the first onset of a new pressure or an increase in pressure brings shock and at least temporary inefficiency, which is generally followed by a leveling off. If stress is unabated, fatigue sets in and ultimately there is breakdown. Prolonged moderate stress, in fact, may be even more damaging than brief intense stress. Thus, there is an interacting effect of the intensity and duration of the stress.

The effects of both the intensity and the duration of the stress are modified by the state of the organism (the resources of the personality). If the personality resources are weak, there may be collapse after even very mild and brief stress. On the other hand, the individual with strong personality resources may rise to increasing heights in performance with both increasing intensity and duration, at least up to a point. Ultimately, however, even the strongest personality will collapse. From this comes the expression, "Every man has his breaking point."

Many factors affect the state of the organism and its capacity for coping with stress. Physical health, the keenness of the sensory organs, mental abilities, personality integration, ego strength, spiritual resources, and the like all have their roles. Previous experience in coping with stress, education and training, and specialized knowledge play their parts. One way of looking at the manner in which these individual characteristics operate to mediate the effects of stressful conditions is through the strategies employed in coping with them. In Chapter 12 an examination is made of some of the typical strategies used in coping with stress. In the chapters that follow, information is presented concerning man's mental operations, the role each plays in formulating and executing these strategies, and how these mental abilities can be developed and freed to function in efforts to cope successfully with life's stresses.

The approach to mental health presented in this book has been made possible by advances in knowledge concerning the nature of man's mental functioning. These advances have come about through a long series of stages and have resulted in an expansion of man's ideas concerning the nature of his mental functioning. For years, psychologists and educators have tried to represent the sum total of man's mental abilities through a single index or number that has come to be called the IQ (intelligence quotient) or MA (mental age). This concept has limited the thinking concerning some of the most vital problems of mental health and has slowed progress in bringing about a more humane education through which all individuals will have a better chance to realize their potentialities.

Many individuals have contributed to these advances. Binet (1909) clearly recognized that there were many important mental abilities not assessed by his measures and that all mental functions are susceptible of development. Binet spoke out quite strongly against the prevailing prejudice of his day against the "educability of intelligence." He remarked that the familiar proverb "When one is stupid, it is for a long time" seems to be taken literally by teachers. He maintained that intelligence is not a single function, individual and of a particular essence, but that it consists of the union of all the little functions of discrimination, observation, retention, imagination, ingenuity, etc., which are plastic and extensible. In experiments with the mentally retarded, Binet described a system of what he called "mental orthopedics," which ranged from the "game of statues" (an exercise in immobility) to exercises in perception, observation, imagination, ingenuity, analysis, and judgment. Binet stressed the fact that his mental orthopedics favored no particular mental ability but an ensemble. He argued that they facilitated discipline; taught the children to regard the blackboard better, to listen better, to remember better, to judge better; brought into play self-respect, emulation, perseverance, desire for success, and all the excellent sensations which accompany active involvement.

Furthermore, Binet severely reproached the predominant methods of education of his day, which brought into play only the memory abilities and reduced the learner to a condition of passivity. On the basis of his observations, he concluded that pupils were rarely called upon to judge anything, reflect upon anything, nor produce anything. They only needed to retain and to reproduce. The ideal pupil recited without making a mistake, and the goal of the teacher was to make the pupil's memory function, to see that he knew what was in the textbook, and to see that he could repeat it cleverly at the examination. Binet pointed out that the result of these deplorable practices for the pupil was a lack of curiosity, a tendency to seek truth solely in the book, an indifference to his environment, a naïve belief in the omnipotence of formulas, lack of adaptation to contemporary life, and a routine mind that is "sadly out of place in an epoch when society evolves with infernal speed." Among the goals in developing the child's mind, Binet included these abilities: to produce and to test ideas on his own, to act spontaneously, to judge for himself, to participate in the life about him, to explain what he sees, to defend his own ideas, to practice making decisions, to learn how to orient himself, to plan his days, to imagine, to invent, to live on his own account, and to feel at once the excellence and the responsibility of free action.

It is unfortunate that Binet's expanded concept of the human mind and its functioning was lost sight of for so long and that such a severely restricted concept of intelligence became associated with the tests he developed. The way for some of the recent advances, however, was kept open by such investigators as Thorndike (1927), Hargreaves (1927), Thurstone (1938), and others. Finally, J. P. Guilford's (1959ab) conceptualization of the structure of the intellect has given us a way of thinking about mental functioning that should pave the way for new advances in mental health, especially in education. Since this conceptualization will be used throughout the remainder of this book, some of its major aspects will be sketched.

By applying common categories of contents, operations, and products throughout the range of intellectual abilities, Guilford has represented the structure of intellect in the form of the three-dimensional diagram shown in Figure 11–1.

Under the dimension of *contents* (or materials), Guilford has included *figural, symbolic, semantic,* and *behavioral* categories. The *figural* category includes visual, auditory, tactual, and kinesthetic materials and thus may be regarded as constituting a general category of *concrete intelligence.* *Symbolic* contents include numbers, syllables, words (word structures, not meanings), and all kinds of code material. Guilford thinks that aptitudes for mathematics and for languages rest heavily upon these abilities. The *semantic* (or conceptual) category consists of meanings in verbalized form. The most commonly used tests of intelligence have been composed primarily of

189

this kind of material. Such tests have frequently been referred to as tests of *verbal intelligence.* Some workers group the semantic and symbolic categories into a common category which they call *abstract intelligence.* The *behavioral* category includes much of what Thorndike (1927) proposed under the category of *social intelligence.*

The kind of mental operations that are performed upon the contents makes up the second dimension of Guilford's structure. Five general kinds of operations have been identified: cognition, memory, convergent produc-

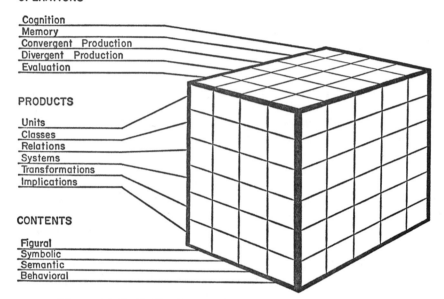

OPERATIONS

Cognition
Memory
Convergent Production
Divergent Production
Evaluation

PRODUCTS

Units
Classes
Relations
Systems
Transformations
Implications

CONTENTS

Figural
Symbolic
Semantic
Behavioral

Figure 11–1. Guilford's Model of the Structure of Intellect (*Used by permission from J. P. Guilford and R. Hoepfner,* Current Summary of Structure-of-Intellect Factors and Suggested Tests. *Los Angeles: University of Southern California, December 1963.*)

tion, divergent production, and evaluation. The first category pertains to the achievement of *cognitions* (awarenesses, perceptions, etc.) and the second involves *remembering* what has been cognized. The two kinds of *productive thinking* have to do with the production of new information from what has been cognized or memorized. *Convergent production* leads to a restricted answer or solution, while *divergent production* leads to several different or possible answers or solutions. The *evaluative* operation consists of determining the correctness, suitability, or adequacy of what has been cognized, remembered, or produced.

190

When certain mental operations are applied to certain contents or materials, various kinds of products result. These products include units, classes, relations, systems, transformations, and implications. *Units* may include figures, symbolic structures, or concepts. *Classes* are aggregates of items of information grouped because of the common properties. *Relations* are recognized connections between units of information. *Systems* are organized or structured aggregates of items of information or complexes of interrelated or interacting parts. *Transformations* are changes in existing information or in its use, as in production. *Implications* are extrapolations of information in the form of expectancies, predictions, antecedents, and consequents.

Beginning with Chapter 13 and continuing through Chapter 22 the materials of this book will be organized on the basis of this conceptualization of the structure of intellect. The focus will be on the mental operations, since it is the author's thesis that if an individual's mental abilities or operations are functioning, he will be able to cope constructively with stress.

Strategies of
Coping with Stress

12

Within his available resources each child invents a unique set of strategies for coping with the demands of life. Most of these strategies are primitive, apparently universal, and overlearned. The adequacy of these childhood strategies receives a severe test when the child enters school for the first time. What is the nature of these strategies and of the testing they receive on the first day of school? What happens if a child's strategies are inadequate to cope with the stress and strain of this new experience? How does the school help such a child learn to cope more effectively with his problems?

Most schools have developed over time a set of practices that have been found to be effective in socializing the child and implementing the adaptation that takes place when the child enters school for the first time. Entering school is one of the big discontinuities in the child's life and thus becomes tremendously important in personality development and mental health. The author has been a strong advocate of the kinds of educational reform that will reduce this and other discontinuities that seem to affect adversely mental functioning and personality development. It has been commonly noted that all, or almost all, children before entering school have achieved considerable experience and skill in such things as exploring, inventing, manipulating objects, questioning, singing, drawing, storytelling, changing things, using them to construct other things, and the like. It is reasonable to expect that mental development would be more continuous and school learning would proceed more smoothly, if we permitted children to continue using these methods in acquiring knowledge instead of insisting that they begin learning in more unnatural and authoritarian ways.

In his 1909 book, Alfred Binet made an almost identical suggestion concerning the education of children. He believed that education and instruction should be grafted on such natural activities as the manipulation of objects, moving them about, changing them, using them to construct other things, drawing, storytelling, and the like. He believed that use of natural activities would enable learning to progress more smoothly and rapidly because children would have the benefit of the start already made by nature. He believed that nature would furnish the activity and that it was the responsibility of the teacher to guide and direct it. Binet apparently found his methods to be successful with mentally retarded children, but this author sees no reason why we should not expect similar methods to be successful with most children at all levels of ability.

STRATEGIES OF COPING OF PRESCHOOL CHILDREN

Few careful studies have been made of the styles of coping used by preschool children in dealing with the demands of their environment. A provocative and carefully done study was made by Lois Murphy in connection with the program of research of the Menninger Foundation. Some of its major findings will be reviewed in this chapter.

On the basis of her observations, Murphy (1957a) has established eight types of strategies used by children in coping with stress. She and her colleagues observed preschool children in a variety of testing situations, including party and play situations. They were also able to observe these children over a period of time coping with separation from their mothers, new situations, authority pressures such as limits, demands to be quiet, demands for compliance, competition with siblings, mother's pregnancy and the anticipation of a new baby, sex-role confusions, illnesses, aggression and competition from peers, special external events such as tornadoes, and anxieties engendered by kidnappings and murders of children that took place in the community during the study. Her categorization of strategies, however, is based only on observations of the children as they were administered relatively standardized tests, both "structured" and "unstructured," intelligence and projective.

Murphy (1962, p. 274) defined coping strategies as "the child's individual patternings and timings of his resources for dealing with specific problems or needs or challenges." Coping strategies include both methods of managing the environment and devices for managing the tensions aroused by stress. Learnings of many kinds are involved and include cognitive mastery, utilization of available resources, self-perception, and the like. If a child's first coping efforts to deal with some external threat fail, tensions aroused by internal upheavals are added to those aroused by the external stress. Subsequent coping devices may then be regarded as "secondary coping." Murphy observed several patterns concerning the differences in the initial coping orientation and the secondary coping efforts. Some children leap first and then settle down to think and make efforts at cognitive mastery after the initial failure. Other children think first and "look before they leap." If secondary coping strategies succeed, the child is free for continued spontaneity. If they fail, defensive rigidity may prevent further exploration and lead to continued frustration, further anxiety, and further defensive attitudes. The situations that call for coping strategies involve encountering something new or not yet mastered (a novel situation, an obstacle, a conflict, etc.). Such situations may be gratifying, challenging, threatening, or frustrating. Some situations involve a combination of these. For example, entering school for the first time might involve both challenge and threat.

The strategies identified in this way by Murphy are as follows (1957a):

1. *Selection from the environment, narrowing the field, choosing what can be coped with; timing the sequences of coping or the period of adjustment to bring the stress within dimensions that can be handled.* In high school and college students, this early-learned strategy is reflected in habits of trying to deal only with the easy items in a test. In a pilot study of the comparative learning of mathematics among 13-year-olds in the Greater London Area and the Greater Twin Cities area, the author found that one factor in the superiority of the London youngsters seemed to be in their lack of hesitancy in dealing with difficult problems. Twin Cities youngsters skipped about on the test, trying to find items they could solve easily. The Londoners sailed right through, taking the problems as they came. This sequence may reflect a cultural difference in the way children are trained to cope with stress. Nevertheless, the tendency to seek to adapt by using first the least expensive energies and then the more expensive ones is probably universal. It is also a wise strategy to bring the stress within some dimension that can be handled. Adaptation does not need to stop at this point, however.

Murphy (1962, p. 98) reports some interesting observations concerning the differences in the strategies children use in preparing themselves to select from the environment the elements with which they will attempt to cope. Children brought into her testing situation were first given large paper cups of juice. Some children regularly gulped their juice and ran off without asking permission of the adults involved, apparently assuming that this new world was theirs to enjoy and explore. By contrast, other children used the initial juice-drinking period as an island of safety. They drank in small, prolonged sips, peering over the edges of their cups at the other children, the surroundings, and the like. They sorted out the various opportunities in terms of what they might like to do or what they could cope with. Other children did not seem uneasy but took their own time in deciding for themselves what they wanted to do. Still others, of course, had difficulty in making any decision as to what to do.

2. *Denial of reality; projecting; using fantasy to avoid the situation.* Examples of adults who deny reality have already been seen in the flood

victims who spanked the children for spilling water on the floor instead of admitting that the house was being flooded, and the combat pilot who thought that he was in a hail storm rather than in a "hail" of enemy flak. When children are asked to think of ideas for improving toys so that they will be more fun to play with, those children who are unable to cope with the problem use the strategy of denial of reality. They insist, in spite of the experimenter's objections, on making the toy a real dog or airplane rather than keeping it a toy dog or airplane.

Murphy (1962, p. 87) reported that 84 per cent of her young subjects recognized limitations in their skills but that at some time about 50 per cent of them used a defense mechanism involving distortion of reality. Over a fifth of them used fantasy in the testing situation, either as a diversion or as an escape. One of the children studied by Murphy (1962, p. 136) lost a part of his finger and adopted denial (an initial hiding or glossing over the loss) as a way of tolerating and working through this stressful experience. Such a strategy, in fact, seems to be rather common in adapting to losses of body parts, severe burns, and the like.

3. *Resisting excessive or unwelcome demands; escaping or evading them.* Flight and fight are the child's most characteristic approaches to excessive and unwelcome demands. Sleep, illness, apathy, feigned lack of understanding, and the like are used by both children and adults.

Most children show the capacity to set limits to demands and pressures from the environment. This is probably a part of what happens when children give themselves a slow warming-up period, taking time for familiarizing themselves with the new situation. Part of their strategy is protecting themselves from overstimulation. Murphy (1962, p. 213) describes a boy who retired to an area in the garage when he arrived at a party. He thus avoided exposing himself all at once to the many people and spaces in the party situation. While he was familiarizing himself with the situation he asserted his areas of mastery by constructing a tall building from blocks.

4. *Tolerating; putting up with; accepting; understanding.* Tolerance, acceptance, and understanding make unwelcome demands less disturbing. A creative acceptance of the limiting effects of the stress results in a healthy basis for adaptation. All coping, and especially this strategy, may be either conforming or creative and transforming. For example, a child may not like a particular toy used in a test situation. He may understand and accept the examiner's expectations that he play with the toy. He may do so only in a desultory, conforming way, or he may imaginatively transform the toy and make it fulfill some unintended function.

5. *Mobilization of extra effort; compulsive repetitions or practice.* Children learn early the strategy of mobilizing extra effort to meet new and difficult demands. It must be recognized, of course, that there are limits to the continued mobilization of extra effort. Compulsive repetition prevents the child from going ahead to cope with additional demands and new tasks.

Compulsive repetition is common in the performance of mentally retarded children on tests of creative thinking but quite rare in the performance of children of normal intelligence in the second grade and above.

The ability to mobilize extra energy or rise to the occasion is apparently closely akin to Selye's (1956, pp. 65–66) concept of *adaptation energy*. Selye maintains that it is as though we had hidden reserves of this adaptation energy in ourselves throughout the body. Selye coined the term *adaptation energy* to indicate that the energy consumed in adaptation is different from the caloric energy received from food. He admits that we have no precise concept of what this energy might be and indicates that he is pursuing some promising research leads concerning this gap in knowledge. Selye has found, however, that the amount of adaptation energy possessed by a person is apparently finite. Individuals can even be trained to adapt to repeated stressors but eventually the adaptation energy runs out. This adaptation energy decreases with age also (Selye, 1956, pp. 66, 303).

6. *Cushioning; protecting self with available gratifications*. Frequently children, in testing situations, make excessive requests for water or trips to the bathroom. These are available gratifications that cushion or protect the child as he copes with stress. The use of play, sleep periods, and the like help to provide such cushioning. In experiments involving children, the author sometimes uses a candy break in the middle of the experiment where he is anxious to sustain effort. Some of the real purpose served by such a practice is illustrated in the query one kindergartener made of the teacher immediately after the author left. He asked, "Do you think Dr. Torrance really gave us that candy because it would make us think better or was it because he liked us?" The real cushioning comes from assurances that they are liked. The assurance may come from a drink of water, a piece of candy, or a friendly pat.

7. *Compensating; giving self leeway with momentary regressions; softening or embellishing the situation imaginatively*. A child may do poorly on one task or fail to mobilize extra effort. To compensate, he may mobilize extra effort on the next problem. If the anxiety mounts, he may giggle, laugh, or otherwise play around with the task, to reduce the anxiety so that he can cope more adequately with the situation. Frequently children make games out of testing situations. All of these are, of course, factors that make problems of test reliability difficult, especially with children, but also with young people and adults.

Apparently momentary regressions accompany both successful and unsuccessful coping with stressful situations. Murphy (1962, p. 88) reports that about 20 per cent of her subjects showed such regressive behavior as mouth or lip play when they were successful and that about 50 per cent regressed under tension. She also reports that performance tests are less threatening to young children than are verbal tests. Apparently there is more opportunity for this protective regression in the performance tests than in the verbal ones. It is well known that various regressive responses are frequently instrumental in coping with problems that call for creative problem solving, even at the level of inventions and important scientific discoveries. According to J. E. Gordon (1963, p. 398), conflict provides the motivation for creative thinking and the behavioral variability involved in reaction to stress provides the possibility of discovering a uniquely useful solution. Increased effort provides the persistence for working at various solutions and regression permits a temporary return to an earlier, less conventional way of thinking from which a creative idea may emerge.

8. *Restructuring; reversing roles; controlling the adult or the situation; making it into something different that can be mastered.* If a child is unable or unwilling to deal with a problem as it is presented, one natural reaction is to restructure the problem in such a way that he can deal with it or find it acceptable. For example, some first grade boys, when asked to think of ways for improving a toy nurse's kit, first changed it to a doctor's kit. The problem was then acceptable to them and they could deal with it without tension. Others, of course, stubbornly said, "I'm not a girl! I don't play with things like that!" No prodding could influence them to think of improvements. This tendency comes out often in the behavior of doctoral degree candidates writing their preliminary examinations. A typical example is to be found in the case of the theological student who was asked to write about the major and minor prophets. He began his response, "Far be it from me, an humble student of theology, to discriminate among those noble individuals, the minor and major prophets. But as for the Twelve Tribes of Israel, . . ." He then proceeded to write for two hours about the Twelve Tribes of Israel.

To reduce the threat to themselves, children often reverse roles and start questioning their testers. It is a common observation of counselors and psychotherapists that clients try to reverse roles when the psychotherapeutic session begins to lead to sensitive areas. Children in testing and learning situations frequently substitute a task they can perform for one that is difficult and develop many strategies whereby they can control the behavior of the adults about them.

It will be noted that some of the above strategies of coping involve changing the realities of the tasks imposed, while others involve coping within the limits of the realities as given. The Murphy studies have also been concerned with sequences of coping constellations. Murphy has found that some children grow step by step and others take more uneven paths. As her research progresses, she believes that creativity in coping will probably be found to involve different constellations of factors, such as these:

1. Range of observation.
2. Discrimination in observation (unusual details).
3. Range and freedom to explore, manipulate, experiment.

4. Range of techniques with people.

5. Wide affective-cognitive range (ability to use and shift between secondary and primary processes and shades in between).

6. Freedom from excessive dependence on *assumed* limits or demands.

7. Large number of ideas.

8. Originality of ideas.

9. Constructiveness with materials (tendency to combine, integrate).

10. Capacity to integrate fantasy and impulse from within with opportunities in the external situations (Murphy, 1957a, p. 4).

An analysis of the factors hypothesized by Murphy to be involved in successful coping with stress reveals that she has included both mental abilities (cognition, discrimination, fluency, originality, flexibility, synthesis, etc., if given traditional labels) and emotional conditions that permit mental abilities to function. The author's preference is to focus on the mental abilities and their functioning and examine the emotional conditions as they contribute to the development of these abilities and to their freedom to function under stress. Before examining this issue further, however, the author will present one of his own conceptualizations.

STRATEGIES OF COPING OF ADULTS

As the author studied man's reactions to one emergency or extreme condition after another (extreme cold, extreme heat, fatigue and sleeplessness, food and water deprivation, danger from the enemy, and the like), several characteristic patterns of coping with stress seemed to emerge. Although these observations were made entirely independently of the work of Murphy and her associates, the strategies were apparently developed early in childhood and overlearned through practice. Their uses may save, enslave, or destroy, depending upon how well they are controlled by higher functions. One group of these strategies is called "risking—avoiding." Others are labeled "mastering—failing," "unloading—overloading," "making peace—denying needs" and "continuing adaptation—surrendering."

RISKING AND AVOIDING

Many students of personality have recognized the importance of risk taking in personality development. Allport (1955), for example, has stated that personality development can take place only through risk taking and variation. Only by testing the limits of his abilities can one achieve a realistic self-concept.

Studying an Air Force population, Torrance and Ziller (1957) developed a series of criteria for identifying individuals having high risk-taking tendencies and those having low risk-taking tendencies. The criteria included tasks involving risks to the subject's status as a survival trainee (heavy penalties for guessing on an extremely difficult examination consisting of items answered correctly by only one or two per cent of the members of previous classes), tasks involving varying degrees of chance for success or survival, tasks requiring choices from alternatives involving different degrees of risk, and a life experience inventory consisting primarily of achievements and preferred activities involving risks of varying degrees. From these data emerged the following personality portrait of the high riskers in contrast to the low riskers:

> The personality pattern of the high risker is characterized by self-confidence, physical and social adequacy, and self-expression. Individuals most willing to take risks feel secure in their own resources and are little concerned that someone may not like them.
>
> They early learned skills which give one status and advantage among his peers—driving a car, dancing, etc. Thus, they are able to face the world with greater self-confidence and less fear. They tend to have been reared on a farm, a rural area, or in a small town rather than in a city. Thus, they were able better to experiment and take risks with less fear and early gained a feeling of power over their environment. They were afforded other experiences which give a sense of adequacy, such as taking overnight trips away from home without parents. They were taught to feel secure in their own resources—started bank accounts at an early age, had fun in changing from one school to another, etc.
>
> They early identified with the masculine role and developed the skills and engaged in the behaviors necessary to validate this role. They engaged earlier in such masculine status-giving activities as smoking, driving a car, playing with snakes, hitchhiking, and the like. They were punished more frequently for bad conduct in school, more of them remember crying as boys, and they were less concerned about pleasing adults. They have also given freer expression to their sexual drives.
>
> High risk-tendency individuals also present a picture of physical adequacy and enjoyment of physical activity. Although they express more enjoyment and claim more participation in almost every active sport, the difference is particularly marked for sports like hunting and fishing.
>
> High riskers also displayed greater social aggressiveness during the developmental years. In grade and high school, they were usually "right in the middle of things." In school, other students expected them to have ideas about what to do and how to do it. They were the ones who helped new students become acquainted. They were the ones who were selected for the major offices in high school and served as captains of varsity athletic teams. They say that they have always enjoyed competition, considered winning important, performed better than usual under stiff competition, and practiced and tried to improve skills when they suffered losses in competition.

Although the personality may develop only through risk taking and testing the limits, avoidance or delay may at times be the best way of coping with stress. From survival research, it would seem that avoidance is likely to be the preferred mode of adaptation under the following kinds of conditions:

1. When the risk is too great and there is not a "fighting chance" of success.
2. When overloading is likely and danger of breakdown imminent.
3. When the psychological cost is too great, i.e., the defenses required are too expensive.
4. When the danger may subside after a lapse of time or when the chances of success will be increased by waiting for the situation to change or by achieving better skills of mastery.

Although avoiding may be instrumental in some cases, it usually represents a noninstrumental response to anxiety and results in decreased capacity to deal with stressful conditions. Avoidance as a strategy of coping with stress apparently is learned in the socialization process when parents use fear to counteract strong tendencies in the child to take risks. Of course, some parents overemphasize this aspect of socialization because of their own fears and inadequacies and do not permit children to engage in normal, safe kinds of exploratory behavior. Unfortunately, inhibitory responses learned in relation to fear and punishment tend to resist extinction more stubbornly than do other responses. Such rigid response patterns apparently become even more rigid with increased stress. Avoidance reactions are also likely to be stronger under stressful than under nonstressful conditions.

In some cases, avoidance behavior may represent an assertion of autonomy and resistance to coercion. Murphy (1962, pp. 208–09) found that avoidance can serve useful preventive or preparatory values for children. She found that this was especially true of children struggling to maintain their own integrity and control. One youngster watched the adults "with a questioning, mischievous, half-defiant gaze that seemed to say, 'You can't make me do anything I don't want to. I'll decide when I'm ready to decide.'" Another child insisted on autonomy at all times as if to say, "I'll do it my own way." It is quite possible that such behavior is a part of the personality pattern of the creative child.

MASTERING AND FAILING

Traditionally, American homes, schools, military services, and the like have trained almost exclusively for victory. For the prevention of breakdowns and mastery of stress, however, individuals need to learn skills for coping with failure or defeat. The British are frequently praised for their success in training men to cope with frustration and failure and to meet such occasions with dignity. One survival story concerns a group of British sailors shipwrecked in the South Pacific in World War II. On one occasion, they were having difficulty in keeping their lifeboat bailed out. To cope with this difficulty they removed their clothes to free themselves of all possible encumbrances. The boat was overturned and their clothes were lost. When they finally reached land they did not know whether it was occupied by the enemy or not. Lest the enemy see them crawling ashore, they marched single file, completely naked across the beach in full dignity.

There seems to be a growing recognition in the United States that youth needs to learn the skills required for coping with the normal, expected sources of stress. Life experience inventory studies suggest that the sequence and readiness for learning this mastery is of special importance. Those who mastered stress best were those who had encountered frustrations and had learned the skills of mastery (driving a car, dating, etc.) at about the predictable age for children in the culture. Those who mastered stress most poorly were those who either had never encountered much frustration and had learned skills of mastery late in life or not at all, or who had encountered frustrations at an early age and prematurely had attempted to learn the skills of mastery. Even in the matter of childhood friends, the low mastery group *always* had plenty of friends. Members of the high mastery group were more likely to have had only a few friends in childhood and more as they grew older.

Since risk taking and mastering of stress imply aggressiveness, such techniques may appear to be threatening to teachers and counselors. In general, emphasis must be placed on the control of aggressive impulses among elementary school pupils and high school students. Thus we have the issue: "When is aggressiveness justified?" In general it seems that aggressive behavior may be justified under the following conditions:

1. When used in self-defense or in defense of others.
2. When directed against the real enemy or true source of frustration. (There may, of course, be times when the counselor or teacher is perceived as the enemy, and the counselor may have difficulty in modifying this perception.)
3. When perceived as wholly justifiable and not accompanied by guilt feelings.
4. When not excessive but adequate in amount.
5. When used at the appropriate time; when the enemy is vulnerable and there is a "fighting chance" of success.
6. When not confused by irrelevant frustrations from the past.
7. When not easily provoked; only when offense is considerable.

UNLOADING AND OVERLOADING

Apparently the human organism has built into its system a number of automatic mechanisms for unloading when stress becomes too great. One of the most obvious is exploding ("blowing a fuse"), usually a regression to some earlier learned and practiced response. Another type of regression is the well-known case of the individual who spoke one language as a child but has for many years spoken a second language exclusively. Under severe stress he may revert to his childhood language. Or take the case of the former Southern beauty who has lost her "Southern accent" except when she becomes angry or upset. Even in dealing with the enemy, a number of Air Force survivors admitted that when the pressure on them was most severe they found themselves using the devices that they had used in managing their parents when they were small boys. A similar type of automatic response occurs as the result of practice and overlearning of emergency procedures. Many flyers maintain that they bailed out and performed many other emergency actions, all of which they were unaware.

Other automatic unloading mechanisms are forgetting, fainting, becoming amnesic, and hallucinating. With these mechanisms the organism prevents overloading of the system and becoming overwhelmed by tension. When such mechanisms occur in students, counselors should recognize what purpose they are serving and assist students in finding more effective means of unloading or preventing overloading.

Another, and sometimes dangerous, unloading mechanism under stress is overdependence upon a leader. This too is a mechanism of which teachers and counselors are well aware. Students under stress want to become overdependent upon them or on some other strong figure in the environment.

The children observed by Lois Murphy coped with problems by selecting from the environment, narrowing the field, and choosing what can be coped with. One of the unloading mechanisms observed in the experiences of survivors of emergencies and extreme conditions is essentially the same. The author has termed this behavior "priority of a single stress." Apparently such priority setting may be both conscious and unconscious. As the author examined reactions to one stress after another, he observed that a single stress almost always assumes priority over all others. In the struggle for survival, such powerful stresses as excruciating pain, extended food and water deprivation, exhaustion, extreme cold, observation of the plight of others, and so on were all pushed out of awareness. At other times, one or the other of the stresses just listed may take over and push aside all others. In general, these seem to be primitive, protective reactions unguided by consciousness. Apparently the need that is most seriously deprived or most essential for survival must be satisfied first. Survival specialists have worked out sets of priorities for various types of situations in terms of what is most essential for survival or according to a sequence that will bring the situation within dimensions that can be handled.

Essentially, this phenomenon has two important implications for educators. The first is the matter of helping the student plan strategies of action according to what is most important and what is least important. The second is in recognizing that a student may be neglecting one aspect of his development because another is claiming priority, perhaps without the student's awareness.

Another useful technique for unloading is adapting by structuring. The very nature of the specific stresses (food deprivation, isolation, cold, etc.) involved in emergencies and extreme conditions dictates different specific adaptive reactions. In spite of this, one single reaction appears to be involved in all of these adaptations and this is the structuring of the situation. The stress produces a loss or disruption of the anchor in reality. Unless some structure is restored, there will be apathy, hopelessness, hallucinations, fear of insanity, or other disorganized behavior. Students who are failing in their school work, interpersonal relations, or jobs need essentially the same kind of structuring to prevent continued failure and ultimate breakdown.

MAKING PEACE AND DENYING NEEDS

Survival is often threatened in emergencies and extreme conditions by concessions to comfort, inability to postpone gratification of immediate needs for ultimate safety, and the like. These frequently result in death and other unnecessary disasters. Men exposed to dangerous emergencies are taught not to endanger their safety by making unnecessary concessions to comfort. At the same time, they are taught to make themselves as comfortable as possible without endangering their safety. In other words, they are taught not to deny their needs but to "make peace" with them to the extent that safety will permit.

Apparently this is what Murphy means when she describes children as cushioning and protecting themselves with the gratifications that are available, compensating for deprivations by momentary regressions, and softening or embellishing the situation imaginatively. Such behavior may also be observed among high school and college students who are taking courses that are too difficult for them, courses that are taught in unexciting ways, and courses in which learning is routine or unchallenging.

Most of the adjustment mechanisms already listed might be regarded as constituting a part of this technique. Sublimation and displacement are examples of "making peace," and repression and withdrawal illustrate "denying needs." The basic problem is in finding acceptable, safe ways of satisfying needs rather than denying them.

CONTINUING TO ADAPT AND SURRENDERING

Will-to-live or ability to continue adapting in the face of repeated frustration and lack of success has long been recognized by medical doctors, psychologists, social workers, school counselors, and others as of critical importance. "Control panic" and "maintain will-to-survive" are the rules of survival training and of training for dangerous occupations. Panic may be regarded as a kind of surrender, at least a surrender of logical control, in the face of absence of an anchor in reality. Will-to-live and continued constructive behavior involve the mobilization of aggressive energies and refusal to give in to physical feelings and to be affected by a variety of personal and group factors. For example, research indicates that will-to-live is maintained by the importance of goals; pressures, particularly from one's own group, that are perceived as legitimate; perception of the difficulties of the situation; internalization of pressures from others, and the like. Resources that appear to help continue the fight include sense of humor, a supporting or survival-oriented philosophy, religious faith, maintenance of dignity and self-esteem, and "having something to live for."

Analogous situations arise in the school when students withdraw from school, drop certain courses, make no effort to "pass," are apathetic in organizations and activities, experience thoughts of suicide, and the like. Truancy, misbehavior in class, other delinquencies, excessive daydreaming, and listlessness may also be symptomatic of surrendering.

A certain type of surrendering can be instrumental in both mental and physical health. Psychiatrists, general practitioners, nurses, and other medical workers are often heard to remark, "Oh, if he could only let himself be sick, there would be a chance or he would get well so much quicker." Even when hospitalization becomes necessary, some individuals deny so strongly that they are ill that they use much of their adaptive energy in the process of denial, leaving little for healing. This is apparently of special importance when adaptive energy is low and rest is necessary for regaining mental or physical health. The patient may even take the prescribed medicine and remain in bed, but be unwilling to permit others to take care of him, assume some of his responsibilities at home or in the office, or otherwise minister to his needs. In such cases, the inability to surrender in this sense militates against recovery.

Aldrich (1955) explains the phenomena described above in terms of the patient's being ashamed or afraid to be dependent. As a result the patient assumes "a synthetic attitude of independence" to avoid and conceal his dependency. When resistance to dependency is strong, a patient may become a serious problem of medical management. Similarly, when a child's resistance to dependency in the classroom is strong, he may become a serious problem in classroom management. This may be a special problem with highly independent children in classrooms taught by an authoritarian teacher who insists upon making children dependent upon her authority. Regardless of the teacher, however, there is the very real problem of getting the child to accept the guidance he needs to prevent his being overwhelmed.

AIDING INDIVIDUALS TO MASTER STRATEGIES OF COPING

In the preceding sections, a brief sketch was presented of the strategies used in coping with life stresses. In this section, an attempt will be made to sketch how schools may aid their pupils in developing more effective ways of coping with some of the most common stresses. It is believed that the conceptualizations that have been presented can be used as guides in helping students make decisions about curricular choices ("hard" versus "soft" courses, etc.), career choices, developing reasonably realistic self-concepts, adapting to the pressures of the peer culture and of the school itself, changing patterns of nonachievement and delinquency, and the like.

PERMITTING RISK

Most of the cases of indecision concerning vocational and educational choice the school counselor encounters are probably individuals who have difficulty in taking risks. Anything new is so threatening that they tend to avoid it or depend too heavily upon counselors, teachers, and parents to decide for them. It is difficult for the counselor or teacher to withstand the temptation of making choices for such individuals, just as it has been for parents and others who have contributed to the making of the situation.

There is, however, a more subtle and perhaps more important aspect of the job of "permitting risk." Students must recognize and accept the seriousness of their situation before it is too late. One of the most dangerous features of behavior in emergencies and extreme conditions is the resistance to accepting the seriousness of the danger. Hesitation seems to operate in almost every type of dangerous situation. It might be said that resistance results from the uncertainty of the situation. The teacher or counselor's problem may be one of gaining acceptance of "scientific facts" or of "reading the handwriting on the wall" as spelled out by low or failing grades, tests results, and the like. The problem is one of helping the student achieve what might be termed "personal validity" rather than just cognition. There are times when this personal validity can be achieved only by a failure experience at the expense of wasted resources. The school's job is to help keep this waste of human resources at a minimum.

DEVELOPING SKILLS OF MASTERY

Fear of the unknown is one of the reasons why high school students avoid risks, resist learning and making changes, are anxious about new experiences, and the like. As already noted, one of the ways of coping with this difficulty is by structuring the situation. Several studies have shown that actual experience is effective in this regard. As described in an earlier chapter, men subjected to brief successive periods of starvation increasingly respond more favorably both physiologically and psychologically (Taylor et al., 1945). Men previously exposed to a survival ration responded more favorably to the ration, even though they disliked it the first time, than those who had had no previous encounter with it (Torrance, 1959c). It is not always possible to provide actual experiences, even in safe situations. Sometimes role playing and other types of practice are helpful.

Even if the above things cannot be done, there are many things that the counselor and the teacher can do to help a student prestructure forthcoming experiences which he approaches with undue anxiety, such as deciding to go to college or choosing a vocation. One of the first steps would be to help him find out what to expect in the new situation, become acquainted with the requirements—in other words, survey the situation and appraise it. Then, the student is in a position to start developing strategies and skills for coping with the new situation. Knowing the requirements of the situation, he can assess his own resources in terms of his capacity for meeting requirements—the scholastic aptitudes, academic or other special preparation, special talents, interpersonal skills, and the like.

Other skills that should receive mention include restructuring situations too big or too difficult to handle, developing the interpersonal skills necessary for coping with the problem, developing patterns of mutual support and encouragement, and decision making.

HELPING UNLOAD

Just as men in emergencies and extreme conditions frequently have to unload accumulated or overwhelming tensions before they are able to recognize the seriousness of the situation, plan ahead, overcompensate, or "go all out," students have to unload before they can even consider vocational and curricular choices. There are more pressing problems, and temporarily problems of vocational choice must be pushed aside. The counselor must permit this to happen, if he is to help the student master the stresses which threaten his mental health. Temporarily, the counselee may be looking for a relationship in which he feels safe, one in which he can relieve tension by "spilling all of his woes." He needs someone in whom he can confide.

After some unloading has taken place, the counselee may then be able to consider his longer-range problems of vocational choice. There still remains, however, the problem of helping him guard against future overloading. This may involve helping him to find more satisfactory relationships with peers or with adults. It may involve helping him differentiate between the important and the unimportant, and the like. In all of these transactions, the counselor has the problem of providing the proper type and amount of structuring, so that progress will take place.

ENCOURAGING THE CONTINUED FIGHT

Teachers and counselors need to understand some of the group or social conditions that aid in maintaining a continued fight. Perhaps one of the most valuable is mutual support. The student with flagging will may be expected to receive encouragement from his fellow students, teachers, parents, and the counselor. There are times when the counselor may find it desirable to solicit the help of these other meaningful persons in a student's life. Leaders of the peer group seem to be especially successful in this regard. In extreme conditions, those who survive longest seem to be those who expend most energy in helping and supporting others. Thus, the student may bolster his own will to survive by giving support to others in his environment.

In attempting to influence the student's behavior and in getting others to try to influence his behavior, the teacher, nurse, or counselor must take care that the pressures exerted are regarded as legitimate, right, and just. Otherwise, they may have an effect the reverse of that intended. There are times, however, when it is difficult to arouse an individual from a state of apathy. Occasionally it is necessary in the interest of salvaging the individual to use shock or countershock to arouse him.

The important thing, of course, is to help the individual to marshal to his own need all the resources he possesses—his religion, his values, his sense of humor, his philosophy of adaptation, his ability to extend support to others and accept support from them, and the like.

Although there may come a time when it is necessary for the parent, teacher, or counselor to arouse an individual to maximum effort, he should recognize that such expensive expenditures of energy cannot be continuously elicited without breakdown. The dangers of the motto "Always do your best!" should be thoroughly understood by the teacher or counselor. He should help the student decide when it is necessary or desirable to utilize the more expensive energies. These energies may have to be used for a while "just to keep in the fight."

Although there may be "tricks" of adaptation applicable to specific situations and specific stresses, the general principles of adaptation for continuing the fight seem to remain the same. For example, one principle is to accept the stress whatever it is and learn to live or cope with it, to exploit it strategically and bend it to one's own advantage.

Another general principle of adaptation is to keep busy and plan activities. This appears to be applicable even to such situations as isolation and reduced stimulation. In fact, reduced stimulation should be treated in fundamentally the same ways as those stresses that produce pain and discomfort. Survivors who had at one time given up hope and were settling down to die have been revived by the sudden conception or presentation of a plan that gave them a fighting chance. Thus, the teacher and counselor's job is to help the student work out a plan of action that will give him a fighting chance.

REHABILITATION FOLLOWING SEVERE STRESS EXPOSURE

Especially deficient is our psychological knowledge about rehabilitation following exposure to intense or prolonged stress. Medically, we know fairly well what is necessary physically to rehabilitate such individuals. We are not quite so fortunate, however, concerning psychological rehabilitation following exposure to severe stress. We seem to know more about what a person who has experienced food deprivation and the like should do than about how to influence him to do what is indicated. We do not know enough about fortifying individuals with the controls needed to "take their medicine." It does seem certain that the more prolonged the stress the more difficult the rehabilitation. The problem of the student who is ineffective, in trouble, or approaching a breakdown is much the same. Counselors and teachers know far more about what he should do than how to influence him to do what is necessary. Again, the more prolonged the stress has been the more difficult it is to help him take the proper action. Infinite patience and love may be required for success.

At present, there seems to be no good reason to believe that everyday problems of rehabilitating individuals who have been deprived of love or esteem are different in principle from rehabilitation following other types of deprivation. In fact, it is extremely difficult to assist an individual long deprived of affection to regain healthy personality functioning.

SUMMARY

In this chapter, two conceptualizations have been presented of the strategies men use in coping with stress. One was based on observations of the behavior of preschool children. The other was based on the study of adult men and women in emergencies and extreme conditions. Murphy conceptualized the strategies of preschoolers as selection from the environment, denial of reality, resistance to excessive or unwelcome demands, tolerance, mobilization of extra effort, protection of self with available gratifications, compensation and embellishment of the situation, and redefinition or restructuring. The author, using data from the experiences of men in emergencies and extreme conditions and stress experiments conceptualized strategies of coping as risking and avoiding, mastering and failing, unloading and overloading, making peace and denying needs, and continued adaptation and surrendering.

Both Murphy's and the author's conceptualizations suggest that most of one's strategies are primitive, early-learned, and practiced; but the evidence suggests that later learning and favorable conditions for growth make possible more effective control of them. General suggestions were offered for aiding individuals through educational experiences to master the strategies required for coping with predictable stresses, to permit risk, to develop skills of mastery, to help unload accumulated or overwhelming tension, to encourage continued effort, and to recuperate after experiences involving severe stress exposure.

Role of the

Cognitive Abilities in

Coping with Stress

13

A distressed teacher writes as follows:

> What can be done for a high school student who is oblivious of practically everything going on in the classroom? He isn't stupid. I have watched him quite carefully. At times he can come forth with quite intelligent answers. The answers given required good reasoning and analysis.
>
> My personal feeling is that somewhere along the line some teacher or parent refused to listen to what he had to say or contribute. Occasionally he has called on me privately and has indicated that he would like to improve his study habits. He is able to take some types of tests well. He is a dreamer and is generally very pleasant in disposition.
>
> He doesn't associate very well with other boys, but he doesn't seem to hold himself aloof. I am not very familiar with his home background.

The teacher who wrote the above account is concerned about the mental health of a student whose cognitive operations are not functioning very well. He is unaware of much that is going on around him. Whenever anything reduces, interferes with, or destroys awareness of any part of one's environment, some anchors in reality are thereby destroyed and one's capacity for coping constructively with stress is reduced. The reader may be familiar with individuals similar to the high school boy described above. Not even the distressed teacher knows very much about this boy as an individual. The reader might like to make some guesses about what kind of person this boy is and some of the possible reasons why he has shut off from his awareness so much of his environment. Before proceeding with this chapter, the reader might try this exercise and after reading this chapter and the next one, evaluate his responses against the concepts presented.

NATURE OF THE COGNITIVE OPERATIONS

Before discussing the role of the cognitive operations in mental health, it might be useful to examine the nature of these operations. As already indicated in Chapter 11, "cognition" will be used to refer to the discovery, awareness, rediscovery, or recognition of information in various forms and to comprehension or understanding. A large number of the abilities (factors) involved in cognitive operations have been identified and measured by Guilford and his associates (Guilford and Merrifield, 1960) and will be described briefly in this section. In sections that follow, attention will be given to other ways of classifying cognitive functioning. The reader should recognize that cognition is used in some books to refer to all mental functioning and is being used in this book in a narrower sense.

VISUAL COGNITION

Visual cognition is one of the ways of knowing units (figures, symbolic structures, concepts) and is sometimes called "speed of closure" (rapidity of completion). One of the tasks used in assessing this ability is the Street-Gestalt Completion Test, which requires the subject to write the names of objects from drawings or blotches suggestive of parts of the objects. Another is the Mutilated Words Test, which calls for the identification of words in which part of each letter has been erased. Visual cognition ability is of critical importance in structuring new physical situations or in restructuring rapidly changing situations, as in an accident or a disaster situation.

AUDITORY COGNITION

Auditory cognition is another way of knowing units. Three tasks are used by Guilford to assess this ability: Haphazard Speech, which requires the subject to write words or short phrases spoken with unusual inflection and pitch changes; Illogical Groupings, which requires the writing of words or a short phrase spoken with a grouping arrangement contrary to sense of the passage; and Singing, which calls for the writing of a short vocal selection sung with piano accompaniment. Auditory cognition is necessary to a person in establishing contacts with the auditory elements of the environment.

FIGURAL CLASSIFICATION

Figural classification is the ability to recognize the class to which a perceived object belongs. One of the tasks used to assess this ability asks the subject to define classes of figures and assign other figures to the correct classes. In the other task, the subject assigns pictures to classes each defined by a group of three pictures. In coping with stress, this ability might be involved in classifying a dangerous animal from a harmless one, a poisonous plant from an edible one, a threatening storm cloud from a nonthreatening one, and the like.

FIGURAL RELATIONS

The eduction of figural relations is the discovery of relationships between perceived objects. The Figure Analogies Test involves the selection of a figure that correctly completes an analogy. The Figure Matrix Test requires the application of rules discovered from changes in rows and columns of a three-by-three matrix of figures to select a figure for a specified cell. This ability is used when a person notes that one object is more pointed, smaller, heavier, or more complex than another and might be expected to facilitate the recognition of dangers and difficulties.

SPATIAL ORIENTATION

Spatial orientation involves the ability of the subject to structure his perception of an arrangement of objects in space. Test tasks include the Guilford-Zimmerman Spatial Orientation Test; Thurstone's Flags, Figures, Cards; and Instrument Comprehension. In the first, the subject is given such problems as indicating how the position of a boat has changed from one picture to another. In the second, the subject has to indicate whether two views of the same object in rotated positions are mirror images. In the third, he has to state which of five pictured airplanes is flying in the direction indicated by reading in two dials. Spatial orientation is obviously important in maintaining anchors in reality under changing conditions.

VISUALIZATION

Visualization is one of the abilities involved in knowing transformations and is used in recognizing what a perceived pattern would look like if rearranged. One of the test tasks is a Paper Form Board in which the subject draws lines on an outline showing how the black pieces will fit together to form a figure presented. In another task, the subject indicates the pattern of holes in a paper that was punched while folded. In a third task, the subject indicates which lettered edges in a drawing of solid figures correspond to numbered edges on dotted "fold" lines in plane diagrams. In a fourth task, the subject indicates the position that depicts the way a clock would look after rotation. Visualization is of obvious importance in adapting to changing physical conditions, deciding upon proposed changes, and reducing the stress involved in coping with changes.

PERCEPTUAL FORESIGHT

Perceptual foresight is a factor for knowing implications. In the Competitive Planning task, the subject completes as many squares as possible for two opponents. In Route Planning, he locates the point through which one must pass in tracing a path from a corner of a printed maze to the goal. In Planning a Circuit, he traces an electrical circuit diagram to determine at which pair of terminals a battery should be placed in order to complete the circuit through a meter. This ability involves the visual exploration of several possible courses of action, preparatory to selecting the most effective one. Such an ability would be involved in finding one's way to safety in dangerous terrain and in other types of situations requiring planned, constructive behavior.

SYMBOL COGNITION

Symbol cognition is another of the factors for knowing units. In Anagrams, the subject makes as many words as possible using only the letters in a given word. The Word Combinations Test requires him to make a new word using the last letters of one word and the initial letters of another word. The Omelet Test requires him to make a word from a given set of letters. Since symbols play such important roles in communication systems, such abilities would appear to be important in maintaining contact with the environment.

COGNITION OF SYMBOLIC CLASSES

Cognition of symbolic classes is one factor for knowing classes. In one test task, the subject states the common features of groups of numbers. In another, he is asked to recognize a pair of numbers that does not belong in a set of four pairs for lack of a common feature. This type of mental functioning is involved in detecting discrepancies and defects, necessary in identifying problems.

SYMBOLIC RELATIONS

Symbolic relations is another of the factors for knowing relations. In one task, the subject is asked to describe a trend based upon relations of letters in a group of words and to apply a rule discovered from the relations of two given pairs of words to select the second member of a third pair. Since the detection of trends is important in recognizing and accepting signs of danger, this type of mental functioning is useful in many kinds of constructive behavior.

SYMBOLIC PATTERNS

Symbolic patterns is one of the factors for knowing systems or patterns and involves the discovery of the complex relationships in a pattern of symbols. In the Circle Reasoning task, the subject is asked to discover rules for marking circles in patterns. In another test, he is asked to find a system

213

in a triangular pattern of letters. This ability is called into play in deciphering a code and in understanding strange rituals in an unfamiliar culture or in a disturbed personality.

COGNITION OF SYMBOLIC IMPLICATIONS

Cognition of symbolic implications refers to the ability to anticipate the consequences of symbolic communications. One test task (Word Patterns) requires the subject to arrange a list of words efficiently in a kind of crossword puzzle pattern. In another (Symbol Grouping) he has to arrange scrambled symbols in a specified order as efficiently as possible in ten minutes. The ability involved is possibly useful in reducing the stresses that arise from ineffective communications in the symbolic area or from unorganized symbolic communications.

VERBAL COMPREHENSION

Verbal comprehension is one of the factors for knowing units. In the Guilford-Zimmerman Comprehension task, the subject selects the word that is most similar in meaning to a given word. In other tasks, he answers questions concerning the content of given paragraphs; answers five-choice vocabulary and information items emphasizing technical knowledge, sports, and mechanical information; and answers five-choice synonym items.

CONCEPTUAL CLASSIFICATION

Conceptual classification is another of the factors for knowing classes. The test tasks require the subject to select the word in a group of four that does not belong; assign given words to one or neither of two classes, each defined by four other words; and indicate whether a sentence conveys fact, possibility, or name.

SEMANTIC RELATIONS

Semantic relations is the ability to see relationships between thoughts or ideas. The tasks call for the selection of a word to complete an analogy after the subject has found the relation in the first pair and has applied the rules discovered from changes in rows and columns in a two by three matrix of words to select the missing word.

GENERAL REASONING

General reasoning is one of the factors for knowing systems. One task calls for the solution of arithmetic-reasoning problems in which numerical computation is minimized. In another, the subject has to find the distance from ship to port considering the influence of several variables. In a third, he has to solve five-choice word problems requiring arithmetic only.

PENETRATION

Penetration is one of the factors for knowing transformations. In one task, the subject has to write six ways in which common objects of a pair are alike. In another, he has to suggest farsighted improvements for social institutions. This type of mental functioning is essential in behaving constructively in situations where superficiality in perception causes difficulty.

CONCEPTUAL FORESIGHT

Conceptual foresight is one of the factors for knowing implications and for anticipating needs or the consequences of a given situation. In one of the test tasks, the subject is asked to write four questions, the answers to which would serve as a basis for making a decision in a conflict situation. In another, he lists as many as six different ways of accomplishing a given task. Conceptual foresight is important in avoiding or reducing the stress involved in making changes in procedures, methods, and policies.

USE OF CONCEPTUALIZATION

Through the detailed conceptualization of the cognitive operations and the examination of the kinds of tests that are used in assessing the effectiveness of their functioning, several values should be realized. First, a conceptualization makes their nature more understandable and their importance in personality development and mental hygiene more apparent. Second, such a conceptualization could very well become the basis for diagnosing and treating difficulties that arise from the malfunctioning of these operations. It might be discovered, for example, that an individual was not adapting because of low awareness in the area of visual cognition. This handicap might be remedied by glasses or visual training. Other deficiencies might be remedied just as easily by measures appropriate to the nature of the deficiency. Not all perceptual difficulties arise from such physical causes, however, as we shall see later in this and the next chapter.

This conceptualization also has almost infinite possibilities for generating ideas for improving the effectiveness of education to cope with the demands and stresses of life in almost all areas. It can also be used as a guide in constructing more useful measures for guiding and assessing educational development. Guilford (1960) has offered some excellent examples of how this conceptualization might be used in improving the teaching of reading, an area in which many difficulties in cognition occur and which generates many problems of mental health. He maintains that the child's readiness to read depends upon basic cognitive abilities. In learning to recognize combinations of letters in syllables and words, the child has to depend upon his ability to cognize symbolic units. Guilford points out that most of the commonly used intelligence tests should not be expected to predict progress of this kind, since this ability is not represented among the tasks included in such tests. Obtaining meaning from the printed symbolic unit involves abilities in the symbolic category, first the meaning of single words, then relations and class ideas. Sentences and paragraphs offer systems of ideas, and poetic and literary writings offer transformations of meanings and vague hints of implications, all of which must be comprehended.

COGNITIVE OPERATIONS IN EDUCATIONAL OBJECTIVES

In the stated objectives of educators, cognitive operations occupy a dominant position. In a study of the social studies objectives of Minnesota elementary and high school teachers, Torrance and Ross (1961) found that about 72 per cent of the objectives clearly fall in the category of cognitive operations. The statement of objectives would begin with "recognize," "be familiar with," "be aware of," "know that," and the like. About five per cent were classified in the memory category; 19 per cent, in the convergent thinking area; one per cent, in the divergent thinking category; and three per cent, in the evaluative category.

Although this study reveals what might be regarded as an over-emphasis on the cognitive operations, personality theorists have long recognized the importance of the cognitive needs in personality development and mental health. Although little attention in research has been given to the cognitive needs for sheer knowledge (curiosity) and for understanding (explanation), we know a great deal about them from common observation.

MASLOW'S CONCEPT OF COGNITIVE NEEDS

Maslow (1954) included the cognitive needs in his hierarchy of basic human needs. In his hierarchy he sees as more demanding the physiological needs (food, water, sleep, rest, sex, etc.), safety needs, affection or love, and status. Thus, in order to activate the cognitive needs in the classroom, teachers must recognize that these more demanding needs must be satisfied reasonably well. Prolonged deprivation of cognitive needs, however, may be expected to produce considerable stress and to result in personality damage.

Maslow (1954, p. 93) maintains that the reason why we know so little about the cognitive needs, their dynamics, and their psychopathology, is that they have not been seen as important in the clinic. Cognitive psychopathology, he points out, lacks the glamour of other psychopathologies and is easily overlooked. Maslow believes that there are true psychopathological

216

effects when the cognitive needs are frustrated. He points to cases in which it seemed clear that the pathology (boredom, loss of zest in life, self-dislike, general depression of the bodily functions, steady deterioration of the intellectual life, of tastes, etc.) was produced in intelligent people.

The need to know and to understand seems to be quite strong in infancy and childhood, perhaps stronger than in adulthood. Maslow contends that children do not have to be taught to be curious but that they can be taught not to be curious. Berlyne (1960) has presented a very useful body of knowledge concerning the role of curiosity in reducing the stress that results from conflict, novelty, uncertainty, complexity, and the like.

BLOOM'S TAXONOMY OF EDUCATIONAL OBJECTIVES

As already indicated, cognition can be conceptualized in a variety of ways. A variety of classificatory schemes have been offered for dealing with the cognitive operations insofar as educational objectives are concerned. One of the best known of these is the taxonomy of educational objectives in the cognitive domain by Bloom (1956) and his associates. They offer a taxonomy both of the kinds of knowledge and the kinds of intellectual abilities and skills that are necessary in dealing with knowledge. They define knowledge as "the recall of specifics and universals, the recall of methods and processes, or the recall of a pattern, structure, or setting" (1956, p. 201).

Bloom's taxonomy has been rather widely used as a guide in constructing achievement tests and has been useful in thinking about educational objectives and mental functioning. In many ways, it is similar to Guilford's Structure of Intellect. Thus, Bloom's taxonomy has not been rejected as an approach for examining problems of mental health and personality development. Instead, Guilford's taxonomy has been chosen as being better suited to such a purpose.

COGNITIVE STYLES

More commonly associated with personality development and mental health is the conceptualization of cognitive functioning in terms of cognitive styles or control principles. Work related to cognitive styles represents a shift in emphasis from personal adjustment to intellectual mastery as a goal of education. It represents only a shift of focus, as it has sought to integrate such fields of knowledge as personality theory, clinical diagnostic testing, psychophysics and Gestalt theory, drives and motivational concepts, and the psychoanalytic concept of defense. The resulting work is easily associated with problems of personality development and mental health in our framework of coping constructively with stress. Of the available conceptualiza-

217

tions of cognitive styles, the author has chosen one that arose from the work of Gardner, Holzman, Klein, Linton, and Spence (1959). A brief description of the following six control principles, styles, or strategies identified in this work will be offered: leveling-sharpening, tolerance for unrealistic experiences, equivalence range, focusing-scanning, constricted-flexible control, and field dependence-independence. Gardner and his associates (1959) use the term "styles" to refer to the interaction or combinations of cognitive controls.

LEVELING-SHARPENING

Leveling has generally been defined as "a low degree of articulation of stimulus field" (Gardner et al., 1959). The leveling tendency might manifest itself by difficulty in extracting figures embedded in larger contexts and easy assimilation of new stimuli into dominant organizations. As a result gradual changes in the stimulus field go unrecognized for a relatively long period of time. Sharpening has been associated with the opposite of leveling, namely, maximal complexity and differentiation of the field. The work of Holzman and Klein (1956) has indicated the desirability of defining leveling and sharpening as modes of organizing a sequence of stimuli. Leveling implies a low level of articulation in a sequence of stimuli, whereas sharpening implies a high level of articulation.

Whereas the Embedded Figures Test has been marginally successful in elaborating the old definition, the Schematizing Test has been more successful in developing the revised definition. The Schematizing Test (Gardner et al., 1959, pp. 23–25) requires judgments of a series of 150 squares which gradually increase in size. Fourteen different sizes of the squares are projected onto a screen in various combinations. The test seeks to distinguish the subject's discriminative sensitivity and his means of reporting it, such as the crudity or refinement of the yardstick he uses, his preference for certain scaling units, and the range of scaled values used.

The defense mechanism of repression is apparently associated with leveling. In both repression and leveling, a new idea or experience assimilates to an older one by virtue of a relationship between them. Thus, the new idea or experience loses its individuality and is unavailable to consciousness as a discrete entity. It seems reasonable to expect that repression as a typical way of coping with stress can occur most easily in persons who use leveling as a characteristic cognitive style. It had been observed by Rapaport, Gill, and Schafer (1945) and by Schafer (1948) that persons using repression as a defense in coping with stress have difficulty in extracting single ideas from memory frames of reference. For example, when asked "Where is Egypt?" in the information subtest of the Wechsler-Bellevue Intelligence Scale, a subject might say, "Somewhere in the East," or when asked "Where is

218

Brazil?" say, "In a jungle somewhere—near Argentina." Subsequent empirical studies by Gardner and his associates (1959) point to a close association between repression and leveling.

TOLERANCE FOR UNREALISTIC EXPERIENCES

Tolerance for instability or unrealistic experiences has been defined as "acceptance of experiences that do not agree with what one knows to be true" (Gardner et al., 1959). Tolerant subjects take their experiences at face value and have relatively little need to mold them in terms of "usual" or "expected" reality. Intolerance for unrealistic experiences is defined as resistance to perceptual or cognitive experiences in which ideational or immediate sense data are in opposition to conventional reality. The Apparent Movement Test and certain measures derived from the Rorschach Ink Blot Test are most commonly used for assessing this tendency. Both types of measures are presumed to indicate the degree to which a person's reality testing rigidly requires the holding onto of forms as they are known to be. Gardner and his associates also used the Aniscikonic Lenses Test, an apparatus developed by Ames in the Institute for Associated Research at Princeton. This test reveals individual differences in the speed with which subjects recognize distortion. Although the research concerning this cognitive control principle is meager, its relevance for coping with stress and maintaining anchors in reality is fairly obvious.

EQUIVALENCE RANGE

Some persons are very detailed in their categorization of experiences and have rather exact standards for judging similarity while others group stimuli into broader categories. Apparently sensitivity to differences per se is not responsible for differences in categorizing behavior. Subjects who group stimuli into broad categories may be aware of subtle differences in stimuli. The differences in categorizing behavior seem to lie in the degree to which subjects are impelled to act upon or ignore an awareness of differences. The object-sorting test, grouping of Chinese ideographs, naming objects, describing people, judging photographs of human faces, and drawing of objects are some of the tasks that have been used in studying equivalence range in the laboratory.

In studies by Gardner and his associates (1959) it was found that subjects high on the equivalence range factor compared with those low on this factor sorted objects into a few large categories, used rather casual criteria for similarity, were aware of and acted on a richer array of connotations of objects, relied on everyday meanings as bases of classification, produced more human content on the Rorschach, produced a larger proportion of human rather than animal responses, used more color and human movement in their responses, and projected more life and activity into the inkblots.

FOCUSING-SCANNING

Focusing involves two major aspects—a tendency to narrow awareness and to keep experiences discrete and a tendency to separate affect from idea. The narrowing of awareness is an ability involved in coping with irrelevancies and distractions that might interfere with accurate performance. The ability to separate affect from idea is used in screening out inner experiences to maintain objectivity and criticality. The initial definition of focusing implied that in extreme focusing irrelevancies are shut out of experience. Research, however, has led to the reinterpretation that the high focuser actually deploys attention to relatively many aspects of stimulus fields. He is broadly aware of many aspects of his environment because he is constantly scanning it. The nonfocuser is actually narrow in his deployment of attention.

The Size Estimation Test and the Picture Sorting Test have been used in studying the focusing principle. The rationale of the Size Estimation Test is that accuracy in size estimation is a function of the degree of attention deployment. A subject who characteristically deploys attention broadly overestimates little in this test; a subject who characteristically limits his scanning largely to the most obvious and interesting objects in the environment overestimates much more.

The defense mechanism of isolation appears to be associated with focusing and scanning. The mechanism of isolation involves the separation of affect from idea, so that potentially unpleasant ideas become more tolerable. Freud himself speculated that isolation involves an overattachment to ideas, words, and things and divests thought of its affective components. There is an excessive emphasis upon logic, attentiveness to spatial and temporal attributes of objects.

A study by Holzman and Klein (1956) suggests a statistical relationship between the presence of isolation as a prominent defense and scanning. Subjects were selected on the basis of a variety of indicators of isolation as a major defense. Eight of the nine men thus identified fell in the extreme-scanning half of the distribution. The results indicate that in isolation, as in scanning, extreme investment of attention in external objects may lead to unusual responsiveness to irrelevant and relevant cues alike.

CONSTRICTED-FLEXIBLE CONTROL

The term "constricted-flexible control" was apparently first used by Klein (1954) to describe individual differences in reactions to stimulus fields containing contradictory or intrusive clues. Constricted-control subjects employ counteractive measures in their attempt to overcome the disruptive effects of intrusive cues. They cope with distracting stimuli by ignoring them in favor of a salient, easily confirmable stimulus attribute. Conflicts are resolved in favor of the most obvious external stimuli, and subjects avoid using feelings or emotional reactions as sources of information. They also tend to resist change and prefer to maintain sets long after they become inappropriate, thus failing to take advantage of all available cues for coping with the situation. Flexible-control subjects appear relatively comfortable when confronted with contradictory or intrusive cues.

One of the tests used to study constricted-flexible control is the Color-Word Test. Part I is a "warm-up" page of color names: red, green, yellow, and blue. The names are printed in black in random order, ten lines to a page. Part II is a page of color strips, rows of red, green, yellow, and blue asterisks that match the arrangement of words in Part I, and the length, position, and color of words in Part III. Four colors and four-color words appear in Part III in contradictory combinations. That is, no color name is printed in its own color. The task of the subject is to read the color names in Part I as rapidly as possible, name the colors of the asterisks in Part II as fast and as accurately as possible, and to read the colors in Part III ignoring the words. An Incidental Recall Test, a Size Estimation Test, and a Free Association Test are also used.

This principle is of special interest in thinking of strategies for coping with stress, since survival or success in coping with stress requires that a person give attention to things that are most essential to survival or success in coping with the stressful condition.

FIELD DEPENDENCE-INDEPENDENCE

The field dependence-independence principle has been defined and studied in connection with personality and mental health by Witkin, Lewis, Hertzman, Machover, Meissner, and Wapner (1954) and closely resembles the constricted-flexible control principle. Witkin and his associates used the concept to account for individual differences in situations described as requiring extraction of an "item" from the field in which it appears. In their original study they used the Embedded Figures Test and others to assess field dependence-independence and the Thematic Apperception Test, the Rorschach Ink Blots, and the Machover Figure Drawing Test for assessing personality.

In brief, Witkin and his associates (1954, p. 469) found that field-dependent people tend to be characterized by passivity in dealing with the environment; unfamiliarity with and fear of their own impulses, together with poor control over them; lack of self-esteem, and the possession of a relatively primitive, undifferentiated body image. Independent performers tend to be characterized by activity and independence in relation to the environment; closer communication with, and better control of, their own impulses; relatively high self-esteem; and a more differentiated, mature body image. The dependent group appear to be quite passive in their strategies for coping with stress while the independents are quite active and constructive in their coping efforts.

Gardner and his associates (1959) in their later study of field dependence-independence used the Embedded Figures Test, the Rod and Frame Test, and the Rorschach Ink Blots. The Embedded Figures Test and the Rod and Frame Test both require that the subject respond to certain cues in the face of competing effects of other cues. In the Embedded Figures Test all of the cues are visual and the subject is aware of his successes and failures. In the Rod and Frame Test, two sets of cues are pitted against each other. Accurate estimation of the verticality of the rod requires that the subject respond selectively to bodily cues and that he not attend to, or in some way actively resist responding to, the misleading frame.

COGNITIVE ABILITIES AND STYLES AND COPING WITH STRESS

There are many obvious relationships between the cognitive abilities and styles as defined in this chapter and problems of coping constructively with stress as outlined in previous chapters. An effort will be made at this point to identify and discuss some of these.

BECOMING AWARE OF DANGEROUS CONDITIONS

Much emphasis has been given in earlier chapters to the dangers of failure to recognize the seriousness of the situation and consequent failure to take adaptive action or delay in taking such action. Although sensitivity to problems is one of the evaluative abilities, there must first be awareness of the condition. If one does not see the red light, hear the siren or other warning, or feel the heat of the stove, the evaluative abilities do not have a chance to function. Perhaps most important in becoming aware of dangerous conditions are such factors as visual cognition, auditory cognition, spatial orientation, perceptual foresight, cognition of symbolic implications, verbal comprehension, conceptual classification, general reasoning, penetration, and conceptual foresight.

REMOVING FEARS OF THE UNKNOWN

It is through the cognitive operations that individuals are able to remove fears of the unknown. Some evidence that indicates that many individuals are literally "scared to death" in unknown or unfamiliar situations has already been pointed out. It has also been shown that people adapt more favorably both physiologically and psychologically to unpleasant situations, if they have had prior experiences in such situations than if they have had no experience at all. This is true, even though the initial experience was not successful.

Hudson (1954) has summarized a number of laboratory and field studies concerned with anxiety in response to the unfamiliar. The subjects of these studies ranged from rats to human beings and showed that adults in all species are sensitive to events, objects, etc., in their environment not immediately recognized as familiar. The response may be curiosity, a series of associations with prior experiences, or marked emotional behavior such as flight, anger, excitement, or anxiety. Rats exposed to a series of strange objects responded with progressively less fear or curiosity as a result of a generalized process of adaptation or learning. The threat (stressor) exists in the perceiver, not in the object. Hudson identified ambiguity as a characteristic common in the perceptual organization of events or objects that are stressful. As a result, Hudson maintains that training for coping with emergencies is valuable, not because it develops the correct behavior pattern per se but because it provides a degree of stability in an otherwise perceptually unstructured situation and thereby reduces anxiety.

Schwartz and Winograd (1954) in their studies of troop participation in atomic maneuvers found that realistic information gained about atomic effects are related to changes in attitudes of confidence or anxiety toward participation in atomic maneuvers or warfare. Similarly, Torrance (1954d) found that the possession of knowledge about how to survive in emergencies and extreme conditions and gains in such knowledge during survival training are both related to expressed confidence in ability to survive and to exert leadership in a survival situation. What seems to be involved in all of these studies is a reduction of fear as a result of knowledge about what would otherwise be unknowns, or as a result of lack of anchor in reality.

STRUCTURING THE SITUATION

Identifying the components of the problem or structuring the situation is essential to successful coping with stress. Essentially this is a cognitive operation. However, after the situation has been surveyed and the individual has become aware of the components of the situation—his condition, the setting, the hostile forces, and the like—evaluation comes into play. The awareness, which has to come first, may involve the various types of foresight, knowing relations, spatial orientation, and the like.

KNOWING WHAT TO DO

The cognitive operations are important in knowing what to do in various kinds of stress-producing situations. Although memory and evaluation may be required, basically, knowing what to do brings into play the cognitive operations. If one knows what others have done or what has worked in similar situations, one is more likely to know what to do when he is confronted with a stressful situation. If he is able to recognize his own unconscious defenses, he gains an additional possibility of control. Knowing the causes of certain kinds of reaction and knowing what to expect in certain conditions improve chances of successful adaptation.

MAINTAINING A SENSE OF WORTHWHILENESS

The cognitive operations figure importantly in several ways in helping an individual cope with stress by maintaining a sense of worthwhileness. The importance of self-esteem in maintaining a will-to-live has already been stressed. A number of different types of psychotherapy emphasize the importance of helping individuals regain confidence in their own perceptions of reality. For example, Rogers (1956) includes in his concept of the fully functioning person openness to one's experiences and acceptance of one's organism as a trustworthy means of perceiving the world. Such a person does not deny, blot out, or distort any perception in order to avoid threat to his self-structure. In other words, he permits himself to be fully aware because he possesses a sense of worthwhileness.

FEEDBACK OF MEANINGS AS A GUIDE TO BEHAVIOR

Since one is dependent upon his cognitive operations for meanings, such feedback is important as a guide to behavior. Study after study has shown that feedback is important in almost every kind of performance, especially performance under stress or changing conditions. In one experiment by Michael and Maccoby (1953), one half of the groups were asked a question and required to give an active, explicit response, overtly or covertly. After a slight pause for responding, subjects were told the correct answer. The other half of the groups gave active responses also but were not given knowledge of the correct response. Instructional time, item for item and over-all, was identical for the two sets of groups. The second set of groups made small but statistically significant gains while the first set of groups made more marked gains, apparently as a result of having received knowledge of the correct response.

Hirsch (1952) compared several forms of knowledge of results in an experiment involving questions posed to students as a participation procedure used with films. He found that there was less effect when students were simply told "right" or "wrong" than when the correct answer was presented. The best results were obtained when the correct response was presented in the context of repeating the question.

An experiment by Angell (1949) was conducted to determine the effect of immediate and delayed knowledge of quiz results on three kinds of learning goals in freshman college chemistry: knowledge of facts and principles, application of facts and principles in nonquantitative problems, and application of facts and principles in quantitative problems. Subjects in one group received immediate knowledge of results by means of a punchboard. Subjects in another group received knowledge of results through the use of IBM answer sheets, which were scored and returned to students at the next meeting of the class following the quiz. Students who used the punchboard, which provided immediate feedback, scored significantly higher on the final examination covering the same material than did the students who received the delayed feedback.

PROVIDING A BASIS FOR PROBLEM SOLVING AND DECISION MAKING

It must be remembered that information is necessary for sound problem solving and decision making. Of course, some investigators argue that productive thinking requires that one cultivate a naïvete. Evidence (Torrance and Harmon, 1961), however, indicates that what one is able to do with information depends to a considerable extent upon his attitude toward the information he possesses. For example, individuals who only "cuss the defects" of the knowledge they possess make little use of it. Rigid adherence to the information one holds may also stand in his way of finding new solutions. The role of knowledge in productive thinking and decision making will be discussed in some detail in Chapters 17, 19, and 20.

USING LESS EXPENSIVE ENERGIES

Arguments have been advanced to support the idea that man tends to adapt first by using his least expensive energies. The author believes that the evidence will support the ideas that in general the cognitive operations represent less expensive energies than the other four mental operations. Thus, in an emergency or under prolonged stress, a person is likely to depend largely upon cognitive operations or upon overlearned (memorized) material. Also, if he knows what to do and does not have to produce new solutions, he will have more energy available for use in coping with the situation. In other words, if his "know how" is able to handle a large percentage of the problems of coping with stress, he has more energy left for productive and evaluative thinking in solving the others.

SPEEDING RECOVERY FROM SHOCK

The speed of recovery from shock may be expected to be increased by the cognitive operations. Knowledge of what to expect and familiarity with possible solutions enable the individual to rise to an occasion more readily and to go all out. Furthermore, the extra energy available for coping with emergencies as a result of such knowledge increases chances of success. This enables an individual to avoid dangerous delays in responding to pressing emergencies.

INCREASING ENJOYMENT OF LIFE

It may also be argued that the more fully aware a person is of his environment the more exciting he will find life. If one is able to see something new in each situation he experiences, he will not suffer the deadening effects of boredom. Many individuals who have survived harrowing emergencies and extreme conditions have found enjoyment in such experiences. Some learned new enjoyments in foods, found a new awareness of the pleasure of exercising their bodies, discovered new kinds of companionship, became aware of abilities they had not previously recognized, saw elements of humor in their predicaments, developed a new awareness of the beauties of nature, and the like. If one finds in everyday life this greater awareness of self and of the external environment, life will be more interesting and exciting; doubtless mental health will be better and more resources will become available for coping with the inevitable stresses.

SUMMARY

The cognitive operations are those mental functions commonly involved in the discovery, awareness, rediscovery, or recognition of information in various forms, and in comprehension or understanding. According to Guilford's conceptualization, the cognitive abilities are visual cognition, auditory cognition, figural classification, figural relations, spatial orientation, visualization, perceptual foresight, symbol cognition, cognition of symbolic classes, symbolic relations, symbolic patterns, cognition of symbolic implications, verbal comprehension, conceptual classification, semantic relations, general reasoning, penetration, and conceptual foresight. The cognitive abilities are important in personality development and mental health. Guilford's conceptualization can form the basis for diagnosing and treating difficulties that arise from the faulty functioning of these mental processes. The conceptualization is also a source of ideas for improving the effectiveness of education.

Other conceptualizations are Maslow's concept of cognitive needs, Bloom's taxonomy of educational objectives in the cognitive domain, and concepts of cognitive styles, such as leveling-sharpening, tolerance for unrealistic experiences, equivalence range, focusing-scanning, constricted-flexible control, and field dependence-independence.

The cognitive abilities and styles are involved in becoming aware of dangerous conditions, removing fears of the unknown, structuring the situation, knowing what to do, maintaining a sense of worthwhileness, feedback of meanings as a guide to behavior, providing a basis for problem solving and decision making, using the less expensive energies, speeding recovery from shock, and increasing the enjoyment of life.

Developing and Freeing the Cognitive Abilities

14

Anyone who has tried to test the limits of his ability to become aware of his environment is shocked to find that he is ordinarily aware of an extremely small portion of what is happening about him. Often a person can see so much more in a photograph of something he has witnessed than he saw in the actual event as he experienced it personally. Why is this?

In this chapter, an effort will be made to present some of the answers to this question. First, the case will be presented for the necessity to exert effort in order to become more open and alive and more fully aware of the world. The necessity for motivation to become more aware will also be discussed. Next, an attempt will be made to summarize what is known through research about factors that reduce or increase the effectiveness of the cognitive operations. Finally, the author will propose some strategies for coping constructively with the factors that reduce awareness.

NECESSITY FOR EFFORT

Even though the cognitive operations may require less expensive energies in general than any of the other mental operations, their full functioning takes definite effort. To become fully aware of his world, a person must be alive, alert, and active, and have constructive attitudes. Awareness as used in this book implies getting under the surface of things, discounting the superficial, and establishing genuine contacts with reality.

CULTURAL DEMANDS FOR EFFORT

In many ways our culture places a low demand on effort. Technology has succeeded marvelously in sparing people from putting forth effort. Advertisements for electrical vibrators and other gadgets urge us to "exercise without effort." Children are discouraged in their efforts to learn more about their environments by cautions that "curiosity killed the cat." Later, such inquiring activities are referred to as "mere idle curiosity." It is even made a moral matter! Parents, teachers, and ministers tell us to "see no evil, hear no evil, speak no evil." They go to great lengths to prevent children from seeing and hearing evil. Thus, they teach in many ways to shut off vast areas of life from awareness and thereby discourage the search for truth.

Dorothy Lee (1960) has described a number of the ways by which various societies develop the motivation to learn. Her thesis is that cultural factors inhibit or encourage the development of the potential to learn—to cognize. She maintains that in her study of other societies, where motivational factors are strong, people in general continue to develop their potential to learn, work at learning on their own initiative, and pursue education until death. Learning occurs in such societies, even though formal education takes place under conditions that we would regard as extremely unfavorable to learning.

Lee found this high motivation in both literate and nonliterate societies. Among the Oglala Sioux she found that children were brought up from infancy to be aware of their responsibility for the camp circle and eventually for the entire universe. To carry out this responsibility they had to develop their capacities to the utmost. This urgency was communicated in such a way that this exercise of potential became something to be developed on one's own initiative. They were taught to use their senses to the utmost—to sit still and listen to that which they could not see; to smell, to touch, and to taste; and to become aware of that which was not obvious to the senses. There was emphasis on the personal, the individual. Everyone had a right to his own private, unfiltered experience. Children were taught to observe and to draw conclusions from their observations.

As a literate society with high motivation for learning, Lee chose the *shtetl* Jews of Eastern Europe. She found in this culture many similarities to the nonliterate Oglala culture. The individual was called upon for tremendous effort in developing capacity to learn or to aid in learning. One must learn in order to perform his duty to God and to carry out his responsibilities to his community. She found that in this culture children consistently learned to read before, according to American ideas, they could be biologically ready. They showed ability to concentrate before they could possibly have a long enough attention span. Originality was valued and exercised even though learning was acquired by imitation and repetition with hard discipline and a multitude of regulations. The learned man was a valued man.

Lee's research, however, does not answer questions about what the teacher can do to motivate learning—to activate cognitive needs—in cultures that do not offer strong incentives like those of the Oglala Sioux and the *shtetl* Jews of Eastern Europe. Thus, let us look at what is involved in activating cognitive needs and the factors in society which affect the desire to learn.

ACTIVATING COGNITIVE NEEDS

Mention has already been made of the position of cognitive needs in Maslow's (1954) hierarchy of needs. Physiological, safety, love, and status needs must be taken care of reasonably well before teachers can expect to activate cognitive needs. Or, cognitive needs may be activated, if the more demanding needs can be attained by achievement in the cognitive area. Generally we have frowned upon using such motivations. Nevertheless, no alert teacher can deny the fact that many of his pupils learn in their struggle to achieve status in the classroom, to win the affection of parents or teachers, or even to satisfy their needs for safety.

When teachers survey the needs of children in the classroom and search for the sources of tensions and anxieties, they almost always omit any mention of the physiological factors. One would wonder, however, if it is safe to assume automatically that these needs are satisfied. Many children do not have enough food, sleep, and rest. In the classroom they may experience discomfort from overheated and poorly ventilated rooms, prohibitions from getting water or relieving bladders, and the like. With the organism's tendency to permit only one strong need to dominate at the time, it is important that teachers be ever cognizant of the fact that children who are fatigued, hungry, thirsty, or deprived of status or love are not likely to be propelled by cognitive needs.

FACTORS AFFECTING DESIRE TO LEARN

Several common, cultural factors have been found to be related to desire to learn.

CULTURAL VALUES ON LEARNING. Mention has already been made of Dorothy Lee's arguments concerning the influence of cultural values on learning. Some schools develop a culture that places little value on learning. This is shown clearly in Coleman's (1961ab) intensive studies of the social climates of ten high schools. These ten schools represented a wide range of communities, ranging from small rural towns to large urban centers. Coleman used instruments that yielded measures of the extent to which various value climates existed in each school. Having good grades was far more important in the status system in some schools than in others. In some schools, athletic prowess, being popular with the girls, or having a car was more important than scholastic achievement in the status system for boys. Similarly, popularity with boys or beauty might be more important in the status system for girls. In general, boys who went all out scholastically were scorned and rebuked for working too hard. The athlete who failed to go all out was scorned and rebuked for not working hard enough.

Tannenbaum (1962) studied the same problem by examining differentially the attitudes of students concerning various aspects of giftedness: the brilliant vs. the average, the studious vs. the nonstudious, and the athlete vs. the nonathletes. He presented 615 juniors in a comprehensive metropolitan high school with written descriptions of stereotyped fictitious students. Each imaginary student was described in three sentences, each sentence exposing one of the two contrasting characteristics. On the basis of the characteristics attributed to each imaginary student, Tannenbaum computed a mean acceptability rating for each type with the following rankings from most acceptable to least acceptable:

1. Brilliant nonstudious athlete
2. Average nonstudious athlete
3. Average studious athlete
4. Brilliant studious athlete
5. Brilliant nonstudious nonathlete
6. Average nonstudious nonathlete
7. Average studious nonathlete
8. Brilliant studious nonathlete

Since students tend to develop along whatever lines they find rewarding, this value system is somewhat disturbing to people who consider educational achievement important. Coleman (1961b) adds that the values of the adolescent society are becoming more important today, since adolescents live more and more in their own society and find the family a less and less satisfying psychological home.

EMPHASES ON KINDS OF LEARNING. A school or a culture may place greater emphasis on certain kinds of learning than on others and may provide rewards accordingly. Such emphasis is likely to limit the areas in which individuals in a culture will become aware. For many years, the culture of the United States placed little value on the learning of foreign languages. Enrollments in foreign language courses decreased. Many colleges eliminated foreign languages as a requirement for admission. Teachers found it difficult to motivate pupils to master a foreign language. Now the situation has changed vastly. The Federal government has provided large grants to establish foreign language laboratories in schools and colleges and to support institutes for training teachers of foreign languages. Similar emphases have shifted values in connection with science and mathematics.

These emphases doubtless affect values on other types of learning such as social studies, literature, and art.

SEX ROLE EXPECTATIONS. Research has consistently shown that in our culture boys and girls differ greatly in what they feel free to learn. For example, Gowan (1957) found twice as much underachievement among boys as girls. Bowman (1960) found three times as many girls as boys among the top ten per cent in grade-point average. The sex differences may be explained by the fact that the openness and sensitivity required in the full functioning of the cognitive operations is a distinctly feminine value in our culture. Young boys are unable to cope with the stressfulness of the taboo against sensitivity without sacrificing their achievement. It is only when boys accept professional and other goals requiring learning that their capacities for awareness are free to develop. Thus, in college, boys begin to show scholastic superiority. Inevitably the reduced awarenesses must take a toll on the mental health of both boys and girls.

In certain areas, cultural taboos limit the awareness of girls, particularly in science and mathematics. Often little girls say, "I'm a girl. I'm not supposed to know anything about things like that." The author heard such remarks repeatedly when he used science toys as stimulus materials in one of his small-group experiments with elementary school children. Fourth and fifth grade girls were especially reluctant to deal with the science toys. During a 25-minute period of free investigation, boys produced over twice as many cognitions as did girls in the first experiments in the spring of 1959. A year later, however, marked changes were noted. In some schools, girls began to feel quite free to deal with these materials, to produce as many cognitions about them as did boys, and to express as much satisfaction in the activity as did boys. Interestingly, however, when the members of five-person groups (usually consisting of two boys and three girls or three boys and two girls) were asked to evaluate the contribution of each member to the success of the group, the evaluation of the contributions of boys was higher than that of girls (Torrance, 1963). Apparently, between 1959 and 1960 a cultural change made it "all right" for girls to "play with" science materials and to enjoy doing so, but the ideas of boys in this area were still more highly valued.

RACIAL AND ETHNIC ORIGIN. A number of studies have shown differences in achievement motivation among different racial and ethnic groups. Rosen (1959) found that Jews, white Protestants, and Greeks scored higher in achievement motivation than did Negroes, French Canadians, and Italians. Some of the author's students working with homogeneous groupings reported that they experienced difficulty in getting non-Jewish students to even stay in high achieving groups. They were unwilling to exert the

231

effort to compete with Jewish students of equal ability. Bowman (1960) found ethnic and racial differences in achievement in extracurricular fields but not in academic fields. Negro students have consistently appeared in large numbers on athletic teams and in the band. In the third grade of a segregated Negro school in the South, the author found that almost all of the boys stated that they wanted to be professional athletes of some type. In most schools, such aspirations are rare among third graders. Anne Roe (1960) has pointed out the relative absence of Catholics among eminent scientists.

SOCIAL CLASSES. In general, studies have shown even greater differences in achievement motivation among the social classes than among racial and ethnic groups. Rosen (1959), for example, obtained such a finding. Even when corrections are made for ability, high school students from the lower socioeconomic classes make much lower grades than those from the middle classes and very few students from the lower socioeconomic classes go to college. Bowman relates a typical incident in which a high school teacher tried to interest a gifted ninth grade boy from the lower socioeconomic class in staying in school. He replied to the teacher, "My brother left school three years ago and is now a bricklayer. He works from six to eight hours a day and makes more money than you do. He doesn't have to grade papers at night. He has a job the year round and doesn't have to go to school in the summer. I have a chance to be an apprentice bricklayer. What more could I want?" (Bowman, 1960, p. 44).

OTHER FACTORS AFFECTING DESIRE TO LEARN. Religion, geographical region, self-concepts, age, and grade have all been found to influence the desire to learn. Some studies (Bowman, 1960) suggest that the desire to learn is strong among Unitarians, Congregationalists, Presbyterians, Episcopalians, and Jews. A greater percentage of high school graduates in the East go to college than in some Southern and Midwestern states. Self-concepts influence what one is likely to strive to know. Certain facts are supposed to be kept from those who are too young or too undeveloped educationally to know.

There are also special problems in motivating highly gifted children and mentally retarded children to learn. Peer pressures against gifted children who excel apparently cause many gifted children to reduce their awareness. Inability to compete in a regular classroom has a similar effect on children of limited ability. The author has been amazed at the performance of low-ability groups when classes are arranged into homogeneous groups according to either mental age or creative-thinking abilities. In five-person groups working with the science toys, the group of lowest ability almost always turned in a good performance and in some classes came up with a larger number of cognitions than any of the other groups.

FACTORS REDUCING COGNITIVE FUNCTIONING

It is convenient to organize the factors that reduce the effectiveness of the cognitive operations into physical and psychological or emotional factors. Among the physical factors are these:

1. Defective senses.
2. Alcohol and drugs.
3. Fatigue and loss of sleep.
4. Pain.
5. Undisciplined or overdisciplined senses.
6. Temperature extremes, hunger, thirst.

Among the psychological or emotional factors are these:

1. Excessive anxiety.
2. Fear, rage, anger, hate, love.
3. Prejudice.
4. Tradition.
5. Taboos.
6. Conformity pressures.
7. Defense mechanisms.

Some of the factors of most direct importance in education will be discussed briefly.

DEFECTIVE SENSES

Man is highly dependent on his senses for knowing about things. Any sensory deprivation limits awareness and is stressful. The organism is deprived of some of the material resources from which the cognitive abilities develop. This reduction in the total functioning places an imposition on the balance and equilibrium of all psychological processes. When one type of sensing is lacking, the operation of all of the others is changed. Apparently such alterations occur naturally and unknowingly, because survival itself would be in jeopardy otherwise.

The degree of sensory impairment, the age at which it occurs, and the like determine the nature and extent of the adaptations that must be made. Usually, the resulting process of adaptation brings about a sharpening of some of the other senses. The basic problem of adaptation, of course, is in maintaining contact with the environment—maintaining one's anchors in reality.

233

THE DEAF CHILD. Myklebust (1960) * reports that the deaf child playing with a toy keeps looking up to scan the environment to assure himself that changes in the environment are not unduly threatening and to determine the meaning of the changes. He also scans whenever there are minor changes in the visual field, such as changes in light. Because he has only one of the senses used in maintaining contact with the environment at a distance he must look up and explore essentially all changes in the visual field. It is only in this way that he can maintain his anchors in reality. Early in life, the deaf child learns through startling, frightening experiences (Myklebust, 1960, p. 52) that environmental changes occur which cannot be monitored visually. He develops greater dependence upon his close senses (smell, taste, and touch). Vibrations also become signals. Nonverbal criteria, such as the Kohs Block Test, indicate that deafness does not influence the cognitive operations.

THE BLIND CHILD. Just as the deaf child uses vision, the blind child uses audition to maintain his contact with the distant environment. He uses it for both background and foreground purposes. Myklebust (1960, p. 53) observes that although the blind child might be speaking to someone he will interrupt his conversation and listen, if he hears a sound in the background. After the background sound has been identified and the situation restructured satisfactorily, he will resume his conversation and play. Often the situation requires further exploration to avoid threat, to satisfy curiosity, and to increase general satisfaction. To obtain the further information, he is likely to use the tactile sense. He may also use his sense of smell in a more direct manner than the deaf child, but he is less dependent upon vibratory sensation than the deaf child.

THE COLOR-BLIND CHILD. The sight limitations of the color-blind child create a multitude of problems. About 2,000,000 people in the United States suffer from some form of color-blindness. By far the majority of these are males and about 99 per cent have color-blindness of the red-green type. Although they cannot be cured, color-blind individuals can be helped to adapt and to make good guesses at distinguishing colors. This defect should be detected early before it has produced psychological difficulties. Any child who shows signs of confusing colors should be referred to a qualified physician. In the classroom the color-blind child finds it impossible to select the correct crayon in art work. On the playground he sees the colors in the target of the dart game as merged and he sees no bull's-eye. Traffic lights may give him trouble. When color is used as a teaching aid, the color-blind child may be penalized for mistakes that are not really his fault.

* Paraphrased from H. Myklebust, *The Psychology of Deafness: Sensory Deprivation Learning and Adjustment* (New York: Grune & Stratton, 1960). By permission.

Any other defect in any of the senses, such as poor depth perception, nearsightedness, farsightedness, or the like, limits one's awareness and brings out changes in techniques of adaptation. If not handled properly, any of these conditions are likely to have negative effects on personality development and mental functioning.

ALCOHOL AND DRUGS

Alcohol and drugs are chemical means of reducing awareness. Included are tranquilizer drugs, sedatives, and narcotics. In using alcohol as a mental hygiene prop, a person tries to blot out awarenesses from which he would like to escape. Research has shown that even small amounts of alcohol produce a kind of tunnel vision. That is, the individual tends to see only what is in front of him. Since so much of one's awareness is destroyed by alcohol, even moderate use of it may make driving an automobile or an airplane a serious danger. The use of alcohol may reduce performance on any kind of job.

Tranquilizers and other drugs can be used with essentially normal individuals during periods of anxiety to restore calm and reduce agitation. A part of the individual's awareness is removed and the world thus becomes less threatening. This respite from prolonged stress gives the individual the time he needs to recoup his resources and develop better strategies for coping with his problems. In more serious cases, the use of tranquilizer drugs may enable the patient to establish communication with a psychotherapist and thus to begin work on his basic problems. Experience has shown that, properly used, drugs can be used to decrease psychomotor activity and to produce mental tranquility without clouding of consciousness or impairment of faculties. But still, parts of one's awareness are temporarily reduced.

FATIGUE AND LOSS OF SLEEP

One of the first behavioral signs of fatigue is that the individual makes errors and is not aware of them. Obviously, this means that he is not aware of some of the customary cues with which he maintains contact with his environment, and mental health is threatened.

PAIN

Individuals severely injured in emergencies frequently fail to discover or report their injuries until long afterwards, although the injuries might ordinarily be disabling. This phenomenon is a further illustration of the ingenious protective function of pain. Man uses small amounts of pain as signals to tolerate certain amounts of pain and to defend himself against excessive amounts. Apparently the organism's basic technique of adaptation to pain is through the cognitive control of focusing or what Schachtel

(1954) calls "focal attention." In various types of discomfort, man shows the capacity to center his attention on one object fully. In pain, focus is on a particular direction, rather than on the whole field. The direction is determined by a particular object (external or internal, such as a thought or feeling). There may be several renewed approaches to the object. Most characteristic, however, is the shutting out of the rest of the field from awareness.

UNDISCIPLINED OR OVERDISCIPLINED SENSES

Both undisciplined and overdisciplined senses may result in shutting out areas of awareness. When the author has asked students or research assistants to make and report observations, he has almost always found that the results indicate that their senses are grossly undisciplined. They are "sloppy" or "careless" in their observations. They do not see one tenth of what happens. This shutting out of awareness of so much of the environment is a reflection of the way they live. Men undergoing survival training frequently say in amazement that their senses have become much keener as a result of the training.

Senses may also be overdisciplined with the explicit purpose of screening out the unpleasant from awareness. A vivid description of this process is given by Colonel E. B. Miller in his account of his experiences on Bataan during World War II:

> I did more concentrating in that last hour of sun treatment than I have ever done before or since. It was a gruelling task—and what a subject to concentrate on! I took each calendar month, day by day, and tried to remember birthdays—holidays—any day that had a special meaning. That concentration must have been deep, because by the time I reached September, the sun was no more, and the cool of the evening was upon us. And my mind was intensely alert. That lesson helped me many times, in the months and years spent in Jap prisons! The body may be imprisoned but not the mind (E. B. Miller, 1949, pp. 223–24).

Education can doubtless go much further than it has in helping children to discipline their senses and thereby improve their cognitive operations.

TEMPERATURE EXTREMES, HUNGER, THIRST

The research concerning adaptation to temperature extremes, hunger, thirst, and the like indicates that the process in each is very much like adaptation to pain and reactions under conditions of fatigue. Awareness is focused on some limited area of experience and all other areas are screened out. Only one of the really basic, strong needs seems to dominate attention at the time. In general, these automatic controls have survival value. At times, however, they may cause a person to neglect too long basic survival

236

needs. For example, one fighter pilot downed on a small island off Korea (Blair, 1955) was so concerned with his safety needs and tried so hard to attract rescue aircraft that he almost forgot to take care of his needs for food. At the end of about two weeks, he noticed that his arms and legs had become almost skin and bones. Suddenly, he realized that he had almost starved himself to death. It was only then that he investigated fully the food resources of the island, finding quantities of rice, beans, and other food. Finally, he chased birds and a cat to eke out a diet.

EXCESSIVE ANXIETY

Since the research on anxiety and learning has seldom given consideration to the intensity and duration of the anxiety, it is exceedingly difficult to interpret. Sarason and his associates (1960), in attempting to summarize studies relating anxiety and intelligence report that studies which show that anxiety interferes with intelligence are more numerous and more sophisticated and impressive than those showing a positive relationship or no relationship. As the author has been able to interpret the evidence, the effects of anxiety on the cognitive operations seem to be the same as for any stress. Small amounts of anxiety are likely to increase the effectiveness of the cognitive operations, but large amounts are likely to result in loss of contact with the environment and confusion. In terms of duration, the sudden onset of anxiety can be expected to reduce greatly the effectiveness of the cognitive operations and to be followed by overcompensation and ultimately by a breakdown of the cognitive operations, if the anxiety is unrelieved.

FEAR, RAGE, ANGER, HATE, LOVE

All of the strong emotions such as fear, rage, anger, hate, and love apparently blot out large areas of awareness and cause some degree of loss of contact with the environment. In all of them, a person is overstimulated in some way, but their effect on the cognitive operations must be seen in terms of the total adaptive situation of the individual. One must look first to the nature of the conditions eliciting these strong responses which engage so much of the organism's energies. Fear provides a good example. William James (1890) stated that fear was stimulated by certain noises, strange men, strange animals, some kinds of vermin, solitude, black things, dark places, holes and corners, high places, certain ideas about the supernatural, and human corpses. It will be noted that all of these stimuli have elements that reduce the individual's contact with his environment, or his anchors in reality. Thus, the organism must cope with conditions that threaten its control. He does not know how to deal with them. Rage, anger, and other strong emotions are elicited by similar kinds of overstimulation. Hate and love are also accompanied by both visceral and psychological signs of emotional excitement. In both, awarenesses may be heightened in certain areas but in general will be limited, as in "focal attention." In other words, the scanning necessary for optimal contact with reality is reduced.

PREJUDICE

Prejudice of any kind—racial, religious, class, professional, and the like—tends to limit and focalize awareness. Prejudice, as defined by Gordon W. Allport (1960, pp. 220–21), is an almost universal syndrome characterized by two essential features. The first is an affective disposition that causes one to lean toward or away from an object (person, idea, place, etc.). The second is the basing of love or hate on beliefs that are wholly or partially erroneous. For example, the belief in witchcraft was based upon an incorrect diagnosis of distress. Once established, the prejudice was maintained by fighting off the awareness of information that might contradict it and emphasizing information that would support it. Both of the characteristics identified by Allport reduce contacts with reality and thereby affect mental functioning.

TRADITION

Traditions, status, family, and the like function in shutting off great areas of awareness in much the same way as prejudices. A tradition tends to remain unquestioned and thus shapes and biases a person's perceptions of reality. The tradition causes him to blot out from awareness information that would show errors in the solution established through tradition. Similarly, persons of status and power have been proved over time to be correct in most instances. Their ideas and information will be accepted without questioning. Thus, a person does not even become aware of the superior ideas or more accurate information of individuals of lesser status. He discredits his own perceptions of reality in favor of those of individuals of high status.

TABOOS

A number of taboos have already been mentioned and have been shown to reduce awareness and contact with reality. Taboos place certain kinds of experiencing off limits and become so practiced that they may act in much the same way as blindness or deafness. A variety of experiments, however, have been conducted to develop ways of reducing such perceptual defenses and increasing awareness. An interesting illustration is afforded by an experiment by Lacy, Lewinger, and Adamson (1953) on foreknowledge as a factor affecting perceptual defense and alertness regarding obscene taboo words. They used a carefully calibrated tachistoscopic method of presenting 15 obscene taboo words and 15 infrequently encountered non-taboo words. The subjects were university graduate students. Recognition thresholds were determined in an effort to test the hypothesis that the speed with which words are reported depends on the nature of the subject's expectations and the time of the presentation and that this dependence is more marked in the case of taboo than nontaboo words. In two studies, each involving 30 subjects, it was found that the taboo words were less easily recognized than the nontaboo words when subjects had no reason to expect to see emotion-arousing words, and that when such an expectation existed the taboo words were the more easily recognized. In helping children maintain optimal contact with reality, teachers may frequently have to arouse expectations for phenomena that are likely to have been blotted out of their awareness by taboos. Such procedures might be especially useful in the training of counselors, nurses, and others whose effective functioning requires that they be aware of emotion-arousing words and experiences.

CONFORMITY PRESSURES

Sullivan's concept of the phases of interpersonal development shows the importance of pressures for conformity. At about age nine, the child develops an accentuated need for consensual validation. He checks his perceptions of reality with other people. Pressures to conformity become an increasingly strong force in his efforts to maintain contact with the environment and easily threaten his anchors in reality. This phenomenon has been demonstrated in a number of studies, but perhaps most dramatically in the experiments of Asch (1958). These experiments indicate that even in matters of fact such as in judging the length of lines only about 25 per cent of the subjects held to their own correct perceptions in the face of majority disagreement. These experiments and their significance will be discussed in greater detail in Chapter 19.

DEFENSE MECHANISMS

In a sense, almost all of the defense mechanisms are devices of the organism for reducing awareness of certain realities in order to remain more comfortable. Thus, all of these reactions reduce or interfere with the cognitive operations. The same may be said for certain personality characteristics such as authoritarianism. For example, a study by Juul (Titus and Hollander, 1957) shows that authoritarian attitudes (as measured by the California F-Scale) interfere with the acquisition of knowledge on child psychology and teaching practices. It was Juul's hypothesis that "many of the concepts and attitudes expressed by teachers and textbooks in courses in child psychology and mental hygiene constitute a serious threat to the equilibrium of the inner world of the authoritarian individual. In organizing his experiences, he is therefore forced to exclude, distort, repress, or otherwise fit every situation, event, and person into his framework and need structure" (Titus and Hollander, 1957, p. 50).

STRATEGIES FOR IMPROVING COGNITIVE OPERATIONS

A variety of training devices has been developed for helping individuals improve their cognitive operations by becoming more fully aware of their environments. Industrial organizations conduct what some of them label "sensitivity training." "Listening training" is another innovation designed to increase awareness and strengthen contact with the environment. Psychotherapy, too, can be looked upon as a procedure whereby one's contact with reality is established and the individual becomes more fully aware.

The strategies outlined in Chapter 12 are all useful in improving the cognitive operations. *Risking* is necessary in becoming aware of or familiar with new stimuli, especially the threatening ones. There are also times when one must stop—even *avoid*—in order to be open, to become aware. *Mastery* of fundamental skills is also necessary before many types of awareness are possible. This is why programs in remedial reading, arithmetic, and the like are so important to the functioning of the cognitive operations. Many other kinds of mastery are also essential to achieving one's potentialities insofar as cognition is concerned. It is also necessary *to fail* and to learn to cope with failure in order to achieve this potentiality. Problems of *overloading* are especially crucial. There are limits to the organism's ability to process information. The information may be presented at too great a speed. The discriminations required may be too difficult. Prior deprivations may have prepared the individual poorly for receiving the information. Too many pieces of information may be presented simultaneously, making it impossible for the individual to process all of them. If overloading occurs, it may be necessary *to unload* by "blowing a fuse," fainting, amnesia, catharsis, or some other similar technique. It may be necessary *to deny certain needs*—especially immediate needs for comfort—in order to maintain full contact with the environment. Or, it may be necessary *to make peace* between conflicting needs for security and cognitive needs. Finally, there are problems of *continuing the struggle* to maintain contact with the environment after fatigue begins to set in.

EDUCATIONAL APPLICATIONS

Numerous pieces of educational research are directly relevant to problems of increasing the effectiveness of the cognitive operations. The technology of constructing achievement tests to assess growth of the cognitive operations in a content area has been fairly well developed. The multiple-choice item is relied upon primarily for this purpose. Many educators erroneously assume, however, that multiple-choice items can be used only to measure the acquisition of facts or definitions or to recognize bits of knowledge. Stecklein (1956) has shown how multiple-choice items can be used to measure a number of other types of cognitions, including applications (relations), recognition of assumptions, comprehension and analysis, recognition of inferences (implications), analogous reasoning, and even operations outside the cognition area. This list could be expanded considerably by using as a guide the factors involved in the cognitive operations, as outlined in Chapter 13.

A number of techniques have been devised for reducing anxiety in classroom examinations of this type in order to free the cognitive operations for more effective functioning. Test constructors have long been advised to make the first few items in an examination easy in order to relieve some of the pent-up anxiety so that the mind can function. McKeachie, Pollie, and Speisman (1955) have experimented with another technique. They encouraged students to write comments concerning the examination items instead of using only the conventional answer sheet. Results showed that students who wrote comments about their questions made higher scores than their controls who used only the conventional answer sheets. The difference was especially significant in the second half of the test, after anxiety resulting from frustration had accumulated. Apparently this device diminished the frustrating effects of failing items during the earlier part of the test. By restructuring some of the items so they could cope with them, the subjects apparently discharged some of the tensions that limit awareness.

SUMMARY

Even though cognition may require less expensive energy than the other mental operations, a high level of cognition requires definite expenditures of energy. Tests have indicated that man is ordinarily aware of only a small proportion of his immediate environment. Research has shown that cultures differ in their emphases on cognition. Theoretically such basic needs as survival, safety, love, and status must be reasonably well satisfied before cognitive needs function naturally. The desire to learn is affected by the values of the culture on learning, emphases on particular kinds of learning, sex role expectations, racial and ethnic origins, social class, religion, geographical region, self-concepts, age, and the like.

Cognitive functioning may be reduced by such physical factors as defective senses, alcohol, drugs, fatigue, loss of sleep, pain, undisciplined senses, temperature extremes, hunger, and thirst. It may also be reduced by such psychological factors as excessive anxiety, fear, rage, anger, hate, love, prejudice, tradition, taboos, conformity pressures, and defense mechanisms.

241

A variety of training devices have been developed for helping persons improve their cognitive operations by becoming more fully aware of their environments (sensitivity training, listening training, etc.). The author proposes the application of strategies of coping with stress: risking, avoiding, mastery of fundamental skills, experiencing failure (accepting challenge), overloading, unloading, denying certain needs, making peace with conflicting needs, and persistent effort.

Role of

Memory in

Coping with Stress

15

In Plato's *Phaedus,* King Thamus bitterly attacked the invention of the alphabet. His argument was that it would produce forgetfulness in the minds of those who learn to use it, because they would not practice their memories. In other words, he was afraid that the minds of men would deteriorate, if they could record things and not have to remember everything. In spite of the fears of King Thamus, the alphabet did not eliminate interest in education concerning the cultivation of the memory. In recent years, however, many educators have vigorously attacked practices that require children to memorize or to remember facts and ideas. The decrease in emphasis on memory in education, nevertheless, appears to have been compensated for by an increase in the number of courses on how to remember in business and industry, the military services, and adult education. Many popular magazines and newspapers carry advertisements of correspondence courses and books on how to improve the memory.

The author of one well-known memory method wrote as follows in 1958:

> A highly developed memory is one of a child's chief assets. It brings him high marks in school and gives him confidence, determination and poise: the keys to personal and social success. Most of all, it gives children an ability which will set the groundwork for their future success in the business and professional worlds (Hayes, 1958, p. 9).

Although Hayes speaks from the bias of a man who is known as a "memory wizard" and teaches courses and writes books on how to develop the memory, it must not be denied that a good memory has its reward. In most schools, the child who recites a poem is still admired more than one who simply reads it or interprets it. The pupil who knows the answer is admired more than the one who knows where to look it up. The mathematician who can do a problem in his head is admired rather than one with a slide rule or calculating machine, or in "original" ways rather than by a strict application of rules. Aside from the rewards of society, memory has obvious values in maintaining mental health. Before going into these, however, let us see what is involved in remembering.

WHAT IS MEMORY?

Since the days of Plato, many scholars have given attention to the nature of memory. Only in recent years, however, have they begun even to identify the different mental abilities involved in remembering or in the nature of the process underlying remembering. Basic to any theory of remembering is a conceptualization of the process that enables a person to use his past experiences. Plato compared memory to an impression upon a wax tablet (Paul, 1959). Ever since that time, various interpretations of memory "trace" have been used in describing the process of remembering. Before discussing these variations and our present understanding of the memory abilities and the process of remembering, let us try to remember something and see what we can learn from the experience.

First, read the following explanation; then look carefully at the photograph on page 245. The boys pictured in the photograph are a part of a group of 50 high-achieving sixth graders being taught how to do research by the author (Torrance and Myers, 1962). To begin to understand the concept of the research process, they had been engaged in finding out what was in the box. After making guesses, shaking the box, smelling the box, assaying its weight, listening to the object inside sliding about, revising their guesses and making new guesses, asking questions, and revising their guesses, they finally determined the identity of the object inside the box. As these boys were caught by the camera, they were verifying their answer by opening the box and examining the object. After this, they were led to formulate the stages in the process and to apply them to the solution of other problems by the research process.

After looking at the picture, answer the questions in the Photographic Memory Test on page 247.

Now that you have tested yourself, try to figure out what happened. What was the nature of the mental operation you performed? What went wrong to prevent your remembering the answers you missed? Were you able to remember some details that had not really come into conscious awareness when you first looked at the photograph? You might find it useful to jot down your own ideas before reading the conceptualization of the memory process and of the abilities involved in memory, according to Guilford's work.

THE PROCESS OF REMEMBERING

As already indicated, most attempts to describe the process of remembering have involved some interpretation of the trace theory which Plato held. In brief, the trace theories in some way assume memory to be the function of a bundle of rigid, unchanging traces (Katona, 1940, p. 104). Each event experienced by a person is supposed to leave a trace behind. These traces are conceived as a true picture or a true copy of the event itself, just as the photograph at the top of page was a true picture or copy of an event. It has also been generally assumed that these traces are stored in definite locations until they fade or become blurred with the passing of time. The concept of traces has also been used in the sense of an aftereffect that is in dynamic interaction with older traces, new processes, and new traces.

Katona (1940, pp. 194–204) uses the term "trace" only as a carrier of the connection between events and thus provides a transition from the more classical trace theories to the structural or schema theories that have been emerging in recent years. He distinguished between "individual traces" and "structural traces," using individual traces to refer to specific items of past experience and structural traces to refer to experiences connected with and derived from the whole character of a process. He maintained that individual traces are characterized by a certain degree of fixation and rigidity and that structural traces are more readily adaptable and flexible. The formation of individual traces, according to Katona, is usually a long and

245

strenuous process, while understanding may lead quickly and with less effort to the formation of structural traces. Structural traces are thought to persist longer than individual traces, which disappear quickly unless reinforced.

Since Katona's concept of traces is derived from their effect, the only proof of the existence of a trace is that remembering is found to be a reconstruction, not a pure construction, or that it represents reproductive thinking rather than productive thinking. Katona uses the example of remembering card tricks. A subject listened to an explanation of the card tricks and several weeks later took tests that indicated that he understood and remembered in a general way the procedure required to perform the card trick. He did not, however, remember the actual words or even the individual steps performed. Thus, the single presentation of the explanation of the card tricks resulted in a structural trace, a general trace including the entire explanation. Of course, the entire procedure could have been learned "by heart," but this would have taken much longer than the formation of a structural trace. The card trick illustration also showed that the structural trace is adapted to many situations, persists for a long period of time, has organization, and represents a condensed version of the events.

Sir Frederick Bartlett (1932) was one of the first investigators to propose a schema theory to replace trace theories. One of Bartlett's major theses was that cognitive functioning cannot be understood unless studied in the light of interests, attitudes, affects, and goals. He supported his thesis by a vast amount of observation in natural situations and by well-controlled experiments. He was particularly critical of research involving meaningless and unconnected materials as stimuli (e.g., nonsense syllables). Bartlett's observations and experiments demonstrated that "the perception and recollection of complex, extended experiences are rarely literal or precise, but are regularly influenced and shaped by processes like 'rationalization,' 'effort after meaning,' and 'fit,' directed by attitudes, interests, and effects" (Paul, 1959, p. 4). Bartlett believed that the process of remembering is complex, and that the mind cannot be considered as a mere storehouse of discrete traces.

As a substitute for the concept of trace, Bartlett borrowed the concept of schema from neurology. Neurologists had defined schema as "an internal postural mode—unified and constantly modified by every incoming sensation evoked by postural changes—which furnishes a basis for the perception and recognition of postural changes" (Paul, 1959, p. 4). Bartlett saw schemata as internal organizations of past reactions and experiences that function as unified and active organs. An essential feature of this conception is that the mind is seen as made up of schemata about the world rather than of images or traces of the world. Thus, recall is not a reproduction *of* a schema, but is an active construction *based upon* a schema.

Recently, Paul (1959) has attempted to extend Bartlett's work and fill

Photographic Memory Test

1. How many of the boys' faces can be seen, at least in part?
2. How many of them are wearing glasses?
3. How many of them seem to be interested in verifying the identity of the object in the box?
4. Is the boy holding the box wearing glasses?
5. Is he wearing a sweater?
6. How many of the boys are wearing ties?
7. Is the boy at the far left wearing a watch?
8. Which boy's left hand is touching the box top?
9. What is he holding with his right hand?
10. Which boy is reaching for the object that has been in the box?
11. How many of the boys show loss of teeth?
12. How many of the boys are visibly apathetic and uninterested in the activity?
13. Are these boys overly restrained by rules for sitting straight in their seats?
14. Is the collar of the boy holding the box unbuttoned?

(Answers on page 249)

in some of the gaps that occurred in it. Paul felt that Bartlett did not give enough attention to process and to individual differences in remembering. Paul's first experiment was a replication of Bartlett's famous study that resulted in the conclusion that reproductions are essentially active reconstructions based on schemata. Bartlett and Paul both used as one of the main stimuli an Indian folk tale, "The War of the Ghosts." To the subjects, this story was unfamiliar in content and style and it has many gaps and ambiguities. Bartlett had used the serial reproduction method of transmitting a story through a chain of subjects, like the spread of gossip or rumor.

In his replication of Bartlett's experiment, Paul attempted to find out whether the gaps and ambiguities of the story were responsible for the tremendous distortions and fragmentations and what role the unfamiliarity of the story played in these distortions. To answer these questions, Paul used the original version of the Ghost Story, a revised version of the Ghost Story in which the gaps and ambiguities of the story are reduced, and the Secretary Story, which is similar in many respects to the Ghost Story but contains more familiar actors and actions. All three stories were transmitted through serial reproduction chains. He found that all three stories underwent considerable collapse and distortion, but that the revised Ghost Story fared better than the original Ghost Story and that the Secretary Story was remembered better than either of the Ghost Stories. He found further that the gaps and ambiguities were crucial places for forgetting and distortion and caused much reshuffling and rebalancing of material. He identified two types of reshuffling and rebalancing: (1) skeletonizations (stripping, fragmenting, and segregating) and (2) importations (the addition of material, often extraneous but seldom conceptually unrelated). From these findings, he drew several tentative conclusions, which he tested further through three other experiments. Explication (reducing the gaps and ambiguities), familiarity, and coherence were the primary variables with which he dealt—all three proved to facilitate remembering, and their absence led to fragmentation, distortion, and forgetting.

Paul (1959, pp. 140–42) reports that he found ample evidence of the active schema process that Bartlett considered so important. He concluded that the phenomena observed can be better conceptualized as active constructions based upon schema organization rather than as the reproduction of a trace system. His conclusion places more emphasis upon the articulating, abstracting, and comprehending aspect of the remembering process. The schema concept further emphasizes that internal dispositions function in neither a passive nor piecemeal way. Instead, these internal dispositions take the form of active processes such as seeking meaning (i.e., connectedness), striving after "fit" (i.e., context), and the like.

An attempt will now be made to relate conceptualizations of mental abilities to the foregoing conceptualizations of the process of remembering.

THE MEMORY ABILITIES

The memory factors that Guilford and his associates (Guilford and Merrifield, 1960) have identified and measured will be described briefly. This is done in the belief that if one has a meaningful way of conceptualizing the abilities involved in remembering, he will be able to figure out more satisfactorily what happens when he remembers.

VISUAL MEMORY

Visual memory is one of the factors involved in remembering or recalling units. One of the test tasks requires the subject to reproduce a geometric design, after having seen it on a flash card. The figure shown in Figure 15–1, though not a part of the test of Reproduction of Designs used by Guilford, has been used in a number of experiments (Koffka, 1935) and can be used to test visual memory. Take a quick look at it, close the book, and see how accurately you can draw this figure. Now check carefully to see how many errors in reproduction you made. What was the nature of these errors?

248

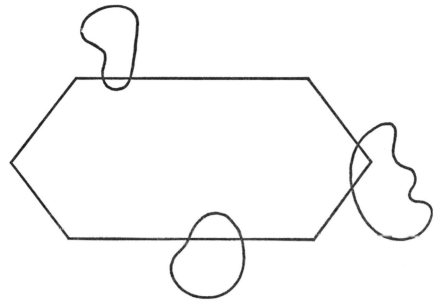

*Figure 15–1. Design for Visual Memory Test Task (From
K. Koffka,* Principles of Gestalt Psychology, *1935, p. 156,
used by permission of Harcourt, Brace & World, Inc.)*

A second task for assessing visual memory is the Map Memory task, in
which the subject must select the map section most similar to the part of a
map viewed previously. Similar types of tasks are found in popular magazines. This kind of memory is of course useful in orienting oneself geo-
graphically and fits nicely into the schema and structured trace concept of
remembering.

AUDITORY MEMORY

Auditory memory is another factor for remembering units. One task is
a test of memory for musical compositions and the other assesses ability to
recognize rhythmic patterns of taps. Involved in both of these tasks is the

Answers to Photographic Memory Test		
1. Eight	7. Yes	11. None
2. Three	8. Smaller boy wearing	12. None
3. All eight	glasses, fourth front	13. No
4. No	row	14. No
5. No	9. Notebook and pen	
6. None	10. Boy at far left	

ability to recall or recognize patterns in perceived sequences of auditory stimuli. Such abilities are important when one's guides to behavior come from sound patterns or sequences.

MEMORY FOR SPATIAL ORDER

Memory for spatial order is one of the factors for remembering classes and falls in the figural column. The Space Memory task requires the subject to identify the form that was located in each of the five sections within five squares previously studied. The Position Memory task requires the subject to recall the position of number-word combinations approximately four hours after the initial administration of the test.

MEMORY SPAN

Memory span is one of the factors for remembering units and involves the ability to recall immediately a series of symbolic elements in correct order after a single exposure. One of the two tasks used to measure this ability requires the subject to repeat a given series of digits, and the other, a given series of letters. The task involving repetition of digits appears in several tests of psychological functioning and is commonly used as an indicator of impairment due to anxiety.

ROTE MEMORY

Rote memory (Guilford, 1959a) is the ability to remember units of material in naturally meaningless connections. In one of the four tasks used as tests of this ability, the subject is asked to recall the number paired with a given picture in a previously presented, differently ordered, list. In a second, he has to recall the number paired with a given word in a previously presented, differently ordered, list. In a third, he has to recall the first name paired with a given last name in a previously presented, differently ordered, list. In the fourth, he is asked to perform a similar operation with colors.

MEMORY FOR IDEAS

Memory for ideas (Guilford, 1959a) is the ability to reproduce previously presented ideas, not verbatim. In one task, the subject is asked questions regarding meaningful details of a previously studied picture. (The Photographic Memory Test, which appears in this chapter, is similar to this task.) In the other task, the subject is called upon to reproduce a brief, one-paragraph story in his own words, after hearing it. Such a task appears in a number of intelligence tests such as the Stanford-Binet and other psychological assessment batteries.

MEANINGFUL MEMORY

Meaningful memory (Guilford, 1959a) is the ability to remember meaningful connections between units of material. In one task, the subject supplies a missing word in each of 40 sentences previously studied. In the other, he recalls the second noun of a previously studied, related pair.

MEMORY FOR TEMPORAL ORDER

Memory for temporal order (Guilford, 1959a) is the ability to remember the order in which events occurred. In one of the tasks to assess this ability, the subject is asked to recall on which of four study pages of a previously administered test each of 48 drawings appeared. In another task, for each pair of test titles, the subject indicates which test was administered first in a battery given three days previously.

Now, the reader might want to reflect again on his performance on the Photographic Memory Test. Basically, this task is one of Memory of Ideas. Actually, however, it is a rather complex task. What other memory abilities were used in making responses? What abilities were not used that might have been useful in this case?

COMMON CAUSES FOR MEMORY FAILURES

Perhaps more important than the abilities and the process involved in remembering are the factors that cause these abilities to fail to function. Some of the more common causes will now be reviewed.

INCOMPLETENESS OF LEARNING

The reader's failure to answer some of the questions on the Photographic Memory Test may have been due simply to the fact that the details had not been correctly, clearly, and forcibly impressed on his mind. He may not have noticed the details in question. Answers to the questions may have required finer discriminations than he is accustomed to making. This incompleteness may have been due to the fact that he was not interested in the situation that had been photographed. Or, there may have been distractions while he was making his observations. Or, some particular feature, such as the lack of desks or the fact that the children were not sitting "properly" in their seats may have attracted all of his attention.

A PROBLEM OF RECALL RATHER THAN RETENTION

The problem may have been one of recall rather than one of retention. Some people believe that, as long as there is no brain injury or atrophy, nothing ever learned is forgotten. The traces remain rigidly. Psychotherapists use various means of helping individuals recover "forgotten" memories. Men who have survived emergencies have frequently told the author that in emergencies they recalled information which they had forgotten long ago, or had forgotten that they had ever known. This is easy to understand in regard to information about survival procedures. One does not like to think of the possibility that he will have to use such information, even denying the possibility. "It can't happen to me!" they say. A person pushes survival out of consciousness because it is frightening. Similarly, one may push aside information that is humiliating or guilt producing. The accumulated scientific evidence seems to indicate that supposedly forgotten incidents may be recalled in exceptional situations such as in emergencies and extreme conditions, dreams, delirium of fever, somnambulism, hypnotic states, and psychoanalysis.

Just as the conditions under which the learning took place may have been distracting, the conditions of recall may have been distracting. A person may have been too cold, too hot, too fatigued, too hurried, or too harassed. The importance of the conditions of recall was dramatically impressed upon the author's mind one extremely cold day in the high Rockies. He and his colleagues were studying problems of retention of briefing information. The subjects had been briefed for about 30 minutes concerning a specific exercise. The researchers tested some of the men for immediate recall in the cold area where they were briefed. Others walked for about 200 yards to spread out the testing before being given their test of retention. The latter group recalled twice as much information as the first group. A similar situation occurred at the end of the day when the subjects were tested for delayed recall. Some of the men were tested outdoors while they were getting water. The others were tested in the warmth of their tents, after they had rested for a short while. Again, the warmed (and in this case, rested) subjects recalled over twice as much information as the cold ones. In both testings, the cold subjects spent fully as much effort and time as, if not more than, the warmed ones. In fact, they seemed to try harder and to strain to call forth the information required.

DEFENSIVENESS

The reader's forgetting of details in the Photographic Memory Test may have been defensive. He may have been disturbed by the fact that these sixth graders were not seated in proper rows and were crowding together. This divergence from common practice may have so distracted him that he was unaware of many of the details. Or, he may have been bothered by the fact that no girls were clearly visible in the picture. The reader may have interpreted this as a kind of discrimination against girls. Or, the children may have seemed to be having too much fun to be really learning. Or the reader may have had some very unpleasant experiences in his own sixth grade.

Research results usually show that pleasant things are remembered better than unpleasant ones, both pleasant and unpleasant things are remembered better than indifferent ones, and some people (pessimists) tend to remember unpleasant things and forget pleasant ones. As a defense against overloading, people also forget innumerable things.

EGO INVOLVEMENT

Individuals tend to remember better those things that are important to them personally—things in which they are ego involved. Thus, the reader may have felt no ego involvement in the situation shown in the photograph. He may have seen in it nothing of any deep concern to him. Instead of teaching gifted children he may teach the mentally retarded, the blind, the deaf, college students, or adults. He may have been indifferent to the contents of the photograph.

OTHER FACTORS IN MEMORY FAILURE

A number of other factors have been found to cause memory failures. One better remembers things which he understands. Intention to remember, confidence in ability to remember, meaningful associations, adequate background, organization, dividing and grouping, and reinforcement by repetition all strengthen memory, and their absence may result in memory failures.

SOME GENERAL PRINCIPLES

On the basis of this quick review, the reader may now want to formulate a set of general principles for improving his ability to remember. The following list compiled by Weinland (1957) may give him a start: *

When a person wants to remember something, he should:

1. Try to see its significance, try to be interested in it or at least in the value of remembering it.
2. Give it his attention, be sure he has it right.
3. Be sure he fully understands it.
4. Intend to remember it.
5. Be confident that he can remember it.
6. Involve the ego, if possible. See its relation to himself.
7. Associate it with other related facts.
8. File it in its proper place in his memory system.
9. See it as a part of a larger whole.
10. If there is a basis for doing so, learn it as part of a small group of related facts.

FUNCTION OF MEMORY IN MAINTAINING MENTAL HEALTH

The function of memory in maintaining mental health is, in many respects, quite obvious. If the reader has any doubts about the stress that can be occasioned by failures in the memory operation, he should try forgetting some important detail.

* From *How to Improve Your Memory* by J. D. Weinland. New York: Barnes & Noble, Inc., 1957. By permission.

One day recently the author found himself under considerable stress because he forgot an important detail. He had known the day before that he would be rushed before the activity and had had the forethought to organize his materials. Just as he was finishing these preparations, it occurred to him that he had forgotten one important detail. He was interrupted at this point, however. Several times during the evening and the next morning, he was reminded of his oversight, but somehow he never managed to take care of the detail. Finally, time for the activity came and he went to the place where the activity was to be held about 20 minutes ahead of time to set up his equipment. As he began these preparations, he realized his omission once more and rushed back to his office. In this rush, he became overheated and uncomfortable. By now, time was getting short and in his rush, he made some mistakes in setting up a piece of equipment, causing it to malfunction. The difficulty had not been overcome by the time the activity was scheduled to begin. Thus, he had at the last minute to alter his plans. He had to skip the first part of the experiment and try to get the equipment to operate during the first activity. Although he managed to complete the activity with reasonable success, it was certainly with increased wear and tear on him and about 140 students. Stress increased his already fatigued condition and he was unable to be productive throughout the remainder of the day and into the evening.

Psychiatrists, clinical psychologists, and other mental health workers pay considerable attention to mental defects. For example, the *American Handbook of Psychiatry* (Arieti, 1959) refers to memory defects in the following kinds of disorders: in aged persons, Alzheimer's disease, arteriosclerotic psychoses, brain trauma, carbon disulfide poisoning, cerebral arteriosclerosis, chronic alcoholism, concussion, diabetes mellitus, general paralysis following head injury, neurodysfunction, Pick's disease, senile dementia, and senile psychosis. Reference is also made to amnesia, the evaluation of memory in the psychiatric examination, and the role of visual and auditory memory in reading retardation.

A number of surveys have been made of psychopathologies of memory. One of the more complete of these was made by Gillespie (1937). He conceptualized the factors involved in remembering somewhat differently from the way Guilford has conceptualized them. He identified eight factors and related each to specific kinds of pathology.

Registration, Gillespie's first factor, is similar to Guilford's cognitive operations. This factor is interfered with in acute organic reaction types (delirium), manic excitement (inattention), and hysteria (global inattention). *Retention* is impaired in the organic reactions. Simple and elementary *recall* is defective in severe organic reactions, and recall as a voluntary act is impaired in such psychogenic conditions as hysteria, in certain organic reactions such as trauma to the head, epilepsy, and Korsakoff's psychosis.

The *time sense,* a fourth factor, is affected in various psychoses with depersonalization and in Korsakoff's psychosis. A fifth factor, *"pastness,"* is impaired in epilepsy and in anesthetic states.

In a sixth category, Gillespie placed *associations* determined by sense organs, appetites, instincts, and interests. These are defective in psychogenic conditions and organic reactions in general. A seventh factor, *imagery,* is affected in early senile dementia and Korsakoff's psychosis. The eighth factor, *awareness of personal identity,* is impaired in hysteria and in connection with depersonalization in various psychoses.

Through surveys such as Gillespie's and more recent ones such as Rapaport's (1950), it seems to be rather firmly established that defects in the memory operations occur in a large number of mental illnesses. These surveys, however, do not seek to establish causal relationships. They do not come to grips with the problem of how failures of the memory operations contribute to various kinds of breakdowns. Common sense, however, suggests that such failures inescapably contribute to the stressfulness of coping with the demands of life and inevitably lead to breakdown if the demands are too great.

MEMORY IN COPING WITH STRESS

The concepts presented in the earlier sections of this text and the author's own experiences in studying adaptation to many kinds of stressful circumstances suggest a number of ways in which memory operations are important in coping with stress.

PROFITING FROM EXPERIENCE

Through the memory operations a person is able to profit from past experiences, successful and unsuccessful. A person is saved not only from past mistakes but is enabled to cope with many problems by using some of his less expensive energies. If a person had to figure out anew solutions to every problem, the energy expenditure would indeed be great. Through the memory operations he is also able to profit from the past experiences of others. Thus, more of his energies can be devoted to constructive rather than survival behavior.

AVOIDING STRESS

Inability to remember and even occasional lapses in memory give rise to much discomfort. Society expects a person to remember names, places, numbers, and the like. Failure to remember to carry out essential acts and to make certain preparations may be embarrassing or even disastrous. In an emergency one has to be able to remember what must be done to survive.

MAINTAINING SELF-CONCEPT

A person must be able to remember identifying characteristics about himself, facts about his liabilities and assets, and the like, or he loses his self-concept and thus his anchors in reality. Without these memories, he is unable to behave appropriately. As a consequence, he either overloads himself or makes no attempts to adapt.

AVAILABILITY OF KNOWLEDGE

Certain knowledge is necessary in coping with almost all problems. Absence of this knowledge prevents or retards adequate adaptive behavior. Since overlearned skills and knowledge represent, in an emergency, one's least expensive energies, overlearning of some skills is necessary for survival. Overlearning is especially valuable when available adaptive energy approaches zero, as in shock and extreme fatigue or exhaustion.

INTERPERSONAL ADJUSTMENT

In earlier chapters, emphasis was placed upon the importance of interpersonal skills in coping with stress. If a person is to behave toward others realistically, rather than as if they have attitudes and characteristics which they do not have, he must be able to remember many things about them. Otherwise, he must inescapably respond to them in a parataxic manner. Inappropriate behavior produces interpersonal stress and eventually breakdown, as is argued by Sullivan and others. Even such a matter as remembering names can be of critical importance in one's social adjustment.

FRAME OF REFERENCE FOR STRUCTURING

Memory provides a person with a frame of reference for structuring new situations and restructuring changed and changing situations. Without such a frame of reference, one's contacts with reality would indeed be precarious. It is also on the basis of memory that one is able to develop new responses.

SUMMARY

Throughout history, most societies have attached much importance to the memory function. Plato was one of the first scholars to give special attention to memory and compared memory to an impression upon a wax tablet, an idea now known as the "trace theory" of memory. For many years, it was generally assumed that these traces or impressions are stored in definite locations of the brain until they fade or become blurred with the passage of time. Katona's work provided a transition from the more classical trace theories to the structural or schema theories that have been current in recent years. He used the term "trace" only as a carrier of the connection between events and differentiated between individual traces and structural traces. He also found remembering to be a process of reconstruction rather than one of construction.

Bartlett was one of the first investigators to propose and test experimentally a schema theory to replace trace theories. He also stressed the importance of interests, attitudes, affects, and goals in remembering. His schema theory was borrowed from the field of neurology. He maintained that recall is not a reproduction of a schema but an active construction based upon a schema. Recently, Paul has attempted to extend Bartlett's work and fill in some of the gaps in knowledge relevant to it. Paul has given greater attention to remembering as a process and to individual differences in remembering. He, too, concluded that memory can be better conceptualized as an active construction based upon schema organization rather than as the reproduction of a trace system. He added emphasis upon the articulating, abstracting, and comprehending aspects of the remembering process.

The memory factors identified and measured by Guilford include visual memory, auditory memory, memory for spatial order, memory span, rote memory, memory for ideas, meaningful memory, and memory for temporal order.

Common causes of memory failures and lack of constructive behavior under conditions of change and stress are incompleteness of learning, interferences with recall, defensiveness, lack of ego involvement, inability to comprehend what is to be remembered, lack of intention to remember, lack of confidence in ability to remember, inadequate background, failure to organize elements to be remembered, and the like.

Inescapably, the maintenance of mental health and constructive behavior under stress requires that individuals remember. Furthermore, it requires at times that individuals overlearn certain skills and facts through practice, repetition, and rehearsal. Otherwise the essential skills and knowledge will be vulnerable to extinction by stress and unavailable for use. There are, of course, limitations to the adequacy of the memory operations in meeting all stresses. It takes more than memory just to cope with stress, but modern theories of memory indicate that remembering is more of a constructive process than earlier theorists had thought. If the memory operations are functioning properly, more energy will be available for the other kinds of functioning required for constructive behavior under stress.

Developing and Freeing the Memory Abilities

16

Nine-year-old Fred is very nervous in school. Anything dealing with memory is difficult for him. He cannot listen to or follow directions. Oral reading is jerky with many familiar words miscalled. His oral communication is full of hesitations filled with "uh-uh's." While he speaks, he scrapes his feet and twists his clothing. While sitting and studying, he chews his shirt tops. He is having extreme difficulty in memorizing number facts and either forgets or blocks on those he has learned. Reading is below grade level, even though the individually administered Stanford-Binet gives him an above-average IQ of 128.

What can an ordinary classroom teacher like me do to help a boy like Fred learn?

Teachers at all levels of education ask this question. It is probably asked more frequently by fourth and fifth grade teachers than any others because it is at this point that teachers and parents begin to worry about the child who cannot read and memorize. It is at this stage that he begins to "bog down" in most schools, if he cannot do these two things. In dealing with such problems, the minds of educators should be attuned to the constant and intrinsic interactions between personality and learning.

Without taking time now to speculate about the reasons for Fred's inability to remember, let us consider some of the basic issues concerning memory disabilities, some of the research findings concerning the conditions that facilitate or inhibit the development and functioning of the memory operations, and how strategies of coping with stress can be used to help one remember.

Although the memory functions that have been studied through research can in some instances be classified according to the abilities identified in the preceding chapter, little attempt has been made to determine the differential effects of a particular condition, procedure, or personality factor on the different memory abilities. Thus, in this chapter no attempt will be made to discuss what is known about developing and freeing the memory abilities in terms of specific memory abilities. Where it is possible to do so, attention will be called to the specific ability or abilities involved.

BASIC ISSUES CONCERNING THE MEMORY OPERATIONS

A basic issue concerning the memory operations is the extent to which defects in the memory operations are a cause of breakdown and the extent to which defects are a consequence of breakdown. The issue shows more obviously in the case of memory than in other mental operations and has received more attention from the mental health professions, perhaps because measures of the memory operations appear to be more objective and more easily determined. There is an observable relationship between a person's memory operations and his ability to cope constructively with life stresses.

Present indications from research (Janis, 1958) are that memory defects should be studied both as causes and as consequences of mental breakdown. It seems more useful to think of them as possible causes of breakdowns. The material presented in the preceding chapter suggests that the memory operations are highly important in coping with stress. The individual who lacks an adequate memory is more likely to break down than is the one with a good memory. Accepting this proposition, one then has to look for the conditions that interfere with the development and functioning of the memory operations.

Anxiety, repression, fear, panic, and fatigue generally interfere with memory. Thus any condition that results in excessive anxiety, repression, fear, panic, or fatigue interferes with memory. The matter is not quite so simple, however. There are matters of the intensity and duration of the stressful condition. There is also the state of the organism. Then, there is the apparent paradox that external stress may both "cause" and "cure" memory disturbances.

Janis (1958, p. 179) points out that one of the best-known facts about psychological stress is that a severely traumatizing experience can give rise to various memory disturbances. In his studies of surgical patients, he found many incidents of memory distortions in connection with recollections of past events with the approach of surgery. He also found many incidents of memory recovery under the stress of surgery or approaching surgery. He found considerable evidence that during the period when the stresses of surgery were the focus of attention, the patient recovered, to an extraordinary degree, details of childhood memories that had hitherto been repressed. Threats of body damage seem to be especially powerful in reviving disturbing childhood memories.

Concerning the recovery of memory under stress, Janis (1958, p. 209) hypothesizes that the need for reassurances about surviving or escaping impending danger may serve as a powerful motivation to recall analogous experiences from the past. Usually such recollections involve instances when the person has either mastered the situation, managed to survive despite exposure to extreme danger, or experienced intense anticipatory fears that subsequently proved to be unwarranted. Since the recall of such instances are likely to increase one's capacity for coping constructively with the situation, the external stress in this case proves to be beneficial. In some cases it provides direct solutions. In others, it reduces anxiety to the extent that the individual is able to produce new solutions.

Many individuals who have survived emergencies and extreme conditions provide much evidence of the type that Janis observed in surgical patients. An interesting experience of this type was recorded by Captain Eddie Rickenbacker (1943) in describing his survival experience during World War II. Rickenbacker and his air crew were stranded on a life raft in the Pacific Ocean at a time when there was little prospect of rescue. He describes the experience as follows:

> My companions clearly began to think of what lay beyond death and to think of it in terms of their own lives.
> They began to tell of what they had experienced in life: their hopes, fears, ambitions, their achievements, their mistakes. I suppose it takes the imminence of danger to release one completely from inhibitions. The talk was entirely honest and, I am sure, entirely frank. What was said will always be locked up in our minds. As far as I am concerned, no hint of those long, man-to-man conversations will ever be revealed. I am sure of one thing, that it did us a great deal of good.*

Whether or not external stress will cause a recovery of memory or a failure of memory depends to a considerable extent upon personality characteristics. Janis points out that some types of people such as compulsives develop acute anxiety whenever they encounter environmental hardships. Such people are likely to experience memory failures. Other people, such as individuals burdened by chronically latent guilt, may react to "real misery" by actually becoming less anxious than usual. In times of extreme hardship and threats of loss of life, psychopathic deviates frequently perform heroically. Their memory operations appear to be more effective than usual.

* From *Seven Came Through* by Edward Rickenbacker. Copyright 1943 by Doubleday & Company, Inc. Reprinted by permission of the publisher.

CONDITIONS THAT FACILITATE OR
INHIBIT MEMORY

In the preceding chapter, Weinland's (1957) principles of memory improvement were presented. An obvious step in improving the memory operations of children would be to apply these principles in teaching. The following suggestions are made by Klausmeier (1961):

1. Foster intent to learn well and remember.
2. Make the original learning meaningful.
3. Provide for satisfying consequences of original learning.
4. Distribute practice and review.
5. Avoid interference and faulty reorganization.
6. Provide for sequential cumulative learning.

All of these principles have been tested and if used intelligently should result in improvements in the memory operations.

From the evidence available, individuals credited with feats of phenomenal memory appear to apply sound principles for remembering. The famous case of Rueckle (Schilder, 1953), who learned a series of 204 digits in seven minutes and 27.8 seconds and 504 digits in 39 minutes and 30 seconds, is a good example. Mueller, who studied Rueckle's performance, credited his achievement to the following six factors:

1. High concentration of attention.
2. Low mental fatigability.
3. Excellent retention.
4. Extremely rapid apperception and reproduction.
5. Particular interest in the field.
6. Use of natural aids to an unusual degree (creation of relationships, schema, and designs).

It will be noted that Mueller's explanation rests partly on the application of principles, partly on the state of the organism, and partly on the basis of strategies or imposition of structure.

PHYSICAL AND PSYCHOLOGICAL STATUS
OF THE ORGANISM

As emphasized in Chapter 15, the state of the organism is important for both retention and recall. An illustration was offered to show that, under the same conditions of retention, men who were cold recalled only about half as much information as those who were permitted to warm up before being asked to recall the information. Excessive cold or heat; discomfort from other physical conditions such as air pressure and poor ventilation in a classroom; fatigue from physical exertion or lack of sleep; pain from injury; and discomfort from hunger, thirst, or other physical deprivations are some of the conditions that inhibit the memory operations.

One should not conclude from this illustration, however, that recall was unaffected by the stressfulness of the conditions under which the information was given. The general principle concerning the intensity of the stress is undoubtedly operative here. Tolman (1951) maintained that things learned under highly stressful conditions tend to be learned "within a narrow or thin cognitive map" and this makes it difficult for a person to admit later modifications in the first learned stimulus-response patterns. Another explanation is simply that when something is learned under highly stressful conditions there are fewer anchors for the mind to grip and closure is likely to be premature.

Various psychological states also inhibit learning. Mention has already been made of anxiety, fear, repression, aggression, and panic. To these we could add mental fatigue from other causes such as frustration, lack of plan, lack of a goal, sustained mental activity, boredom from repetition, lack of interest, and the like. In fact, any condition of the organism that reduces contact with the environment, such as sensory defects and prejudice, may be expected to inhibit the memory operations.

An example of the way by which prejudice inhibits memory is to be found in the well-known experiment on the learning and forgetting of procommunist and anticommunist material by Murphy and Levine (1958). In this experiment, students with procommunist and those with anticommunist attitudes were identified. Both groups were then given procommunist and anticommunist materials to read, and their recall of the material was tested immediately. This procedure was repeated for three successive weeks and recall tests were given for five weeks after this. It was found that the anticommunists remembered more anticommunist material than did procommunists, and the procommunists remembered more procommunist material than did the anticommunists. These differences were maintained throughout the five-week period.

Obviously, teachers can control some of the factors that interfere with memory. Where attitudes, feelings, and emotions affect what is being retained, the problem is somewhat more difficult. Teachers are not always able to present to children only materials that are pleasant or that are in harmony with their attitudes and values. In some cases, improving the memory operations may involve such fundamental changes as can be accomplished only through psychotherapy.

In attempting to increase the chances that children will be able to remember what they are taught, teachers must be ever alert to individual differences in the reactions of children to threatening or fear-arousing stimuli. Thus far, there is no very dependable information concerning the kinds of individual differences that affect memory operations. Perhaps more research concerning this problem has been done with the anxiety variable than any other single variable. Yet the results concerning anxiety are not clear-cut. It is the author's opinion that the reasons why the results are not more consistent and clear-cut is that research on this problem has not been guided by any general theory of stress. While most studies suggest that there is a curvilinear relationship between anxiety and ability to remember, some studies show inverse relationships of a linear variety. For example, Chansky (1958), using scores on the Taylor Manifest Anxiety Scale, found an inverse relationship between anxiety and ability to recall information read. When reading was done under threatening conditions, the relationship between anxiety and recall of information was stronger than when the conditions were nonthreatening. In some research (Waite, Sarason, Lighthall, and Davidson, 1958) subjects are dichotomized on the anxiety variable, precluding chances for the emergence of the findings predictable from stress theory.

It is possible, however, that anxiety may not be the most important variable to study in learning how to maximize learning through individualizing instruction. Goldstein (1959) used the coping-avoiding variable in studying responses to fear-arousing propaganda. He identified two groups of people, "copers" and "avoiders," on the basis of a sentence-completion test. Each subject was exposed to a propaganda lecture with either a strong fear appeal or a minimal fear appeal. The results showed that a strong fear appeal received greater acceptance among copers than among avoiders and that the minimal fear appeal received greater acceptance among avoiders than among copers.

It may turn out, however, that teachers will have to depend upon research using both anxiety and coping variables for information that will be useful in dealing with problems of individual differences in performance under stress. One such study was conducted by Lowe (1961), who compared interference proneness with individual differences in modes of coping with anxiety. Stress was induced by exposing subjects to failure on a task on which they were motivated to do well. Preferred mode of coping with anxiety was determined from the relative emphasis of the subjects in recalling successes and failures (Failure Recall Ratio). Subjects were classified as goal oriented or ego oriented in coping with failure. Interference proneness was determined by a 19-item questionnaire assessing the subjects' susceptibility to the interference of anxiety in mental functioning. A variety of tests of mental functioning were used but tests of memory tended to be predominant.

Subjects who had been classified as goal oriented in coping with anxiety improved their performance significantly following failure, while the ego-oriented subjects showed no significant increase. Also, subjects classified as highly prone to the interference of anxiety in mental functioning showed an increase in the number of errors after failure, while the less interference-prone group actually showed a decrease in errors after failure. There was greater variability in the performance of subjects in the middle ranges of goal orientation and interference proneness. This variability suggests that subjects with no marked preferences in coping techniques are inconsistent in their use of these techniques or that variables such as intensity of stress must be introduced in order to clarify the picture. The results certainly emphasize the necessity for distinguishing between the different effects of anxiety in evaluating the effects of frustration on mental functioning.

USE OF ALL OF THE SENSES

As already stated, anything that reduces the contact of the senses with the environment tends to inhibit the memory operations. People usually think, however, only in terms of seeing and hearing, and classroom planners limit their concerns to good lighting, elimination of interfering noises, and the like. Other senses are involved in memory in a number of ways. First, there are various kinds of memory: visual, auditory, tactual, olfactory, gustatory, muscular, and motor. In various kinds of learning, senses other than sight and hearing are used. The learning of physical skills, such as operating a motor vehicle, dancing, and tennis, requires many kinds of memory.

Using all of the senses in learning a task gives more anchors in reality and thus facilitates remembering. For example (Weinland, 1957), the military services have found that verbalizing the process of cleaning rifles facilitates memorizing the process.

Some individuals appear to remember best what they see, others what they hear. It is better, however, if the senses reinforce one another, thus strengthening contacts with reality. Apparently, visual imagery is very strong in young children, but generally becomes weaker after the age of fourteen. Some adults retain this special ability, however, and are said to have a "photographic memory" or "eidetic imagery." Ruch (1953) cites the example of a law student with eidetic imagery who was charged with cheating on an examination because he had reproduced with accuracy material from a textbook. He offered to prove his innocence by duplicating the feat under observation. After five minutes' study of new material he wrote down four hundred words of it exactly as printed.

F. C. Bartlett (1932), who has studied visual and auditory memorizers, has presented interesting characterizations of these two types. Those with a visual preference learn rapidly and are confident in reproducing what they have learned. Their approach is direct. They visualize the material as presented and depend relatively little upon grouping, comparisons, or secondary associations. They make more errors in reproduction than they realize but remain confident, regardless of objective accuracy. Those with an auditory preference tend to grasp signs or cues and fix them with descriptions. They use classifications, associations, and comparisons more than do the visualizers. In recalling, they respond with uncertainty even when their memory is accurate. An individual who has a strong preference in either direction might do well to recognize the weaknesses of his type and try to strengthen the ability that is weaker. Yet, when success is important he is certainly wise to rely upon the sensory modality that for him is most dependable.

Visual aids can strengthen memory. Very complicated data can be made clear by a diagram. A chart gives a structure, which increases the student's contacts with the material being presented. Making his own visual aids can be a great aid to the student's memory by serving several purposes. He clarifies facts and relationships by simplifying them and arranging them logically. He makes certain that he understands the facts and absorbs the information in more than one way. Thus, he has more anchors that reinforce the information in memory. He also heightens his interest in the information through ego involvement.

The use of efficient reading techniques, writing or taking notes on what is to be remembered, and recitation are also well-tested means of improving the memory operations. Many suggestions concerning these methods will be found in standard textbooks on how to study.

PRACTICE AND OVERLEARNING

If information and skills are to be used under stressful conditions, they should be overlearned, that is, practiced until they have become "fixed" well beyond mere mastery. Since the effects of practice are likely to be counteracted by fatigue, practice should be spaced. Intense activity following learning can inhibit recall, because of the immediate interference with what has been learned. It has been demonstrated that unfinished tasks are remembered better than finished tasks (Zeigarnik, 1927).

In some cases, however, behavior that appears to be the result of practice and overlearning may in actuality be the result of early learning. Since first-learned behaviors are often overlearned, it is sometimes difficult to differentiate which factor is involved when an early-learned behavior appears under stressful conditions. A large body of research information (Barker, Dembo, and Lewin, 1941; Mowrer, 1940; O'Kelly, 1940) indicates that there is regression in behavior following stress. This topic has already been discussed in some detail in the first part of this book. Nothing, however, has been said concerning first-learned behavior. An experiment by Barthol and Ku (1959) indicates that some of the results of early learning are due to the primacy of the learning rather than to the fact that behavior was overlearned. The experimenters selected the tying of a bowline knot because there are two dissimilar methods of achieving the end result. Subjects were carefully screened to determine whether or not they already knew either of the methods. The 18 subjects were divided randomly into two groups. Both groups were taught both methods of tying knots but in opposite order. In a later stressful situation (at 1:00 A.M. on Sunday immediately after returning from a dance in one case, and at 9:00 P.M. on another day after finishing a difficult final examination), subjects were asked to "tie a knot." Sixteen of the 18 subjects tied a bowline by the method learned first. One of the two divergent subjects later recalled that he had actually learned the second-learned method years earlier and had forgotten about it. The other began to tie the knot according to the first-learned method but then recalled the other, simpler method and changed.

DEVELOPING A SCHEME OR PATTERN

Something that has been structured is easier to remember than something unstructured. Developing a scheme, organization, or pattern aids memory by increasing the contacts with reality. Structuring also reduces overloading and relieves the strain that results from overloading.

Although this fundamental principle has been demonstrated in a variety of ways during the past 300 years, the work of George A. Miller (1956ab) has been quite useful in elaborating the principle in modern applications. Miller discusses the work of René Descartes, the seventeenth-century philosopher who in his *Rules for the Direction of the Mind* was concerned about the overload on the memory in the following of a long argument. A person trying to hold each step of a long argument in mind as he proceeds to the next step is likely to lose his way in the sheer mass of detail, as does the plane-geometry student who has to listen to a detailed, 45-minute proof of a theorem. As a solution, Descartes proposed some rules for organizing material so that it can be remembered better. The drawings in Figure 16–1 of the fanciful heads represent an artist's interpretation of the idea Descartes proposed.

A nineteenth-century philosopher, Sir William Hamilton, observed that if marbles are thrown onto the floor, a person cannot view more than six at once without confusion. If a person sees six marbles, he can usually name their number without counting. With more marbles, however, he often makes mistakes. Miller, in his experiments, has applied and extended the rules of Descartes, Hamilton, and others to the binary number system, computers, small-group phenomena, and other modern-day problems (1956, 1958).

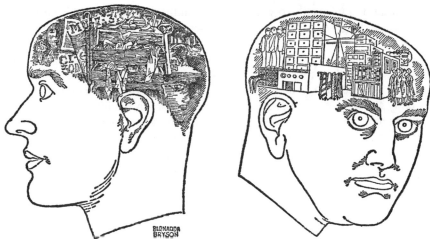

Figure 16 1. Fanciful heads drawn by Bernarda Bryson to depict René Descartes's Rules for the Direction of the Mind. *The individual at the left has presumably not had the benefit of the rules, whereas the man at right has. (From G. A. Miller, "Information and Memory,"* Scientific American, *August 1956, 195, 46. Reprinted by permission, Copyright © 1956 by Scientific American, Inc. All rights reserved.)*

DEVELOPING NEW CONSTRUCTS

George Kelly (1955) approaches matters of personality development in terms of a psychology of personal constructs. According to Kelly, man looks at his world through transparent patterns which he creates and then tries to fit over the realities of which the world is composed. Although the fit is not always accurate, man would be unable to make any sense out of such an undifferentiated homogeneity without patterns. Man continues to try to improve his constructs by increasing their number, by altering them to improve the fit, and by organizing them. Kelly emphasizes strongly the idea that one remembers what is structured and forgets what is unstructured.

PRESENTATION OF MATERIALS

The principle of structure should provide much guidance to writers, curriculum specialists, and teachers in organizing and presenting material that is to be remembered. Sometimes a question arises concerning the amount of detail that is necessary for optimum retention. Almost all communications are redundant. Some people argue for eliminating redundancy, while others argue that detailed information with examples and illustrations is necessary. Research in the field of information theory has shown that some redundancy is necessary for retention. Without it, the mind is unable to process information adequately.

267

In an unpublished experiment by the author and some of his survival research colleagues, a few of these issues were explored. In one set of instructions, the experimenters gave only the necessary information. In a second set, they gave descriptive detail. In a third, they added examples and illustrations. Rather consistently they found that men were able to retain more of the second set of instructions than either of the other two. Apparently the first does not provide enough anchors in the information to be remembered. The third has essentially the same effect as the first because there is too much detail. The excess detail prevents the learner from establishing adequate anchors in the information. Such detail may be distracting, may be so great as to be overwhelming, and may overload the system.

OTHER FACILITATORS AND INHIBITORS

Many other very useful concepts about the improvement of the memory operations have been advanced and tested. The author has selected only a few, some of the ones he has found most useful in thinking about the problem. Others may be equally useful.

Ebbinghaus, Thorndike, Hull, and others have developed and tested what have been referred to as "laws of learning." For example, Ebbinghaus worked with the laws of Similarity, Contrast, and Spatial or Temporal Contiguity. Strong needs to remember may facilitate memory. Thus, rewards are important. The evidence here is rather clear and consistent. People tend to learn and develop along whatever lines they find rewarding. Thus, if a teacher wants students to memorize, he must test them and grade them on memory.

Various kinds of memory devices and systems have thrived. Nearly all of the memory systems, Weinland (1957) points out, were developed before the days of printing. Rhymes, numbering, alphabetical ordering, abbreviations, pigeonholing, acrostics, paired associates, and association chains are some of the simpler and more frequently used devices. Sometimes the addition of the system leads to overloading.

Apparently the people who remember the most are curious and explore particular things of their own choosing. Their egos are involved in the information that they acquire. Far more than interest, however, is involved in remembering.

USING STRATEGIES FOR COPING IN REMEMBERING

Since it is quite apparent that memory is aided by ability to control anxiety and by the establishment of anchors in whatever is to be remembered, it is to be expected that the strategies for coping with stress will be useful in improving the memory operations.

RISKING AND AVOIDING

Both risking and avoiding appear to be useful in certain situations in improving the memory operations. Risking has been emphasized in some programs of training designed to improve the memory operations. Nichols (1960) * recommends a risking technique in listening training. He explains that people think about four times as fast as they talk. Normal conversation rate is about 125 words per minute and slows down to about 100 words per minute before an audience. Thinking speed is between 400 to 500 words per minute. As a result, Nichols contends, people remember only about 25 per cent of what they have heard after two days. To counteract this loss, one of his suggestions is to anticipate the speaker's next remarks; try to guess what he is going to say. A correct answer or an error will strengthen memory, Nichols' research shows. The uncertain type of memorizer, which Bartlett describes as the auditory type, could probably profit most by this kind of training.

The strategy of avoiding is likely to be most useful when vast amounts of unimportant information, conflicting or interfering information, intense activity following learning, and the like are involved. Risking may interfere when there is little chance of success in remembering because the material to be remembered is too difficult, too unfamiliar, or too great in amount. A person who is fatigued, preoccupied with other problems, hungry, thirsty, or in great danger, should probably postpone efforts to memorize. Avoiding may also be a good strategy if there is danger of overloading, if the psychological cost is too great, or if some basic skill needs improvement first. Avoiding may be pathological when applied to memory, if it represents apathy, procrastination, a fatalistic attitude, denial of the need to remember, or fear of new experiences.

Teachers and others can assist children in learning sound techniques of risking and avoiding by showing them the connection between behavior and its consequences, criticism and encouragement, defining the limits, and the like.

MASTERING AND FAILING

The strategies of mastering and failing are useful in improving the memory operations. One of the techniques recommended by Nichols in listening training is to underline mentally the examples or facts the speaker

* Paraphrased from "What Can Be Done about Listening?" from *The Supervisor's Notebook,* Vol. 22, No. 1, Spring 1960. Copyright © 1960 by Scott, Foresman and Company. By permission.

uses to illustrate his point. This action represents an aggressive, mastering, taking-over approach on the part of the listener.

The basic strategies that have been outlined for coping with any type of defeat or failure are useful in coping with the difficulties involved in remembering. Restated in terms of memory problems, these include the following:

1. Accept the fact that the material must be remembered in order to achieve something that is desired.
2. Analyze and accept what is necessary in order to remember the required material.
3. If there has been failure in remembering, adopt a more powerful method, go all out, using more effective or expensive energies for a short period.
4. Try to identify the cause for the memory failure; eliminate the inadequacies that appear to have caused the failure.
5. Apply the psychology of making progress to efforts to memorize; measure the movement toward the goal.
6. Decide upon a definite target and adopt long-range and short-range goals; adopt revised or new goals, if needed.

If a teacher has the problem of helping a child who is having unusual difficulty in memorizing, some of the principles suggested by Redl and Wattenberg (1959) should prove useful. The child may need help in getting over a specific hurdle. Prompting may be the solution. Or the teacher may need to help the child understand the material to be remembered. If the child is learning a skill, the teacher may have to rehearse the child step by step and help him develop a routine. Support from routines may also be needed in other kinds of remembering that seems too difficult. If a memory task has proved too difficult, the teacher may need to help the child save face with the group. As a final resort, the teacher may have to remove the memory requirement.

OVERLOADING AND UNLOADING

According to Nichols' findings concerning listening and memory, making mental summaries every three or four minutes should help avoid overloading. The listener can constantly condense and structure the material, keeping it from becoming overwhelming.

In the hands of the intelligent teacher, the strategies of overloading and unloading should be very useful in helping children to improve their memory operations. In a sense, it is a matter of increasing or decreasing stress in accordance with the needs. At times, when a child becomes a behavior problem because his work is too easy, overloading may be necessary in determining what his capacity is. If a child is a behavior problem because he is not ready to remember the material, it is too difficult for him, or the language of the material is too remote from his developmental level, the teacher can reduce the load or stress.

Overloading as a teacher strategy may be harmful, however, if it results from memory assignments badly planned, poorly explained, or unfairly judged.

DENYING NEED AND MAKING PEACE

Improving the memory operations may bring about a conflict between the so-called pleasure principle and the reality principle. A child may be so pleasure oriented or have such short-time perspective that he makes concessions to immediate comfort and sacrifices more important goals. In some situations, the teacher should provide opportunities for the satisfaction of some basic need before he expects a child to retain information, as already indicated in the discussion of the effects of various kinds of physical and psychological discomfort on memory.

CONTINUING TO ADAPT AND SURRENDERING

A child may begin a memory task with much enthusiasm but be ready to abandon it, when he discovers that it will require prolonged effort. If this happens, the teacher can apply some of the tried principles for sustaining effort. These include the following:

1. Try to develop determination based on a firm decision to memorize a particular set of materials.
2. Help the child see the value of memorizing the materials and provide suitable rewards, both intrinsic and extrinsic.
3. Do whatever can be done to improve the physical and emotional state of the child. If he is fatigued, let him rest. If he has lost enthusiasm, stimulate his interest.
4. Make sound use of mutual support from the group, as well as group pressures.
5. Help the child find a new approach.
6. Help him see the goal as an attainable one.
7. Arouse him to all-out effort, at least for a short period.
8. Use his natural curiosity and the excitement of discovery as a motivating force.

STRESSES ARISING FROM THE EXPLOSION OF KNOWLEDGE

An especially difficult problem of today's teachers arises from the explosion of knowledge in all fields during the past decade. It has often been charged in recent years that educators have been so concerned with the population explosion that they have virtually ignored the explosion of knowledge. As a result, today's schools are filled with antiquated methods, obsolete textbooks, and uninformed teachers. Many observers point out that teachers are trying vainly to fill the minds of the young with information that is no longer true. All of this, of course, creates stressful conditions for both teachers and pupils and leads to future difficulties for those students who accept as true much of the information they are taught. Frequently, it leads to failing grades and teacher-student conflicts for those who are less dependent upon the teacher for their information.

Perhaps one of Margaret Mead's arguments (1951) will help to explain some of the dynamics of this problem. She maintains that children of five have already incorporated into their everyday thinking ideas that most of their parents and teachers will never fully assimilate. In 1951, she pointed out, during the lifetime of ten-year-olds the world had entered a new age, the hydrogen age. Soon this would be followed by the space age. Mead mused that teachers who never heard a radio until they were grown up have to cope with children who have never known a world without television.

This problem became apparent to the author recently when he was involved in developing some experimental materials for fourth graders. An attempt was being made to present the story of America's rocket pioneer, Robert Goddard, as realistically and as powerfully as possible in a tape-recorded drama. When teachers were asked about the appropriateness of the materials, almost all of them said that the vocabulary and the concepts were too difficult for fourth grade children. They said that fourth grade pupils could not grasp such concepts as "thrust," "liquid fuel," "interplanetary travel," "research," "guided missile," "field-test," and the like. Their fears were virtually groundless, however. In field trials involving about 1500 fourth graders, no such complaints were made by the children. They had grown up with these concepts; the teachers had not.

How this problem affects the mental health of pupils is illustrated by the case of Kenneth, who won eight state and national awards for original achievements in science during his junior and senior years. Yet there was constant turmoil between Kenneth and most of his science teachers, and most of his high school science grades bordered on failure. A college teacher who worked with Kenneth when he was in the seventh grade asserted that Kenneth knew more physics and chemistry at that time than did physics and chemistry majors in college. Somewhat fearfully, Kenneth approached his high school physics teacher following his first examination, inquiring about some of the answers that the teacher had marked as incorrect. Kenneth knew that his answers were correct according to some of the more up-to-date sources he had been studying. Fortunately for Kenneth, the physics teacher proved to be honest and open-minded and told Kenneth that he would study the problems in the newer sources and give him an answer the next day. Accordingly, the teacher found that knowledge in physics had changed since his last courses in college physics and that Kenneth's answers were correct. The chemistry teacher, however, insisted on sticking to the answers that he himself had learned in college. Thus, Kenneth was continually torn mentally between giving the false answers taught by the teacher and the correct information obtainable in more up-to-date and authentic sources.

APPLICATION

Now that some of the basic issues concerning memory disabilities, the conditions that facilitate and inhibit the memory operations, and the use of strategies for coping with stress in improving memory have been discussed, the reader might go back to the case of Fred, described briefly at the beginning of the chapter. Reread the case and then review the contents of this chapter by trying to find ideas that could be applied in helping Fred to become more effective in his efforts to remember "number facts" and master other tasks dealing with memory. Of all of the ideas that might apply, the reader should choose the one that might be most productive. This can be written on a separate sheet of paper along with a list of reasons why this idea might be successful. Ideas other than those presented in this chapter may also be chosen.

SUMMARY

Perhaps because measures of memory appear to be more objective and more easily determined than measures of the other mental operations, such measures have been widely used as indicators of impaired mental functioning. It is difficult to determine in many cases whether impaired memory caused or resulted from mental breakdown. Generally, memory defects should be studied both as causes and as consequences of mental breakdown.

Anxiety, repression, fear, panic, and fatigue generally interfere with remembering. People manifesting certain personality characteristics suffer memory impairment under stress while people with other characteristics appear to function at a higher level than usual. It is generally accepted that remembering is facilitated by the intent to learn well and remember, the meaningfulness of the original learning, the provision of satisfying consequences of the original learning, distribution of practice and review, avoidance of interference and faulty reorganization, and the provision of sequential cumulative learning. The physical and emotional comfort of a person also affect remembering.

Remembering under stress is likely to occur if all of the senses have been involved to the extent possible in the original learning, if there has been practice and overlearning, if a pattern or scheme has been developed, if new constructs have been added, if materials have been presented in an organized way, and if the schemes or constructs used are sufficiently simple. Specific uses were identified for such strategies as risking and avoiding, mastering and failing, overloading and unloading, denying needs and making peace, and continuing to adapt and surrendering in using the memory operation in coping with stress. Stresses arising from recent explosions of knowledge in almost every field are of special significance to teachers in their efforts to behave constructively.

Role of
Convergent Thinking in
Coping with Stress

17

"Thinking is the reward for learning, and we may be systematically depriving our students of this reward as far as school is concerned," writes J. S. Bruner (1959, p. 187).

In the preceding four chapters, the concern has been with "learning." In the next six chapters the concern will be "thinking." Bruner and others have said that the greatest reward for learning is being able to use what has been learned—thinking. They have said that school should help children to "leap the barriers from learning to thinking." What then is the difference between learning and thinking? What happens when a person thinks that is different from what happens when he learns? Lorge (1960) has compiled an interesting set of verbs that people use in trying to describe what happens when they "learn" and what happens when they "think." Consider carefully these two lists:

LEARNING FOR MASTERY	THINKING (solving problems, making decisions, inventing, creating)
attend, orient	concentrate
observe, regard	seek, search
relate, recall, associate	ascertain, analyze
abstract, conceive, conceptualize, generalize	deliberate, contemplate, ponder, meditate
comprehend, understand	speculate, consider, guess, imagine
review, reorganize	judge, reason, surmise, infer, hypothesize, deduce

275

LEARNING FOR MASTERY	THINKING
know, believe	restructure, plan
evaluate, appreciate	solve, discover
	verify, decide, conclude, confirm, act, resolve

Lorge pointed out that the verbs in the two lists seem to parallel one another in sequence and suggest a comprehensive structure for the behaviors subsumed under the concepts of "learning for mastery" and "thinking." He sees in them quite different emphases and goals, however. Thinking is described as an active process. It seeks, searches, solves, discovers, and verifies. Thus, because of its active nature, thinking probably requires more expensive energies than learning.

THE THINKING PROCESS

Both learning and thinking have been described as processes. Although the above lists may be regarded as descriptions of these processes, there have been a number of attempts to conceptualize the thinking process more simply. One of the more familiar conceptualizations of the nature and process of thinking is John Dewey's (1933). He used the term "reflective thinking" to label what he considered the best kind of thinking—"the kind of thinking that consists in turning a subject over in the mind and giving it serious and consecutive consideration." To Dewey, this process involved a succession of things thought of, with one thought leading to another. He saw it as restricted to things not directly perceived (cognized) and as aimed at a conclusion. Dewey maintained that the origin of thinking is some perplexity, confusion, or doubt, and that to appeal to anyone to think is futile unless the person has some difficulty that troubles him or upsets his equilibrium. Once the difficulty is sensed, the next step is the search for some way out—the formation of some plan, hypothesis, or theory to account for the problem and the consideration of some solution for the problem. Past experience and a fund of relevant knowledge supply the suggestions for solutions, making it futile to exhort a person to think when he has no previous experiences that involve some of the same conditions. The suggestions that emerge from such data, however, have to be examined critically. The thinker must be willing to endure suspense and to undergo the trouble of search. Thus, the process of thinking conceptualized by Dewey may be thought of as a five-step process: (1) felt difficulty, (2) location and definition of difficulty, (3) suggestion of possible solutions, (4) consideration of consequences, and (5) testing of the solution.

More recently, Hullfish and Smith (1961) conceptualized the process of reflective thinking in much the same way as Dewey did. They see it as having the following four phases (pp. 43–44):

(1) The presence (and recognition) of a problem situation, such as on-going activity being halted by an unusual or unexpected change.

(2) Clarification of the problem, such as determining the cause of the unusual or unexpected change.

(3) Hypotheses formed, tested, and modified, such as casting guesses or predictive statements in the form of "if-then" propositions.

(4) Action taken on the basis of the best-supported hypothesis.

Polya (1945), a mathematician, has conceptualized the process of thinking in the following four steps: (1) understanding the problem, (2) working out connections between known and unknown, thus deriving a plan of solution, (3) carrying out the plan, and (4) examining the solution. Johnson (1955) has offered the following three-step process: (1) preparation, (2) production, and (3) judgment. Merrifield, Guilford, Christensen, and Frick (1960) have conceived of the total problem-solving or thinking process as having five phases: (1) preparation, (2) analysis, (3) production, (4) verification, and (5) reapplication. In reviewing the recent research on thinking and problem solving, Gagne (1959) classified the research according to the phase with which it was concerned and came up with the following categories: (1) reception of the stimulus situation, (2) invention or formation of the concept, (3) determining the courses of action, (4) making the decision, and (5) verification.

The foregoing conceptualizations show very little difference. Johnson's steps are broader than the others, but actually include the same behaviors. Since the relationship of the thinking abilities that will be discussed in this and the succeeding five chapters is more apparent in Merrifield, Guilford, Christensen, and Frick's conceptualization, it will be elaborated somewhat.

PREPARATION. During the preparation stage, a problem arises, is sensed, and is recognized as a problem. The person becomes aware that things are not as they should be. He may have enough information to understand the general nature of the problem and its urgency. He may remember relevant information.

ANALYSIS. In this second stage, the individual receives and develops information that relates to the problem. The data are based upon both situation and goal. Through analysis, the individual becomes better acquainted with both the situation and the goal requirements. From the information about the situation, he deals with the consequences; from the goal information, he deals with the necessary causes or antecedents.

PRODUCTION. In the production stage, alternative solutions are generated. As more information is amassed and clarified concerning the situation and the goal, what it will take to bridge the gap between them begins to

277

emerge. Relationships become clearer and a set of possible solutions is developed.

VERIFICATION. In the fourth stage, a tentative solution may be rejected. If the first attempt succeeds, the problem is solved and no longer exists. The rejection is on the basis of the individual's standards of success.

REAPPLICATION. To accomplish the fifth stage there must be a return to earlier stages to select or generate another tentative solution. Depending upon the difficulty, there may be much backtracking at this stage, as there might be at any other stage. It may recur a number of times, either until the problem is solved or until the individual feels that he has exhausted the possible alternatives.

In convergent thinking, the problem has a correct solution, a single best solution, or an approved solution. In other words, the emphasis is on getting the correct answer, the proper behavior, or the approved attitude.

THE CONVERGENT THINKING ABILITIES

The convergent thinking abilities that have been identified and measured by Guilford and his associates (Guilford and Merrifield, 1960) will be described. It is believed that this information will be useful to teachers, parents, and counselors in helping others learn to solve problems, to "get the right answers." By suggesting, hinting, and questioning, a teacher can lead children through the phases of understanding the problem, preparation, analysis, production, verification, and reapplication. If the teacher understands the nature of the abilities involved in this kind of thinking, he should be able to do a much better job of suggesting, hinting, and questioning. These activities will be directed toward the mobilization of these abilities.

FIGURAL REDEFINITION

Figural redefinition (Guilford and Merrifield, 1960) is sometimes known as "flexibility of closure" (ability to shift to varied approaches in closing or completing figures). It involves the ability to redefine figural material, overcoming the "set" or expectation established by "closure." Four tasks are used for assessing this ability. In the Concealed Figures task, the subject indicates which of four complex geometrical figures contain a given geometrical figure. In Penetration of Camouflage, he has to locate faces hidden in pictures. In the Hidden Pictures task, he has to find human or animal pictures hidden in a scene, as rapidly as possible. In the Hidden Figures task, he is asked to indicate which of five figures is hidden in a given figure. This ability should be especially useful in restructuring situations when coping with stresses that result from sudden or unexpected changes, or even gradual changes, and in making the most of limited resources.

SYMBOL SUBSTITUTION

Symbol substitution (Guilford and Merrifield, 1960) is one of the factors for producing figural implications. In one task (Form Reasoning) the subject is asked to solve simple equations in terms of familiar geometric forms. In the other, Sign Changes, he is asked to solve simple equations involving the substitution of one arithmetic operation for another. This ability should be especially useful in coping with problems involving changes in a system or process and in integrating these changes into one's behavior.

SYMBOLIC CORRELATES

Symbolic correlates (Guilford and Merrifield, 1960) is a factor for producing symbolic relations. In one test task, Correlate Completion II, the subject is asked to apply a rule discovered from the relations of the letters of two given pairs of words to write the second word of a third pair. In the second task, Letter Series, he has to indicate which letter properly continues the sequence of a series of letters. This ability is useful in adapting to situations that require the discovery of rules involved in coping with a difficulty.

CONVERGENT PRODUCTION OF SYMBOLIC SYSTEMS

Convergent production of symbolic systems (Guilford and Merrifield, 1960) is the ability involved in producing systems of numbers, words, or other symbols. One of the test tasks designed to assess this ability, Operations Sequence, requires the subject to state the order in which numerical operations should be performed in going from one number to another. In another, Word Changes, he is asked to state the order in which given words must be placed in order to go from a starting word to a goal word, changing one letter at a time. This ability is useful in a variety of kinds of trouble-shooting thinking where a series of operations is involved.

SYMBOLIC REDEFINITION

Symbolic redefinition (Guilford and Merrifield, 1960) is the factor for producing symbolic transformations. Although it is one of the convergent production factors, it is thought to be one of the abilities involved in creative thinking. One task, Camouflaged Words, requires the subject to find the name of the sport or game concealed in a sentence. For example, one sentence might be: "Cowardice is not a soldierly attribute." The answer is "dice." Another task, Word Transformation, involves the indication of new divisions between letters in a series of words, forming a phrase, to make a new series of words. This ability appears to be important in restructuring situations under conditions of impending danger, sudden or severe changes, or unexpected events, and in situations where resources are quite limited.

NUMERICAL FACILITY

Numerical facility (Guilford and Merrifield, 1960) is another factor for producing symbolic implications. The test tasks involve familiar mathematical operations, addition, division, subtraction, and multiplication; and numerical operations (all four operations). This ability should be useful in avoiding becoming overwhelmed by demands that involve mathematical operations.

CONCEPT NAMING

Concept naming (Guilford and Merrifield, 1960) is one of the factors for producing semantic units. In one task (Picture-Group Naming), the subject is asked to provide a class name for a group of five pictures. In a second (Word-Group Naming), he is asked to give a class name to a group of five words. In a third (Seeing Trends I), he is asked to describe a meaningful trend in a group of words. This ability is used under stress when a person is able to call forth a solution, if he can label properly the phenomena with which he must cope. Concept naming simplifies the data to a degree that he can cope with them.

CONVERGENT PRODUCTION OF SEMANTIC CLASSES

Convergent production of semantic classes (Guilford and Merrifield, 1960) involves the production of classes instead of units, as in the preceding factor. The Word Grouping task calls for the subject to put a list of words into a unique set of categories. The Figure Concepts task requires the formation of groups from a large number of pictured objects. This ability should be useful in adapting to stress in much the same way as concept naming.

SEMANTIC CORRELATES

Semantic correlates (Guilford and Merrifield, 1960) calls for the production of semantic relations. Spearman (1930) and others considered this type of thinking to be a part of the very essence of creative thinking. In Guilford's work, semantic correlates falls in the convergent production category and is not regarded as an important ability involved in creative thinking. Vocabulary Completion, one of the tasks designed to assess this ability, involves the production of a word that fits a given definition and begins with a given letter. Inventive Opposites calls for the writing of two antonyms for a given word, the first letter being given. A third test task (Associations III) requires the production of a word that is similar in meaning to two given words. The ability involved in tasks such as these should be helpful in retrieving information from past experiences and relating the demands of the present situation to other tested or recommended solutions.

ORDERING

Ordering (Guilford and Merrifield, 1960) involves the production of semantic systems. The Picture Arrangement task, a fairly familiar one in psychological testing, requires the subject to indicate the correct sequence of pictured events presented in scrambled order. Sentence Order, a second task, requires the subject to arrange three sentences in a sensible order, and a third (Temporal Ordering) requires him to list steps in appropriate order to complete a given project. Ordering is another way of reducing a situation to dimensions with which one can cope, and the ability involved in these tasks should be important in structuring and restructuring complex or confusing situations.

SEMANTIC REDEFINITION

Semantic redefinition (Guilford and Merrifield, 1960) involves the production of semantic transformations. In one task (Gestalt Transformation), the subject is asked to indicate which of five listed objects has a part that will serve a specified purpose.

A second task (Object Synthesis) calls for the naming of an object that could be made by combining two specified objects. In another (Picture Gestalt), the subject is asked to indicate which object in a photograph will serve a specified purpose. Like all of the redefinition abilities, this ability should be useful in restructuring rapidly changing situations and in seeing other than intended uses of common objects.

DEDUCTION

Deduction (Guilford and Merrifield, 1960) involves the production of semantic implications. One of the test tasks, Sequential Association, requires that the subject indicate the best order for four words to produce a chain.

In a second task, Attribute Listing II, the subject is asked to state the necessary attributes of an object that is to serve a certain purpose. Deduction ability should be highly related to success in recognizing what must be done in a situation involving danger, newness, or complexity.

OTHER CONVERGENT PRODUCTION ABILITIES

Guilford's descriptions omit many of the convergent thinking abilities. Of special interest to teachers, counselors, and others concerned about personality development and mental health are abilities which lie in what

Guilford terms the behavioral content area. Unfortunately, little progress had been reported in the measurement of these abilities at the time this book went to press. Abilities in the behavioral content area, however, are receiving major attention by Guilford at this time and promising developments seem to be emerging. Included in this area are human interactions where awareness of the attitudes, needs, desires, moods, intentions, perceptions, and thoughts of other persons and of oneself is important.

Education has traditionally placed great emphasis upon conformity to behavioral norms. This emphasis, as well as many other factors, makes the convergent thinking abilities important in personality development and mental health. Generally, however, teachers will have to devise performance tests or situational tests in order to assess pupils' convergent thinking abilities in the behavioral content area. They may, however, find Guilford's tests useful as models which can be applied to children at various educational levels.

Also largely missing from the measures already developed are those which deal with implications, "extrapolations of information in the form of expectancies, predictions, known or suspected antecedents, concomitants, or consequents" (Guilford and Hoepfner, 1963, p. 2). The abilities involved in producing implications are also of special interest to educators. Imaginative teachers, however, can develop tasks in connection with traditional curricular content. Bruner (1959) has described a number of such tasks observed in elementary schools. One teacher presented in dramatic form the beginnings of the Whiskey Rebellion and then said to the pupils, "You now have enough to reconstruct the rest of the story. Let's see if you can do it." In the teaching of the geography of the North Central states, fifth graders were given maps showing only the rivers, lakes, mountains, and natural resources. They were asked on the basis of these data to decide where the major cities, highways, and railroads should be located. Then they were called upon to defend their choices and finally were permitted to check their solutions with the geography books. Such activities encourage children to organize and use minimal information to draw a maximum number of inferences.

COMMON FAILURES IN CONVERGENT THINKING

In Chapters 14 and 16 some of the factors that affect cognition and memory were discussed. Since cognition and memory are involved in convergent thinking, it is obvious that whatever causes error in these operations also causes error in convergent thinking. Thus, there seems no need for a lengthy review of factors having their origin in difficulties in cognition and memory.

In 1922, Boraas presented a conceptualization of the most common factors affecting thinking. He described one set of factors as obstacles to the development of initiative in thinking. Among the factors that prevent thought from occurring are these: fears, monotony, drudgery, superstition, customs and traditions, conventionality (uncritical imitation of contemporaries), slavery to rules and proverbs, subjection to authority, and slavery to details (inability to organize and systematize one's work). Fears, monotony, and drudgery seem to be emotional factors that interfere with thought. The next five factors involve paralyzing conformity and the last one results in lack of structure. All of them involve some loss of anchors in reality and paralyze thinking.

In a second set of factors, Boraas (1922, pp. 53–55) placed sources of errors in convergent thinking. In these factors, thinking occurs, but the individual does not obtain the "correct" answer because of some error. Boraas lists the following sources of error:

1. Sensory defects such as color blindness.
2. Lack of information about the characteristics of sensations.
3. Inability to concentrate attention on the important aspects of things.
4. Instinctive interests causing bias (differences among men and women concerning fighting).
5. First impressions that linger and influence later judgments.
6. Bias caused by previous experience or training.
7. Emotional excitement.
8. Common human weaknesses (laziness, strictness, haste, caution, etc.).
9. Self-interest.
10. Prior opinions.
11. Lack of experience and information.
12. Persistent attitude such as pessimism, optimism, conservatism, or progressivism.

In trying to conceptualize the problems of common failures in convergent thinking in the educational setting, it seems useful to think first in terms of the factors in the situation that cause such failures and second the problems of the thinker himself. In the first, the intensity and duration of the stress are involved; in the second, the state of the organism.

COMMON STRESSES CAUSING FAILURES IN THINKING

Among the common stresses responsible for failures there are both physical and social conditions. One of the early controversies in research concerning thinking involved physical conditions. The story is told of the feud between Thorndike of Columbia University and Adams of Yale. Thorndike concluded from his experiments that cats were incapable of thinking, whereas Adams had concluded that cats can think. Adams had one of his assistants obtain by some devious means detailed plans of Thorndike's experimental apparatus and procedures. Adams still found that cats can think. Finally, the controversy was resolved when someone noted that Thorndike kept his cats hungry and ran his experiments in the stressful atmosphere of a large city. Adams, on the other hand, fed his cats adequately and conducted his experiments in the peace and quiet of New Haven. Thus, Thorndike's cats tried to go directly to the food, whereas Adams' cats sat and thought and figured out how to approach the food. One might ask, "What right did Thorndike have to expect his cats to think?" Similarly, after visiting classrooms that are crowded, stuffy, overheated, or confused, the author has asked, "What right have we to expect these children to think?" Upon leaving some attractive, well-lighted, well-ventilated schools, he has had the opposite reaction, "Why shouldn't these children think?"

There are some conditions over which teachers have little control. Many of the physical conditions that cause failures in thinking, however, can be greatly improved by teachers and others interested in stimulating thought. These will be discussed at length in Chapter 18.

The social conditions in a classroom or other group may cause failures in thinking. Either conformity to group opinions for conformity's sake or disagreement for disagreement's sake may interfere with correct solutions to problems. Problems of creating the group conditions that are conducive to sound thinking will also be discussed in the next chapter.

The materials of instruction may also be responsible for failures in thinking. Russell and Groff (1955) have discussed this problem in relation to reading. They maintain that, although simple perceptual judgments can be improved by practice, personality and experiential factors vitally affect a child's perception of what he reads and thus of how he thinks. The teacher has little control over these factors since they have their roots in early experiences in the home and in the neighborhood. He insists, however, that a wise teacher can be aware that a story about a happy home may be rejected by a child who comes from a broken home or that a boy in the sixth grade may find escape in sports stories to compensate for his own inadequacies in sports. As a result, different children will perceive very different things in what they read and will differ in their interpretations.

PERSONALITY PROBLEMS CAUSING FAILURES IN THINKING

In considering common personality problems causing failures in thinking, one is concerned with the third set of factors that mediate the effects of stress, the state of the organism. Raths (1960) has presented a very useful conceptualization of the characteristic patterns of children who are chronic nonthinkers and are behavior problems as a result. He describes the following eight types of nonthinking youngsters:

THE VERY IMPULSIVE CHILD.   Raths believes that the very impulsive child needs frequent opportunities to think and that he needs a curriculum which requires comparing, summarizing, observing, criticizing, analyzing, imagining, problem solving, interpreting data, doing research, and the like. All of these activities slow down the impulsive person, who is prone to premature closure.

THE OVERDEPENDENT CHILD.   The overly dependent child continually asks the teacher for help and seems to be unable to proceed until he receives the teacher's approval. Raths believes that such a child needs a great emphasis upon the thinking-type situation. His contention is that, as this child works on his own observations, his own summaries, and his own comparisons, he will learn how to use his mental abilities and will become more independent. Such a child needs to learn the skills for determining for himself when he makes mistakes and for correcting them.

THE RIGID CHILD.   The rigid child does not want to try a new activity or method. He lacks flexibility, and the narrowness of his approach almost precludes thinking. Raths recommends for such a child a variety of assignments requiring many diverse thinking functions. Such a child, however, may have been overconditioned to authority acceptance and be reluctant to explore new ways.

THE CHILD WHO MISSES THE MEANING.   Some children frequently do not catch the meaning of a situation. In summarizing, Raths points out, they are likely to repeat every tiny detail because they do not see the larger meanings. Such a child, he says, may need more experiences in interpretation, analysis, and criticism.

THE LOUD, DOGMATIC, AND OVERASSERTIVE CHILD.   Another nonthinking type seems to be cocky and overconfident of his views and conclusions. He wants to win or to dominate and often gets his way through his arrogance. For such a child, Raths recommends a regimen of thinking situations, coding of his thinking so he can see it and appraise it for himself. Under such conditions, Raths feels that this type of child will reduce the bombast of his behavior and develop greater sensitivity in the analysis of problem situations.

THE UNDERCONFIDENT CHILD.   Another type of nonthinking child has little confidence in his ability to think. He may want to suggest something but he is afraid that it will not be well received. He might be laughed at or ridiculed. He is afraid that his thoughts are not worth listening to. Unable to appraise his own solutions, he is quiet and withdrawn in thinking situations. For him, Raths recommends rigorous training in thinking to develop his courage to say what he thinks, what he believes, and what he is for or against. Such a child needs to regain his confidence in his own senses to perceive reality.

THE CHILD UNABLE TO CONCENTRATE ON MEANS AND ENDS. Another nonthinking child is unable to connect means with ends. He does not see the connection between the immediate doing and the long-range goal. He says that he tries hard but always makes some mistake. Raths recommends for such a child a rigorous and long-range exposure to thinking situations. Teachers, Raths explains, need to examine this child's thinking carefully, to code it for him, and to reflect it to him. In this way he can learn to appraise his own thinking more realistically.

THE ANTI-THINK CHILD. Raths maintains that some children do not want to think. They want everything spelled out for them in detail. They want the teacher or the counselor to tell them what to do. Such children are action-oriented and lesson learners. As Raths explains, they find it uncomfortable to suspend judgment, consider alternatives, or examine the relationships of means to ends.

Anxiety is the personality variable that has perhaps been used most frequently in studying the relationship between problem-solving performance and the state of the organism. An experiment by Dowis and Diethelm (1958) illustrates how personality factors can interfere with convergent thinking and how experimental research in this area can be conducted. Dowis and Diethelm state that their experiment deals exclusively with the type of thinking that occurs when an individual modifies his behavior in terms of the predictive value of information. In their conceptualization of the variables involved they see anxiety in psychiatric patients as prolonged intense stress. They are careful to point out, however, that other experiments have shown that nonclinical subjects exposed to anxiety-producing stress show a loss in flexibility of intellectual function and problem-solving behavior.

The subjects of the Dowis and Diethelm study were 15 hospitalized psychiatric patients, all less than 50 years old and free of brain pathology. All patients were tested once during a prolonged period of intense anxiety and again when clinical observations indicated that the patients were relatively free of anxiety. The testing and clinical observations were done separately. The test used was the Wisconsin Card Sorting Task, which resembles in many ways some of the tests of convergent thinking that have been described in this chapter. Subjects were instructed to sort each of 60 response cards into one of the four stimulus cards on the basis of similarity to one of the stimulus cards. After each placement, the subject was informed as to whether he was "right" or "wrong." A number of variables were involved in both single placements and sequences of placements. Three phases were involved in the testing procedure: (1) a prestress period during which the examiner administered the procedures for determining the discovery of stimulus variables and for determining their utilization; (2) a stress period during which the problem was made systematically unsolvable; and (3) a poststress period during which (1) was repeated.

It was found that more trials were necessary to modify behavior in accordance with predetermined criteria of success (convergent solution) when the subjects were intensely anxious than when they were moderately anxious. The experimentally induced stress of the second phase of the testing affected performance in the same way. Through the experiment, Dowis and Diethelm devised a method analyzing performance produced by experimental conditions. In summary, they identified and differentiated inefficient strategies in the following manner:

1. Each of a series of inefficient placements was reproduced in order to determine the sequential relationships among the stimulus bases of response, reinforcement, and subsequent decisions to change or not change.
2. On the basis of these relationships, a unifying strategy was stated.
3. The strategy was analyzed to determine what use, misuse, or nonuse of available information was implied.
4. Terms were found in psychological and psychiatric literature which implied the use, misuse, or nonuse of information (e.g., rigidity, confusion, perseveration, faulty memory, narrowing of perceptual field, negativism, etc.).

Dowis and Diethelm's method should be useful in studying pathological thinking reactions to the general environment, among essentially normal as well as clinical subjects.

Experiments involving problem solving requiring different types of convergent thinking indicate that anxiety as a state of the organism may function differentially in success in convergent thinking. In general, it seems that anxiety within limits may facilitate or impede convergent thinking depending upon whether the organism must be open to receive and integrate new information or must be closed to extraneous information. One such experiment was conducted by Maltzman, Fox, and Morrisett (1953), using the Taylor Manifest Anxiety Scale as a measure of anxiety. They used two different types of problem-solving situations involving the establishment of mental sets.

In the first experiment, the Luchins' water-jar problem was used to establish a set for a particular method of solution. It was found that the tendency to change to a more direct method of solution was inversely related to the level of anxiety determined by the Taylor Manifest Anxiety Scale. There was a coefficient of correlation of $-.27$ between anxiety score and number of direct solutions. It was also found that using the median score as a cutoff point, the more anxious subjects had significantly fewer solutions than the less anxious subjects.

In the second experiment, the problem consisted of anagrams having solutions referring either to some aspect of nature or eating. During the training phase, subjects received an equal number of trials with eating- and nature-set anagrams. They were then presented with only one of these categories in the test series. It was found that subjects with high anxiety scores made significantly fewer errors than subjects with low anxiety scores. Apparently success on the water-jar problems involves letting information in and being free to change the set. In the anagrams problem, success requires that the subject hold a particular set and not let anything else in to interfere. Thus, it appears that highly anxious persons are likely to perform better than less anxious ones on tasks that require adherence to an established set, while less anxious subjects are likely to excel on tasks requiring shifts in set.

CONVERGENT THINKING IN COPING WITH STRESS

Convergent thinking and behavior rank high among the objectives of teachers in almost all subject matter areas. In a study of the social studies objectives of elementary and secondary teachers, the author found that about 21 per cent of the objectives could be classified in this category. Only the cognitive operations claimed a greater percentage. In a small sample of elementary teachers, he found that a majority of their objectives in language arts could be classified as requiring convergent thinking and behavior. Thus, it would certainly appear that teachers consider it important that children be able to think and behave convergently in coping with life's stresses.

Thinking convergently, thinking as others think, has its advantages. First, it requires less expensive energies generally than the other thinking operations. It is usually the easiest and quickest way. It is also usually the most efficient method for the individual with limited ability because it enables him to act on the thoughts of the best minds in his group. In some ways, it is the most effective for the process of the group—at least, it saves time. Intolerance of disagreement, however, may reduce the quality of the group's productions, as will be seen in the next chapter.

The roles of convergent thinking in coping with stress are fairly obvious. Quite clearly, survival often requires agreement on many matters.

To some degree a person must conform in his thinking for life in a civilized society. In many situations, there is only one correct solution, or the group must agree upon one best solution in order to act. The ability to find such a solution is essential in coping successfully with stress. If an individual or group is unable to arrive at this "best solution," the effects of stress will accumulate and become overwhelming.

Convergent thinking has rather high rewards. Having the same answers as others have brings social approval, status, and the satisfaction of certain needs. This type of thinking enables the individual to maintain rapport with his environment, to make the socially or culturally approved response, and to profit from the experience of others. All of this, of course, reduces tension both for the individual and for the group in which he is a member.

SUMMARY

One of the most important rewards of learning (cognition and memory) is to be able to use what has been learned in thinking. The verbs associated with and used to describe thinking require greater activity and expenditure of energy than do those associated with and used to describe learning. The thinking process has been described by men like John Dewey, Hullfish and Smith, Polya, Johnson, and Guilford and his associates in terms of steps or stages. All of these writers include some kind of preparatory stage in which there is a felt difficulty followed by some attempt to locate and define the difficulty (define the problem). Then comes an idea-getting stage of some kind during which a variety of possible solutions are produced. In some way, these possible solutions are considered and the more promising ones tested, modified, or corrected.

The convergent thinking abilities identified and measured by Guilford are figural redefinition, symbol substitution, symbolic correlates, convergent production of symbolic systems, symbolic redefinition, numerical facility, concept naming, convergent production of semantic classes, semantic correlates, ordering, semantic redefinition, and deduction. Urgently needed is a better understanding of and measures for assessing abilities in the behavioral content area and in the production of implications, since such abilities are likely to be especially useful in constructive behavior under stress.

Among the more common factors that paralyze convergent thinking are fears, monotony, drudgery, superstition, customs and traditions, conventionality, slavery to rules and proverbs, and inability to organize and systematize one's work. Among the more common sources of error in convergent problem-solving are sensory defects, ignorance of the characteristics of sensations, lack of concentration on important aspects of the problem, biases, erroneous first impressions, emotional excitement, human weaknesses, self-interest, lack of experience and information, and persistent attitudes such as pessimism, optimism, conservatism, or progressivism. Both physical and psychological conditions causing discomfort are likely to interfere with correct solutions. Among the more common personality problems causing failure in convergent problem-solving are extreme impulsiveness, overdependence, rigidity, disorientation, dogmatism and overassertiveness, lack of confidence, inability to concentrate, and aversion to thinking.

Convergent thinking and behavior rank high among the objectives of teachers and bring high rewards in other areas. Intolerance of disagreement, however, may reduce the quality of solutions. Nevertheless, constructive behavior frequently requires convergence on many matters.

Developing and Freeing the Convergent Thinking Abilities

18

Twenty Questions is a well-known game. Someone thinks of an object that must be an animal, vegetable, or mineral. Then, by a series of questions, the player or group has the problem of determining the object the leader has in mind. The player begins by determining whether the object is an animal, a vegetable, or mineral. He can then focus his questioning more keenly and converge upon the correct solution by gradually limiting the possibilities. If the player cannot determine the correct answer with twenty questions, he loses. If he arrives at the correct solution in less than twenty questions, he wins a bonus.

Another game is Hot and Cold. The player is sent from the room. The group then decides upon some object in the room. The player returns to the room and tries to discover what object the group has decided upon. When he goes in the direction of the object—being hot—the group applauds loudly. When he is going away from it—being cold—the applause is soft. With this help, any school-age child can find the object within a few minutes.

NECESSITY FOR GUIDANCE

What would the games be like with different rules? In playing Twenty Questions, what if the player could ask no questions and had to get the correct answer to begin with? What if the answers were sometimes correct and sometimes incorrect? What if he were punished severely for every question he asked? What if the answers were given in a language he could not understand?

In playing Hot and Cold, what would happen if there were no applause or other signals of "hotness" or "coldness"? What would happen if the applause were inconsistent—applause at times and no applause at others? What would happen if the applause at times were true and at times false? What would happen if some members of the group had in mind one object and others had in mind a different object?

In these two games and their alternative conditions are found many of the factors involved in creating the conditions necessary for developing and freeing the convergent thinking abilities. In other words, there are problems of giving adequate instructions, having clear goals, giving consistent guidance, being free to explore and to make mistakes, and the like. Playing the two games would be uncomfortable under any of the alternative conditions suggested. There would be no anchors in reality, and seeking correct solutions would be extremely frustrating. Players would either give up, take an extremely long time to find solutions, or find solutions entirely by chance.

In the preceding chapter, some of the conditions that cause failures in convergent thinking or problem solving were reviewed. In earlier chapters, the conditions necessary for developing and freeing the cognitive and memory operations were reviewed. All of these matters obviously are important in developing and freeing the convergent thinking abilities. In this chapter, an effort will be made to summarize some ideas that are relevant to the problem, giving special attention to group problem solving and the use of coping strategies to improve problem-solving effectiveness.

PRINCIPLES FOR AIDING CONVERGENT THINKING

Since much of the research that has been done under the label of problem solving involves convergent thinking, the author will draw almost entirely from this body of literature. This area of research has a long and respectable history. Since problem-solving research involves "correct" answers, the results are less debatable than are those of many other types of research, and are considered to be more firmly anchored in reality. Most of the earlier experiments involved puzzles. Later the Gestaltists introduced new types of problem situations. These usually involved the use of animals in some type of novel situation in which the direct approach to the lure was blocked but an indirect route was left open and the various points and interrelations were visible to the subject. More recently, the trend has turned in the direction of human beings and games. Always there is a correct, best, or school-approved solution.

In spite of firm anchorings in reality, however, the outcomes of such research have been criticized. In regard to animal research, Bertrand Russell (1927) maintains that all of the animals that have been observed have behaved in such ways as to confirm the ideas held by the observer before he initiated the observations. Moreover, these animals have displayed the national characteristics of the observer. Animals studied by American psychologists rush about frantically and at last achieve the desired result by chance. Animals observed by German psychologists, on the other hand, sit still and think, and at last evolve the correct solution out of their inner consciousness.

Although much of value has been learned from the problem-solving behavior of animals, the study of the problem-solving behavior of human subjects has become increasingly important. There is considerable convergence in the findings both in animal and human studies and in the American and German ones. In these convergences, teachers, counselors, and parents will find much guidance for creating the kinds of experiences that will facilitate the development and functioning of the convergent thinking abilities.

Unfortunately, almost none of the research on convergent problem solving has employed designs that make possible very clear interpretations concerning the effects of the intensity and duration of stress upon problem-solving effectiveness. As one would expect, however, a particular stress may improve performance on one task and interfere with performance on another. Reynolds (1960) has reported just such a study. Two different types of tasks, the Thurstones' Test of the Space Factor and the Mirror Drawing Test were used. The stress in both cases was an oral report of failing or poor performance (bottom 20 per cent of a comparable group). No difference appeared between the failure-stressed and control groups in the single-decision space problems. A difference did appear, however, in the mirror-star problem, a more complex task. Reynolds suggests that the stress group's increased motivation resulted in improved performance on the single-decision space problems, but that the beneficial effects of increased motivation were lost as the stress interfered with the more complex and poorly-learned cognitive strategies used in the solution of the mirror-star problem. He suggests that the interference effects of stress increase directly with the complexity of the strategy and inversely with the degree to which the strategy has been learned.

Fortunately there has been a variety of studies to ascertain what factors make problems more difficult. Duncan (1959) in his review of recent research on human problem solving lists the following: an increase in the number of response items held constant, an increase in the number of stimulus-response or total items, and response availability (the number of response items from which the correct response for each stimulus must be selected). In terms of stress concepts, the variables involved all introduce overloading in some way.

There have also been a relatively large number of studies involving state-of-the-organism differences and problem solving. Many of them have involved sex differences and most of these have indicated the superiority of males over females. Of the recent studies reviewed by Duncan (1959) nine experiments revealed some kind of problem-solving superiority for boys and men in comparison with girls and women of similar characteristics. The other three studies reviewed by Duncan showed either no sex differences or few sex differences in problem solving. An important study by Milton (1957), however, suggests that it is sex-role identifications, not sex itself, that is important in determining problem-solving effectiveness. Milton partialled out, in a covariance analysis, Terman-Miles masculinity-femininity scores (i.e., corrected statistically for them) and found that sex was not a significant factor in problem solving. She argues that sex-role identification begins early in childhood and that such differences as occur between boys and girls in problem solving result from past experiences. Nevertheless, the differences are great enough to suggest greater emphasis on problem solving in elementary school as a method of improving the school learning and mental health of boys. It is well known that girls excel boys in reading ability, vocabulary, and many other educational skills during the early school years, and that boys have more personality disturbance during this period. It is also well known to those who have done systematic observation of classroom processes that problem-solving behavior rarely occurs in either the elementary or high school classroom. Thus, boys have little opportunity to achieve in the classroom in a kind of intellectual activity in which they excel.

Among the other individual differences investigated in recent research on problem solving are age differences, reasoning ability such as described in the preceding chapter, motivational variables such as anxiety and the achievement need, intelligence, and analytic habits.

SOME CONVERGENCES FROM PROBLEM-SOLVING RESEARCH

Educators have long agreed that children should be taught how to solve problems and that they should be given school experiences in solving problems. In actual practice, however, efforts have not materialized as might be expected. One obvious reason is that there has been confusion concerning what constitutes a problem. For example, some algebra and geometry teachers say that they give their students problems to solve when in actuality they are only asking them to reproduce solutions given in the textbook or by the teacher. A problem exists for the problem solver when he confronts a situation where he must find a solution for which he does not have immediately available the methods, the information, or both without further thinking.

As pointed out in the preceding chapter, there is considerable agreement concerning the steps or sequences in the problem-solving process. These steps have already been outlined and discussed. Dewey, Parker, Boraas, and others have tried to spell out for teachers, counselors, and others what they should do in order to stimulate and guide individuals in convergent thinking. The suggestions offered by these scholars flow directly from these steps.

Russell (1956), after summarizing a vast body of research concerned with children's thinking, offered a more detailed set of suggestions or hints for teachers and parents in helping children solve problems. These too may be tied in with the steps in the problem-solving process. In abbreviated form his hints are as follows (Russell, 1956, pp. 375–76):

1. Encourage children to present their own problems, not admonish them to think clearly.
2. Motivate them to solve problems. The problem solver must feel that the task is important to him.
3. Remember that the process can be taught because it involves factors that can be controlled and can be learned through experience.
4. Be aware of the level of difficulty at which the problem can be presented. The individual's and the group's level of aspiration gives clues to the complexity of problems that may be successfully presented.
5. Avoid presenting ready-made solutions. Time and patience are not always inexhaustible but they are certainly desirable.
6. Develop meanings in the problem area as a first step.
7. Call attention to any material in the stimulus situation that is not perceived, and to the objective to be attained.
8. Encourage children to modify the objective as it becomes clearer through experience.
9. Assist them in using inductive-deductive methods in cases where definitions, rules, and other generalizations are to be mastered.
10. Encourage them to raise questions, check sources, and otherwise evaluate ideas.
11. Give opportunities for observation and time for using memory in solving problems.
12. Help children face, not avoid, basic personal problems by guiding them in an early search for solutions.
13. Teach older children to recognize some of the common errors of logic.
14. Help remedy difficulties (faulty reading, errors in computation, etc.) with specific techniques.
15. Generalize and verbalize the scientific method with older children to provide them with a possible series of steps for solving problems.
16. Have children test solutions in action.

STRATEGIES OF CONVERGENT THINKING

As games and game theory models have been brought into problem-solving research, the concept of strategies of problem solving have begun to come into prominence. Bruner, Goodnow, and Austin (1956) in their research on thinking have shown that four main strategies or plans of action come into play when people attack problems. These strategies operate by *simultaneous scanning, successive scanning, conservative focusing, and focus gambling.* In *simultaneous scanning,* the problem solver tries to keep before him all of the possibilities that have not been eliminated previously. Each piece of evidence that comes into awareness and each new organization or reorganization of data that takes place is used to support, confirm, or disconfirm the possibilities. In *successive scanning,* the problem solver tests one hypothesis at a time. He limits his choice to those instances that provide a positive test of his hypothesis. In both types of scanning, the individual is ultimately able to converge upon the correct, best, or most acceptable solution. In *conservative focusing,* the individual finds a positive instance (one receiving a "yes"). He then makes a sequence of choices, each of which alters but one attribute value of the first positive instance and tests whether each change yields a positive or a negative response. In *focus gambling,* the problem solver uses a positive instance as a focus and then changes more than one attribute at a time. In both cases, he is able to converge or "zero in" on the correct or best solution. To implement and reinforce these four strategies, the teacher will need to recognize the thinking and guessing responses made by pupils.

STIMULATING THINKING ABOUT A LONG PROBLEM

Almost all of the problems with which school children are confronted require only a few minutes to solve. The division of the school day into short periods, each with something different scheduled, makes the presentation of longer problems difficult. Some elementary schools have broken away from the shackles of such schedules in order to provide opportunities for long problems. The introduction of the core curriculum in some high schools and some of the various plans for team teaching and individual study now being activated make the use of long problems a possibility. The value of long problems has been recognized by some educators for a long time, although there is little evidence that much has been done to provide children with such problems. Boraas in 1922 offered nine reasons for stimulating children to think about long problems (pp. 193–95):

1. Children gain firsthand experience with a long problem in such a way as to realize its nature and thereby be saved from attempting, later in life, to deal with long tasks as if they were like the little school tasks set from day to day.

2. They learn the art of breaking up a big problem into smaller problems by asking questions and analyzing it into its elements.

3. They learn to suspend judgment until all of the evidence is in.

4. It gives an opportunity for cooperative thinking, demonstrates the value of such thinking, and shows ways and means of doing it.

5. The problem serves as a nucleus for much valuable information which will be likely to remain with the pupils because the problem to which it is related will remain.

6. It provides opportunity for gathering material under conditions quite similar to those of everyday life.

7. It gives real practice in oral and written composition.

8. It gives opportunity for conflicts of opinion, for debates in which the purpose is that of discovering the truth

9. It gives practice in organizing the information obtained into a systematic whole, the children evaluating the various parts and assigning to them their proportionate amount of space.

Although the author knows of no systematic or scientific test of the claims made by Boraas concerning the values to be realized by stimulating children to think about long problems, they are supported by "common sense" and are certainly not contraindicated by the experimental evidence available. They are of special significance in the light of some of the major conceptualizations of this book. They are especially relevant to the concern that has been expressed as to the need to learn to cope with prolonged stress. It is quite likely that many breakdowns and failures in problem solving in life situations result from failures to help children master the kinds of skill Boraas was concerned about. Perhaps this failure is what causes long problems to be unnecessarily stressful.

RIGIDITY AND PROBLEM SOLVING

Considerable attention in problem-solving research has been given to the problem of rigidity. Rigid approaches to problem solving reduce chances of success. Researchers, however, have experienced difficulty in demonstrating that there is a general, pervasive factor of rigidity or flexibility in problem solving. Some people who are very rigid in persisting with an established method of solving certain types of problems are quite flexible in solving problems in other areas. For example, one can be quite flexible in solving problems in the science laboratory but extremely rigid in solving everyday problems in his personal life and social problems in the community.

A number of specific research findings have interesting implications for teaching children problem solving. Goldner (1957) found that rigidity and flexibility are rather consistent characteristics of individuals in meeting tasks that are similar in nature. If the problems are varied in nature, this consistency is not found. The problem of the teacher, counselor, or parent then becomes one of helping the individual discover what types of problems are approached with rigidity, then helping him to understand its causes and learn to employ more flexible approaches to such problems.

Prior experience with an object, set of materials, people, or situations sets up certain expectations that are difficult to overcome. In one study Birch and Rabinowitz (1951) found that past experience with objects keeps individuals from using them in different ways when they encounter a problem where the objects must be used in a different manner from the original experience. Luchins (1942) and others have found that when individuals are taught to solve a series of related problems by one method they continue to use that method in solving other problems, even in the face of repeated failure with the method.

SUPPORTIVE CONDITIONS FOR THE INDIVIDUAL PROBLEM SOLVER

Investigators concerned with problems of anxiety and problem solving have provided some interesting leads concerning the creation of group conditions that will support the individual problem solver. Shands (1960) found that the interfering effects of anxiety upon problem solving may be prevented either by the availability of a pattern of behavior for coping with the problem or by the availability of the pattern of a relationship with another person. He maintains that it is especially important in stressful situations that the individual have available a supportive pattern of relationships in order to carry out the complex mental processes of problem solving. An important aspect of the anxiety-arousing situation is the fact that it involves making a selection from various possible patterns of behavior. This problem is apparently diminished whenever the situation includes one or more supportive individuals on whom he can depend for cues as to appropriate responses.

Individuals look to teachers, counselors, parents, and peers for clues to help them structure problem-solving situations. Preschool and primary children usually look to parents and teachers and, as they progress to the intermediate grades, to their peers. As shown in the chapter on the development of interpersonal skills, this stage is marked by an increased concern about consensual validation. The necessity for conforming to adult authority continues throughout this period, however. Adolescents express strong needs for breaking habits of conforming to authority, and their behavior may cause parents and teachers even greater concern than did the earlier break at about the beginning of the intermediate grades.

As teachers, parents, and counselors come to understand and respect adolescent needs for status, they will be able to create the conditions necessary to support adolescents in finding the correct or best solutions.

CONDITIONS FOR GROUP PROBLEM SOLVING

Both in school and in life outside of school, much of the problem solving is done in groups. In school, a whole class or a small group is asked to solve problems. Sometimes, the solution must come from group consensus. The factors of affect, power, communication, and goal, discussed in earlier chapters, are important, especially where stress is involved. The size of the group, the nature of the problem, and the importance of the problem to group members are also salient. Teachers and others interested in developing more effective processes for convergent problem solving in groups may be helped by a series of studies conducted by this author and his colleagues (Torrance and Ziller, 1958). This research was based on studies of the problem-solving behavior of groups in emergencies and extreme conditions and in laboratory experiments involving some type of stressful condition. Some of the highlights of this research will be summarized briefly.

In successful group problem solving there is almost always a leader to give structure to the situation. In emergencies and extreme conditions, leaders seem to feel a greater need than usual to seek the judgments of group members, perhaps because the group provides an anchor in reality. At the same time, there are indications that group members under stressful conditions are more willing than usual to place their lives in the hands of a strong leader who promises to solve their problems for them. In spite of the haste with which many solutions must be reached under stress, the evidence seems to indicate that even in extreme emergencies leaders can profit from the ideas of group members in finding solutions.

On the matter of leadership techniques, it appears (Ziller, 1957a) that group members react most favorably and productively to a group problem-solving situation under conditions permitting self-determination and reinforcement from an authority figure (leader, teacher, parent, etc.). Groups using leader-centered techniques of problem solving (in which the leader has no knowledge of the group's ideas or opinions prior to stating his own) are more reluctant than group-centered problem-solving groups to make a decision involving risk of the lives of group members. It should be of especial interest to adults that group members in problem-solving situations

299

want to know how their leaders stand. They want to be free to disagree with the leader but they also want to know and consider the leader's ideas. Having the leader's opinions seems to be a necessary part of the structuring required for healthy group conditions in solving problems.

In any group where members work together over any length of time, some achieve more ability to influence the solutions of problems than others. Over time, they demonstrate that they are usually "right." A dangerous point is reached, however, when the group assumes that the high-status members are correct and that the other members need not even think. This condition seems to occur in almost all types of groups, whether the power structure is an official one or an informally developed one. The evidence (Torrance, 1954c) shows that influence on solutions requiring group convergence is in line with the power structure of the group, and that differences in power or status interfere with the quality of the problem solving. In groups having an official power structure, the effects of power differences are lessened when the groups are temporary rather than permanent.

In three-man groups with well-defined power structures, the occupant of each power position tends to be assigned or assumes interaction behaviors characteristic of his position. The person with highest status appeals to solidarity, obtains and evaluates suggestions. The person of intermediate status tends to be freer to disagree than either of the others. The lowest status member seems to be afraid to disagree and tends to withdraw from the problem-solving process.

Teachers, counselors, and parents need to be sensitive to the effects of status or power differences in group problem solving. Even in the kindergarten, this factor may prevent a group from finding the correct solution. For example, one parent recently told of such an experience by his five-year-old daughter. The child had been permitted to demonstrate her telescope to the class. Not understanding the child's explanation, the teacher undertook to demonstrate the telescope but pointed the wrong end of the telescope to the sun. Since the teacher must always be "right," the child was afraid to point out this error and as a result lost all interest in school learning, at least temporarily. This is an example of how deference to power may prevent correct group solutions.

Evidence from accounts of actual experiences of groups in emergencies and extreme conditions and from experiments shows that group tolerance of disagreement makes a positive contribution to convergent problem solving (Torrance, 1957a). The disagreement must, of course, be task centered rather than person centered. Preventing disagreement from becoming person centered presents serious problems in some groups. Even though a member is always "right," his ideas may be disregarded or rejected by the group, if he is disliked. If the leader can help the group understand the functions of disagreement, it will be easier to create conditions of tolerance for disagreement of a task-centered type. In research by the author and his colleagues, the following functions of disagreement were identified:

1. *It increases the range of alternatives.* The evidence (Ziller, 1955b) indicates that the wider the range of alternatives considered, the more likely is the solution of the group to be correct or superior.

2. *It decreases chances of misunderstandings.* If members of a group do not feel free to communicate their real opinions, they are likely to be misunderstood. Misunderstandings affect not only the quality of the solution but the mental health of the group members. This phenomenon is dramatically illustrated in a study in which a group of about thirty men who had survived a severe blizzard were interviewed (Torrance, LaForge, and Mason, 1956). At a critical stage following the blizzard, the instructor led the men down an unfrozen creek and continued the trek in subzero weather for about four hours before stopping to pitch camp for the night or to dry out. As a result, eight members of the group suffered severe frostbite. Almost without exception, the interviews revealed that the men thought at the time that the correct thing to do was to stop and dry their feet and that they wanted to do just this. They felt, however, that a protest would be useless as the instructors had made it clear that instructor judgment was not to be questioned. Each instructor also maintained that he wanted the group to stop, make a fire, and dry feet and footgear. They did not order trainees to do this because the trainees appeared apathetic and would do nothing to take care of themselves. Thus, instructors apparently misinterpreted as apathy the men's unwillingness to disagree.

3. *It increases willingness to take calculated risks.* Solutions requiring greater personal risk for the welfare of the group were reached in groups in which the problem solving was shared with the group rather than when the leader shouldered the major responsibility (Ziller, 1955a). This phenomenon may also be observed in the classroom. When permitted to do so, children will frequently choose a superior solution, even though it requires more work and more expensive energies than the teacher himself would think of imposing upon them. Apparently two important factors are at work. Knowing where other members of the group stand clears up misunderstandings and encourages the choice of more expensive, though superior alternatives. Knowing that the group supports him, the leader takes courage in making the more risky decision. Similarly, the teacher, knowing that his pupils are willing to accept the need for working harder, will select the superior solution.

4. *It increases willingness to accept the group's solution.* Frequently executives and leaders who attempt to apply democratic procedures complain that everyone seems to go along with their suggested solutions at a

meeting, but they discover later that the members of the group did not really support them after all. The result is that the agreed-upon solution is ineffectively carried out. In experiments where individual judgments were obtained both before and after group discussion and solution, there tended to be a higher degree of consensus when the solution was preceded by greater expression of disagreement (Ziller, 1955b). Apparently, individuals feel that their ideas have been considered and are consequently more willing to accept the group solutions.

Disagreement, of course, has possible negative effects, if there exists any negative identification among members of the group.

Difficulties in problem solving may be encountered if the leader differs too sharply in values or personality from the other members of the group (Torrance, 1958a). For example, an authority-oriented leader may be very effective in leading an authority-oriented group, but ineffective in leading a group with a democratic orientation. Similarly, a leader with a democratic orientation is likely to be despised and considered weak and unworthy of following by an authority-oriented group, but he may be quite effective in leading men with a democratic orientation. Evidence indicates that highly authoritarian leaders (as identified by the California F-Scale) tend not to profit from critiques of their performance and to overestimate the superiority of the group's solutions. It has also been found that nonhomogeneous groups tend to produce higher quality solutions than do homogeneous groups.

Leaders most willing to assume risks for the group tend to be relatively unconcerned about group opinions, relatively authoritarian, high in self-esteem, and high in level of aspiration (Ziller, 1955a). Although group opinion may give a leader the courage to attempt a more difficult task or solution, the leader must recognize any tendency for the group to be overanxious to take risks. In emergencies and extreme conditions, he may have to exercise a restraining influence when risk is not necessary for the accomplishment of the group's mission. Similarly, a teacher or parent may have to use his restraining influence to prevent children from undertaking solutions for which they are totally unprepared.

In groups of up to six persons, the research evidence indicates that increasing size seems to contribute to increasing quality of group solutions (Ziller, 1957b). In most tasks, however, groups of four and five members tend to depart from this linear trend. Groups of six appear to be most consistent in the quality of their solutions from problem to problem. Groups of six almost always work out some kind of organization or division of labor. Groups of four or five rarely do. Teachers would probably do well to train small groups, especially groups of four and five, how to organize their efforts more effectively.

APPLICATIONS TO EDUCATIONAL PROBLEMS

A problem of teachers, school counselors, psychologists, and administrators is to help children achieve enough convergence in their behavior to meet the demands of society and to get along with groups well enough to permit them to work out satisfactory solutions. Throughout history, the most favored means of obtaining convergent behavior has been through punishment and coercion. Even today, a large number of parents and educators believe that the only way to control the behavior of children, young people, or adults is through punishment and coercion. They fail to consider the implications for personality development and mental health.

Feelings of insecurity and inadequacy are naturally increased by discipline that makes a person feel acutely the differences between himself and the authority executing the discipline. Force in the form of punishment has this effect, since the person being disciplined usually lacks the ability to oppose the force brought against him. Children, of course, use such counter weapons as crying, disobedience, overactivity, refusal of food, lack of control of elimination, and mild aggressions such as holding the breath or banging the head. Usually the parent or teacher uses additional force (punishment) to oppose the counter weapons. School-age children also use refusal to learn as one of the counter strategies against coercion.

Rich (1946), in examining the mental health problems resulting from force and punishment, maintains that in America we have a tradition that maintains that the only way to control or alter a child's behavior is to punish him. Some authorities also maintain that this same tradition has dominated the treatment of the mentally ill (Joint Commission on Mental Illness and Health, 1961) in the United States. Panken (1946), in discussing the menace of coercive education, insists that people who are charged with the education of children can best serve children if they treat them as personalities. He insists that each child craves respect for its mind and person and that the developing mind is nourished by sympathetic understanding and participation in its hopes, dreams, and ambitions.

One of the big lessons of the ages is that some individuals simply do not profit from punishment. The more they are punished the more they behave in nonconforming and unconstructive ways. The implication of the research and theory described in this chapter is that educators do have for their guidance some very constructive clues for developing and freeing the convergent thinking abilities. A responsive environment is more likely to result in healthier convergent behavior than is a coercive environment.

SUMMARY

Successful convergent thinking or problem solving is impossible or extremely unlikely without adequate clues or guides to behavior. Little of the research concerning convergent problem solving has employed designs that make possible interpretations concerning the effects of the intensity and duration of stress. The scattered evidence, however, indicates that the general guides outlined in the first part of the book hold for convergent problem solving. Research has identified the major factors that make problems more difficult and thus more stressful beyond certain limits. These include an increase in the number of response items held constant, an increase in the stimulus-response or total items, and response availability. A majority of the studies involving sex differences shows superiority of boys and men over women and girls.

There is general agreement among educators that children should be taught problem solving. Education writers have long offered very specific and sound suggestions for accomplishing this goal. Observations of the classroom process indicate, however, that little problem-solving activity occurs in classrooms. Research such as that of Bruner, Goodnow, and Austin should give teachers useful clues for this type of teaching. Especially lacking in school situations studied are problem-solving activities of a sustained nature.

A number of studies indicate that personality rigidity reduces chances of success in problem solving. Studies also indicate that supportive conditions improve chances of successful problem solving, especially under conditions of stress. Some of the group conditions identified as favorable to convergent problem solving are the presence of a leader who helps to give necessary structure to the situation, self-determination by group members with reinforcement from a leader, consideration of solutions by all members regardless of status or power, and willingness to disagree. Willingness to disagree aids in the solution of correct solutions because it increases the range of alternatives, decreases chances of misunderstandings, increases willingness to take calculated risks, and increases willingness to accept the group's solutions. As long as disagreement is task-centered rather than person-centered it is likely to contribute to successful convergent thinking. Such conditions cannot be achieved through punitive, coercive discipline.

Role of
Divergent Thinking in
Coping with Stress

19

Divergent thinking involves the production of new information from what has been cognized or memorized, just as does convergent thinking. In contrast to convergent thinking, however, divergent thinking involves thinking in terms of possibles instead of driving for the one "correct" or "accepted" solution. It goes off into different directions, making possible changes in the method of problem solving and departures from the known solutions; it leads to a diversity of solutions where more than one solution may be acceptable or even desirable.

THE DIVERGENT THINKING ABILITIES

The abilities involved in divergent thinking are somewhat different from those involved in traditional tests of intelligence or scholastic ability, such as the Stanford-Binet, the Wechsler Intelligence Scale for Children, the California Mental Maturity, the Otis, and the Kuhlmann-Anderson. The findings by Hargreaves in 1927 on this issue have continued to be supported. When he scored his tests of imagination for fluency of ideas, with emphasis on quantity rather than quality, he obtained rather high correlation with scores in intelligence tests. In addition to the appreciable amount of the general factor "g" (general rather than specific ability), he found a considerable group factor in common with other measures of imagination. The "speed" factor was also found to be important in fluency. When these same tests of imagination were scored for originality, denoting novelty and uncommonness, Hargreaves found very little relationship to "g."

In work with preschool children Andrews (1930) found that the correlations between IQ and imagination and between mental age and imagination are low enough to indicate that very little relationship exists between intelligence and imagination. Most recent investigators have found small but statistically significant relationships between measures of creative thinking and well-known measures of intelligence or academic aptitude. Barron (1957) reports a coefficient of correlation of .33 between his measure of originality and the Concept Mastery Test. Flanagan (1959) obtained a coefficient of correlation of .39 between his measure of ingenuity and the Guilford-Zimmerman General Reasoning Test.

Using Terman's Concept Mastery Test with his selected groups of highly effective persons, MacKinnon (1960) found little relationship between intelligence and creativity. On this measure, the architects, one of the most creative of his groups, earned a mean score of only 113 with a range from 39 to 179. Among these architects, he obtained a coefficient of correlation of −.08 between scores on the Concept Mastery Test and creativity in architecture as rated by a panel of five architects. MacKinnon reports that this value is not far different from the correlation between intelligence and creativity in his other creative groups. In general, however, all of MacKinnon's highly creative subjects may be considered as intelligent. Apparently some minimal level of intelligence seems to be necessary for outstanding creative achievement in any field. This level probably differs from field to field, but has been estimated by MacKinnon, Roe, and others as being around an IQ of 120.

In the author's work at the University of Minnesota, coefficients of correlation have been computed according to educational groups, sexes for each educational group, and separately for different measures of intelligence or academic aptitude. In general, coefficients of correlation are higher for girls than for boys and higher in unselected groups than in highly talented groups (high-achieving, high-ability, and high-IQ children, graduate school groups). With the Stanford-Binet in one elementary school, mean coefficients of correlation of .16 and .17 in successive years were obtained between mental age and total score on a battery of creative thinking tests. Other coefficients of correlation between measures of intelligence and creative thinking obtained by the author and his associates are summarized below. It is of special interest to note that there is a high coefficient of correlation within the lower ranges of intelligence. Since both measures are group tests, it is doubtful that either measure yields a true measure of the subjects' potential.

If, from Table 19–1, gifted groups (upper 20 per cent) were selected separately on the basis of the measure of divergent thinking and separately on the basis of the traditional measure of intelligence or academic promise, the overlap would range from 23 to 52 per cent. In other words, one would miss on the average about 70 per cent of the upper 20 per cent on divergent thinking, if one were to rely upon the traditional measures of intellectual promise.

Table 19–1.

GROUP	NUMBER	MEASURE OF INTELLIGENCE OR SCHOLASTIC APTITUDE	CORRELATION COEFFICIENT
Grades 1–6	354	Otis Quick-Scoring	.32
Grades 5 and 6	238	Kuhlmann-Anderson	.27
Grades 5 and 6	110	California Mental Maturity	.24
Grades 7–12	272	Lorge-Thorndike	.27
High Achievers (Grade 6)	30	Stanford-Binet	.03
Grade 9 (Upper 20% IQ)	21	Otis Beta Test	−.11
Grade 9 (Lower 20% IQ)	20	Otis Beta Test	.73
Counselors	70	Miller Analogies	.10
Counselors	70	Ohio State Psychological	−.02
Graduate Class (Educ. Psychol.)	75	Miller Analogies	.11

If the divergent thinking abilities are different from those measured by traditional tests of intelligence or scholastic aptitude, what then are they like? The factors thus far identified and measured by Guilford and his associates (Guilford and Merrifield, 1960) will now be described.

WORD FLUENCY

Word fluency is the ability to produce divergent symbolic units. Four tasks are currently being used (Guilford and Merrifield, 1960) to assess this ability. In a suffixes task (Suffixes W-1), the subject is asked to write within a four-minute period as many words as he can which end with a specified suffix. A similar task with prefixes (Prefixes W-2) is also used. In a third task (First and Last Letters W-3), the subject writes words beginning with a specified letter and ending with a specified letter. In a fourth task (Word Fluency), the subject writes words containing one specified letter. The subject is required to produce rather than to recognize or reproduce responses. What is produced must meet certain requirements.

EXPRESSIONAL FLUENCY

Expressional fluency is the ability to produce divergent symbolic systems. One task, Expressional Fluency, involves writing four-word sentences when the first letter of each word is given. Simile Interpretations calls for the completion of a sentence that states an analogous idea. Word Arrangements calls for the writing of sentences containing four specified words. Again, it will be noted that responses must be produced within specified limits.

IDEATIONAL FLUENCY

Ideational fluency is ability to produce divergent semantic units and is one of the abilities involved in almost all test batteries designed to assess the creative thinking abilities. This ability is sometimes referred to as "copious ideation" or "free-wheeling" and refers merely to the number of ideas produced. Although some people maintain that mere quantity of ideas is relatively unimportant, there are strong arguments for the viewpoint that "quantity yields quality." Alfred North Whitehead, Thomas Alva Edison, Alex Osborn (1963), and others have subscribed to this point of view. Research in social psychology (Ziller, 1955b) indicates that greater variation or divergency in alternatives leads to superior group decisions.

In one of the tasks (Guilford and Merrifield, 1960) used in assessing this ability, the subject is asked to write as many ideas as possible about a given topic in five minutes. In another, he is asked to write as many words as possible about a given topic in six minutes. In a third task, he lists, during a period of two and one half minutes, the names of as many things as he can think of that are round or could be called round. In a fourth task, he writes the names of things that fit broad classes, the task being divided into three parts, each lasting four minutes.

ASSOCIATIONAL FLUENCY

Associational fluency (Guilford and Merrifield, 1960) is the ability to produce divergent semantic relations. One task, Controlled Associations, requires the subject to write as many synonyms as possible for given words. A second, Simile Insertions, calls for the writing of adjectival completion for a simile. A third (Associational Fluency) calls for the production of a word that can be associated with two given words.

FIGURAL SPONTANEOUS FLEXIBILITY

Figural spontaneous flexibility (Guilford and Merrifield, 1960) is the ability to produce divergent figural classes. It was formerly interpreted as "rate of fluctuation of ambiguous figures." The tasks used in assessing this ability have been rather widely used in psychological testing and were developed by L. L. Thurstone (1944).

The first task, Cube Fluctuations, calls for the subject to indicate the number of changes in perspective of an ambiguous cube. The second requires the subject to indicate the number of alternations from one illusion to another while observing the shadow of a rotating rectangular blade. A third task, Retinal-Rivalry Reversals, requires the subject to indicate the number of reversals perceived when a blue field is presented stereoscopically to one eye and a yellow field to the other eye.

308

FIGURAL ADAPTIVE FLEXIBILITY

Figural Adaptive Flexibility (Guilford and Merrifield, 1960) is the ability to produce figural transformations. Two of the well-known Match Problems are used in assessing this ability. One requires the subject to indicate three or four different patterns of a specified number of matches that can be removed to leave a specified number of triangles or squares. The second calls for him to indicate several different patterns of matches that can be removed to leave a specified number of squares. A third task, Planning Air Maneuvers, requires the subject to select the most direct path in "skywriting" letter combinations. It consists of 20 items to be completed in sixteen minutes.

SEMANTIC SPONTANEOUS FLEXIBILITY

Semantic Spontaneous Flexibility (Guilford and Merrifield, 1960) is the ability to produce divergent semantic classes. One task, Brick Uses, calls for the writing of a variety of kinds of uses for bricks. This task has been used also as a test of ideational fluency with bricks or other common objects as stimuli. While the fluency score is determined by the number of ideas produced, the flexibility score would be the number of different categories into which the uses produced would fall. A second task, Alternate Uses, requires the subject to list different peculiar uses for common objects.

Many people get set on one approach and cannot break away from it. For example, in the author's studies "tin cans" has been used as the stimulus in the Unusual Uses task. In spite of the fact that "unusual, clever, interesting" uses of tin cans are requested, many subjects are unable to break away from the idea that tin cans are used as containers. For example, 87 per cent of the responses given by a sample of 71 schizophrenic subjects apparently on the road to recovery fell in the container category. In a relatively large sample of college sophomores and juniors, the percentage was 33 and in a sample of elementary school children, 17. In a class of 100 graduate students, the percentage was 40, indicating lower flexibility than the younger students but far greater flexibility than the mental patients.

ORIGINALITY

Originality (Guilford and Merrifield, 1960) is the ability to produce divergent semantic transformations. It has also been variously defined as the ability to think of unusual or new ideas, to break out of the mold, and to get off the beaten path. In most studies, originality has been operationally defined in terms of statistical infrequency. It has also been defined in terms of remoteness of association, cleverness, and the like.

In one task (Plot Titles), the subject is asked to write titles for short stories and only clever titles are accepted. In a second (Symbol Production), he is asked to produce symbols to represent given activities and objects. In a third (Remote Consequences), he is asked to list remote consequences for a specified event, remoteness being assessed in terms of distance in time, space, or sequence of events. In the fourth (Riddles), he is asked to give clever solutions to riddles. The ability involved in these test tasks is thought to be related to ability to produce new and unusual solutions to problems. In terms of stress behavior, it would be hypothesized that a person scoring high on these test tasks would be likely to show what is commonly termed ingenuity in coping with the stressful situation. In other words, he would be able to find clever, surprising, and unexpected solutions that would enable him to behave constructively in the stressful situation.

Numerous people other than Guilford, including the author, have devised tests of originality. Almost all of them use statistical infrequency as a major criteria but also require that a response be relevant and useful in terms of the problem.

SEMANTIC ELABORATION

Semantic elaboration is the ability to produce divergent semantic implications. One task, Planning Elaboration, requires that the subject fill in as many details as necessary to make a briefly outlined activity work successfully. A second, Figure Production, calls for the subject to add to given lines in order to produce a meaningful figure. The score is based upon the number of details produced.

OTHER MEASURES OF DIVERGENT THINKING

The divergent thinking measures described in the foregoing section have been used primarily with adult and college-level subjects, although limited use of them has been made with high school students. Under a variety of labels such as imagination, originality, ingenuity, and creative thinking, many other tests of the divergent thinking abilities have been devised. A few of the methods that have been used with children will be sketched briefly in the sections that follow.

METHODS OF MEASUREMENT IN EARLY CHILDHOOD

A variety of methods have been used to assess the divergent thinking abilities of young children. McCarty (1924) used drawings; Abramson (1927) used ink blots and concrete observations; Grippen (1933) used paintings and verbalizations while painting, a procedure called the "constant contact method."

Andrews (1930) used a great variety of methods and observations and classified many types of imaginative or creative behavior. Three of Andrews' tests were presented tachistoscopically with the task of forming new products (transformations). The following kinds of observations were made of the imaginative play of children from two to six: imitation, experimentation, transformation of objects, acts of sympathy, dramatizations, imaginary playmates, fanciful explanations, fantastic stories, new uses of stories, constructions, new games, extensions of language, appropriate quotations, leadership with plan, and aesthetic appreciation.

Markey (1935) employed observational methods to evaluate performance in a variety of standardized situations and tasks, such as a housekeeping game, the fanciful naming of visual stimuli, leadership in imaginative games, block building, and the like. Some of the *Minnesota Tests of Creative Thinking,* which will be described in the next section, have also been used at the kindergarten level.

In all of the attempts to assess the divergent thinking abilities, the correlation tends to be low between measures of divergent thinking ability and traditional measures of intelligence. Markey sought in various ways to explain away the relatively low correlation between the measures. Andrews recognized more clearly the difference between the two types of measures and concluded that "very little relationship exists between intelligence and the fantastic imagination of the young child."

METHODS OF MEASUREMENT DURING THE ELEMENTARY SCHOOL YEARS

Although investigators of divergent thinking during the elementary years have used a variety of measures, no single investigator has used a variety with a single sample of subjects. Typical of early efforts was Kirkpatrick's (1900) work with ink blots. Colvin and Meyer (1906) used compositions, giving attention to such qualities as invention, sense of humor, imaginative power, and perceptive power. Simpson (1922) used fifty sets of four small round dots, representing the four corners of squares, as the stimuli for constructions that assessed fluency, originality, and flexibility. The methods of McCarty, Abramson, and Grippen have already been mentioned. Harms (1946) employed a test requiring the representation of words (mostly various actions) by single lines in grades one through twelve.

Since 1958 the author and his associates have been engaged in a continuing program of development and research related to the identification, development, and utilization of creative talent. Most of the tests would qualify as tests of divergent thinking under Guilford's conceptualization. Although attention has been given to the period from kindergarten through graduate school, concentration thus far has been on the elementary school period. A variety of tasks have been devised and, though the work is far from complete, an effort is being made to develop a comprehensive approach to the measurement and development of these abilities.

At first, the author sought to adapt for use with children some of the tasks developed by Guilford and his associates (1951). The first work was with two alternative forms consisting of the following six Guilford-type tasks: unusual uses, impossibilities, consequences, problem situations, improvements, and common problems. Adaptation was accomplished by substituting objects or situations more familiar to children. Thus, subjects were instructed to think of unusual uses of tin cans or cardboard boxes instead of bricks, and to imagine all of the things that might possibly happen "if animals and birds could speak the language of men," instead of what would happen "if all national and local laws were suddenly abolished."

Almost simultaneously, experimentation was begun with several other kinds of tests. The test tasks were constructed on the basis of analyses of the reported experiences of scientific discoverers, inventors, writers, and other types of creative persons. An attempt was made to construct tasks that would be models of the creative process, each involving several different kinds of thinking. The author has tended in the direction of fairly complex tasks which have features that make use of what is known about the nature of the creative thinking processes, the qualities of creative products, the creative personality, and conditions that facilitate or inhibit creative behavior. Very early in this work, both verbal and nonverbal tasks were included. The repertoire of tasks has continually been broadened. To the Circles Task has been added Squares and Parallel Lines, various versions of the Incomplete Figures Test, the Picture Construction or Shape Test, a Manipulative Design Task, and the Science-Toy Test (Torrance, 1962).

The verbal tasks have involved a variety of objects and materials that stimulate the senses of sight, hearing, and touch. The Ask-and-Guess Test calls for questions about gaps in knowledge about the events occurring in a picture, and hypotheses about possible causes and consequences of the pictured events. Similar uses have been made of excerpts from films. The Product Improvement Test calls for novel ideas for improving such objects as children's toys, instruments used in one's vocation, and the like. In most cases, the objects in question have been presented for examination. The concept of the well-known Consequences Test has been adapted by presenting new improbable situations along with drawings for what is called the "Just Suppose Test." The Sound Effects Test makes use of tape-recorded sound effects, a progressive series of warm-ups, and other built-in features based on research findings. The author is now developing tests based on tape-recorded dramatized accounts, using both fantasy and reality materials. As an example of the former he is using the story of "Giovanni and the Giant." Each time the Giant maneuvers Giovanni into a tight spot, the tape is stopped for pupils to write their solutions. "Polar Pilot," the story of Richard Byrd, is being used in a similar manner.

The results of these tasks make it clear that some individuals respond more imaginatively to things they hear, while others achieve greater heights when responding to things they see. Some individuals are free, spontaneous, and bold in their thinking when permitted to transmit their ideas in figural symbols, but are paralyzed and impoverished if they have to express their ideas in words. For others, the reverse is true. These individual differences become increasingly important in the consideration of the clinical uses of such tests.

COMMON PROBLEMS IN DIVERGENT THINKING

Since each person is unique, it is to be expected that each individual's thinking will be unique or divergent. Being unique or divergent, however, is an extremely uncomfortable state, as social psychologists such as Asch (1958) have demonstrated. Frequently, divergence in thinking makes the person a minority of one. Since being a minority of one is so uncomfortable, the individual must either repress his divergent thoughts or learn to cope with the tensions that arise from being "different" in his thinking. Such repression may lead to actual personality breakdown. Expression of divergent ideas, however, can lead to loneliness, conflicts, and other problems of adjustment. First, some of the problems that result from divergent thinking and then some of the ones that result from repressing such thoughts will be identified and discussed.

PROBLEMS RESULTING FROM DIVERGENT THINKING

SANCTIONS AGAINST DIVERGENCY. Many of society's coercive influences against divergency are illustrated in the story of Pepper, the Flying Monkey, recounted in the first chapter. The divergent thinker is especially in trouble if he lacks some characteristic considered important in his society. Such is the plight of Roarless, a silent lion, in the following story:

> Once there was a lion named Sylvester. Everyone in the jungle called him Roarless. The reason they called him that was because he never roared.
> One day he was walking along in the forest when he met his pal, Tom. Tom was a lion too. He was roaring all the time. "Roarless, why don't you ever roar like the rest of the lions?" said Tom.
> But Roarless just kept walking along. Then he met his other lion friend, Tim. "Roarless, why don't you ever roar like the rest of the lions?" said Tim.
> But as usual Roarless just kept walking along.
> All the lions in the jungle were asking the same question. Since they were all doing this, Roarless was getting a little fed up. He turned around and gave the biggest roar that they had ever heard. Then all of the animals in the jungle called Roarless, Sylvester.

PRESSURES TO BE WELL ROUNDED. The divergent thinker is likely to have lagged in some phases of his development. Many investigators in a

313

variety of fields have been disappointed in not finding that outstanding individuals in a field under study are well-rounded, "all-American" boys. The verbal abilities of the creatively gifted child frequently will be below some of his other abilities. He may even have difficulty in learning to read or write. Perhaps the most inventive and imaginative child tested by the author is a boy who has had unusual difficulty in learning to read, yet his store of information and his ability to use it imaginatively in solving problems and developing ideas is fantastic.

This problem is particularly acute at the fourth grade level. In a number of cases, fourth graders identified by tests as highly creative have been re-evaluated by teachers. Teachers have then discovered that these children are far more knowledgeable and thoughtful than the teachers had imagined. The author was particularly struck by a comment made by the examiner after testing orally a fourth grade boy. The examiner stated: "This boy impresses me as the kind of individual who will become a top executive who can dictate to five secretaries at the same time without becoming confused." The boy's responses gave evidence of high inventive level, flexibility, and originality. However, he had a serious reading disability and ranked near the bottom of his class on the written test of creative thinking.

PREFERENCE FOR LEARNING ALONE. Divergent thinkers prefer to learn on their own, and society has been slow to grant such opportunities. In one study (Torrance, 1964) it was found that children will do a great deal of writing on their own, if properly motivated. In another (Fritz, 1958) it was found that gifted children in a split-shift school showed more growth in language development, science, and social studies than did gifted children under a full-day schedule. Only in spelling was there significantly less growth among the split-shift children (seventh graders). In still another study (Torrance, 1964) it was found that children in a split-shift school engage in a large number of learning activities on their own.

ATTEMPTING DIFFICULT TASKS. Divergent thinkers want to move ahead of or to move in different directions from their peers. Ideas about educational "readiness" and equality of opportunity, however, prevent teachers from permitting children to move in these divergent directions. These conflicts are exemplified in Harold Benjamin's (1956) satire of the conflict between the educational mountaineer and the educational plainsman. The mountaineer wanted to develop a crippled six-year-old's personality by teaching her tap-dancing. The child could move her right foot only by dragging it on the floor, but she could lift her left foot off the floor and move the toe and heel. The plainsman complained that this was undemocratic, that if tap-dancing was good for one child it was good for all the children. The mountaineer replied that he was not teaching tap-dancing but that he was teaching a shy child to be more confident and to get her first secure moorings.

In another case, the educational mountaineer wanted to develop the six-year-old of high intellectual capacity by encouraging him to study osmosis. Again, the plainsman complained that osmosis is a high school subject and that this is where it should be taught to everybody. Again, the mountaineer countered that he was not teaching osmosis but that he was teaching a child who is a great genius to be in truth the great genius that he is.

A very frequent theme in the imaginative stories of children is related to this problem. The young animal or fowl asks, "When can I roar? When can I crow? When can I quack? When can I fly?" Almost always, the answer is, "When you are a little older." Parents and teachers are always afraid that the young one might not be ready to learn and that he would be forever scarred by even the most temporary failure.

A common experience in the lives of many highly outstanding individuals has been their ability to cope with failure and frustration. Certainly, almost all highly creative scientists, inventors, artists, and writers have attempted tasks that were too difficult for them. Had they not attempted such tasks, it is quite unlikely that their great ideas would have been born.

SEARCH FOR UNIQUENESS. The children who think divergently seem to create problems for themselves by trying consciously to be different—by searching for their uniqueness. Barron maintains that creative individuals reject the demands of their society to surrender their individuality because "they want to own themselves totally and because they perceive a short-sightedness in the claim of society that all its members should adapt themselves to a norm for a given time and place" (1958, p. 163).

One way in which the creative individual searches for his uniqueness is through his vocational choice. Getzels and Jackson (1960), for example, found that their highly creative subjects (divergent thinkers), compared with their highly intelligent ones, gave a greater number of different occupations and more "unusual" or rare occupations. Their attitudes toward adult success were also different, the divergent thinkers being less concerned with conventional standards.

THE PSYCHOLOGICAL ESTRANGEMENT OF CREATIVE CHILDREN

From the foregoing it should be obvious that a large share of the divergent thinker's adjustment problems are likely to be centered in his psychological isolation and estrangement from his peers and teachers. It will be no news that peer groups exercise severe pressures against their most creative members. In no group thus far studied has the author failed to find relatively clear evidence of the operation of these pressures, though they are far more severe in some classes than in others.

When the most superior divergent thinkers of each sex in each classroom selected and matched for sex and IQ with other children in the same classroom, three characteristics stood out as differentiating the highly divergent from the less divergent ones. First, there was a tendency for them to gain a reputation for having wild or silly ideas. Their teachers and peers agreed on this. Second, their work was characterized by its productivity of ideas "off the beaten track." This divergence came out as a differentiating characteristic both when the number of unique details and when the number of nonessential details were considered. It explains one of the difficulties of teachers and peers in evaluating the ideas of divergent children and perhaps explains why they show up no better than they do on traditional intelligence tests. Their ideas simply do not conform to the standardized dimensions, the behavioral norms, on which responses are judged. Third, the divergent children were characterized by humor and playfulness. All of these characteristics help explain both the estrangement and the divergent production.

PROBLEMS RESULTING FROM REPRESSION OF DIVERGENT THINKING

FAULTY OR UNCERTAIN SELF-CONCEPT. The obedient, convergent-thinking child is likely to grow up with a lack of confidence in his own thinking, to be uncertain of his self-concept, and to be overly dependent upon others in making decisions. The importance of freedom to test one's limits through experimentation and exploration has already been discussed in earlier chapters.

LEARNING DISABILITIES. Children who repress their divergent thinking may develop serious learning disabilities. They learn to repress their natural tendency to learn creatively by questioning, guessing, exploring, and experimenting. They are afraid to make errors. When prevented from learning creatively by going in divergent directions, some children will lose interest in learning and refuse to learn by authority. Elizabeth Drews (1960) has given an excellent example of such a boy:

> Tim, a fourth-grader, gave every evidence of developing into a scientist. His interests ranged from electricity through crustaceans and birds to geological specimens. Most of these interests were displayed in one way or another on, in, and around his desk. He had dry cells, rocks, an abalone shell from California, and a robin's egg from the year before.
>
> His previous teacher had encouraged his far-ranging interests and his willingness to share with his classmates. This year he had a new kind of teacher, a young man just out of military service, who was accustomed to neatness and discipline and took a jaundiced view of Tim's projects.

316

> One day the teacher ordered the boy to take the clutter home and keep it there. Tim did, but his heart was broken. From that time on, he refused to learn. When he took his standardized achievement tests, he ranked below grade level! His only educational venture in the classroom for the rest of the year was to learn the Morse code and teach it to his classmates.

We also find such learning disabilities in the stories of children about animals and people with special disabilities. One told a story of a lion that would not roar. He was afraid to try to roar because he thought his roar might not sound like a lion.

BEHAVIOR PROBLEMS. Many children who score high as divergent thinkers are behavior problems in the classroom. In the early grades, the author found in his studies at Minnesota, such children received several times as many nominations as ones who "think of the most ideas for being naughty" as the average or as the highly intelligent and less creative child. Sometimes, after a child gains this kind of reputation, teachers and classmates are unable to see even his good ideas as anything but silly or naughty. Perhaps as unfortunate is the tendency for some divergent children to repress their ideas or keep them secret.

Catherine Patrick (1955) has offered some interesting hypotheses concerning the thinking of the psychopathic personality. She explains that such an individual has experienced severe conflicts. Faced with difficult problems and being distressed and unhappy, the psychopathic deviate finally has a hunch. According to Patrick, this "wonderful idea" gives him such pleasure after his severe unhappiness that he clings to it and is loath to undergo the discouragement inherent in the final stages of revision and verification. Because he shrinks from testing his solution, he spends hours elaborating upon it instead of verifying and revising it. Or he rushes out and applies his erroneous solution and gets into difficulty.

Two ongoing studies of the creative thinking abilities of delinquent youths suggest that the latter course of rushing out and applying an idea without developing it is likely to be more frequent. Patricia Will (1964) studied a sample of delinquent adolescent girls. On several of the measures of divergent thinking, these girls performed as well as or better than other girls their age. They showed an amazing deficiency in ability to elaborate (about 1.2 standard deviations below average) or to develop the details of an idea. They also showed some difficulty in producing ideas for improvements. Even within this special sample, the degree of emotional disturbance as judged from the Minnesota Multiphasic Personality Inventory was found to be associated with inability to elaborate. Results from a similar study of delinquent boys also emphasize this inability to elaborate and work out the details of an idea. If these studies can be further substantiated and elabo-

317

rated, they may provide useful clues for the prevention and rehabilitation of the psychopathic deviate.

It seems, then, that the divergent thinker with behavior problems is likely to have three major deficiencies in his thinking. First, he jumps to a premature closure or actually thinks of too few possibilities. Second, he fails to test and revise his hunches or hypotheses. Third, he fails to elaborate or think through the details of a plan causing even good plans and intentions to fail or to result in delinquent behavior. Consequently, he fails to learn from experience.

NEUROTIC CONFLICTS. Apparently one consequence of the repression of divergent thinking is neurotic conflict. Some students of creativity have maintained that one must be neurotic in order to be creative. Most personality theorists and psychotherapy theorists, however, have seen neurotic conflict as inimical to creative thinking. Some, like Rank (1932), however, have maintained that the "neurotic type" may be more creative and sounder psychologically than the "adapted type," who is aware of no problems but is well adapted to the status quo. To Rank, the "creative type" has a healthy personality and lives fully and completely in harmony with his potentialities and interests.

Some neurotic artists and writers have refused psychotherapy for fear that they would lose their creative spark. Kubie (1958), Roe (1959), and others cite evidence that this belief is erroneous. Kubie argues that the neurosis is "the most banal and undistinguished component of human nature." He contends that only when an individual is not hamstrung by conscious fear and guilt that the preconscious processes operate. "The contribution of preconscious processes to creativity," Kubie (1958, p. 37) explains, "depends upon their freedom in gathering, assembling, comparing, and reshuffling of ideas." He concludes that creative activities can be used as one ingredient in the therapeutic process but that creative activity alone can never cure.

PSYCHOSES. If creative needs are strong and if their repression is severe or prolonged, tension is likely to be overwhelming and psychosis a possible result. The process by which this occurs is apparently varied. A common feature, however, is a lack of verification or revision in divergent thinking or a paralysis in thinking.

There are a number of other ways in which psychotic and creative divergent thinking must be differentiated. As a consequence of the way a creative person is treated by society, he develops some traits that resemble those of psychotics. For example, a highly creative individual because of the very superiority of his thinking and production may be threatening to others. As a result he may experience in actuality a great deal of persecution. His reaction to this reality may be very much like the behavior of the

318

paranoid personality, at least in some respects. Or, in order to accompli significant creative work, an individual may have to behave in ways that a judged as withdrawn or schizophrenic. As Barlow (1952, pp. 140–41) has pointed out, scientists who withdraw from society and absorb themselves in research, often make epoch-making discoveries because they are able to concentrate on their problems without social distractions. The shy, sensitive poet may transform society's ridicule and dislike for him into rhythms of great beauty. Musical composers frequently assume certain schizoid-like traits. Their source of inspiration may be found in the fantasy and day-dreaming they use in their adaptation to stresses. Such behaviors, however, are vastly different in other ways from truly psychotic behavior.

ROLE OF DIVERGENT THINKING IN MENTAL HEALTH

Now that some of the consequences of both expressing and repressing the divergent thinking abilities have been examined, one may ask, "Is the development of the divergent thinking abilities worth it? What is their role in mental health?" From the ideas already presented, it will be agreed that there is little doubt but that prolonged, enforced repression of a person's divergent thinking may lead to actual breakdown of personality. For one thing, the stifling of divergent thinking cuts at the very roots of satisfaction in living and ultimately creates overwhelming, paralyzing tension.

Research concerning divergent thinking is yielding more and more confirmation of the above ideas. One set of evidence comes from a study (Hebeisen, 1960) of a group of schizophrenic subjects who at the time they were administered a battery of divergent thinking tasks were apparently on their way to recovery. Their tremendous inflexibility, blocking, and lack of imagination was amazing. They seemed afraid to think. For example, over 80 per cent of a control group of normal subjects responded to all of the divergent thinking tasks and subtasks while less than 25 per cent of the schizophrenics did so. About 60 per cent of the schizophrenics blocked on four or more of the tasks or subtasks, whereas none of the normals blocked on this many. Their fear in thinking divergently is also shown in the data already presented concerning their inability to depart from the "container" category on the Tin Cans Uses task. One schizophrenic subject gave the following record:

1. To put food in
2. To put soup in
3. Tomato soup in
4. Campbell's soup in
5. Bean soup in

The container response is the safe response. Everyone knows that tin cans are made to put food in.

Clearly, the partly-recovered schizophrenic patients studied lacked some important resources for coping with life's demands. One would suspect that this lack explains why they broke down to begin with, although it cannot be proved by the data available. For this reason, some of the roles of divergent thinking in coping with stress and preventing breakdown will be reviewed.

COPING WITH CHANGE. We are living in a world in which the rate of change is increasing rapidly. Over 60 per cent of the foods now on the market were not on the market ten years ago, and 80 per cent of the foods that will be on the market five years from now are not available today. Ninety per cent of the medicines now in use did not exist 25 years ago (*Time,* May 26, 1961); 75 per cent were nonexistent ten years ago. These data give us an index of the rate of change to which individuals must accommodate. It is impossible then to prepare children to cope with all of the demands they will meet. They must indeed think divergently, not only to make the changes that move society forward but to respond constructively to the changes.

AVOIDING FRUSTRATION OF UNWORKABLE SOLUTION. Frustrated individuals continue to use methods that have repeatedly proved to be unsuccessful. These people have been led to expect that *one* method is best. If they were flexible in their thinking they would try different approaches. If they were original in their thinking, they would be able to "get out of the rut" and come through with some approach that had escaped others. History too reveals that man has many unsolved problems which he continues to try to solve by methods that have repeatedly failed. Thus, mankind might avoid much frustration by using more divergent thinking in solving problems. Perhaps some of the problems are not insoluble after all.

COUNTERACTING FATIGUE. Fatigue has many causes other than physical exertion. It may be caused by the lack of an idea, a plan on which to base hope. Men in emergencies and extreme conditions frequently report that they felt completely exhausted, only to pick up great spurts of energy when they suddenly thought of some "wild idea" that gave hope of escape from their predicament. The plan or strategy often *has* to be a "wild" one, one that they have never used before. Common objects have to be used for purposes far different from their intended ones.

GAINING CONFIDENCE FROM ALTERNATIVE PLANS. One can relax somewhat—at least be less desperate—if he has in reserve some alternative plans or ideas for solving his problems. Thus, ideational fluency and flexibility operate to give extra energy for executing problems and to increase chances of successful coping. As shown in the last chapter, men tend to make better decisions if they have a larger number of possibilities from which to choose.

AVOIDING SHOCK FROM UNANTICIPATED EVENTS. If one has thought out in advance a large number of possible consequences, he is more likely to be ready for whatever happens and not be shocked by it. Thus, if one has been divergently productive, he is able to reduce the dangerous lag in performance that comes when a sudden or unexpected demand or event occurs. If one has been curious about the causes and consequences of various actions, he is less likely to be "caught off guard" in an emergency.

AVOIDING "HOPELESS CHOICES." If one is able to think of many possible outcomes of his behavior, he is less likely to make choices that give no hope of success. One can prevent calamities by thinking of possible consequences ot one's actions.

INCREASING ENJOYMENT OF LIFE. If one is free to think in terms of his own uniqueness, he is more comfortable, more fully himself—a more authentic person. Life will be more varied, more interesting, more exciting. He sees other people in their uniqueness, respects it, and as a result finds others more interesting, exciting, and worth while. Thus, his relationships with others are more enjoyable. He is able to accept his own limitations creatively rather than cynically, and he thereby uses his resources more fully.

SUMMARY

The divergent thinking abilities are those involved in the generation of new information from given information, where the emphasis is upon variety and quantity of output from the same source. These abilities are also likely to be involved in what has been called transfer. As they have been measured, these abilities have only a slight relationship to measures of intelligence or mental age, especially in the upper ranges. These abilities include various kinds of fluency, flexibility, originality, and elaboration. A variety of devices have been produced for assessing these abilities, but in general they have not been made generally available for use in operational school situations.

Some of the common problems that result from the exercise of the divergent thinking abilities stem from society's sanctions against divergency and pressures to be well rounded. Divergent thinkers often prefer learning and working alone, attempting difficult tasks, searching for uniqueness. Highly creative children are often estranged from their teachers, peers, and parents, probably because they fail to obtain adequate response from them.

Some of the most common problems resulting from the repression of the divergent thinking abilities are faulty or uncertain self-concepts, learning disabilities, behavior problems and delinquency, neurotic conflicts, and even psychoses if repression is too severe and/or prolonged.

The divergent thinking abilities seem to be especially critical in coping constructively with change, avoiding frustration from unworkable solutions, counteracting fatigue at critical times, gaining confidence from alternative plans, avoiding shock from unanticipated events, avoiding hopeless choices, and increasing enjoyment of life.

Developing and
Freeing the
Divergent
Thinking Abilities

20

How much uniformity does this society need for safety?

It needs only that uniformity which the achievement of its greatest goals require. It demands security of life and health for its people. It demands wide opportunities for its people in work and play, in song and prayer. It must provide each individual with maximum aids to the development of his powers to contribute in every way possible to the great goals of his people. . . .

How much deviation does this society require for progress?

It requires just as much deviation, just as many uniquely developed peaks of ability, just as much idiosyncrasy as the attainment of its goals will allow and need. All societies are wasteful of the capacities of their people. That society which comes closest to developing every socially useful idiosyncrasy in every one of its members will make the greatest progress toward its goals. (Benjamin, 1956, pp. 36–37.)*

The above quotation from Harold Benjamin's 1949 Inglis Lecture at Harvard University is an eloquent plea for the cultivation of divergent talents. He characterizes the problem as one of determining the degree of caution needed to protect the society's goals and the amount of daring required to advance the society toward these goals. The problem of this chapter is to outline some ways of developing and freeing the divergent thinking abilities.

Since many of the concepts presented in this chapter are the same as those the author has used in discussing the necessary conditions for creative growth, the reader should keep in mind the distinction between "divergent thinking" and "creativity." The distinction made by Guilford is perhaps clearer than any other that can be offered at the present time. According to

* From *The Cultivation of Idiosyncrasy* by H. Benjamin. Used by permission. Copyright 1949 by the President and Fellows of Harvard College.

his most recent conceptualization (Guilford and Merrifield, 1960), all of the divergent thinking abilities are involved in creative thinking. Creative thinking is thought to include also the redefinition abilities, which fall into the convergent production category, and sensitivity to problems, one of the evaluative thinking abilities. Thus, even though "divergent thinking" cannot be equated with "creative thinking," it still constitutes a major core of creative thinking. The author will use this chapter to present some of the conclusions he has reached as a result of six years of research on the creative thinking abilities, most of which would fall into the divergent thinking category.

LISTS OF CONDITIONS FOR IMPROVING DIVERGENT THINKING

From the reviews of authors such as Patrick (1955) and Russell (1956) it is possible to compile a catalog of the conditions necessary for improving divergent or creative thinking. For example, the following are listed in the index of Patrick's book under "ways of improving creative thinking":

1. Acquisition of information
2. Answering one's own questions
3. Awareness of influence of professional habits
4. Beneficial recreational activities
5. Caution and accuracy
6. Criticism of own work
7. Encouragement to think creatively
8. Enough time to solve problems
9. Favorable habits of living
10. Favorable physical condition
11. General cultural background
12. General curiosity
13. Mood
14. Motivation
15. Notebook habit
16. Optimism with avoidance of worry
17. Patience
18. Periods for reverie and autistic thinking
19. Periods of sleep and rest
20. Personal attitudes
21. Problems sufficiently difficult
22. Readiness to work for long periods
23. Readiness to accept new ideas
24. Relaxation of routine
25. Self-confidence
26. Sense of humor
27. Standards of work

28. Temporary changes of work
29. Wide-awake attention and interest

Classroom Procedures

30. (Applying) available information
31. Avoidance of prejudices and biases
32. Correct thought models
33. Credit for original answers
34. Development of general curiosity
35. Differences between fact and theory
36. Objective records of periods of reverie
37. Opportunities for creative work

Parental Assistance

38. Child's self-confidence in value of ideas
39. Encouragement to (find) answers (to) own questions
40. Materials to express creative thought
41. Praise for original work

David Russell (1956, pp. 380–87) has also outlined specific suggestions for improving the creative thinking of children. He reports that, as result of a series of meetings, the California School Supervisors Association in 1950 summarized the ways in which teachers may encourage the creativeness of children. The California supervisors concluded that the teacher may encourage creative thinking by:

1. Strengthening pupils' awareness of their own abilities
2. Watching for signs of readiness to be creative
3. Following the interests of children instead of imposing the standards of adults.
4. Fostering exploration and experimentation.
5. Using teacher-pupil planning as a way of aiding growth.
6. Teaching the techniques of problem solving, critical thinking, and evaluation.
7. Assisting with the tool skills which are necessary to many forms of creativity.
8. Maintaining emphasis on intrinsic rather than extrinsic rewards.
9. Interpreting the program to parents so that school and home may work in harmony for the optimum growth of boys and girls.

The many lists of ways of improving divergent or creative thinking are overwhelming in their detail. As the author has mulled over these lists and stacks of original data, he has concluded that it would be sufficient to include all of these ideas under one heading—the prevention of anything that would keep the individual from being fully alive. Just as long lists are overwhelming, such a single generalization is too inclusive to be genuinely

325

useful. Thus, an effort has been made to think of the problem in terms of the personality factors and social conditions that can interfere with divergent thinking and in terms of the classroom conditions that can be influenced by teachers in healthy ways. Consideration will be given first to some of the personality factors and then to some factors in nature and society that seem to affect the development of the divergent thinking abilities. Afterwards, several experiments involving classroom manipulations which proved to be successful in fostering divergent thinking will be reviewed.

PERSONALITY ATTRIBUTES OF DIVERGENT THINKERS *

Maslow's portrait of the self-actualizing person (1954) and Rogers' concept of the fully-functioning person (1961) may be seen as models of the productive divergent thinker. In essence, Maslow and Rogers picture the healthy personality as one who has become free to become his potentialities and who is different both from the "normal, well-adjusted" person and the unhealthy person. Being different is a key personality characteristic of the divergent thinker—the self-actualizing person, the fully-functioning person, and the creative person. He is not different for the sake of being different but is different because he has to be different in order to cope constructively with the pressures of his environment and to become his potentialities.

As indicated in the first chapter, the awesomeness of being different is well understood by most children by the time they reach the fourth grade. Yet creative achievement requires that a person be different, so let us now examine some of the particular ways in which productive divergent thinkers are different.

They are always puzzled about something and are seeking answers.

One of the most common characteristics of the divergent thinker is his persistent tendency to search for the answers to the questions and problems that puzzle him. Since he is attracted to the unknown and the unusual, his questions are many and are often embarrassing. The author and his associates have now assembled data from about a dozen states and eight countries outside the United States (India, Western Samoa, Germany, Malaya, Canada, Australia, the Philippines, and Greece) concerning the characteristics of the ideal child. "Always asking questions" ranks uniformly rather low among the 62 characteristics in the checklist, thirty-ninth among both parents and teachers in the United States. Subjects were asked to check each of the 62 characteristics which they considered desirable and should be encouraged, double check the five most important characteristics, and draw

---

* The ideas summarized in this section are discussed in greater detail in the author's article, "The Creative Child," in *The Difficult Child*, edited by J. S. Roucek, published by Philosophical Library, 1964. Pp. 1–17.

a line through all characteristics considered undesirable. Rankings were determined by assigning a weight of two for a double check, one for a single check, and minus one for characteristics having a line drawn through them. Only in Western Samoa was the ranking for "always asking questions" better than thirty-first. To the Samoan teacher, however, "always asking questions" means asking if what they have done is all right or if what they are doing is what the teacher wants done. Even asking for permission to do something is disfavored, and sometimes strongly punished. One of the reasons why asking questions causes a child to be considered difficult is that such questions disturb carefully planned classroom procedures and organization. Of the 62 characteristics in the checklist, the most universally discouraged and punished is "disturbs class procedures or organization."

Even among the most creative persons in modern history (Goertzel and Goertzel, 1962), harsh treatment has often been the reward for asking questions about puzzling phenomena. Tom Edison's teacher did not like the kind of questions Tom asked (Guthridge, 1959; Josephson, 1959). As a result, Tom spent many mornings on the low stool in the corner of the schoolroom. After three months, the teacher decided that young Tom was mentally "addled." The teacher became enraged one morning when Tom observed that a certain river ran uphill instead of downhill as do most rivers and asked how water could run uphill. The teacher slammed his book shut, pounded his desk with his fist, came over to Tom with his eyebrows going up and down, and said, "Thomas Alva, you always ask entirely too many questions. You are 'addled.' " By now Tom had begun to regard himself as a hopeless dunce, and his father had begun to have vague anxieties about Tom's stupidity. His mother, however, recognized the boy's talent for asking difficult and puzzling questions as a valuable one. Young Tom stopped going to school and, with his mother, found study easy and exciting.

Albert Einstein also suffered a great deal from his proclivity for asking questions about things that puzzled him (Hammontree, 1961). His mother apparently loved and encouraged this tendency. His father was occasionally somewhat exhausted by it, but nonetheless accepted it and responded with liveliness and understanding. The boy found no such response in the German schools he attended, however, and disliked school intensely until he found one in Switzerland where his questions were respected. At the Luitpold Gymnasium in Munich teachers did not like him because he asked so many questions, and they sometimes thrashed him when he asked. Insight into the reasons why this questioning characteristic makes a child difficult is reflected in the interview between Einstein and his science teacher on the day he became a school "dropout." The teacher asked young Einstein to remain after class and told him that he was a "bad" influence on the other students, causing them to lose respect for the teacher. The teacher had apparently compiled a list of the embarrassing questions Albert had asked. His list included such questions as: "Why can't we feel the earth move?" "What is space?" "What keeps the world from flying into pieces as it spins around?" The teacher confessed that he could not answer Einstein's questions and that no one else could. He then reported that it was the consensus of the teachers in the school that young Einstein should withdraw from the school.

It is unfortunate that these teachers and the many others throughout history who have been tortured by the puzzling questions of young people could not have recognized this characteristic as a tremendously valuable one. There is no reason why such questions should be threatening to teachers and cause them to lose respect.

They attempt difficult and dangerous tasks.

Another common characteristic of the divergent thinker is his tendency to attempt tasks that are too difficult for him. He is forever testing the limits of his abilities, the situation, and his resources. On the ideal-pupil checklist, "attempting difficult tasks" has not been held in very high regard among teachers and parents. "Preference for complex tasks" ranks thirty-fifth among teachers in the United States and thirty-seventh among parents. Similar rankings are noted in all eight of the other countries studied. "Attempting difficult tasks" ranks nineteenth among teachers and twenty-second among parents in the United States, with only the German teachers giving it a rank among the top twelve characteristics. "Willingness to take risks" ranks thirty-sixth among both parents and teachers in the United States and holds a similar position in the other countries for which data have been compiled.

The boyhoods of Edison, Ford, Einstein, Franklin, and Byrd are filled with accounts of attempts to accomplish tasks that were too difficult for them. Usually they calculated the risks rather carefully, but all inevitably made mistakes or experienced dangers that placed them in the category of "difficult children."

Young Tom Edison in his enthusiasm for the study of lighter-than-air gases incurred the displeasure of even his mother, when his friend Michael became ill from drinking Seidlitz gas to make him float. On this occasion, Mrs. Edison made Tom go to bed without supper and told him that he would have to destroy all of the bottles in his laboratory. She relented, however, in the matter of the destruction of his laboratory. During his adolescence, he lost his railroad job when there was an explosion in the laboratory he had on the train. He was re-employed later after promising to leave his laboratory at home.

Young Benjamin Franklin toyed with danger when he devised a kite that would drag him along the water as he floated. On one occasion, the kite drew him backward, dragging his head under water. He became so tired from hanging onto the kite string that he might have been drowned had he been a less powerful swimmer. Franklin also fashioned himself a set of paddles, which he strapped onto his hands and feet with leather and used in swimming. He was able to calculate the risk, however, and discarded them when they proved to be too heavy. It seems to be characteristic of highly creative people that they test carefully the limits of their abilities, the situation, and the materials and methods they devise.

An unwillingness to attempt difficult jobs has been found to be an important factor in poor mental health and lack of achievement among college students of high ability. Berger (1958), for example, found that one large category of gifted, underachieving college students set high standards for themselves, lacked wholeheartedness in their efforts, believed that they should be able to achieve at a high level with little effort (achieving through hard work was not especially creditable in their eyes), and were unwilling to risk being wrong, being disappointed, or doing poorly.

They become absorbed in their thinking.

A third common quality of the divergent thinker is the high degree of absorption in his thinking. He frequently becomes so preoccupied with his ideas that he is inattentive to whatever is going on around him. He may be considered absent-minded. His parents and teachers find such behavior annoying and may forbid the absorbing activity. Such a complaint is frequently made concerning the child who is most outstanding on tests of creative thinking. Apparently what happens is that he gives himself over so completely to the problem with which he is concerned that he ignores distractions that he considers less important.

They are honest.

Honesty is the very essence of the creative personality. Adults, perhaps unconsciously, condition children through the home, school, church, and community to be less than honest. Certainly independence in judgment, courage in convictions, emotional sensitivity, intuition, and openness to experience are all important in being oneself and are seriously impaired by subtle conditioning to dishonesty. Unfortunately, however, none of these characteristics are very highly valued by United States parents and teachers, according to the results of the ideal-pupil checklist. Quite interestingly, independence in thinking is highly valued, ranking second among teachers and seventh among parents; but independence in judgment ranks twenty-first among both teachers and parents. The productive divergent thinker must be able to make independent judgments and to have the courage to stick to his conclusions and to work toward their achievement, even though he may be a minority of one at the beginning. Being courageous is valued even less than independent judgment among teachers (twenty-ninth), although it ranks eighteenth among parents. Emotional sensitivity ranks forty-seventh among both teachers and parents in the United States, and being intuitive ranks thirtieth among teachers and thirty-fourth among parents.

An incident from the early life of Albert Einstein illustrates how honesty may create problems for a child. He was sometimes ridiculed by his peers for being honest and was nicknamed "Honest John." On one occasion Albert was so absorbed in his dreams and thoughts that he failed to notice a group of passing soldiers. One of the officers asked the other boys who Albert was. They said, "Oh, that's 'Honest John.' " When asked to explain, the boys told the officer that "because Albert is not very bright, he always tells the truth, even if it gets him into trouble." The officers then called Albert over and taunted him for not playing soldier with the other boys. Albert explained that he did not want to play soldier and that he was not going to be a soldier. This enraged the officer who made Albert tell him where he lived. Albert was told by both the officer and his parents that he would have to be a soldier. This frightening incident apparently gave Albert an intense desire to escape from Germany.

They may appear to lack consideration for others.

Both parents and teachers in the United States rank "being considerate of others" as the most important of the 62 characteristics included on the checklist. This great importance attached to being considerate of others certainly identifies some of the reasons why most teachers do not like creative or divergent thinking children. They often appear to be lacking in this virtue. They may sacrifice their lives in an effort to help others, to work for the good of others, to serve their country, or to benefit humanity. There are times, however, when they become so involved in the problems on which they are working and consider these problems so important that they do not take the time to be polite to others. Placing this characteristic at the top of the hierarchy of values may reflect an overemphasis on conformity to the thinking of others and could be carried to such an extreme that it could work seriously against the freeing of the divergent thinking abilities. It is interesting to note that being altruistic, actually working for the good of others, is rather disfavored on the checklist, ranking forty-first among teachers and forty-second among parents in the United States.

Other characteristics make divergent thinkers different.

The foregoing are only a few of the qualities of creative persons or divergent thinkers. Some others will be mentioned without comment. The divergent thinker is both more shy and more bold. He is often timid and shy in social relationships but bold in the conception and execution of ideas. He is both more primitive and more cultivated. He is more destructive and more constructive. He is madder and saner. Usually, he is strongly determined, committed, industrious, and hard-working, possessed of a sense of humor and a high degree of sincerity. He is a self-starter but sometimes late in completing his work, playful, emotional, adventurous, affectionate, never bored, spirited in disagreement, unwilling to accept the judgments of authorities, visionary, and willing to take risks. He may also appear haughty and self-satisfied, though the reverse is almost always true. He may like to work alone and to strive for distant goals.

DIVERGENT THINKING AND ANCHORS IN REALITY

The real crux of the mental health problem of the divergent thinker is the threat that divergent thinking imposes upon a person's struggle to maintain his anchors in reality. Being an independent thinker often makes a person a minority of one, an uncomfortable state of affairs. It is this threat that causes many people to surrender their individuality and become extreme conformists. Crutchfield (1962, p. 135), for example, found that the extreme conformist is generally quite anxious, insistent on securing a safe and stable environment, desirous of avoiding uncertainty and ambiguity at high cost. The extreme conformist is searching for strong anchors in his environment, and the group is prepared to offer him these strong anchors in exchange for his undeviating acceptance of its judgments and its established beliefs. Crutchfield also reports that the extreme conformist is assailed by doubts concerning himself and these make him timid about expressing his ideas that diverge from the group's. As a result, he tends to defer to the judgment of others and is demoralized in the face of what seems to him the superior judgment of the group. This happens even when his perception of reality is accurate and his judgments are correct. The real difficulty comes, however, when he becomes so dependent upon the group's perceptions and judgments that he no longer makes any effort to use his own senses in maintaining contact with his environment.

SOCIAL AND CULTURAL CONDITIONS AFFECTING DIVERGENT THINKING *

The social and cultural conditions that will be discussed here became apparent to the author as he developed and administered tasks for eliciting divergent thinking among children. To the extent possible, he then tried to

* The ideas presented in this section are discussed in greater detail in *Guiding Creative Talent* by this author and published by Prentice-Hall, Inc., in 1962.

design studies or reanalyze existing data to obtain confirming or disconfirming evidence.

SUCCESS ORIENTATION

It has been alleged that the United States has a success-oriented culture and that military and civilian education does not prepare individuals to cope with frustration and failure. Everything frustrating must be prevented. As children performed tasks individually, the inhibiting effects of the preoccupation with prevention became apparent. They were illustrated dramatically in the Mother Hubbard problem, which asks the subject to think of all of the possible things Mother Hubbard could have done when she found her cupboard bare. The children showed a growing preoccupation with prevention reaching its height in the third grade. When confronted with this problem, third graders tended to give a blank stare, and say, "What do you mean 'What could she do?' ? She shouldn't have let it happen. She should have counted her bones. If she was getting low and didn't have any money, she should have gone to work." They were paralyzed, however, in their consideration of alternative solutions once she was in the predicament.

PEER ORIENTATION

Anthropologists describe our culture as the most peer-oriented in the world. Evidence of the inhibiting effects of peer pressures to conformity on creative thinking is obvious and widespread. Investigators find it when they observe children, when they conduct experiments, when they do sociometric studies, and when they study the creative writing of children. These phenomena are probably responsible for the sharp drop found in the developmental curves in the fourth grade and again in the seventh. At about the time a child reaches the fourth grade, his need for consensual validation is intensified. He becomes almost afraid to think until he finds out what his peers are thinking.

Unusual or original ideas, outstanding performance, and almost any kind of divergent behavior becomes the target of peer pressures to conformity. This struggle is symbolized in the following story of a flying monkey by a sixth grade girl:

> My brother was born a day before I was. But there was something wrong with him. He had wings! Can you imagine that? A monkey with wings!
>
> He could fly where other monkeys couldn't get to, so they teased him. Well, he got tired of being teased and I got tired of being his brother (because, of course, I was teased too). We decided to fly to some other place. So I climbed upon his back and away we flew.
>
> The other monkeys were sorry then because my brother then called the "flying monkey" had always gotten the best bananas for them.

> Everyone was sad, even my brother and I. We couldn't find any-
> where to go and he was getting tired. Finally, we turned around and
> started walking back.
>
> When we got back everyone was happy again! But sometimes, for
> spite, the "flying monkey" wouldn't get the bananas for the other mon-
> keys and then the teasing would start again.
>
> Finally, he learned how to keep his "wings" out of sight. After
> that he hardly used them and was never teased again.

In many of the stories, the flying monkey is lonely, no one will play with
him, no one likes him, because he can fly and they can't. It is as plain as
that! It is only by some heroic action such as flying all of the other monkeys
to safety when the jungle catches afire that he can win the acceptance of his
peers.

Peer orientation is symbolized in a somewhat different way in the story
of the "Green Pig," written by a creative fifth grade girl:

> Once upon a time in a far-off land, there was a magic farm that
> no one has ever visited. Many different animals lived there. The odd
> thing about these animals was that they were different colors from
> regular animals.
>
> The cows were pink, the horses were purple and the hens and
> chicks were blue! All the pigs were green. That is, all except for one
> little fellow who was just plain pink. Nobody wanted to be near him or
> play with him because he wasn't green. And this little pig was very,
> very sad.
>
> One day, as he was walking along, he saw a great big puddle of
> mud. He splashed and rolled in it. When the little pig came out of the
> puddle, he was all *green!* And he stayed green for the rest of his life.
> And all of the other pigs began to play with him.

We do not have to look to stories of flying monkeys and green pigs for
this kind of material. Perhaps it is more comfortable to do so.

The problem of the educator is to create a climate that will permit a
healthy type of individualism and divergent thinking along with necessary
conformities. He can do this in a number of ways. One of them is providing
the divergent thinker with a "sponsor" or "patron."

Almost always wherever creativity occurs, and persists, there is some
other individual who plays the role of "sponsor." The sponsor is someone
who is not a member of the peer group, but possesses prestige or power in
the same social system. He does several things. Regardless of his own views,
the sponsor encourages and supports the child in expressing and testing his
ideas, in thinking things through for himself. He protects the child from the
counter reactions of his peers long enough to permit him to try out some of
his ideas. He can keep the structure of the situation open enough so that
originality *can* occur. The sponsor may be a teacher, a principal, an older
child, an adult leader in a youth organization, or the like.

The school must provide opportunities for using the divergent thinking abilities. The opportunity to do original work must be present in laboratories, classrooms, and shops, as well as in the procedure of the instructor himself. Teachers cannot expect to develop divergent thinking only by causing pupils to memorize, to repeat facts, to reproduce processes, or to prepare for some higher level of education.

SANCTIONS AGAINST QUESTIONING AND EXPLORATION

Although teachers generally recognize the need for children to ask questions and in other ways inquire about the wonders and mysteries about them, they still do a very brutal job of squelching such tendencies. They have many devices for putting the curious child in his place. They tell him that "curiosity killed the cat" and refer to it as "mere idle curiosity." Cats are very skilled in calculating the risk and learn what they are capable of doing; most children never have this chance. The author has also observed that curious people are never idle.

Exploring, inquiring behavior, so important in creativity, begins before the child's first words are uttered. A baby handles things, shakes, twists, and turns them upside down. These infantile manipulations are apparently forerunners of the process that may later lead to creative work in science, art, or some other field. Even in laboratory experiments there is a significant relationship between degree of manipulation and quantity and quality of inventive response. To develop divergent thinking, parents should permit and encourage children to manipulate, to play around with objects, words, and ideas, to the extent possible within the limits of safety. Educators can do much to arrange the conditions wherein failure is not so threatening. Some interesting and promising work is also being done on training children in skills of questioning and inquiry (Suchman, 1962).

OVEREMPHASIS OR MISPLACED EMPHASIS ON SEX ROLES

One of the most consistent findings concerning divergent thinking during the past 60 or 70 years (Torrance, 1962) has been the finding that boys excel girls in some kinds of creative thinking and that girls excel boys in others. Almost always these differences can be explained on the basis of differences in the way the culture treats boys and girls. Rarely do women become scientific discoverers, inventors, or composers. Overemphasis or misplaced emphasis on sex roles, however, exacts its toll on the creativity of both sexes and creates serious problems of adjustment to highly creative individuals of both sexes.

Creativity, by its very nature, requires both sensitivity and independence. In our culture, sensitivity is definitely a feminine virtue, while independence is a masculine value. Thus, the highly creative boy may appear to be more effeminate than his peers and the highly creative girl may appear more masculine than hers. Roe (1959), Barron (1957), and others have cited evidence in support of this conclusion. In longitudinal studies the author has found interesting examples of children who sacrifice their creativity in order to maintain their "masculinity" or their "femininity," as the case may be.

This cultural block to creativity comes out in many places. The author first observed it in the Product Improvement Test, in which children are asked to think of all the ideas they can for improving common toys so that they will be more fun to play with. In the first grade, boys excelled girls on the fire truck while girls excelled boys on the nurse's kit. Many of the boys refused to think of anything to make the nurse's kit more fun, protesting "I'm a boy! I don't play with things like that!" Some of the more creative boys, however, first transposed it into a doctor's kit and were then quite free to think of improvements. By the third grade, however, boys excelled girls even on the nurse's kit, probably because by this time girls have been conditioned to accept toys as they are and not to manipulate and change them.

DIVERGENCY EQUATED WITH ABNORMALITY

Once even leading thinkers believed "genius" and "madness" to be associated with one another. Almost all inventors, composers, creative scientists, and other eminent men were regarded as insane. Although these beliefs were discredited long ago, somehow the belief has persisted that any divergence from behavioral norms is an indication of something abnormal or unhealthy and to be corrected at all costs. This is in spite of definitions of the truly healthy personality as being different both from the "normal or average" personality and the unhealthy, and theories of psychotherapy which stress self-fulfillment and creative living.

The imaginative stories of children suggest that children are taught very early that divergent characteristics or behavior are signs of mental illness. In one story, the flying monkey's father pleaded with him not to fly because others would think he was "crazy."

Children who have divergent characteristics or display divergent thinking are likely to have an especial need to feel that someone understands them. They also find tremendously stressful unrelenting pressures to conform or to develop into well-rounded personalities.

WORK-PLAY DICHOTOMY

Another characteristic of our culture that serves to block the development of divergent thinking is the work-play dichotomy. One is supposed to enjoy play and is considered queer if he does not. Also, one is supposed to dislike work and is considered peculiar if he does not. Perhaps one of the reasons why teachers give children few opportunities to learn divergently is that children enjoy divergent learning and "fun" makes teachers uneasy. School is supposed to be work. In schools with an austere, no-fun atmosphere there is little evidence that the creative thinking abilities are used in learning. Many classrooms need more "mental sunshine."

Perhaps the greatest reward for learning is thinking—doing something with what has been learned. Children enjoy taking tests of creative thinking ability. One kindergarten class greeted their teacher when she returned the day after the testing with: "Gee, you ought to have been here yesterday. That man sure did work us hard, but gee was it fun!" A fourth grade class, when the recess bell rang, protested, "Don't make us stop. This is more fun than recess, anyway!"

Another interesting clue comes from a study differentiating the highly intelligent from the highly creative. In one school (Torrance, 1962), there was a difference of 25 IQ points between these two groups (the upper 20 per cent in the group on these two measures) but no difference in their measured achievement. Ordinarily one could say either that the highly creatives are overachieving or that the high IQ group is underachieving. The teachers, however, rated the high creatives as being less ambitious and hard-working. Yet with IQ's averaging 25 points lower and being less ambitious and hard-working, they still learned as much as their more intelligent classmates. Apparently they had been learning through activities that appeared to adults to "be playing around." Apparently this is one of their ways of learning.

The author was also interested in the reactions of some of the teachers in the creative writing experiments. In drawing up a list of suggested titles, the author was anxious to think of titles that would spark the imagination of the children, be new to them, permit them to regress, and bring out their concepts about divergent characteristics and behavior. Thus, he selected such topics as "The Flying Monkey," "The Lion That Won't Roar," "The Cat That Won't Scratch," "The Woman Who Won't Talk," and "The Man Who Cries." Some teachers objected that these titles were not suitable for boys and girls to write about, because they wrote about silly things and were not realistic. They also objected about the de-emphasis on correct spelling, good handwriting, and mechanics.

It will doubtless be some time before understanding of the creative process will make it possible for teachers to discard some of their rigidity and constriction and accept the conditions necessary for what Maslow and others call "primary creativeness." Contrasted to secondary creativeness, primary creativeness has as its primary source the preconscious, is a source of new discovery and original ideas, and comes from people who are able to play, fantasy, laugh, be spontaneous, and accept their human weaknesses. Secondary creativeness comes primarily from the conscious from people who are rigid, constricted, afraid of their unconscious, cautious, overcontrolled, orderly, and unfriendly to all types of emotional expression.

EXPERIMENTALLY INDUCED CONDITIONS AFFECTING DIVERGENT THINKING

Only a few years ago, it was commonly thought that productive divergent thinking (scientific discovery, new ideas, inventions, etc.) had to be left to chance. Indeed many people still think so. Yet it is difficult to imagine how well-informed persons can still hold this view. The amazing record of inventions, scientific discoveries, and other creative achievements—the products of divergent thinking—resulting from deliberate methods of ideation should convince stubborn skeptics. The records amassed through creative problem-solving methods (Osborn, 1963; Parnes and Harding, 1962), synectics (W. J. J. Gordon, 1961), and bionics (Small, 1962) are impressive. Experiments involving these deliberate methods of improving the quality of divergent thinking have also been consistent and convincing (Maltzman, 1960; Parnes and Meadow, 1960; Torrance, 1963).

Although a variety of materials have been used in the original experiments that will be reviewed the basic design has been the same for most of them. Groups have been divided by some random procedure for the types of experimental training under study. The training has been followed by a task requiring some type or types of creative thinking. In most of the experiments, results have been analyzed separately for each grade, generally from grades one through six, and totaling about 400 subjects in each experiment.

TRAINING IN PRINCIPLES

Several experimenters (Maltzman, 1960; Parnes and Meadow, 1959, 1960; True, 1956; and Nicholson, 1959) have demonstrated that adults can be trained to use various principles and thereby improve significantly their divergent thinking. In one of the earliest experiments in this area, the author tried to determine whether or not children can be trained during a 20-minute period to apply a set of principles and thereby increase the quantity and improve the quality of their ideas. He used the principles developed by Osborn (1963), such as making an object larger, making it smaller, rearranging, combining, adapting, changing color, giving motion, giving odor, changing shape, giving sound, and the like. In the experimental condition, practice was given in thinking of ideas to improve a toy fire truck so that it would be more fun to play with, and was followed by training in generalization based on a square that had been "improved" by all these methods and the establishment of connections between the "square model" and improvements on the fire truck. Examples of the modified squares are shown in Figure 20–1. The test task involved thinking of ideas for improving a toy stuffed dog.

In all grades there was a consistent tendency for the trained subjects to produce more responses, more flexible records, and more clever or original responses than the untrained ones. The differences between the first and fifth grades, however, did not reach statistical significance, except for greater flexibility in the fifth grade.

It was concluded that pupils in the early school years, with the possible exception of the first and fifth grades, can in a short time be taught a set of principles that will enable them to produce a larger number of ideas, achieve greater flexibility of ideation, and produce a larger number of clever or original ideas. Longer and/or spaced periods of training would probably produce more conclusive results.

MOTIVATION FOR QUANTITY VS. QUALITY

Using the same experimental setup as described above, one group was motivated for quantity ("Think of as many ideas as you can; don't worry about how good they are") and the other for quality ("think of the cleverest, most interesting, and most unusual ideas you can").

In the first three grades there was a consistent trend for the motivation to produce "clever, interesting, and unusual" ideas to be more effective than motivation for quantity ("Think of as many ideas as you can; don't worry about how good they are." There was a consistent trend in the opposite direction in the fourth, fifth, and sixth grades. Acceptable levels of statistical significance were achieved only in the second and fourth grades, however. Although these findings are not very convincing, Osborn's principle of motivation for quantity without regard for quality appears to be inappropriate for use in the first three grades. It may have value, however, above the third grade. Similar experimental procedures have been used successfully with first grade pupils (Cartledge, 1962) and mentally retarded children (Rouse, 1963).

COMPETITION

The setup described above was used to study the effects of competition. Under competitive conditions, a prize was offered for the children in each grade who thought of the most and "best" ideas. Under noncompetitive conditions, no prize was offered.

At every grade level, children under competitive conditions produced a larger number of ideas, showed greater flexibility, and produced more clever ideas. At all grade levels the differences were statistically significant.

In a second experiment (Torrance, 1963), competition was pitted against a warm-up experience in which children practiced on the fire truck

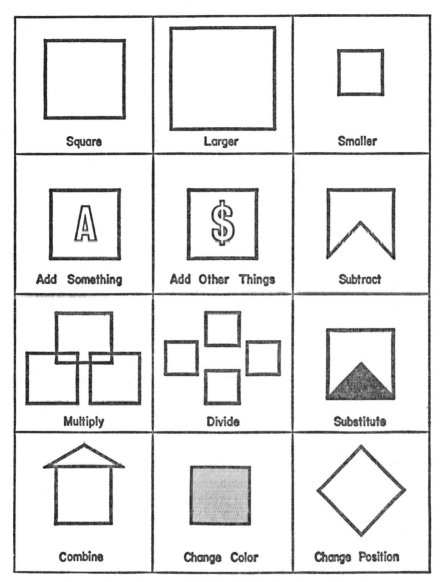

Figure 20–1. Examples of Modification of Square to Illustrate Principles for Developing New Ideas (From page 139 of Education and the Creative Potential *by E. P. Torrance and published by the University of Minnesota Press, 1963. Used by permission of the University of Minnesota Press.)*

before being asked to think of ideas for improving the toy dog. There was still a fairly consistent tendency for children under competitive conditions to excel those under the warm-up conditions. Results were statistically significant in only the first (fluency), second (flexibility), third (fluency and flexibility), and fourth grades (fluency and flexibility). Thus, it appears that the children above the fourth grade may be as responsive to some kinds of warm-up experience as to competition, and that a warm-up experience at least in part compensates for lack of competition in the first four grades.

UNEVALUATED VS. EVALUATED PRACTICE

In a set of experiments (Torrance, 1964) using the Shape Picture Completion and Incomplete Figures Tests, the author and his associates experimented with unevaluated and evaluated practice. In the first condition, the children were urged to experiment, to try out various things, not to be afraid of messing up their materials, and the like. They were assured that the practice would not count toward their winning the prize on the test task later. Under the evaluated condition, the children were given helpful suggestions during and following the practice session and no assurance was given that the practice work was "off the record." The instructions were designed to encourage two types of creative thinking: originality and elaboration. The products were evaluated for these and other creative qualities.

In general, the unevaluated practice was more effective than evaluated practice in encouraging creativity in the first three grades but not in the upper grades. On one task (the Shape Task), however, unevaluated practice was also more effective in the fourth grade. In the first grade, however, the evaluated condition produced greater originality than unevaluated practice.

On the basis of these findings, it may be concluded that, generally speaking, children in the primary grades will respond favorably to unevaluated practice or freedom from immediate evaluation. It had been observed previously that timid children in the primary grades responded favorably in the individual testing situation when urged to do it "just for fun."

It is not possible to say what would happen in the upper grades if unevaluated practice were continued. Responses in the present experiment might have been conditioned by the children's prior experience in being evaluated all of the time. They may have been skeptical about the experimenter's assurances.

CRITICAL AND CREATIVE PEER EVALUATION

In an experiment to assess the effects of critical and creative peer evaluation (Torrance, 1964), the same experimental setup as described above was used. In the Critical Peer Evaluation condition, the children were asked to criticize one another's work following each practice exercise. Emphasis was placed on defects or faults. In the Creative Peer Evaluation condition, the children were asked to suggest other possibilities that would have made another's products more interesting, more unusual, or added other ideas.

From kindergarten through third grade, there were no statistically significant differences on either of the two tasks. Most of the differences were statistically significant, however, in the fourth, fifth, and sixth grades. It is thought that these results indicate that children in the kindergarten and primary grades are not bothered by the opinions of their peers but that negative criticism in the fourth, fifth, and sixth grades puts a definite damper on creative thinking.

CREATIVITY TRAINING AND IMPROVEMENT OF CREATIVE WRITING

In an experiment conducted by Myers (1960), a random half of the children in a class were given intensive training in creative thinking over a period of four months but no training in creative writing. The other half were given training in convergent problem solving. As measured by pretests and posttests of creative writing, the children who had been given creativity training showed greater growth than their controls.

More recently, exercises developed by Myers and Torrance (1961, 1962) have been tested in a variety of situations. In most cases, the results have shown that pupils who participated in these exercises made greater gains on creative writing and developed more positive attitudes toward divergency than did similar children not exposed to this kind of classroom activity. Highly creative teachers, however, have been shown to be more effective in bringing about creative growth through exercises of their own than less creative teachers using the creativity training exercises.

In another experiment, teachers were urged to try out a number of ideas for developing divergent thinking through language arts activities. Although the controls reported using as many of these ideas as the experimentals, interesting results were obtained. When these teachers were split at the median on the number of ideas tried out and the performance of their pupils compared, the results were not significant. Teachers participating in the experiment had been administered the Personal-Social Motivation Inventory, which yields a score defined as "Creative Attitude." Participating teachers were divided at the median into a "high creative" and "low creative group." It was found that the high creative tried out a larger number of the ideas included in the manual entitled "A Collection of Ideas for Developing the Creative Thinking Abilities Through the Language Arts." It was also found that their pupils showed significant growth in creative writing, whereas the pupils of those in the lower half actually showed a slight decrement between the pretest and posttest of creative writing.

341

HOMOGENEOUS AND HETEROGENEOUS GROUPINGS

Fourth, fifth, and sixth grade classes in three schools were divided into five-person groups (Torrance and Arsan, 1963). Some classes were divided homogeneously and some heterogeneously in two schools on the basis of creativity and in the other school on the basis of IQ. Each group was given the Science-Toy task. During the initial 25-minute period, the group was instructed to experiment and try to discover as many uses, intended and unintended, of the toys as possible and to demonstrate and explain as many scientific principles as possible. The second 25-minute period was devoted to the demonstrations and explanations.

When the groups were divided heterogeneously on the basis of creativity, there was a strong tendency for the more creative members to initiate the most ideas and to demonstrate and explain the most principles. The tendency was a linear one. No such linear tendency was observed when the basis of heterogeneity was IQ. In fact, the low IQ children tended to do as well as the high IQ ones. In both of the homogeneous conditions, the low groups tended to go all out and excel or equal the high groups. In general, the groups composed of average and slightly below average ability tended to perform most poorly.

In this same experimental setup (Torrance, 1964) the problem of social stress in homogeneous and heterogeneous groups within classes for creative activities was studied. Observers' records were carefully analyzed for signs of social stress and signs of positive, productive interaction. The following terms were counted as indications of disruptive social stress:

> Bickering, fighting, squabbling, uncontrolled behavior, disorder, disorganization, domination, squelching, reprimanding, loss of temper, apathy, refusal to cooperate, loss of interest, sarcasm, disruptive talking, and joking.

The following were considered signs of positive, productive interaction:

> Cooperating, helping, working together, organizing, absorption in task, praising one another, respecting others' ideas, listening, considering others' ideas, trying out others' ideas, communicating ideas, consulting with one another, congenial, interested, questioning, curious.

Significantly more signs of social stress were observed in heterogeneous than in homogeneous groups in all three schools. It was concluded that teachers, by their choice of homogeneous or heterogeneous groupings within a class, may influence the degree of social stress in groups working on creative tasks. At times, heterogeneous groups may be desirable; at others, homogeneous groups may be more effective.

In the heterogeneous groups formed on the basis of tests of divergent thinking, a number of interesting findings resulted from an analysis of the pressures exerted by the group on the most divergent member and the counter strategies adopted by that member. In one school, the experiment was extended downward to the second grade. From second through sixth grade there was a decreasing tendency for group members to work alone, especially the most divergent thinkers, rather than as a part of a group. Their tendency to work alone persisted fairly strongly through the fifth grade, at which point the tendency for groups to organize began to emerge as an important technique of control. Techniques for controlling the most divergent member included open aggression and hostility, criticism, rejection, ignoring, the use of organizational machinery to limit scope of operation and to impose sanctions, exaltation to a position of power involving excessive "paper work" and administrative responsibility, and the like. Adaptation techniques of the most divergent members included compliance, counteraggressiveness, indomitable persistence, apparent ignoring of criticism, clowning, silence, apathy, preoccupation, inconsistent performance, filling the gaps when others faltered, solitary activity, and the like.

THE "IDEA-TRAP"

The "idea-trap" plan promoted by Osborn (1963), Clark (1958), and others was applied to the creative writing activities in one school from grades three through six (Hiller, 1961). Using a weekly magazine, named by the children "Ideas of the Week," as a motivating device, children were encouraged to write on their own. In the demonstration experiment, it was found that most children (over 90 per cent) responded favorably to this plan, generating much enthusiasm and developing increased appreciation of the value of their own ideas and those of their classmates.

REWARDING CREATIVE THINKING

It is known through research that children and adults learn and develop along whatever lines they find rewarding. Most of the rewards of society are given to those who conform to the behavioral norms. In a recent study, the author found that about 60 per cent of the language arts objectives for the activities of a particular day were concerned with conformity to behavioral norms. Less than nine per cent were related to creative thinking.

To help teachers in rewarding creative thinking, a manual entitled *Rewarding Creative Thinking* was developed by the author and his colleagues specially for use in this project. A set of six principles was also developed and used in an in-service training program in a field experiment. Briefly, these principles are as follows:

1. Treat questions with respect.
2. Treat imaginative, unusual ideas with respect.

3. Show pupils that their ideas have value.
4. Give opportunities for practice or experimentation without evaluation.
5. Encourage and evaluate self-initiated learning.
6. Tie in evaluation with causes and consequences.

Manual users were also asked to describe and evaluate specific attempts of their own in applying these principles. Many teachers responded favorably to workshop experiences and suggestions provided by manuals. Skillful application of these principles appeared to lead to creative growth.

A comparison of the logs of the most and least effective mathematics teachers in 1959–60 revealed almost the same picture (Torrance, 1964). A more detailed analysis of the evaluative thinking of these teachers was then made. It was found that the least effective teachers reported more praise or positive evaluation and also more negative criticism than did the more effective ones. The more effective teachers reported far more troubleshooting or hypothesis-making behavior than their less effective colleagues. They consistently tried to put their finger on difficulties and advanced hypotheses concerning the cause and nature of the difficulty and about ways of remedying the difficulty.

ATTITUDES TOWARD WHAT IS KNOWN

Two opposing views are widely held concerning the role of information as a basis for divergent thinking. Some authorities maintain that the more knowledge one has the more likely is he to produce valuable divergent ideas. They base their arguments on the fact that more new relationships and combinations are possible and that the depth of knowledge will enable the thinker to recognize the significance of apparently chance events. Others maintain that the less knowledge one has the more likely is he to think of divergent ideas. His thinking is not "set" and there is no difficulty of "getting off the beaten track."

The author's research and that of Hyman (1961) indicate that the ability to think of divergent ideas is not dependent so much upon the amount of knowledge itself but upon the attitude one has toward what he knows. In one study (Torrance, 1964), educational psychology students who read research articles creatively excelled those who read similar articles critically in the quality of their original ideas and in their ability to make creative applications of the subject matter of the course. In another (Torrance and Harmon, 1961), memory, evaluation, and creative reading sets had differential effects on performance on tests assessing various kinds of achievement (recognition or multiple-choice, memory or completion, creative applications, and decision making or evaluation). In all cases, the creative or divergent thinking set resulted in superior performance on the creative application parts of the examination. Hyman (1961) has conducted experiments that have shown that "constructive attitudes" ward prior information compared with a "critical attitude" produced solu tions, on both related and unrelated problems, that were rated significantly more original.

SUMMARY

During recent years there has been an increasing recognition of the necessity for diversity among the people of a nation. Several lists of conditions for improving divergent thinking have been compiled. Most of these conditions can be related in some way to a person's becoming more fully alive and able to live more fully and completely in harmony with his abilities and interests.

Many of the divergent thinker's personality problems arise from his being different from his associates. He tends to be always puzzled about something, to be in search of answers. He attempts difficult and dangerous tasks and becomes at times completely absorbed in a task. He is honest, even when honesty gets him into trouble, and at times he appears to lack consideration for others. Much of the pressure from being different comes from the difficulty in maintaining satisfactory anchors in reality.

Some of the social and cultural conditions that appear to affect divergent thinking include undue success orientation, peer orientation, sanctions against questioning and exploration, overemphasis or misplaced emphasis on sex roles, divergency equated with abnormality, a work-play dichotomy, and the like.

Experiments show that the quantity and quality of divergent thinking can be improved by teaching children a set of principles, motivating for original and elaborate ideas, competition and warm-up, unevaluated practice, creative peer evaluation rather than critical peer evaluation, homogeneous grouping, cultivating the "idea-trap" habit, and developing constructive attitudes concerning available information.

Role of
Evaluative Thinking in
Coping with Stress

21

Our young people come out of schools, in many cases, without intellectual legs to stand upon, without learning the techniques of coming to agreement on controversial issues, without knowing how to marshal and mobilize facts and thinking for the purpose of making decisions, without adequate clues to the situations in which they are to live, and at a loss intellectually, morally, and vocationally (Weber, 1953, pp. 121–22).

To the extent that Weber's charges are true, young people coming out of American schools are inadequately prepared to cope with the common predictable and unpredictable stresses of everyday life. Even less attention is given in classrooms to the evaluative abilities than to the divergent thinking abilities. Except for sporadic and scattered interest in "critical thinking," educational literature reflects little interest in the development and use of these abilities. When elementary and secondary teachers are asked to state the objectives of courses, units, and daily activities, there is little evidence of such concern. By stretching a point and including all objectives remotely related to critical thinking, assessing, selecting, judging, comparing, contrasting, and the like, one can include about three or four per cent of the objectives given in elementary and secondary social studies and elementary language arts. If one omits "critical thinking," the percentage drops to below one half of one per cent. Almost none of the objectives hint of the ability to make decisions.

It is estimated that the evaluative thinking abilities in general require the use of more expensive energies than do the productive thinking abilities. The productive thinking abilities must always be called into play before the evaluative abilities have a chance to operate. Some individuals use less expensive energies by evaluating their decisions upon only the most obvious

346

alternatives. Others develop formulae of various types and attempt to evaluate alternatives in a very mechanical fashion. Even graduate students who are called upon to make critical appraisals of research apply formulae which they use to pronounce as invalid any piece of research ever done or to be done in the future. It is an extremely rare doctoral candidate who can evaluate a piece of research thoughtfully and make calculated decisions about what parts of it can be used in practical situations and how it can be used without too great a risk.

THE EVALUATIVE THINKING ABILITIES

Guilford and Merrifield (1960) define the evaluative abilities as those involved in reaching decisions or making judgments concerning the goodness (correctness, suitability, adequacy, desirability) of information in terms of criteria of identity, consistency, and goal satisfaction. Thus far, Guilford and his co-workers have identified and developed measures for only a few of these abilities.

FIGURAL IDENTIFICATION

Figural Identification is the ability to evaluate figural units and has been known traditionally as "perceptual speed." One of the tasks used to assess this ability is the Guilford-Zimmerman Perceptual Speed Test, which requires the subject to find the pictured form that is the same as the given one. A second task, Identical Forms, was developed by L. L. Thurstone (1944) and requires the subject to find the form that is identical to the given form. This ability comes into play in coping with stressful situations where discriminations must be made rapidly, where signs of danger must be detected in changing situations, and the like.

SYMBOLIC IDENTIFICATION

The ability to evaluate symbolic units (Guilford and Merrifield, 1960) is called symbol identification and has been known traditionally as "speed of symbol discrimination." In one of the test tasks (Letter "A" Sd–1), the subject has to check a list for words having the letter "a" in columns of 40 words each. In a second task (First Digit Cancellation Sd–2), he is asked to indicate, in a row of 30 digits, each digit that is like the first one in the row. A third task (Scattered X's Sd–3) calls for the circling of the seven X's among letters scattered over a page. All three tasks were originally developed by the Educational Testing Service. Tasks of this type are commonly found in tests of clerical aptitude.

The two abilities for evaluating units involve processes that are simpler and require less energy than the others. Performance of tasks of this type, however, are quite vulnerable to stress. The author has found that such

347

distractions as recorded noises or a simple competing task quickly lead to decrements in performance. Small degrees of fatigue result quite rapidly in an increase in errors of perception or discrimination and/or in decreased speed.

SYMBOL MANIPULATION

Symbol manipulation (Guilford and Merrifield, 1960) is the ability to evaluate symbolic relationships. In one task, the subject has to decide whether symbolically presented "if—then" statements are true or false. In another, he has to indicate which interchange of arithmetic operations will make an equation correct. It is generally thought that this ability is important in learning mathematics. It is logical, however, to expect that it is also important wherever one must make decisions involving "if—then" situations and/or the interchange of operations and coping with stresses which involve the evaluation of possible consequences of new procedures or contemplated changes.

LOGICAL EVALUATION

Logical evaluation is defined (Guilford, 1959a) as the ability to use logical relationships in testing the correctness of meaningful conclusions. It is the factor involved in evaluating semantic relations. The factor was originally reported by Thurstone (1938) who called it "deduction." One task is the well-known False Premises type of test, which requires the subject to indicate which conclusions are logically correct for syllogisms (nonsensical statements). Items of this type appear in a number of group intelligence tests. A second task calls for him to choose the correct conclusion that can be drawn from two given statements (formal syllogisms). The third task, Inference Test, requires the selection of the most justified conclusion that can be drawn from a given statement.

Both symbol manipulation and logical evaluation involve essentially the task of making decisions about the soundness of a conclusion in terms of its logical consistency with given information. Such abilities apparently come into play in making independent judgments and would obviously be related to performance under stressful conditions.

EXPERIENTIAL EVALUATION

Experiential evaluation (Guilford, 1959a) is the ability to evaluate the various aspects of a situation in terms of internal consistency. It is the factor involved in evaluating semantic systems and may be associated with the process of testing theories on the basis of case study data, life experiences, and the like. For example, the method of internal consistency was used by Freud and other personality theorists who have relied upon clinical data for generating and testing hypotheses.

348

In one of the tasks designed to assess this factor, the subject is asked to point out two incongruities in sketches of common situations. In another, he is called upon to select for a given situation the action leading to the most desirable consequences.

JUDGMENT

Judgment is defined by Guilford (1959a) as the ability to make wise choices of action in a somewhat ambiguous situation. It is the factor involved in evaluating semantic transformations. In one test task, the subject has to select the best solution to a practical problem. In a second, he has to make quantitative estimates based upon common experiences.

Though never widely used in aptitude testing, a number of tests of practical judgment and estimation have been devised and used to a limited extent. For example, Boraas in 1922 (pp. 43–44) outlined the kinds of measures possible in this area. His eleven categories and examples of each are as follows:

1. *Judgments of quality,* such as color, sound, taste, touch, and temperature. *Examples:* The cloth is blue-green. That is the fragrance of lilies. This water has a temperature of about 60 degrees.

2. *Judgments of quantity,* such as size, weight, pressure, and amount. *Examples:* This piece of board is six feet long. That tree is about 50 rods from the house. The hog weighs about 275 pounds. The bin has about 175 bushels in it. That wheat will run about 15 bushels to the acre.

3. *Judgments of time and speed. Examples:* According to the position of the sun, it is now two o'clock in the afternoon. The man is driving 20 miles per hour.

4. *Judgments in regard to the relation of the parts to a whole. Examples:* . . . This is an apple seed. The manager is elected by the board of directors and makes his report to them.

5. *Judgments of cause and effect. Examples:* He learned his lesson because he studied attentively, not because he kept on so long. The board bulges because it is wet on one side . . .

6. *Judgments of economic values. Examples:* This land is worth $185 per acre. . . . A shoe like that is worth about $6.50. This breed of poultry will bring a better price as broilers than the other kind.

7. *Judgments of social values. Examples:* Mr. X has done more for this community than any other man. This poolroom is demoralizing some of our young men . . .

8. *Judgments of esthetic values. Examples:* Yards look better with the fences removed . . . That wall will look better if you hang a picture in the space next to the window . . .

9. *Judgments about governments. Examples:* This candidate will not make a good official, but that one will . . . The government should regu-

late the railroads. The Federal Government should equalize the educational opportunities in the various states.

10. *Judgments about religious values. Examples:* Christianity helps people to live cheerfully and helpfully . . . Mr. X is correct enough in his beliefs, but he does not live according to them.

11. *Judgments about persons. Examples:* John is naturally slow and can master only a minimum assignment . . . I admire Lincoln more than Washington.

In the years since 1922, general education has for a variety of reasons avoided giving attention to the exercise of the judgment abilities. Some of the specialized areas of education have, therefore, had to give special attention to developing the kinds of judgment essential to certain activities. For example, agriculture, home economics, and other vocational or trade areas have given special attention to judgments of quality, quantity, time, speed, and relations of the parts to a whole. In general, making judgments has been frowned upon. In many situations, students have been carefully conditioned to refrain from making judgments. Personnel and clinical psychologists have emphasized the assessment of persons. Reliance, however, has been upon the use of objective assessment devices rather than upon the thinking abilities and processes required in using the instruments to arrive at judgments or decisions concerning persons. There has been a great deal of recent interest in the processes of interpersonal perception and judgment in social psychology research (Tagiuri and Petrullo, 1958).

SENSITIVITY TO PROBLEMS

Guilford (1959a) defines sensitivity to problems as the ability to recognize that a problem exists; he sees this ability as important in creative thinking. It is the factor involved in evaluating semantic implications. This ability is of tremendous importance in coping with stress, because adaptive action cannot be taken until the individual has recognized that a problem exists or that the situation is dangerous.

One task calls for the subject to suggest two improvements for common appliances, such as telephones, bicycles, and the like. A second, Seeing Problems, calls for the listing of possible problems that might arise in connection with a common object, such as a candle or a bar of soap. A third, Seeing Deficiencies, requires that the subject point out the way in which a described plan or activity is faulty.

THE EVALUATIVE THINKING PROCESS

The evaluative thinking process, as it has been described and studied (Johnson, 1955), does not differ greatly from the general problem-solving process already described. Since there are a number of different emphases, it seems useful to approach the process from this vantage point. In brief, the first stage, preparations for effective evaluating, includes exploring the problem, deciding what questions to ask, deciding upon the most profitable set of observations, and making hypotheses. The actual evaluating includes fact finding, idea finding, judging facts and ideas, and organizing data for evaluation. Each of these aspects will now be discussed briefly, and then the role of the evaluative abilities and the evaluation process in coping with stress will be examined. In the next chapter, some of the problems of improving these abilities and processes will be discussed.

PREPARATION FOR EVALUATION

It is often said that a question well put is half answered. It is indeed important to know what questions to ask, and some interesting research is now being done on devising methods for teaching children how to ask good questions (Suchman, 1961ab). Questioning is a skill that few teachers and supervisors have mastered.

Preparation for evaluation is itself a process. There are several rich sources of information concerning this process: experiments on association and problem solving, studies of creative thinking, studies in risk taking and decision making, and the like. Some of the thinking abilities already listed figure prominently in this process. One of these is orientation, the ability to see an order or trend in a mass of information and to recognize what is pertinent to the situation. Exploratory activity is commonly referred to as investigatory responses (Berlyne, 1960). The responses activate manipulation, which brings about changes in external objects or situations. The exploratory experiment is one example of this type of behavior.

Materials developed in three of the Minnesota studies will serve to illustrate some of the problems in the preparation process.

The first pertains to the problem of deciding what questions to ask. One of the tests developed in the studies of creative thinking will illustrate this aspect of the process. This is the Ask-and-Guess Test. The subject is confronted with a picture. He is asked first to think of all of the questions he would need to ask in order to find out everything that is happening in the picture. He is given one restriction: his questions must be ones that cannot be answered by looking at the picture. The subject must survey the situation, determine what questions he can answer from what is given, identify the gaps in information, and then ask questions to obtain the missing information. Questions range from "global" ones, which involve only very general hypotheses, to questions that have well-formulated hypotheses built into them (Yamamoto, 1962). In an unfamiliar problem, the subject probably has to start with a few "global" questions. As he gains experience, he soon learns to ask more specific and penetrating questions that will most economically provide him with the data needed for evaluation. In the "guessing" phase of this test, the subject is instructed to think of all possible causes (things that happened previously to cause the events in the picture) and then to think of all possible consequences (things that might happen because of the events). The kinds of thinking activities involved in this task illustrate a desirable kind of preparation for evaluation.

The psychology of the preparation for thought may also be regarded as an elaboration and application of the psychology of set. One of the teacher's problems in evaluating a student's performance would be to decide what set to use in making observations and collecting data. For example, in evaluating such performance, should the teacher assume a memory set and try to remember everything that the student does, that is, try to soak up all available information about the student? Or should he assume a creative-thinking set, observing all of the ways in which the student might improve, thinking of all possible explanations of his behavior, all possible consequences of his behavior, and the like? Or should he assume an evaluative set, evaluating the correctness, suitability, adequacy, and desirability of the student's behavior in terms of whatever criteria he has determined to be relevant?

An experiment conducted by Torrance and Harmon (1961) indicates clearly that the set which students assume in reading course requirements affects the kinds of achievement that will result. To the extent that one can generalize from these findings, one would say that for purposes of evaluation or decision making, one should assume an evaluative set. The other sets are superior for other purposes. For example, if one's purpose is to teach and develop, the creative set would perhaps be most effective.

Much has been said in educational literature about the need for the evaluation process to pervade the teaching process. The author has long held this point of view and has devised a variety of ways of helping teachers to implement it. In earlier attempts, he has been painfully aware of failure. Through a recent study (Torrance, 1964) he discovered one possible reason for this failure. Since this study involves the troubleshooting type of evaluation or hypothesis making which characterizes the preparation process, this study will be described briefly.

The data of this study are the daily logs of teachers participating in the 1958–59 and 1959–60 experiments of the Minnesota National Laboratory for the Improvement of Secondary Mathematics. Teacher effectiveness had been determined from the regression coefficients of posttest achievement scores of pupils on pretest achievement and aptitude scores. In other words, effectiveness is determined by how much the teacher's pupils learned per unit of resources they had to begin with.

First the daily logs of the five most and five least effective teachers in the 1958–59 experiment were analyzed to determine the types of mental operations represented by the teacher and pupil activities reported. Guilford's mental operations (cognition, memory, convergent thinking, divergent thinking, and evaluation) were adopted for this purpose. The more effective teachers reported significantly more of the thinking activities (convergent, divergent, and evaluative) than the less effective ones.

A new scheme was then devised to analyze the evaluative behavior of these teachers as reflected in the daily logs. The three categories used were negative evaluation, positive evaluation, and hypothesis-making evaluation. The more effective teachers reported far more of the hypothesis-making activity, whereas the less effective ones reported more negative and positive evaluation. The logs of the 14 most and 14 least effective of the 127 teachers participating in the 1959–60 experiments were analyzed with almost identical results. Detailed examination of the hypothesis-making behavior of these two groups indicates that the hypothesis making of the less effective teachers tends to be too general, stereotyped, and vague to be of real value. They also tended to report hypotheses as having been tested rather than as having possibilities for solution. There were also scattered indications that teachers whose evaluations were predominantly positive may have actually been unaware of the difficulties their students were experiencing in learning. Hypothesis making involves an awareness of the deficiency coupled with a constructive idea concerning its cause and/or remedy.

IDEA FINDING

It is hoped that the need for idea finding has already become clear. Idea finding does not have to be left to chance. There are a number of rather well-formulated principles which, when properly applied, improve substantially the output of ideas. One of these (Osborn, 1960) is the principle of suspended judgment or suspended evaluation. The reader probably knows this as the "brainstorming principle." This principle may be applied to both individual and group idea finding and has been demonstrated repeatedly to produce superior results (Meadow and Parnes, 1959; Parnes and Meadow, 1960). In fact, when individuals adhere to the principle of suspended judgment they generate almost twice as many good ideas as when they allow judgment concurrently to interfere (Osborn, 1960). Successful courses for training individuals and groups in the principles of idea finding have been developed by the Creative Education Foundation and other agencies.

Idea finding (production) and judgment (evaluation) have usually been studied separately, but Johnson and his associates have recently begun to study their interaction. Johnson and Zerbolio (Jennings and Johnson, 1963) demonstrated that subjects who practiced the production of plot titles improved their judgment of plot titles. Johnson and Jennings (1963) showed that subjects shifted readily from the production of plot titles to the judgment of these titles. They also found that the accuracy of the judgments of the subjects of their own productions conformed to predictions based on judgment of objects supplied by the experimenter. In still another experiment, Jennings and Johnson (1963) had subjects produce small angles and then judge a standard series of angles. They had another group produce large angles and then judge the standard series of angles. The results showed that the two groups differed in the scales of judgment used, apparently because of the different contexts established during production. In a similar experiment, run in reverse sequence, it was found that the context established during the judgment of angles influenced the production of angles. Jennings and Johnson also demonstrated the same effects regarding the judgment and production of short statements describing offenses.

ASSESSING DATA FOR EVALUATION

Important as they are, fact finding and idea finding together are not enough. The "goodness" of these facts and ideas must be assessed. It must be assumed that the preparation for evaluation has accomplished three things (Johnson, 1955):

1. The thinker has been alerted for action at the appropriate time.
2. The stimulus objects, data, or materials of evaluation have been specified.
3. The form of the evaluative response or the alternative response categories has been specified.

Assuming that the evaluator is now prepared to evaluate, the important question becomes: What does he evaluate? If the evaluation is a simple one, like evaluating which of two pupils is taller, the preparation emphasizes just one aspect or dimension of the stimulus objects, such as the size. In experimental research investigators have been concerned chiefly about three characteristics of the stimulus objects: perceptual (what is seen), affective (what is felt emotionally), and abstract (what is conceived).

When evaluation is based on *perceptual* characteristics, the evaluator gives his attention to some specified attribute of the object of evaluation, such as length, weight, color, loudness, intensity, and area. Instruments for measuring such attributes have been well worked out.

If the evaluator is concerned about *affective* characteristics, he will report his likes and dislikes, how pleasant or unpleasant something looks or smells to him, how intensely he wants something, how strongly he reacts for or against something. This is perhaps the most primitive and effortless way of reacting to the environment and constitutes a large share of casual conversation. Instruments in this realm are less well worked out than in the perceptual area, but some preference for objects, colors, musical intervals, and foods can be rather accurately measured. Methods such as paired comparisons, order of merit rating, and the like are fairly well advanced.

354

The evaluator may have to direct his attention to *abstract* or conceived characteristics. Teachers, counselors, administrators, and other mental health workers are continually being asked to make evaluations concerning the personality characteristics of individuals. They are asked to rate individuals on such abstract qualities as sociability, honesty, cheerfulness, aggressiveness, and the like. In making such evaluations, the thinker has more to do than in making the other types of simple evaluations. He must abstract a trait such as sociability from a jumble of past and present impressions occurring in many different contexts. There are multiple possibilities for interference because things are similar or dissimilar in respect to so many abstract properties. Thus, more effort is required to maintain a set and to resist interference. It is possible, however, to study and evaluate two concepts as same or different just as two sugar solutions may be tasted and judged same or different.

A number of technical developments are useful in assessing abstract or conceptual characteristics. These include various scaling procedures, measures of central tendency, measures of variability, correlation, significance of differences, anchoring procedures, and the like.

Most of the evaluations made in fostering personality development and mental health are not simple ones. A teacher makes complex evaluations when he decides that a particular child needs help in coping with his difficulties. His preparation for making these evaluations may be quite general and indefinite, an unanalyzed result of years of experience. It may, however, be quite explicit. He may write down the factors that caused him to be concerned about the child's mental health. Often the criteria to be used are quite specific. Regardless of the degree of explicitness or source of the criteria of evaluation, there are still the issues of what affects the judgments and what are the relative weights of such factors.

From the research that has been devoted to this problem, it is possible to extract a few general principles of evaluation. A few of these will be reviewed (Johnson, 1955, pp. 294–300): *

1. The first principle is obvious but important. *The evaluation may be influenced by things to which attention is not directed by explicit instructions or by logical implications of the materials being evaluated.* Man's irrational nature is well known. It is rarely possible to discuss rationally, without striking prejudices, such commonplace things as health, clothes, Negroes, Jews, social class, money, sex, marriage, some diseases, wage scales, and so on through a long list that varies from time to time, place to place, school to school. Few people can think clearly and honestly about many of these things, and they inevitably intrude into evaluations in dealing

---

* Abstracted from *Psychology of Thought and Judgment* by Donald M. Johnson (New York: Harper & Brothers, 1955). By permission of Harper & Row, Publishers.

with problems of personality development and mental health. In other words, these biases are not supposed to affect one's evaluations, but they do.

2. The second principle is somewhat similar. *The evaluation may be influenced by things which the evaluator cannot or does not report.* For example, it seems rather certain that one's immediate intuitive evaluations of personality are based in part upon subliminal cues which may depend upon memory impressions too vague to be reported. Repression may increase this effect.

3. Several studies indicate that *most evaluators give extra weight to suggestions, judgments, opinions, and the like attributed to people whom they regard as experts.* It is even possible to manufacture a temporary expert in a laboratory by making one person appear more successful than the others. In the author's research with combat aircrews, this effect has been demonstrated quite clearly (Torrance, 1954c) in decision-making experiments. For example, in B-26 crews, it was found that gunners just as frequently as pilots had the correct or best solutions to problems. Yet gunners seldom influenced the decisions of crews, even though the problems did not involve the areas of the pilots' special expertness.

4. *Most judges give extra weight to suggestions, judgments, and opinions attributed to a majority of a group with whom they identify.* Very early in life a child starts depending upon consensual validation for his judgments and guides to behavior. He does not admit to consciousness of his judgments until he finds out what others think. This is illustrated in the story of the children who were trying to decide whether their baby rabbits were girl rabbits or boy rabbits. After some argument, one said, "I know how you can tell. Let's vote on it." Children should learn that there are better ways of making some evaluations than "voting on it" and that the majority may be in error.

5. *When the evaluation called for is avoided because of its difficulty or for any other reason, evaluation of some other aspect will be made.* As shown in earlier chapters, a person confronted with something too difficult selects out some part with which he can cope successfully. Some of the easiest things to evaluate are the least important. For example, a teacher may find it easier to evaluate a child's creative writing on the basis of evenness of margin, correctness of spelling and capitalization, and the like than on the basis of such creative qualities as picturesqueness of speech, vividness, personal involvement, originality of plot or ending, surprisingness, humor, individuality of style, imagination, perceptive sensitivity, versatility of style and word usage, new and refreshing symbolism, and the communication of a mood. Similarly, school administrators may find it easier to evaluate teacher effectiveness on the basis of the neatness of their classrooms, the quietness of their pupils, and their promptness in submitting

reports than on the basis of the personality growth and mental health of their pupils.

6. A special case of the fifth principle may be stated as follows: *when an abstract evaluation is called for, an affective evaluation is commonly given.* As already indicated, maintaining a set toward abstract characteristics of a complex behavior or situation to be evaluated is difficult and tedious for many people. Thus, they use the more primitive affective evaluation. This tends to occur when teachers are asked to evaluate the growth or status of pupils relative to the complex mental processes discussed in this book. For example, teachers are likely to overevaluate the creativeness or problem-solving ability of highly conforming pupils and to underestimate such abilities among pupils who are nonconforming and upset the orderliness of classroom organization and procedure. The author asked one group of teachers to evaluate their pupils in terms of curiosity and gave them several specific criteria to use in judging curiosity. Although these teachers approached their task seriously and made careful judgments on the basis of the criteria, they were at first rather uncomfortable about their evaluations. A typical comment was, "I hate to list some of my best students in the low group on curiosity. They are the best in the class in spelling, arithmetic, and reading, but they really are not curious at all. They never ask questions, rarely seek new experiences, and do not persist in examining and exploring things in order to know more about them. I suppose I just like them better, and I really do not like some of the ones I placed in the high group. I certainly would not have rated them this way if you had simply asked me to name my five most curious and five least curious pupils."

7. *When the evaluation called for is straightforward and easy, the evaluator is likely to maintain his set for that judgment and not be diverted into something else.* Evidence for this principle comes from many experiments (Johnson, 1955, p. 298) and experiences. One decision-making experiment (Torrance, 1953) has demonstrated that better decisions result when groups are trained to focus attention during evaluation sessions on factors that have been found to be most important through research than when methods not involving such structuring are used. Teachers tend to evaluate the creativeness of their pupils on the basis of the elaborateness and fanciness of the things that they produce (qualities that call for relatively straightforward and easy evaluation) rather than on the basis of their inventiveness and originality (qualities that call for rather complex evaluations).

ORGANIZING DATA FOR EVALUATION

The seven principles for identifying the factors that influence evaluations and for determining the strength of each do not tell the whole story. The next problem is one of organization. What does the evaluator do to get his facts and ideas into shape for evaluation? A few common organizing principles can be described.

1. A SINGLE STIMULUS DIMENSION AS FIGURE. Although evaluations of height are systematically related to measured variations in height, this relationship does not tell all that the evaluator did. Obviously experience plays a part in the organization of the material for evaluation. An experienced teacher or coach, for example, has learned what defects to look for in the performance of a student or player and what deviations can be tolerated in evaluating a performance. That aspect of the performance in which the teacher, coach, counselor, nurse, or principal has most frequently found defects probably stands out as figure for him (i.e., predominates above or obscures all other aspects of a performance). The situation may be changed by in-service education or supervision, however, and some other aspects may become figure for different reasons. In selecting athletes for a team, a coach may concentrate on a few highly desirable or highly undesirable qualifications. This method may cause him to ignore some outstanding characteristic of a particular athlete which might have been more important than all of the other qualifications combined.

2. ALGEBRAIC ADDITION. A person making a complex evaluation may try to add the effects of all pertinent variables, whether positive or negative. He adds up the advantages and disadvantages, the correct actions and errors, the credits and debits. The result may give him a first approximation, but this assumption of additivity should be critically examined. The adding-up process may lead to a hazardous evaluation.

Three principles are important in using the principle of additivity:

(a) Errors based on this principle may not be due to failure of the principle but to the use of scales of unequal units. An extreme example of a hazardous evaluation is that of a candidate for parole in a prison who has only one demerit on his prison record and that is for the murder of a guard compared with a candidate who has ten demerits, all for minor infractions such as being three minutes late for a job, unpolished shoes, or an incorrectly folded blanket. A less extreme case of an error of this type is an evaluation of "failing" given by a teacher to a composition that the teacher herself recognized as the best-written composition submitted by members of her class. She had instructed pupils to write two paragraphs on a particular topic. This pupil had thought of a clever way of treating the topic and presented her idea in a well-organized, excellently written paragraph. The error of adding unequal units is especially hazardous in evaluations which determine success or failure in rather absolute terms. For example, a teacher failed to promote a third grade girl, although this girl regularly outdid every pupil in the class in arithmetic and spelling, read far above her grade level, and learned many things on her own initiative. The girl had failed to turn in a number of her assignments, had lost her notebook, and had received low grades in conduct for whispering in class, interrupting the teacher, and being out of her desk.

(b) Errors in evaluation occur when qualities important in achieving success in a particular program are given no more attention than qualities having little relationship to success in that program. A boy who is enthusiastic about science and is truly expert in many areas of science may be excluded from his school's science club because he does not have a B-plus average. A candidate may be admitted to engineering school on the basis of a high grade-point average, although he has low grades in the few courses he had in high school mathematics and has a strong aversion to mathematics and science. Children may be selected for special programs for gifted children on the basis of performance on intelligence tests and teacher grades. Yet in the special program, they are taught by discovery methods and much emphasis is placed on experimentation, self-initiated learning, creative problem-solving, and decision making. Children selected on the basis of high scores on tests of creative or divergent thinking are given programmed learning materials designed to prevent errors by permitting only tiny mental leaps, whereas they are accustomed to making large mental leaps and then testing and correcting their solutions and are skilled in doing this.

(c) Errors in the data used in making evaluations may be so great that precise evaluations cannot be made. A coach may find that his evaluations of the motivations of candidates for a team are unreliable (contain error). On the other hand, he can obtain reliable measures of various physical and mental characteristics, past performance, and personality characteristics, all of which have predictive value. Although the coach knows that motivation is important in athletic performance, he would reduce his errors in selection by comparing one prediction with another and arranging them so that the difference between predictions is largely relative to the errors in the data. Of course, he might continue to seek more reliable indicators of motivation. In many cases, precise evaluations should be avoided. This is particularly true when judges are able to assess, with accuracy, extremely high and extremely low degrees of a quality. In such cases, error may actually be reduced by studying the extreme cases for which reliable assessment is possible.

3. SERIAL EVALUATION. Many evaluations are difficult because there is too much information to organize. The evaluator may consider each item serially, not adding pros and cons, but using each piece of information in different ways. At least two such types of organization have proved useful: the *checklist* and the principle of *successive hurdles*.

One of the most common evaluation problems is the decision of readiness for a critical activity. Aircrews have a very detailed flight-checklist. The pilot memorizes a list of items to check before the take-off, and another to check before the landing. A teacher might have a checklist of the critical skills and techniques a child must have before he is prepared to undertake a new experience or an activity involving known dangers.

The principle of successive hurdles is also useful. When the performance of a college student has been evaluated as unsatisfactory, the counselor may ask, "Can this student be salvaged for further college work?" If the answer is "No," the matter is closed. If the answer is "Yes," the counselor goes on to the next hurdle: "Is there a defect in his earlier education?" If the answer is "No," that issue is closed. If the answer is "Yes," the counselor goes on to the next hurdle: "Can the defect in education be remedied?" If the answer is "No," the issue is closed. If the answer is "Yes," he goes on to the next hurdle until he reaches a decision upon which he can act.

Experiments by Johnson and Jennings (1963) showed that serial analysis slowed the subjects but did not reduce the quality of the solutions. Johnson's methodological conclusion is that the solution of certain problems can with advantage be analyzed into functional units shorter than the problem-solving episode but longer than the single response. Judgment along with preparation and production of ideas yields a broad but differentiated outline of problem solving.

4. JUDGMENT BY GENERAL IMPRESSION. Many studies indicate that the various aspects of a complex evaluation are not judged separately for what they are worth, even though the instructions may call for separate judgment. The evaluator gets a general impression, perhaps from one striking aspect, and makes evaluations predominantly on that basis, ignoring the other aspects or treating them as minor deviations that do not count. This is the well-known "halo effect." Some people have argued that for practical purposes, as in selecting employees, this over-all impression is all that is required and is more valid than several analytical judgments. The little evidence available (Johnson, 1955, p. 312), however, indicates that evaluators are at least more consistent when they make these analytical evaluations than when they make judgments on the basis of general impressions. In other words, synthesis is more successful, if it has been preceded by analysis.

In a more recent report, Johnson (1963) concluded that the evidence for halo effect resulting from judging operations is questionable. In the reanalysis of some of his earlier data Johnson found that some of his differences could be due to objective variations in the information available to the different judges rather than to the judging operation itself.

5. COMPARING COGNITIVE PATTERNS. The types of organization already discussed have involved separation of the aspects of a complex

evaluation. At times, it is profitable to consider patterns rather than separate aspects. A symptom might have quite a different meaning if accompanied by one kind of behavior from what it would have if accompanied by another. The physician examining a patient in a coma makes his evaluation by an organization of the facts he observes. He knows the pattern of symptoms of head injury, of diabetic coma, of alcoholic intoxication, and other possibilities. If any one aspect of the patient's behavior suggests head injury, he checks for other signs that will corroborate this diagnosis. He assembles all his information into a pattern and matches this pattern with the familiar symptom pattern.

In trying to discover the remedy for a behavior problem in the classroom, a teacher might have to follow a similar pattern approach. He may identify the problem and begin trying to detect the accompanying behaviors. He may do this by comparing the child's pattern of behavior with some model established by experience or by contrasting the effective with the ineffective pattern of behavior. Having a frame of reference is useful.

Many ways of structuring and restructuring the facts and ideas used in evaluation have been developed. The ones suggested herein are only a few.

EVALUATIVE THINKING IN MENTAL HEALTH

As the thinking abilities involved in evaluation and the process itself have been discussed, much of the role of evaluative thinking in mental health has unfolded. Emphasis has been on the importance of recognizing the existence of a problem. Recognition requires the kinds of discrimination involved in figural and symbolic identification. After a person has made accurate discriminations, he must evaluate relationships before he can recognize the seriousness of the situation. Evaluating sets of relationships, judgments, and sensitivity to problems then becomes the very essence of the initial process of adapting to stressful situations. It is only as these abilities operate that adaptive action can be taken.

MAINTAINING ANCHORS AND ADEQUATE STRUCTURE

The importance of maintaining anchors or contacts with the environment and the need for adequate structure have also been emphasized. Here too the evaluative process is intimately involved. In the preparatory phase, a person needs orientation abilities in order to see trends, to recognize the important variables operating, and to bring about adequate structure. He must use perceptual foresight and prediction abilities to see beyond what is happening at the moment and to explore visually several possible courses of action, preparatory to selecting the most promising. He must see beyond the immediate and obvious and anticipate the needs or consequences of a given situation, in order to prevent shock and frozen panic.

MAKING CHOICES UNDER CONDITIONS OF UNCERTAINTY

Judgment has been defined as the ability to make wise choices of action in a somewhat ambiguous situation. The very essence of coping with stress is making wise choices under conditions of uncertainty, risk, or relative lack of structure. Such choices are highly important in preventing frustration, fatigue, and collapse because they help the person to avoid or reduce the stressfulness of an emergency and to extricate himself from the predicament when it occurs.

WILLINGNESS TO ACCEPT LIMITATIONS

Through evaluation the individual is able to learn from experience and to avoid past mistakes. He can reduce the number and seriousness of his errors and can cope more effectively with stress. He can learn when he must summon his more expensive energies in order to succeed. He can learn to test his limits and those of the situation. He can calculate better the risk he is taking and thus be better prepared to cope even if failure results. He can react more favorably because he has recognized in advance that he might not succeed and is prepared with alternative strategies. He is also less likely to be disappointed or demoralized by failure and is consequently more invulnerable to the various mental health hazards of failure.

The foregoing dynamics are involved in a study conducted by E. M. Berger (1962) at the University of Minnesota Student Counseling Bureau around a variable he labeled "willingness to accept limitations." Using a simple sixteen-item inventory, Berger identified University of Minnesota students with a high or "healthy" willingness to accept limitations and those with a low or "unhealthy" willingness to accept limitations. In general, students with a healthy willingness may be described as denying that they have extremely high standards for themselves, admitting that they make wholehearted efforts to achieve, admitting that they are willing to try their best despite a risk of not doing well, and acknowledging that hard work in achievement is creditable. Such students do not demand that they be absolutely "successful," and they accept the fact that some of their abilities are not as good as others and that some things require more effort. They also accept the fact that, despite their best efforts, they will not always be "outstanding," that there will inevitably be some disappointment, some failure to achieve objectives.

Berger hypothesized that other things being equal, those high-ability college students who are more willing to accept limitations, will achieve at a higher level. His definition of high ability was high school rank at the eightieth percentile or over. The Willingness to Accept Limitations Inventory was administered during the freshman orientation period. Students were paired to be as similar as possible on high school rank, college aptitude (score on American Council on Education Psychological Examination), and size of high school, and as different as possible on Willingness to Accept Limitations. Among male students in the College of Science, Literature, and the Arts, Berger found that on the average about one full grade-point average separated those showing a healthy acceptance of their limitations from those showing a lack of acceptance of limitations. The results were less convincing for men in the Institute of Technology and women in the School of Science, Literature, and the Arts, though still definitely in the direction hypothesized.

EVALUATING AND CORRECTING FOR BIASES

Biases of various kinds can cause the cognitive, memory, and productive thinking operations to get off track. If one is able to evaluate his biases, he will frequently be able to correct for them or even avoid the ill affects of them on the other mental operations. Apparently biases or unconscious motivations as they interfere with the evaluation abilities show up in such characteristics of decisions as the improper ordering of the usefulness of alternatives, estimates of extreme desirability of alternatives, failure to consider long-range consequences, and omission of or inadequate attention to noxious aspects of the evaluation process.

In their study of personality factors affecting decision processes, Brim, Glass, Lavin, and Goodman (1962, pp. 54–58) examined nine different beliefs, most of which had been shown to be of significance in earlier research. These beliefs are as follows:

1. The degree of mastery which one believes he has over his environment.
2. Whether events occur through some natural order or whether they are caused by supernatural or mystical causes (Belief in Supernatural Causes and Belief in Animism).
3. Whether or not the world is viewed as predictable (Belief in Predictability of Life).
4. Whether events which occur in the world are mostly good or mostly bad (Four Scales of Optimism and Pessimism).
5. Complexity of causal relations between events in nature (Belief in Multiple Causation of Events).
6. Emphasis which should be placed on consideration of future events, compared with the past and present (Future Time Orientation).
7. Value placed upon originality and creativity (Anti-Traditionalistic Orientation).
8. Degree of goodness or badness and of the probability or improbability of events.

9. Value assigned to being thoughtful and deliberate in considering courses of action, compared with the value placed on spontaneity and impulsivity (Belief in Thinking Before Acting).

Many of the implications of these biases or beliefs for behavior under stress will be fairly obvious and can be assessed by available research. Many others will need further testing.

ORGANIZING AND SIMPLIFYING STRUCTURE

Organization of a mass of data simplifies the structure, reduces the load on the mental operations, and makes it easier to cope with the situation. Evaluation is also operative in separating the important from the unimportant, in unloading, and in conserving energy or focusing it on the important tasks.

The ability to tolerate complexity without undue stress may be dependent upon the ability to organize and simplify the structure of what would be an overwhelming mass of data. For example, organization enables a classroom teacher to individualize instruction in the classroom, or at least make differentiations among the instruction given different types of pupils. The author has been interested in the ways by which teachers differentiate instruction for highly creative children and for less creative children. In one study, he divided into three roughly equal groups the fifth grade pupils of 19 teachers in one school system on the basis of pupils' scores on a battery of tests of creative thinking. In studying under- and overachievement as judged by discrepancies between mental age (as measured by an intelligence test) and educational age (as determined by standardized achievement tests), he noted vast differences in patterns among teachers. Under some teachers, the highly creative pupils overachieved and the less creative ones underachieved, while the reverse was true for other teachers. Under a few teachers, both the highly creative and the less creative pupils overachieved. Teachers in the third category had exceptionally high scores on a measure labeled Tolerance for Complexity. The author's guess is that teachers in the first category are overwhelmed by the complexity involved in differentiating instruction for different types of learners and insist that all learn in about the same way.

TESTING DIVERGENT POSSIBILITIES

While divergent thinking should be encouraged in attempts to solve problems, there are dangers of unrealistic decisions. Thus, the evaluative abilities have to function in order to maintain adequate contacts with reality by testing the divergent ideas that have been produced. Only when the individual is able to trust his own judgments is he able to cope adequately with life's stresses.

364

SUMMARY

The evaluative abilities are given even less attention in the schools than are the divergent thinking abilities, with apparently less than one per cent of teacher's objectives being concerned with this area of achievement. It is also estimated that the exercise of the evaluative thinking abilities in general requires more expensive energy than any of the other types of mental operations. The evaluative thinking abilities are called into play in making decisions concerning the goodness (correctness, suitability, adequacy, desirability) of information in terms of identity, consistency, and goal satisfaction. Among these abilities are figural identification, symbolic identification, symbol manipulation, logical evaluation, experiential evaluation, judgment, and sensitivity to problems.

Evaluation involves the following phases: preparation (exploring the problem, deciding what questions to ask, deciding upon the most profitable set of observations, and making hypotheses), idea finding, assessing data, and organizing data. Problems associated with each of these aspects can be identified and discussed in relation to coping constructively with stress.

The evaluative abilities are important to mental health because they are used in maintaining anchors in reality and adequate structure, making choices under conditions of uncertainty, willingness to accept limitations, evaluating and correcting for biases, organizing and simplifying the structure of the situation, and testing divergent possibilities.

Developing and

Freeing the

Evaluative

Thinking Abilities

22

In 1922, Julius Boraas wrote that he had made more than three thousand visits to schools and classes in rural, graded, and high schools, as well as colleges and universities, but that he had never witnessed what he called a judgment recitation. By "judgment recitation" he had in mind a session to develop the evaluative abilities, in which the aim is to "train the pupils to judge correctly by having them make comparisons, determine relative importance or values, weigh evidence, or test inferences and conclusions regarding things, persons, situations, or ideas" (Boraas, 1922, p. 37).

The author's experiences and the surveys of the objectives of teachers suggest that Boraas would have little better chance of observing such a recitation today. Although teachers have emphasized "getting the right answer" and "having the right attitude," these answers have been predetermined and taught by authority. The student does not arrive at them through the exercise of the evaluative thinking abilities and the processes of evaluation described in the preceding chapter. The student makes no leap across the barriers from learning to thinking in arriving at the solutions and attitudes he seeks.

The beginning of the 1960's saw an unprecedented interest in creativity in education and in the development of the creative thinking abilities. While such interest is long overdue and far from universal, it is disturbing to anyone interested in personality development and mental hygiene that there has been no comparable interest in decision making and the development of the evaluative thinking abilities. It is this lack of skill in evaluation that causes the superior divergent type of thinker so much difficulty. The type is well known—highly intuitive, imaginative, and even brilliant, but lacking in sound evaluation or common sense. In elementary school, his ideas are called "silly," "wild," "crazy," or "naughty." Even when his ideas are outright brilliant and sound, they are likely to be labeled as "nutty." This person has a major problem in developing and freeing his evaluative abilities.

Educators, however, cannot be blamed too severely for not showing concern about teaching children how to decide. Although the decision-making problem is as old as life itself, man has been slow to develop a body of knowledge about how decisions are made and how the process of making them can be improved. For example, in his final comment concerning a symposium on uncertainty and decisions, Shackle (1954) wrote: "Yet decision-making, the focal creative psychic event where knowledge, thought, feeling, and imagination are fused into action, seems to have received only the most casual glances of scientists and scholars" (p. 100).

USING KNOWLEDGE ABOUT DECISION MAKING

At the time Shackle wrote the words quoted above, there had already developed considerable interest in the study of decision making. Von Neumann and Morgenstern (1947) had already written their famous treatise on the theory of games and economic behavior. Economists, mathematicians, philosophers, logicians, and psychologists had begun to develop and test theories concerning decision making. Since that time interest has been fairly well sustained. Practical interest, however, has come primarily from the fields of business and industry. A little interest has been shown by military groups but has never been very powerful or consistent. Even less has been shown by such mental hygiene groups as counselors, guidance workers, psychiatrists, clinical psychologists, and the like. Almost none is reflected in the professional literature of teachers and administrators.

One possible reason why educators have ignored this body of knowledge is that its language is highly technical and specialized. Thus, good translators are needed to make the knowledge that exists meaningful to educators. Although no such attempt will be made in this chapter, the author will identify a few concepts that should be of value to those who are interested in the relationship of decision making to personality development and mental health.

Bross (1953) has presented an interesting historical account of man's decision-making operations. Man was created as a decision-making animal; a biological mechanism for decision was a necessity for his survival. The human animal finally came to substitute a cultural mechanism for decision for the biological one. The pooling of experiences and transmitting them to the young, required less expensive energies of the decision maker. Experiences within a culture, however, were not all concordant, and as a result contradictory instructions placed a severe strain on the young decision maker. Nevertheless, cultural mechanisms for decision making led to advances in civilization. As societies became more complex, there arose a class of professional decision makers—kings, generals, and priests. One advantage of this development lay in the fact that it generally takes less expensive energy to make a decision when someone else must bear the consequences. Many of these professionals, however, botched their jobs, resulting in a distrust.

The professionals developed a number of intellectual decision systems and these came into vogue. They simplified things and gave a structure that could be comprehended by other men. There was a pressing need for simplicity. From these efforts have come elaborate models of the real world. One of the earliest was the devil theory. Decisions were made on the basis of whether or not an action would please the gods and frustrate the devil. According to Bross, the next model was Reason, and the latest is Science.

History has shown the inadequacies of the biological decision-making mechanisms, of the professional decision makers, and of reason. This generation must learn how to use the concepts of science in making decisions. A few of the concepts presented by Bross provide clues and will be reviewed briefly.

One may conceive of the decision maker as a machine into which information flows and out of which comes a recommended course of action. The machine has three systems: the predictive system, which generates the various alternatives; the value system, which handles various conflicting purposes; and the criterion, which integrates the other two components and selects an appropriate action. The pragmatic principle must be used in constructing the decision maker and testing it. Thus, decision makers that will be able to stand up under stress must have carefully constructed systems. They must be carefully tested.

Bross has discussed several possible rules for action and has introduced such concepts as "calculated risk," "sequential decisions," and the like, all of which have important implications for coping with stress. In the calculated risk there is the implication that "the favored action is not guaranteed to lead to a desired end, but rather that it seems more likely to do so than the alternative actions" (Bross, 1953, p. 102). Furthermore, the term "calculated" indicates that this conclusion was reached by a deliberate analysis of the situation, historical precedents, and the like. The two principal criteria for making decisions on the basis of calculated risk are maximizing the expected gain and minimizing the maximum risk.

Many complex decisions require a series of decisions, leading to the concept of "sequential decisions." At each stage a decision is made as to whether to continue the experiment or to make a terminal decision. Some theorists have advocated that nations make more use of the sequential decision in arriving at problems of international peace. Educators might well consider ways of devising situations in which children are permitted to make sequential decisions about such concerns as art, science, and curricular choices. Perhaps vocational and educational counselors have always tried to help their clients to develop strategies for making sequential decisions about their choices. Some counselors, however, feel compelled to make "final" decisions. Perhaps a greater tolerance can be developed for sequential decisions, as well as skills in making them. Such efforts should result in healthier personality development and mental functioning.

The traditional emphasis on making "final" or "ultimate" decisions has been highlighted by Davis (Thrall, Coombs, and Davis, 1954). He pointed out two major preoccupations concerning decision problems that have persisted for over two thousand years. The first is the concern as to whether or not a given action or decision would be good, right, or likely to achieve some desired effect. Philosophers, he points out, have presented these problems in the form of dilemmas. If there were more than two alternatives available, the decision maker usually hewed to a "mean." The second of these preoccupations is found in the implicit assumption that decisions are to be made on the basis of one *known* situation. It is now more generally recognized that decision makers must allow for information whose accuracy is only probable and in no sense absolute. Theories of preference and utility may also help to resolve some of the difficulties involved in the question of stating what "the desired effect" is to mean.

It is the author's belief that many of the concepts being developed in decision theory will prove valuable in developing and freeing the evaluative thinking abilities and consequently in contributing to personality development and mental health. Thus far, these concepts have not found their way into textbooks in educational psychology, mental health, and the like. It is to be hoped that good translators will soon communicate this growing body of knowledge to the diversity of individuals interested in promoting mental health.

SUGGESTIONS FOR IMPROVING EVALUATION

One of the most common pieces of advice given about improving evaluation is to "suspend judgment" and to "keep an open mind." The wisdom of this advice, however, depends upon what happens while judgment is suspended and one is keeping an open mind. It would seem that suspending judgment and keeping an open mind improve evaluation only when hypotheses are being actively produced and tested during this period. Then, of course, one is no longer really suspending judgment. He is playing around with a possible solution and testing it. In general, however, the author is somewhat suspicious of people who keep open minds. In one experiment he found that so-called open-minded people may be less likely to be influenced by objective facts than those who had presumably "made up their minds" or had formulated some hypothesis. So, instead of teaching students to keep an open mind, it would probably be wiser to tell them to go ahead and guess, make a tentative evaluation, and then test it, finding out what the consequences will be. This advice, of course, has to be tempered by consideration of the danger involved in the testing.

Several other pieces of research have influenced this conclusion. Teachers and counselors frequently try to force individuals to suspend judgment and to prevent haste by forcing them to delay before beginning problems. Rokeach (1950) studied the influence of haste in working the Luchins water jar problems already described. He forced his subjects to delay before starting work for periods ranging from 10 to 60 seconds. Apparently, the enforced delay interrupted the set and allowed competition from other sets, thereby causing a decrement in performance.

The value of picking out one solution and playing along with it to test its validity is demonstrated in an experiment reported by I. J. Lee (1954) for obtaining agreement where there is a deadlock within the group. Essentially, the procedure required that each side give a full hearing to the other side of the issue without the interruptions of counterarguments, denials, and refutations. Questions of clarification, implications, and the like were permitted. In other words, the group was caused to entertain the idea that each side may be correct and to test each hypothesis, using the information that its advocate could marshal. Lee reported unusual success with the technique.

As in the case of memory, there are a number of rather trite and well-worn bits of advice that can be given by teachers, counselors, and others to improve the evaluative operations. The teacher, counselor, or administrator could hang on his wall a neatly lettered sign reminding himself and others to "Think." Usually this is about as useless as telling a troubled person not to worry. One could even draw up a list of feasible procedures which, if followed, would improve the quality of evaluative operations. These might include such things as the following (Johnson, 1955, p. 482): *

1. Avoid certain kinds of foods, or take some kind of drug or vitamin.
2. Improve your working conditions—soundproof your walls, open a window, arrange your office more conveniently, and the like.
3. Plan your evaluative work for a certain preferred time of day. Work in 45-minute periods. Schedule your activities in optimal sequences. Alternate productive activities with evaluative activities.
4. Study the common errors and successful solutions of others.

* Abstracted from *Psychology of Thought and Memory* by Donald M. Johnson (New York: Harper & Brothers, 1955). By permission of Harper & Row, Publishers.

5. Adopt a set to attend to certain things and ignore others. You can do this by writing down a rule or guide to follow.

It would probably be more useful to provide experiences in applying systematically some fundamental principles for improving the evaluation processes. A few of these will now be outlined.

1. ANALYSIS OF EVALUATIVE THINKING. One can apply some of the recommendations just listed, such as improving working conditions, and evaluations will improve in quality. Much better results can be expected, however, if attempts at improvement are based on an analysis of one's evaluative thinking. One can use some method for locating the difficulties or errors in evaluation. Here are four possibilities to consider (Johnson, 1955, p. 483): *

a. The nature of the final result, especially if there are errors in the evaluation, may permit inferences about the place where the error occurred.
b. If the evaluation procedures can be examined separately, direct observation of the defective procedures may be possible.
c. The source of the error may be located *ex post facto* by correcting it. If the conditions are improved, for example, and the final result is improved, there must have been something wrong with the preparation.
d. The source of the error may also be determined by discovering and becoming aware of consistent personal biases.

In summary, the over-all strategy for improving evaluative thinking should consist of analyzing the operations involved, identifying and diagnosing the weaknesses, and applying efforts to improve the points of greatest weakness.

2. IMPROVEMENT OF THE EVALUATIVE THINKING ABILITIES. Obviously techniques for solving arithmetic problems can best be improved by working arithmetic problems. But one never knows whether the problems of evaluation he will face tomorrow will be like those he faced yesterday. The world is changing so fast that it is difficult to apply past experience to the present or to the future. Thus, it is desirable to seek techniques of improvement that the evaluator can transfer to a wide range of problems. Efforts of this sort should be directed at the improvement of the evaluative thinking abilities, just as they have been for the productive thinking abilities.

Improvement might take place through *changes in objectives, curricular content,* and *evaluative practices* that include consideration of the evaluative behavior of students.

The present status of objectives relevant to evaluation and decision

* Abstracted from *Psychology of Thought and Memory* by Donald M. Johnson (New York: Harper & Brothers, 1955). By permission of Harper & Row, Publishers.

making has already been discussed. The objectives are important since they serve as a guide to the behavior of both the teacher and the pupils in choosing activities. The author has also found that when students read their assignments with an evaluative set, they perform better on examinations that require them to make decisions and support those decisions with sound reasons.

Little development of the evaluative thinking abilities is likely to occur unless they are given an opportunity to operate. This is especially important since the evaluative operations appear to call for more expensive energies than do the other operations. The need for making changes in curricular content to include such opportunities is apparent from many observations and studies. An early study of this nature was reported by Stevens (Boraas, 1922, pp. 9–10). When she asked teachers of history why they were teaching history, the most customary answer was that "history develops judgment." She reported, however, after observing hundreds of classrooms, that among questions formulated by teachers very few called for judgment. She wrote that she had found such questions as, "Was the king right in imposing the stamp tax upon the colonists?" Such a question might be interpreted as an appeal for a possible judgment by pupils. It cannot be a genuine judgment, however, when all of the textbooks distinctly revealed marked censure of the king. According to stenographic records of history lessons, the percentage of questions that could possibly involve the element of judgment ranged from five per cent to 22 per cent.

Several types of exercises should be especially useful in developing the evaluative operations. One type calls for discrimination concerning the significant aspects of the behavior or object being evaluated. It should give practice in arranging various pieces of information so as to produce the most convenient total combination. It should also require estimations of the relative value of various qualities.

If people are to develop their evaluative abilities, it will be essential to assess their performance on problems requiring judgment and decision making. For example, the author has found that students who are told that they will be examined and graded on decision-making questions before reading an assignment will perform significantly better on this type of examination than those not so instructed. It is also important that students learn to question and evaluate their own judgments and decisions. If the teacher makes a practice of telling pupils every time they express an erroneous opinion or judgment, they will depend upon him to tell them when they are incorrect. In coping with life's stresses they will usually have to detect and correct their own mistakes. There are many ways in which teachers can help children to evaluate their own work. Evaluation should include far more than correcting spelling and arithmetic drills, using an answer key. Children can be taught to evaluate their compositions, their solutions to social studies problems, and the like. From early childhood it is possible to teach children the skills and strategies of detecting and correcting their errors.

Teacher-constructed examinations, as well as standardized ones, can give greater emphasis to the evaluation of skills in judging and making decisions. The lack of such items in common practice was dramatically called to our attention by Boraas in 1922 (pp. 6–8), Getzels in 1960, and others.

3. ATTENTION TO PREPARATION FOR EVALUATION. All available evidence indicates that preparation for evaluation is very important but that this function is frequently skipped. It is almost certain that a person could improve his evaluations by giving more attention to preparation. What facts, concepts, and principles are pertinent has to be determined for each type of evaluation. The collection of facts is not enough. It is necessary to formulate the problem so that the facts can be organized in such a way as to be brought to bear on the required evaluation. A teacher, counselor, or administrator should try to identify individuals who plunge into evaluations without due preparation and give them special practice in preparation procedures.

Much more than practice in the preparation procedures may be required, however. Some very fundamental skills of questioning and inquiry may be needed. The work of Suchman (1961a) in developing the basic skills of inquiry has already been mentioned. On the basis of a thoroughgoing analysis of the inquiry process, he has constructed a set of training procedures and devices. The program draws upon three techniques: (1) the structuring of an operational schema, (2) guided practice, and (3) feedback and reinforcement. Through the first, the child is given a systematic basis for his approach to data gathering. He has a search plan that is independent of the specific situation. Suchman (1961a) reports that this gives the child a feeling of security in attacking a new problem and thereby reduces blocking and strengthens inquiry. Through guided practice, the schema takes on new meaning, and in the process the child invents new search models. Motivation, which is maintained through feedback and reinforcement, gives anchors in reality, reducing the stress sufficiently to enable the individual to continue attempts to solve the problem.

At the heart of the training program is a set of motion picture films of physics demonstrations that pose problems of cause and effect. Typical of the films is one that demonstrates a bimetallic strip. The strip is held in a Bunsen burner flame and bends downward after a few moments. It is then placed in a tank of water where it straightens out immediately. The strip is then turned over and held in the flame again. It then bends upward and again straightens out when placed in the water.

Pupils are shown the films and told to determine why the events took place as they did. They may ask questions that can be answered by "yes" or "no." The teacher answers each question but gives no explanation. The pupils must think through and organize their questions in such a way as to obtain the needed information. Each question must be a concrete hypothesis. Whenever a pupil thinks he has the correct explanation, he may offer it. If it is inaccurate or incomplete, the teacher then shows him why and permits the group to continue its inquiry.

Suchman (1961b) reports that the fundamental weaknesses in children's inquiry are their low productivity (inability to generate enough questions to obtain the necessary information), low autonomy (fear of assuming responsibility for autonomous inquiry), and lack of discipline (lack of understanding of experimental design and rules of logical inferences). In order to overcome these weaknesses, children are taught through a series of stages a set of strategies of inquiry.

4. CONTROL OF EMOTION. As already suggested, there are many emotional factors that interfere with the evaluation process. But how does one control his emotions, or get others to control theirs? Although there are no simple answers to this important question, there are some fairly standard procedures that help. One such method is to ventilate the difficulty—tell somebody about it. Talking may not clear up all of the quirks of the personality, but it should help to display the biases that are relevant to the evaluation under consideration. If one is aware of a prejudice, it is less likely to affect his evaluations. The danger, of course, is in overcorrecting. For those who want to go that far, there is psychotherapy. Briefly, some other suggestions are:

1. Separate yourself spatially from the stimulus that arouses the strong emotion.
2. Develop a genuine interest in the problem at hand.
3. Schedule easy problems of evaluation that have no emotional involvements first and then the more difficult ones in which emotional distortion is possible.

In order to help a child regain control and cope constructively with stress, a teacher may need to give what Redl and Wattenberg (1959) call "situational assistance." The assistance should be of a type that enables the child to regain control by reducing, at least temporarily, the stressfulness of the situation. Techniques include the following:

1. Helping the child over the hurdles.
2. Restructuring the situation.
3. Giving support from routines.

4. Using nonpunitive exile.
5. Using restraint.
6. Removing distracting objects.
7. Anticipatory planning.

In spite of such disadvantages as lulling the teacher into thinking that a problem has been solved, such techniques prevent trouble, and they free energy for thinking.

Problems of intensity and duration of stress are especially important in considering the matter of emotional control. A major problem is to decide what degree of motivation to strive for in giving problems requiring evaluation. Johnson (1955, p. 489) thinks that in general the production of new ideas (as in convergent and divergent thinking) requires a greater degree of arousal than does judgment (the evaluative operations). He compares these two types of mental operations in Figure 22–1. It will be noted that even in judgment he recognizes the need for some degree of stress. Johnson is less concerned about trying to determine the optimum emotional arousal beforehand than he is to watch for signs for the disabling effects of emotion. Among such signs would include repression of pertinent data or their implications and loss of flexibility in reorganizing the data or in shifting the set.

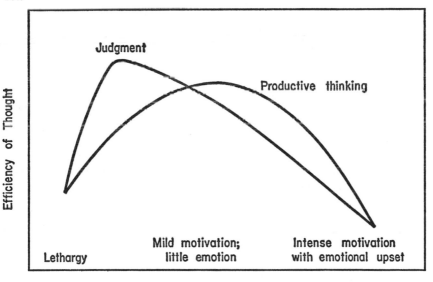

Figure 22–1. Hypothetical Curves Schematizing the Effects of Motivation and Emotional Involvement on Two Thought Processes (From Psychology of Thought and Judgment *by Donald M. Johnson, Harper & Brothers, 1955. By permission of Harper & Row, Publishers.)*

5. IMPROVEMENT OF JUDGMENT. Work on obtaining agreement between two or more evaluators has led to a number of methods for improving judgment. A simple procedure is to have two judges work independently, then get together and check points of agreement and disagreement, discuss reasons for disagreement, and then work independently again. There may be need for practice on making the fundamental perceptual judgments. It is also helpful to keep records of initial judgments so that one can compare them with later judgments and to compare judgments with some kind of objective measure, such as a test result or other measure of performance. The identification of common errors greatly steps up the results of training. Using a checklist, judging one factor at a time, examining the data of complex evaluations from several points of view and in several contexts, and improving the form in which the evaluation is expressed are other procedures for improving evaluations.

The above ideas will of course have to be modified for use with children in helping them improve their judgments.

6. IMPROVEMENT OF CRITICAL THINKING. The evaluative operations may be improved through the use of critical thinking, that is, logical reasoning and the avoidance of common fallacies in judgment. Russell (1956), Johnson (1955), and others believe that the critical thinking abilities begin early and develop gradually. Russell believes that parents and teachers can start with preschool and primary grade children in encouraging their development. Teachers can plan experiences that help children develop critical attitudes toward the statements and materials that are presented to them. Teachers, however, are generally afraid to encourage such attitudes. One of the chief hazards to critical thinking in childhood is lack of experience and inadequacy of concepts. Critical thinking while reading is mentioned frequently as one way of improving this ability. Russell concludes, however, that individuals will learn responsibility for their conclusions only when they are required to test them in actual practice.

The work of Wellington and Wellington (1960) is a good example of special attention to the matter of teaching for critical thinking at the high school level. Wellington and Wellington believe that each person possesses a basic aptitude for becoming a "good teacher" and that there is a basic method of teaching that all good teachers employ. They see in each facet of the teaching process implications for teaching critical thinking. They describe the teacher's task as one of discovering "more precisely the ways of teaching which will promote learning through reasoning and judgment" (Wellington and Wellington, 1960, p. 26). Their conceptualization of the critical thinking and problem-solving process is essentially that which has permeated this book. A problem situation represents to them an unstructured or unmapped region of life space. The individual does not know how to go from the things granted or assumed to the goal and as a result feels uncomfortable and insecure. He continues to feel insecure until this region of his life space has been structured so as to permit him to solve the problem.

Wellington and Wellington believe that it is the teacher's responsibility to lead the class into problem situations, making students aware of a difficulty and helping them to perceive how it relates to what they already know. The teacher must then lead them through the process of defining the problem, making it their problem, and deciding how to approach it. Then follows the research phase, which may involve reading, listening, experimenting with and manipulating equipment and symbols, travel, and talk. This is followed by hypothesizing in the light of the new evidence and the appraisal of the hypotheses. Finally, there is a personal judgment with commitment to action. This process can be elaborated through discussion techniques, small-group approaches, laboratory and experimental methods, multisensory techniques, lectures, planning activities, discipline, and evaluation or grading.

7. IMPROVEMENT OF GROUP PROCEDURES OF DECISION MAKING. The suggestions given in Chapter 18 for improving group problem solving in general are also applicable for improving decision making.

USE OF STRATEGIES IN IMPROVING EVALUATION OPERATIONS

The strategies for coping with stress that have been used throughout Part Four should be useful in improving the evaluation operations and will be reviewed briefly in this context.

RISKING AND AVOIDING

The strategies of risking and avoiding are especially useful in developing and freeing the evaluative abilities. By risking and testing his limits, the individual develops a realistic appraisal of his abilities. In the same way, he learns the limitations and potentialities of his environment. He cannot make sound decisions without realistic concepts of himself and his environment. Young people who are unable to make educational and vocational choices are usually exceptionally afraid of taking risks and have not developed realistic concepts of themselves and their environment.

In developing strategies of risking and avoiding, the general rules for determining when each is pathological should be useful. In general, risking is pathological when (1) there is no chance of success or when there is little chance in relation to the value; (2) when risking involves flagrant, inexcusable violations of laws such as those against robbery, forgery, murder, and the like; or (3) when the timing is incorrect because of lack of preparation or not knowing the odds. Avoiding is pathological when it results in such conditions as apathy, indecisiveness, failure to take any adaptive action, excessive procrastination, a fatalistic attitude, denial of reality of dangers, flight into the past, flight into illness, seclusiveness, or isolation.

Where known or unknown risks are involved in decisions, problems of mental health are almost always involved. In helping a child make decisions, the teacher may have to help him reduce the risk before a decision can be reached. It may be possible to pretest some of the possible decisions before a final decision is reached. It may also be possible to introduce some of the element of a "second chance." It may be possible to offer an opportunity to alter the course of action or in some way to reduce the child's losses so that failure will not be so overwhelming or ruinous. Sometimes it is possible to commit oneself in principle but to test the decision on a trial run or experimental basis. Teachers, administrators, and counselors need to keep these principles of the second-chance factor in mind in regard to their own decisions. They need to be alert to the earliest signs of error, deviation, or failure, which may call for corrective action or a modification of the decision.

The technique of limited commitment (Cooper, 1961) is especially useful whenever the cost of failure is great—when the decision is a high-risk one. Other than trying to think through the possible consequences, there are several possible alternatives within the strategy of limited commitment. It is sometimes practicable to divide the action in such a way as to commit a minimum of resources until the decision maker can determine how things will work out. Setting up a simulated situation on a small scale may give an opportunity to identify weaknesses in the plan of implementation and to make modifications before full action is taken. As another alternative, Cooper (1961, p. 139) suggests that the decision maker monitor the experience by evaluating carefully each subtarget and use the information this yields as a basis for correcting both preceding and succeeding steps. This procedure is similar to sequential decision making, which has already been discussed.

Avoidance of decisions may become pathological among children as well as among high-level executives. It is the strategy of decision by default. The executive somehow manages to find something that must take priority. In the conscious or unconscious hope that the problem will disappear, he may refer it to others for comment. He may even assign it to a committee. Even then, he will find something else that needs to be done or some new question that should be answered. If all else fails, he may praise the virtues of delay. The decision maker feels insecure for some reason, perhaps because of fear of the unknown or fear of failure. In the home or in the classroom, the child may employ similar maneuvers to avoid making a decision.

The obvious corrective action in helping a reluctant decision maker is to find the cause of insecurity. The basis of the insecurity may be a deep-rooted psychological blockage that will not yield to help from a teacher, parent, supervisor, or higher executive. The problem may sometimes be relieved by letting the decision maker know where he stands personally and how far he can go in exercising his judgment. If every mistake counts against a person, he is likely to feel insecure about any decision. The decision maker should be told as much as possible about the decision. It may be necessary to press the decision maker into taking some preliminary or trial actions so that he can move to successively deeper involvements. Since nothing succeeds like success, the reluctant decision maker can actually gain confidence by building on his experience in particular kinds of situations as well as in coping with action problems generally (Cooper, 1961, p. 67).

Whether the child is impulsive and fails to calculate the risks or is reluctant to make any decisions, he almost always needs guidance in learning the strategies of risking and avoiding in decision making. The child needs help in strengthening his ability to see the consequences of his actions. Redl and Wattenberg (1959) suggest a number of devices for accomplishing such a goal. The adult can make direct appeals, showing the connection between conduct and consequences, or he can give dramatic illustrations. He can offer criticism and encouragement and help the child define the limits, or he can himself define certain limits for the child. The adult should use what Redl and Wattenberg call post-situational follow-up after the consequences of a decision have been felt. He cannot assume that a person will learn automatically from experience. The adult may need to interpret the child's behavior in terms of causes and consequences. On a number of occasions, the author has suggested to counselors and teachers that they cultivate in children the habit of thinking of as many possible causes and consequences of their behavior as possible.

MASTERING AND FAILING

The necessity for achieving fundamental skills of mastery should already be obvious. These include the fundamental skills of inquiry and decision making already discussed in this chapter. Some of the strategies for coping with defeat and failure should also be mastered. Among these are the following:

1. Analyze and accept the requirements for success in achieving a solution.
2. Develop higher or new appropriate skills.

3. Adopt a more powerful strategy.

4. Go all out, using the most effective, though expensive, energies for a short period.

5. Form the habit of learning from failure experiences.

6. Use the psychology of making progress (improvement, growth, movement toward goal).

7. Decide upon definite targets, using both long-range and short-range goals.

8. Adopt revised or new goals, using the principles of sequential decisions.

The basic underlying cause of failure to develop skills of mastery is fear of the unknown or a lack of anchors in reality. Children must be permitted to engage in experiences in which there is a chance that they may fail or dislike the activity. Chances of success can, of course, be increased by prestructuring new experiences, restructuring tasks that are too difficult, giving feedback concerning success, and creating an environment in which there is mutual support and encouragement among members.

Cooper (1961, pp. 205–20) urges that decision makers master a set of ten analytical skills and suggests ways by which these skills can be mastered. In brief, these skills and the suggested kinds of practice are as follows: *

1. *Frame-of-reference facility* (availability of an organized body of information, experience, and opinions, which serves as a background for examining new problems). This facility requires the storage of information and experience, practice in clustering and relating the various bits of information, and reflective analysis.

2. *Associational perception* (ability to see likeness, relatedness, and interdependence). To acquire this skill, Cooper suggests clustering of facts, making extended notations, and making continued inputs.

3. *Sequential perception* (ability to see events and phenomena in a time relationship). Suggested practice includes action involvement and reflective analysis.

4. *Elaboration* (ability to supply the details in a plan). The development of this skill takes practice in action involvement, extended notation, and ranking.

5. *Generalizing* (ability to draw central principles from the mass). To develop this skill, Cooper suggests practice in clustering, outlining, and validating.

6. *Symbolizing* (ability to express thoughts, quantities, matter, and relationships in abstract or symbolic forms). The development of this skill

---

* Condensed from *The Art of Decision Making* by Joseph D. Cooper. Copyright © 1961 by Joseph D. Cooper. Reprinted by permission of Doubleday & Company, Inc., and The World's Work (1913) Ltd.

calls for practice in the symbolic disciplines such as mathematics, statistics, art, and use of analogy.

7. *Organizing* (ability to arrange or constitute in interdependent parts, each having a special function or relation to the whole). This skill calls for practice in clustering, outlining, ranking, and validating.

8. *Strategic sensing* (ability to identify key facts, thoughts, or events upon which other such phenomena will depend). To become skilled in strategic sensing, Cooper suggests practice in gaming, outlining, and ranking.

9. *Goalmindedness* (ability to relate thought and action to goals, to perceive and formulate new goals). Practice in counseling, forecasting, and validating are calculated to develop this skill.

10. *Objectivity and skepticism* (ability to rise above personal or emotional attitudes and to depart from prior conclusions, especially to adapt thinking and attitudes to new conditions). This skill requires practice in counseling, inquisitiveness, involvement-detachment, and validating.

In spite of all efforts to master the skills of decision making, no matter how these may be conceptualized, inevitably there will be failures. Usually the reaction to failure or the occurrence of error is to fix the blame. Mere condemnation of the error maker, however, is usually a waste of time. Whenever a person fails, he should make an effort to gain something from the failure. Anything short of perfection involves some degree of error. If the action as a whole is successful, the minor failures are usually tolerated. In the interest of mental health and increased ability to cope with stress, one of a number of alternatives might be followed in working with the child who fails or makes mistakes. Permit the errormaker to correct his own mistakes, whenever possible. Furthermore, teach him the skills for finding out how he makes a mistake and how to correct it. He can learn from his experiences, and he can maintain a favorable self-concept. Above all, make it easy for the child to admit that he has made an error instead of feeling that he must conceal his error. Admission reduces the error and frees the child to think of new possible solutions and to evaluate them more objectively.

UNLOADING AND OVERLOADING

Overloading of any type can result in serious defects in decision making. In fact, decision making may be more vulnerable to overloading stress than any of the other mental operations. As a consequence, unloading may be necessary before the evaluative operations can function properly. Unloading may be a prerequisite to recognizing the seriousness of a situation, planning, considering problems of adjustment, and the like. In helping children unload so that they can resume their evaluative functioning, the teacher may use such devices as humor, gripe sessions, planful ignoring, and the like. School programs can be designed to permit opportunities for unloading through scheduling, curricular arrangements, and planning of activities. For example, physical education and music classes can help children to unload, as can other activities. Time for thinking can be scheduled.

A major aspect of the problem of overloading is related to time and to ways of organizing activities in such a way as to save time. Wise use of time is a goal of the business executive, the teacher, the school principal, the counselor, and the psychologist. Much of the advice usually given ambitious executives seems to be rather generally appropriate. The following are six steps frequently suggested to business executives for organizing to save time (Nation's Business, 1960):

1. *Analyze your own job performance the way you would someone else's.* Are you able to do all that you say you will? Do you meet deadlines? Do you check facts carefully? If this analysis shows that your job has become too big and that you have spread yourself too thin, you may have to make some tough decision to regain control. Concentrate on your most important objectives and let other people do the other jobs, or let them go undone.

2. *Do more jobs alone.* Doing work in groups or by committees is time-consuming. It takes time to prepare for meetings, to hold meetings, to keep the committee informed of progress after meetings, and to write committee reports. Not all committees can be eliminated, of course, but many of them can be.

3. *Cut down on routine.* Effective executives will not allow themselves to be occupied with routine. Obsession with routine is usually found in an enterprise that grows faster than the leader is willing to delegate routine tasks.

4. *Look ahead in time stages.* A job becomes more manageable when the planning ahead is done in stages: tomorrow, next week, next month, next year.

5. *Subdivide your working day.* If a person's appointment calendar swallows up his entire day, he has no time to do his other essential work. He usually ends up by taking his job home with him day after day. If he schedules time for these other tasks, he may gain some relief.

6. *Keep the priorities flexible.* Priorities are forever shifting in any job. Things that are important today may be less important tomorrow. Many people become buried under a job by working hard on the wrong things.

Frequently unloading can be accomplished by simplifying a job, that is, by looking at the job in new ways, selecting a problem, breaking it down into details, questioning each detail, developing better ways, and applying the improvements. This procedure is not possible until the person overcomes his resistance to change, his resentment of criticism, his insecurity, or his complacency.

MAKING PEACE AND DENYING NEEDS

Many problems of evaluation and decision making arise from conflicts between the needs of the individual and the demands of the situation. The common effects of such conflicts frequently cause the evaluative operations to "go wrong" and these should be understood. Some of the more common effects of conflicts are frustration, short-time perspective, competition, rivalry, hostility, fatigue, and focus on parts rather than the whole. Such effects may lead to dangerous concessions to immediate comforts and a short-circuiting of healthy evaluative processes.

Some of the more common aids in resolving conflicts and abetting the evaluative operations are the following:

1. Use of objective information.
2. Counteracting the threat in some way.
3. Remembering that time may shift the balance and change the odds.
4. Being willing to endure and not surrender.
5. Recognizing that the problem may take mental effort (the use of more expensive energies).
6. Strategic withdrawal.

Teachers and counselors may have to help individuals resolve conflicts before they can expect evaluative operations to function effectively.

In making a decision, an important consideration is gaining acceptance of the decision and this involves the strategies of making peace and denying needs. What qualities of a decision are likely to make it accepted or rejected? Cooper (1961, pp. 91–92) has suggested a set of such qualities that might serve as a guide in developing strategies in this category. He has concluded that people are likely to support decisions of the following types:

1. Actions that contribute to the reaching of important goals, where the individual identifies himself with organizational goals.
2. Actions that further the interests of the individual, whether official or personal.
3. Actions that would seem "right" because they accord with the way things are done or because the facts and their logical analysis are overpowering.
4. Actions that represent the mode, the group will.

CONTINUING TO ADAPT AND SURRENDERING

Learning the fundamental skills involved in evaluation makes rather heavy demands upon adaptive energies, and their development may at times be hindered by failures to continue adaptive action. Conditions of mutual support, legitimate pressures, and teaching the strategies of continued adaptation would seem to offer greatest promise. Learning how to make clear-cut decisions can prevent much of the loss of will to continue adaptive effort. Making decisions can bring relief which frequently gives the individual a new grip on the situation.

Much of the research that has been done on independence of judgment is relevant to the problem of continued adaptation in the exercise of the evaluative abilities. In many studies, it is clear that the subjects do in fact "give up" and stop trying to make judgments on their own. To some extent, the results of these studies can be explained on the basis of the false or inappropriate anchors which subjects are given in the experiments. Much more than false anchors seems to be involved, however. Let us examine three of these experiments.

Among the best known of these studies is the series conducted by Asch (1955, 1958). In all of Asch's experiments, subjects were given false anchors in the form of deliberately incorrect judgments by collaborators of the experimenter. In one of these experiments, subjects were asked to make judgments in the presence of varying numbers of other people, all of whom gave incorrect judgments concerning the lengths of lines. Thus, each subject found himself a minority of one. Asch found that his subjects could continue to make rather active judgments in the presence of one or two dissenters, as is indicated in Figure 22–2. Errors in judgment increased markedly, however, when subjects found themselves opposed by three or more persons. Thus, it appears that the size of the majority that opposed them had an effect on the subjects. With a single opponent the subject erred only 3.6 per cent of the time; with two opponents he erred 13.6 per cent of the time; with four, 35.1 per cent; etc. Having more than four opponents, however, did not seem to have much more deleterious effect than having just four.

Deutsch and Gerard (1955), through a series of ingenious experiments using a modification of the Asch situation, have provided additional information about the normative and informational social influences upon individual judgment. They found that social influence on individual judgments is greater when the individual is a member of a group than when he is among an aggregation of individuals who do not compose a group. They found that normative social influence is reduced when the individual sees that his judgment cannot be identified and when there is pressure to conform to his own group. Deutsch and Gerard also showed that the more uncertain a person is about the correctness of his judgment, the more likely he is to be susceptible to both normative and informational social influences in making judgments. Also, the more uncertain he is about the correctness of the judgments of others, the less likely is he to be influenced by their judgments.

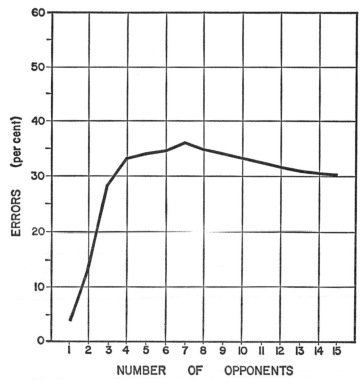

Figure 22–2. Size of Majority and Percentage of Errors in Judgments (Adapted from S. E. Asch, "Opinions and Social Pressure." Scientific American, November 1955. Reprinted by permission. Copyright © 1955 by Scientific American, Inc. All rights reserved.)

Crutchfield (Levy, 1962) has conducted a series of experiments on independence of judgment in which subjects were placed in cubicles instead of face-to-face groups. The judgments reported to subjects were standardized, tape-recorded ones, though each subject assumed that the judgments he was hearing came from the other subjects being tested at the same time. Crutchfield found that some subjects almost immediately stopped making judgments of their own and simply went along with the unanimous opposition on every item. Others yielded on virtually no items. He identified the following personality characteristics of the individual who continued to make independent judgments under these conditions: high ego strength or ability to cope with emotional stress, greater insightfulness and realism in self-conceptions, less anxiety, greater emotional spontaneity, less rigidity, and less authoritarianism. These clues should suggest some ideas about the cultivation of the ability to continue making independent judgments.

385

SUMMARY

Although the 1960's have seen increased interest in the development of the divergent thinking or creative thinking abilities in education, there has been no such upsurge of interest in developing the evaluative abilities and decision-making skills. The growing body of knowledge concerning the decision process, group decision making, and the like should soon give a scientific base for sound developments along this line.

The principle of suspended judgment is a way of improving decisions. Other principles for improving decisions include careful and systematic analysis of evaluative thinking, improvement of the evaluative thinking abilities, adequate attention to preparation for evaluation, control of emotions that interfere with the evaluation process, improvement of judgments, improvement of critical thinking, and the improvement of group procedures in making decisions. The role of risking and avoiding, mastering and failing, unloading and overloading, making peace and denying needs, and continued adaptation and surrendering are important in using the evaluative abilities in mediating the effects of stress.

Education for
Constructive
Behavior

23

In this book, the reader has been asked to explore the concept of constructive behavior as the prime criterion of mental health and as a goal of education. Adjustment and adaptation, however, have dominated thinking about mental health and education for so long that the acceptance of constructive behavior as the prime criterion of mental health and as a goal of education will require considerable reorientation. The dominance of adjustment in mental health and education is symbolized by the titles of the textbooks now in use in education courses on mental health. The word "adjustment" appears in the title of almost all of them—psychology of adjustment, personality adjustment, personal adjustment, adjustment and personality, and the dynamics of adjustment.

A few of the mental health textbooks appearing in the 1960's, however, have shown trends in the direction of the basic theme of this book—that is, constructive behavior and functioning in harmony with one's potentialities. For example, Bonney's *Mental Health in Education* (1960), devotes chapters to initiative, social drive, and group-centered and altruistic behavior, after first devoting several chapters to school adjustment, defensive adjustments, self-adjustment, conformity, and adaptability. Seidman's book of readings, *Educating for Mental Health* (1963), contains selections on creativity, problem solving, and raising sights to higher horizons. A number of textbooks in a variety of fields of education show increased emphasis on educating for creative behavior and the realization of potentialities.

NEED FOR EMPHASIS ON CONSTRUCTIVE BEHAVIOR

The needs of our day seem to require this shift of emphasis. New knowledge concerning the human mind and its functioning, the psychology of stress, social psychology, and creativity provide many insights, which can guide the developments required by a shift of emphasis. Much of the research in social psychology warns that such a shift may be long overdue. In earlier chapters, the studies of Asch (1952, 1955, 1958) were described to show how erroneous majority judgments destroy the perceptions of intelligent and well-educated people even in matters of fact. A number of social psychology studies have also warned of the dangers of overacceptance of or obedience to authority. We have had little sympathy for the guards and attendants of the death camps and gas chambers of Nazi Germany who defended themselves during trial with the statement, "I did nothing wrong. I simply obeyed orders." Yet recent studies warn that obedience can be so deeply ingrained in many intelligent and highly schooled Americans that it over-rides their training in ethics, sympathy for fellow humans, and moral conduct.

Smith's (1959) study, described in detail in an earlier chapter, hints of this danger. Milgram's (1963) recent study provides a more dramatic and disturbing warning. This study shows how social conformity and submission to authority can permit people to perform acts of cruelty on command. Milgram's subjects were forty male volunteers who believed that they were participating in an experiment on memory and learning. These men were between the ages of twenty and fifty and came from such diverse occupations as postal clerk, high school teacher, salesman, engineer, and laborer. The experimenter was a 31-year-old high school biology teacher who maintained an impassive and stern appearance throughout the experiment. He was aided by a mild-mannered and likable man, who acted as a "victim." He told each subject, together with the "victim" masquerading as another volunteer, that the purpose of the experiment was to study the effects of punishment on learning, particularly the differential effects of varying degrees of punishment and various types of teachers. The drawing of lots was rigged so that the volunteer was always the teacher and the "victim" was always the learner. The victim was strapped to a complex apparatus labeled "Shock Generator." The teacher-volunteer was given a sample 45-volt shock to demonstrate the apparent authenticity of the machine.

A row of thirty switches on the apparatus was labeled from 15 to 450 volts in 15-volt steps. Groups of switches were labeled from "slight shock" to "danger: severe shock." Through instructions, the teacher-volunteer was led to administer increasingly severe punishment to the learner-victim, who by prearrangement gave incorrect answers to three out of four questions and received shocks as punishment for his errors. When the punitive shock reached the 300-volt level, the learner-victim pounded on the walls of the room in which he was bound. At this point, the teacher-volunteer was told to continue after a five-to-ten-second pause. After the 315-volt shock, the pounding occurred again. After that, there was silence and no further answers reappeared on the four-way signal box. The teacher-volunteers were still verbally encouraged to continue right up to the maximum level of voltage.

Twenty-six of the forty subjects completed the series, finally administering 450 volts to the now silent victim. Only five of the subjects refused to obey the experimenter's commands beyond the 300-volt level. Four more subjects stopped after the 315-volt shock; two, after the 330-volt shock; and one each at 345, 360, and 375 volts. Some of the subjects voiced concern for the learner-victim, but the majority overcame their humane reactions and continued as ordered right up to the maximum punishment. One observer described how an initially poised businessman entered the laboratory smiling and confident. Within 20 minutes he had been reduced to a twitching, stuttering wreck approaching nervous collapse, simply because his deeply ingrained conditioning to obey those perceived as legitimate authorities came into strong conflict with his disposition not to harm other people. Some of the subjects remained calm and unmoved throughout the experiment.

This entire range of responses is represented in the reactions of teachers who have written me or talked with me about unjust and punitive treatment they have had to administer to some pupils. A majority of them have justified their behavior by saying, ". . . but what could I do? I have to do what my superiors tell me to do!" A few have literally fought for pupils who were unjustly treated: in some cases they have been vindicated and have held their jobs; in other cases they have been fired or placed in an inferior position. A third group, seemingly, have not recognized anything "wrong" about their unjust and inhumane treatment of children.

DETERMINANTS OF CONSTRUCTIVE BEHAVIOR

In this book, an effort has been made to present a somewhat original conceptualization of the determinants of constructive behavior and to show how an understanding of these determinants can be used to increase the chances of constructive behavior, especially through educational experiences. According to this conceptualization, personality and mental breakdowns occur when the demands of the stresses, internal and external, pressing upon a person exceed the personality and mental resources available for constructive response. A common characteristic of all stresses is a reduction in a person's contacts with his environment, guides to constructive behavior, or anchors in reality. Any stressful condition (lack of social contact, confusion, monotony, overstimulation, and the like) may lead to any of a great variety of possible consequences, and any one of these possible consequences may be caused by any of the specific kinds of stressful conditions. What the consequences of any given condition will be depends upon the duration and intensity of the stress and the personality and mental resources of the person.

Stress may have both beneficial and injurious effects. If we begin with theoretically complete relaxation and from there increase the intensity of stress, performance will increase up to a point. After that, if the intensity of the stress is great enough and is continued unabated, a resulting disorganization brings about sharp decrements in performance and collapse. With the onset of a new stress or a sharp increase in intensity, a temporary shock effect or sharp drop in performance occurs. Then comes a period of over-compensation or all-out effort, after which there is recovery and settling down to the customary level of performance. Of course, if the stress continues, fatigue and collapse finally occur. All of these processes may be speeded or retarded by the status of the person's personality and mental resources. Prolonged mild stress may be more damaging and lasting in its effects than brief periods of intense stress.

Although this conceptualization of constructive response to stress does not provide precise prediction, it may offer many useful guides to behavior. The results of many of the stress studies reported here have to be accepted with caution because they have not taken into consideration such key variables as the intensity and duration of the stress and the status of the subjects' personality and mental resources. This failure makes the accumulated literature on the psychology of stress confusing: some studies indicate that behavior improves with the application of stress and others show the reverse.

PERSONALITY RESOURCES AND THEIR DEVELOPMENT

Personality resources for responding constructively to change and stress have been conceptualized in a variety of ways by personality theorists. Educators need to understand the nature of personality resources and the process through which they develop. One way of viewing personality resources is through the concept of ego strength and the stages of psycho-sexual development. Another way is through the concept of nonparataxic interpersonal relations (behaving toward others realistically in terms of their abilities, attitudes, interests, motivations, and the like). Just as ego strength is achieved through the psychosexual stages of development, the development of nonparataxic relations is attained through progressive stages of cognitive development and mastery of interpersonal skills. Some theorists conceptualize both personality and mental development as a continuous process, while others see both types of development as occurring in successive stages, such as the stages of psychosexual development and the stages of interpersonal development. In a relatively discontinuous culture such as we have in the United States, most kinds of development seem to be discontinuous and can be conceptualized according to stages. Each stage seems to be brought about by new and usually increased demands (stresses) and accompanied by temporary periods of regression or nonconstructive behavior. When a child is unprepared to meet these new stresses, lacks the ability to meet them, or is provided inadequate guidance in meeting them, various types of breakdown may occur. Alternative ways of conceptualizing stages of development involve such variables as affection or feeling for others, vocational and career development, and developmental tasks. All of them may be viewed as a process of meeting life stresses with constructive behavior and of functioning according to potentialities and interests.

When development goes wrong and there is impending breakdown, either major or minor, there are usually numerous warning signs. A person's defenses usually blind him to these signs. There are some reasonably objective and reliable ones which parents, teachers, school nurses, school psychologists, counselors, and others can use in detecting impending breakdown and seeing that children are provided the help that will make it possible for them to cope constructively with stress. Any indication that a person is not behaving constructively or is performing far below his potential and outside of his interests might be regarded as a warning that the developmental process is to some extent going wrong. Any of the following should alert workers: signs of lack of mental, emotional, or social growth; learning difficulties; intense isolation or rejection; persistent and recurrent difficulties; and unresponsiveness to remedial procedures. Behind all of these indicators is some loss of anchor in reality or inadequate guides to behavior.

CONSTRUCTIVE GROUP BEHAVIOR

By viewing groups as entities, the foregoing concepts can be applied to constructive group behavior and group breakdown. Nonconstructive behavior and ultimate breakdown occur in groups when there is inadequate structure or loss of anchors in reality. There may be lack of structure both of the group itself and of the task to be accomplished. In either case, loss of anchors or guides to behavior make it difficult or impossible for group members to know what to do. The processes—in intensity and duration of stress—seem to be essentially the same for groups as for individuals. Groups may be thought of in terms of the forces that hold them together and give them organismic properties. These forces may be conceptualized as affect, power, communications, and goals. Signs of impending breakdown may be examined according to the functioning of these four variables.

MENTAL RESOURCES AND THEIR DEVELOPMENT

A person's resources for constructive behavior may also be conceptualized by his mental abilities. At least since the turn of the century, there has been a growing recognition among those who study the functioning of the human mind that intelligence or mental functioning is not a single function. Binet, at least as early as 1909, insisted that intelligence is not a single function, individual and of a particular essence, but that it consists of all of the little functions of discrimination, observation, retention, imagination, ingenuity, and the like, which are plastic and extensible. A number of eminent scholars, nevertheless, insist that intelligence is a unitary function and refer to it in terms of "g," or general mental ability, and consider it as fixed and its development as genetically predetermined. The investigations of men like Thorndike, Thurstone, Hargreaves, Guilford, and Taylor yield evidence strongly in favor of the theory advocated by Binet.

Of the available models of the human intellect, Guilford's structure of intellect was chosen as the basis for examining the mental resources for coping with change and stress. This model pictures the intellect in the form of a three-dimensional cube made up of five types of mental operations acting upon four types of content (figural, symbolic, semantic, and behavioral) and six types of products (units, classes, relations, systems, transformations, and implications). This model provides a basis for describing in considerable detail man's mental abilities and in developing methods for assessing their functioning.

Before children have developed their mental resources to a degree that would enable them to cope constructively with stress, they nevertheless develop a variety of strategies for dealing with their life stresses. As these abilities develop, however, their behavior becomes more constructive. Apparently, however, many of their primitive, early-learned strategies continue to be used in adulthood when stress is intense or prolonged. In sudden emergencies, these early-learned strategies for controlling the environment seem to be a major resource. In adaptation to stress over time, however, abilities developed through later experiences are called into play. The author maintains that it is a responsibility of the school to aid individuals, through educational experiences, to master the skills and strategies necessary for coping with predictable stresses.

From most of the conceptualizations of the problem-solving process, it is easy to see how the mental operations conceptualized by Guilford and treated in detail in this book become engaged in the process of behaving constructively to change and stress. In fact, Guilford (1964) himself has attempted to show this through a recent conceptualization of a typical instance of problem solving. First a person's attention is aroused and directed to some phenomena. He then draws upon his memory storage and tests his new cognition. At this point, a danger or a problem is sensed and structured as the person continues to draw from his memory storage and to evaluate the degree and nature of the danger. Possible answers are then generated, bringing into play the productive thinking abilities. As he generates possible answers, the person continues to draw upon his memory storage and to evaluate both what he produces and what he retrieves. He may then search for new information or cognitions. He then evaluates or tests these new inputs and continues to draw from his memory storage before again bringing into play his productive thinking abilities to generate new answers, which in turn are tested and communicated. In this process many different types of information may be pulled from the memory storage and discoveries may be communicated at various stages.

RESPONDING CONSTRUCTIVELY TO NEW EDUCATIONAL PRESSURES

In recent months numerous educational changes have been proposed, many of which will introduce new stresses both to educators and to children and young people. It is to be hoped that knowledge of the psychology of stress will enable educators to make decisions that will enable them and the children to behave constructively. There are pressures to teach children to read sooner; develop a higher level of physical fitness; keep potential drop-outs in school; lengthen the school day, week, and year; determine a child's academic future at an earlier date; provide an increasing amount of instruction on a mass basis; rely increasingly on programmed learning in skill areas; utilize computers and other machines to help group, teach, and test children; assign more work and require a higher level of performance from every child; provide compensating opportunities for the culturally disadvantaged; and to teach more patriotism and love of country. The list could, of course, be extended considerably. These examples are enough to emphasize the fact that educators need to understand the psychology of stress and learn how to help children use their personality and mental resources to respond constructively. They must also weigh carefully the intensity and the duration of the stresses, which these new demands will place upon teachers and learners. Otherwise, increased rates of breakdown are inevitable. Although the knowledge needed is far from complete, the author has confidence that there is enough knowledge to provide useful guides to behavior to those who serve children and young people and, furthermore, that educators can use this information intelligently and thereby behave increasingly more constructively, rather than just adaptively, in response to change and stress.

393

References and

Index to Authors of

Works Cited*

Abramson, J. "Essai d'Etalonnage de Deux Tests d'Imagination et d'Observation." *Journal de Psychologie,* 1927, pp. 370–79. **310**

Aldrich, C. K. *Psychiatry for the Family Physician.* New York: McGraw-Hill Book Co., 1955. **204**

Allen, M. S. *Morphological Creativity.* Englewood Cliffs, N. J.: Prentice-Hall, 1962. **60**

Allport, G. W. *Becoming.* New Haven, Conn.; Yale University Press, 1955. **198**

————, P. E. Vernon, and G. Lindzey. *Manual, Study of Values,* 3rd ed. Boston: Houghton Mifflin Co., 1960. **5, 238**

Andrews, E. G. "The Development of Imagination in the Pre-School Child." *University of Iowa Studies of Character,* 1930, *3,* 4. **89, 101, 107, 305, 310**

Angell, G. W. "Effect of Immediate Knowledge of Quiz Results on Final Examination Scores in Freshman Chemistry. *Journal of Education Research,* 1949, *42,* 391–94. **224**

Applezweig, D. G., and M. H. Applezweig. *Stress and Behavior: I. The Behavior Interpretation Inventory.* New London, Conn.: Department of Psychology, Connecticut College, 1954. **49**

Argyris, C. *Personality and Organization.* New York: Harper & Row, 1957. **181**

————. "Organizational Leadership." In L. Petrullo and B. M. Bass (Eds.), *Leadership and Interpersonal Behavior.* New York: Holt, Rinehart and Winston, 1961, Pp. 326–54. **181–182**

Arieti, S. (Ed.). *American Handbook of Psychiatry.* Vols. I and II. New York: Basic Books, 1959. **254**

Asch, S. E. *Social Psychology.* Englewood Cliffs, N. J.: Prentice-Hall, 1952. **97, 388**

————. "Opinions and Social Pressure." *Scientific American,* November 1955, *193*(5), 31–37. **384, 388**

————. "Experimental Investigation of Group Influence." In *Symposium on Preventive and Social Psychiatry.* Washington, D. C.: Walter Reed Army Institute of Research, 1958. Pp. 17–25. **239, 313, 384, 388**

Back, K. "Influence through Social Communication." *Journal of Abnormal and Social Psychology,* 1951, *46,* 9–23. **169, 180**

Baker, G. W., and D. W. Chapman (Eds.). *Man and Society in Disaster.* New York: Basic Books, 1962. **164**

Barker, R. G., T. Dembo, and K. Lewin. "Frustration and Regression: An Experiment with Young Children." *University of Iowa Studies in Child Welfare,* 1941, *18,* 1. **265**

* The numbers in **bold face** at the end of each reference indicate the page(s) on which a given reference is cited or discussed.

Barlow, F. *Mental Prodigies*. New York: Philosophical Library, 1952. **319**

Barron, F. "An Ego-Strength Scale Which Predicts Response to Psychotherapy." *Journal of Consulting Psychology*, 1953, *17*, 327–33. **66**

————. "Originality in Relation to Personality and Intellect." *Journal of Personality*, 1957, *25*, 730–42. **306, 335**

————. "The Psychology of Imagination." *Scientific American*, 1958, *199*, 151–66. **315**

Barthol, R. P., and N. D. Ku. "Regression Under Stress to First Learned Behavior." *Journal of Abnormal and Social Psychology*, 1959, *59*, 134–36. **266**

Bartlett, F. C. *Remembering*. London: Cambridge University Press, 1932. **246, 264**

————. *An Experiment on Flying Fatigue*. London: Air Ministry, Flying Personnel Research Committee, April 1940. **58**

————. "Fatigue Following Highly Skilled Work." *Procedures of the Royal Society, London, Ser. B: Biological Science*, 1943, *131*, 247–57. **58**

Baughman, E. E., and G. S. Welsh. *Personality: A Behavioral Science*. Englewood Cliffs, N. J.: Prentice-Hall, 1962. **130**

Bayley, N. "On the Growth of Intelligence." *American Psychologist*, 1955, *10*, 805–18. **115**

Benjamin, H. *The Cultivation of Idiosyncrasy*. Cambridge, Mass.: Harvard University Press, 1956. **314, 323**

Berger, E. M. "A Hypothesis Concerning the Relation of a Type of Underachievement in College to an Aspect of Self-Acceptance and to Aspects of Normal Development." Paper presented at meetings of the American Psychological Association, Washington, D. C., 1958. **329**

————. "Willingness to Accept Limitations and College Achievement: An Application of Personality Concepts." Minneapolis: Student Counseling Bureau, University of Minnesota, 1962. (Dittoed) **362**

Berlyne, D. E. *Conflict, Arousal, and Curiosity*. New York: McGraw-Hill Book Co., 1960. **217, 351**

Bexton, W. H., W. Heron, and T. H. Scott. "Effects of Decreased Variation in the Sensory Environment." *Canadian Journal of Psychology*, 1954, *8*, 70–76. **36**

Binet, A. *Les Idées Modernes sur les Enfants*. Paris: E. Flamarion, 1909. **188, 192–193**

Birch, H. G., and H. S. Rabinowitz. "The Negative Effects of Previous Experience on Productive Thinking." *Journal of Experimental Psychology*, 1951, *41*, 121–25. **298**

Bischof, L. J. *Interpreting Personality Theories*. New York: Harper & Row, 1964. **15**

Blair, C. *Beyond Courage*. New York: David McKay Co., 1955. **237**

Blake, R. R. "The Other Person in the Situation." In R. Tagiuri and L. Petrullo (Eds.), *Person Perception and Interpersonal Behavior*. Stanford, Calif.: Stanford University Press, 1958. Pp. 229–242. **97**

Bloom, B. S. (Ed.). *Taxonomy of Educational Objectives: The Classification of Educational Goals. Handbook I: Cognitive Domain*. New York: Longmans, Green & Co., 1956. **217**

Blum, G. S. "A Study of the Psychoanalytic Theory of Psychosexual Development." *Genetic Psychology Monographs*, 1949, *39*, 3–99. **77, 78**

————. *The Blacky Pictures: A Technique for the Exploration of Personality Dynamics*. New York: Psychological Corp., 1950. **77**

Bombard, A. "I Sailed Across the Atlantic in 65 Days Without Food or Water." *Argosy*, May 1954(a), *338(5)*, 23ff. **40**

————. *The Voyage of the Herétique*. New York: Simon and Schuster, 1954(b). **40**

Bonney, M. E. *Mental Health in Education*. Boston: Allyn & Bacon, 1960. **387**

Bonney, W. C., and C. E. George. *Studies of Adaptation Level Phenomena in Personality*. College Station, Tex.: A & M Research Foundation, 1958. **119**

Boraas, J. *Teaching to Think*. New York: The Macmillan Co., 1922. **283, 296, 349, 366, 372, 373**

Bowman, P. H. "Personality and Scholastic Underachievement." In A. Frazier (Ed.), *Freeing Capacity to Learn*. Washington, D. C.: Association for Supervision and Curriculum Development, 1960. Pp. 40–55. **231–232**

Braddon, R. *The Naked Island*. Garden City, N. Y.: Doubleday & Co., 1953. **52**

Brim, O. G., Jr., D. G. Glass, D. E. Lavin, and N. Goodman. *Personality and Decision Processes*. Stanford, Calif.: Stanford University Press, 1962. **363**

Brooks, H. L. *Prisoners of Hope*. New York: L. B. Fischer, 1942. **51**

Bross, I. D. *Design for Decision*. New York: The Macmillan Co., 1953. **367–368**

Bruner, J. S. "Learning and Thinking." *Harvard Educational Review*, 1959, *229*, 184–92. **275, 282**

————. "After John Dewey, What?" *Saturday Review*, June 17, 1961, *44(24)*, 58–59f. **16**

————, J. J. Goodnow, and G. A. Austin. *A Study of Thinking*. New York: John Wiley & Sons, 1956. **296**

Buehler, C. *Der Menschliche Lebenslauf als Psychologisches Problem*. Leipzig: Hirzel, 1933. **107**

Burton, W. H., R. B. Kimball, and R. L. Wing. *Education for Effective Thinking*. New York: Appleton-Century-Crofts, 1960. **125**

Cannon, W. B. *The Wisdom of the Body*. New York: W. W. Norton & Co., 1939. **41, 48**

Cartledge, C. J. "Training First Grade Children in Creative Thinking Under Quantitative and Qualitative Motivation." Master's thesis. Emory University, 1962. **338**

Cartwright, D. "A Field Theoretical Conception of Power." In D. Cartwright (Ed.), *Studies in Social Power*. Ann Arbor: Research Center for Group Dynamics, University of Michigan, 1959. Pp. 183–220. **177**

Cassel, R. N. *The Ego Strength Q-Sort Test*. Chicago: Psychometric Affiliates, 1958. **66**

————, and B. L. Hariman. "A Comparative Analysis of Personality and Ego Strength Test Scores for In-Prison, Neuropsychiatric and Typical Individuals." *Journal of Educational Research*, 1959, *53*, 43–52. **66**

Chansky, N. M. "Threat, Anxiety and Reading Behavior." *Journal of Educational Research*, 1958, *51*, 333–40. **263**

Clark, C. H. *Brainstorming*. Garden City, N. Y.: Doubleday & Co., 1958. **343**

Coch, L., and J. R. P. French, Jr. "Overcoming Resistance to Change." *Human Relations*, 1948, *1*, 512–32. **163**

Cohen, A. R. "The Effects of Situational Structure and Individual Self-Esteem on Threat-Oriented Reactions to Power." Doctoral dissertation. University of Michigan, 1953. **55, 181**

References and Index to Authors of Works Cited

Cohen, A. R. "Situational Structure, Self-Esteem, and Threat-Oriented Reactions to Power." In D. Cartwright (Ed.), *Studies in Social Power*. Ann Arbor: University of Michigan, 1959. Pp. 35–52. **181**

————, E. Stotland, and D. M. Wolfe. "An Experiment Investigation of Need for Cognition." *Journal of Abnormal and Social Psychology, 1955, 51*, 291–94. **176**

Cohen, E. A. *Human Behavior in the Concentration Camp*. New York: W. W. Norton & Co., 1953. **55**

Coleman, J. S. *Social Climates in High Schools* (Cooperative Research Monograph No. 4). Washington, D. C.: U. S. Government Printing Office, 1961(a). **229**

————. *The Adolescent Society*. New York: Free Press of Glencoe, 1961(b). **229, 230**

Colvin, S. S., and I. F. Meyer. "Imaginative Elements in the Written Work of School Children." *Pedagogical Seminary*, 1906, *13*, 84–93. **311**

Cooper, J. D. *The Art of Decision Making*. Garden City, N. Y.: Doubleday & Co., 1961. **378, 379, 380, 383**

Crutchfield, R. S. "Assessing Persons Through a Quasi Group Interaction Technique." *Journal of Abnormal and Social Psychology*, 1951, *46*, 577–88. **155**

————. "Conformity and Creative Thinking." In H. E. Cruber, G. Terrell, and M. Wertheimer (Eds.), *Contemporary Approaches to Creative Thinking*. New York: Atherton Press, 1962. Pp. 120–40. **331**

Davis, S. W. "Stress in Combat." *Scientific American*, 1956, *194*, 31–35. **28, 29**

————, and J. G. Taylor. *Stress in Infantry Combat*. Chevy Chase, Md.: Operations Research Office, John Hopkins University, 1954. **28, 56–57**

Deane-Drummond, A. *Return Ticket*. London: Fontana, 1955. **55**

Deutsch, M. "A Theory of Cooperation and Competition." *Human Relations*, 1949(a), *2*, 129–52. **171, 175**

————. "An Experimental Study of the Effects of Cooperation and Competition Upon Group Process." *Human Relations*, 1949(b), *2*, 199–231. **171, 175**

————, and H. B. Gerard. "A Study of Normative and Informational Social Influences Upon Individual Judgment." *Journal of Abnormal and Social Psychology*, 1955, *51*, 629–36. **384**

Dewey, J. *How We Think*. Boston: D. C. Heath & Co., 1933. **125, 126, 276**

Dombrose, L. A., and M. S. Slobin. "The IES Test." *Perceptual and Motor Skills*, 1958, *8*, 347–89. **68**

Dowis, J. L., and O. Diethelm. "Anxiety, Stress, and Thinking: An Experimental Investigation." *Journal of Psychology*, 1958, *45*, 227–38. **286, 287**

Drews, E. M. "Freedom to Grow." *NEA Journal*, September 1960, *49(6)*, 20–22. **316**

Duncan, C. P. "Recent Research on Human Problem Solving." *Psychological Bulletin*, 1959, *56*, 397–429. **293, 294**

Duncanson, D. L. "The Relationship of Role Expectations and the Behavior of School Superintendents in the State of Minnesota." Doctoral dissertation. University of Minnesota, 1961. **95**

Durrell, D. "Pupil Team Learning: Effect of Team Size on Retention of Knowledge." Paper presented at meetings of American Educational Research Association, Chicago, Ill., February 23, 1961. **169**

Dyer, F. L., T. C. Martin, and W. H. Meadowcroft. *Edison: His Life and Inventions*. Vols. I and II. New York: Harper & Row, 1929. **110**

English, O. S., and G. H. J. Pearson. *Emotional Problems of Living*, Rev. ed. New York: W. W. Norton & Co., 1955. **71, 107**

Fenichel, O. *The Psychoanalytic Theory of Neurosis*. New York: W. W. Norton & Co., 1945. **70, 71, 72, 73, 75**

Festinger, L. "Informal Social Communication." *Psychological Review*, 1950, 57, 271–82. **183**

———. "Theory of Social Comparison Processes." *Human Relations*, 1954, 7, 117–40. **180**

Fiedler, F. E. "Assumed Similarity Measures as Predictors of Team Effectiveness." *Journal of Abnormal and Social Psychology*, 1954, 49, 381–88. **97**

———. "Interpersonal Perception and Group Effectiveness." In R. Tagiuri and L. Petrullo (Eds.), *Person Perception and Interpersonal Behavior*. Stanford, Calif.: Stanford University Press, 1958. Pp. 243–57. **97**

Field, S. M., and S. W. Davis (Eds.). *Fatigue and Stress Symposium*, Chevy Chase, Md.: Operations Research Office, Johns Hopkins University, 1953 (*Technical Memorandum ORO–T–185*). **143**

Flanagan, J. C. "The Relation of a New Ingenuity Measure to Other Variables." In C. W. Taylor (Ed.), *The Third (1959) University of Utah Research Conference on the Identification of Creative Scientific Talent*. Salt Lake City: University of Utah Press, 1959. Pp. 104–23. **306**

Flugel, J. C. "Humor and Laughter." In G. Lindzey (Ed.), *Handbook of Social Psychology*. Cambridge, Mass.: Addison-Wesley Publishing Co., 1954. Pp. 708–34. **172**

Franklin, B. *Autobiography*. New York: Heritage Press, 1951. **110**

French, J. R. P., Jr., and B. Raven. "The Bases of Social Power." In D. Cartwright (Ed.), *Studies in Social Power*. Ann Arbor: Research Center for Group Dynamics, University of Michigan, 1959. Pp. 150–67. **175**

Freud, S. *The Psychopathology of Everyday Life*. New York: The Macmillan Co., 1914. **15**

———. "Instincts and Their Vicissitudes." In *Collected Papers*. Vol. 4. London: Hogarth, 1925. Pp. 60–83. **70**

Fritz, C. E., and H. B. Williams. "The Human Being in Disaster: A Research Perspective." *Annals of the American Academy of Political Science*, 1957, 309, 42–51. **50**

Fritz, R. L. "An Evaluation of Scholastic Achievement of Students Attending Half-Day Sessions in the Seventh Grade." Unpublished master's paper. University of Minnesota, 1958. **314**

Fromm, E. *The Sane Society*. New York: Holt, Rinehart and Winston, 1955. **15**

Funkenstein, D. H., S. H. King, and M. E. Drolette. *Mastery of Stress*. Cambridge, Mass.: Harvard University Press, 1957. **28, 29, 49, 57, 100**

Gagne, R. M. "Problem-Solving and Thinking." In P. R. Farnsworth and Q. McNemar (Eds.), Palo Alto, Calif.: *Annual Reviews*, 1959. Pp. 147–73. **277**

Gantt, W. H. "Pavlovian Principles and Psychiatry." In J. H. Masserman and J. L. Moreno (Eds.), *Progress in Psychotherapy. Vol. II. Anxiety and Therapy*. New York: Grune & Stratton, 1957. Pp. 140–46. **31, 35**

Gardner, R. W., P. S. Holzman, G. S. Klein, H. B. Linton, and D. P. Spence. "Cognitive Control: A Study of Individual Consistencies in Cognitive Behavior." In G. S. Klein (Ed.), *Psychological Issues*. New York: International Universities Press, 1959. **218, 219**

Getzels, J. W. "Non-IQ Intellectual and Other Factors in College Admission." In K. E. Anderson (Ed.), *The Coming Crisis in the Selection of Students for College Entrance.* Washington, D. C.: American Educational Research Association, 1960. **373**

Getzels, J. W., and P. W. Jackson. "Occupational Choice and Cognitive Functioning: Career Aspirations of Highly Intelligent and Highly Creative Adolescents." *Journal of Abnormal and Social Psychology,* 1960, *61,* 119–23. **315**

Gillespie, R. D. "Amnesia." *Archives of Neurology and Psychiatry,* 1937, *37,* 748–64. **254**

Glaser, K., and L. Eisenberg. "Maternal Deprivation." *Pediatrics,* 1956, *18,* 626–42. **37**

Goertzel, V., and M. G. Goertzel. *Cradles of Eminence.* Boston: Little, Brown and Co., 1962. **327**

Goldner, R. H. "Individual Differences in Whole-Part Approach and Flexibility-Rigidity in Problem Solving." *Psychological Monographs,* 1957, *71,* 450. **298**

Goldstein, K. *Human Nature in the Light of Psychopathology.* Cambridge, Mass.: Harvard University Press, 1940. **15**

Goldstein, M. J. "The Relationship Between Coping and Avoiding Behavior and Response to Fear-Arousing Propaganda." *Journal of Abnormal and Social Psychology,* 1959, *59,* 247–52. **263**

Gordon, J. E. *Personality and Behavior.* New York: The Macmillan Co., 1963. **197**

Gordon, W. J. J. *Synectics.* New York: Harper & Row, 1961. **60, 337**

Gowan, J. C. "Dynamics of Underachievement of Gifted Students." *Exceptional Children,* 1957, *24,* 98–101. **231**

Graybiel, A. "Long-Range Studies of Naval Aviators." *ONR Research Review,* August 1957, pp. 15–21. **56**

Greene, R. W. *Calvary in China.* New York: G. P. Putnam's Sons, 1953. **51**

Grippen, V. B. "A Study of Creative Artistic Imagination in Children by the Constant Contact Procedure." *Psychological Monograph,* 1933, *45(1),* 63–81. **310**

Grosvenor, G. "Peary's Explorations in the Far North." *National Geographic Magazine,* 1920, *37,* 319–22. **141**

Guerlain, R. *They Who Wait.* New York: Thomas Y. Crowell Co., 1943. **153**

Guilford, J. P. *Personality.* New York, McGraw-Hill Book Co., 1959(a). **189, 250, 251, 348, 349, 350**

————. "Three Faces of Intellect." *American Psychologist,* 1959(b), *14,* 469–79. **189**

————. "Frontiers of Thinking That Teachers Should Know About." *Reading Teacher,* 1960, *13,* 176–82. **215**

————, "Basic Problems in Teaching for Creativity." Paper presented at the conference sponsored by the United States Office of Education on Creativity and Teaching Media, La Jolla, California, August 31–September 3, 1964. **392**

————, and R. Hoepfner. *Current Summary of Structure-of-Intellect Factors and Suggested Tests.* Los Angeles: University of California, 1963. **282**

————, and P. R. Merrifield. *The Structure-of-Intellect Model: Its Uses and Implications.* Los Angeles: Psychological Laboratory, University of Southern California. 1960. **190, 211, 248, 278, 279, 280, 281, 307, 308, 309, 324, 347, 348**

————, R. C. Wilson, P. R. Christensen, and D. J. Lewis. *A Factor-Analytic Study of Creative Thinking. I. Hypotheses and Description of Tests.* Los Angeles: Psychological Laboratory, 1951. **312**

Guthridge, S. *Tom Edison, Boy Inventor*. Boston: The Bobbs-Merrill Co., 1959. **327**

Hall, C. S., and G. Lindzey. *Theories of Personality*. New York: John Wiley & Sons, 1957. **15**

Hammontree, M. *Albert Einstein: Young Thinker*. Boston: The Bobbs-Merrill Co., 1961. **327**

Hare, A. P. *Handbook of Small Group Research*. New York: Free Press of Glencoe, 1962. **180**

Hargreaves, H. L. "The 'Faculty' of Imagination." *British Journal of Psychology, Monograph Supplement*, 1927, *3*, 10. **189, 305**

Harlow, H. F. "The Nature of Love." *American Psychologist*, 1958, *13*, 673–85. **118**

————. "The Heterosexual Affectional System in Monkeys." *American Psychologist*, 1962, *17*, 1–9. **118, 119**

Harms, E. "The Psychology of Formal Creativeness: I. Six Fundamental Types of Formal Expression." *Journal of Genetic Psychology*, 1946, *69*, 97–120. **311**

Harris, I. D. *Emotional Blocks to Learning*. New York: Free Press of Glencoe, 1961. **116, 117**

Harris, W., R. R. Mackie, and C. L. Wilson. *Performance Under Stress: A Review and Critique of Recent Studies*. Los Angeles: Human Factors Research, 1956. **24, 145**

Hartmann, H. "Ego Psychology and the Problem of Adaptation." In D. Rapaport (Ed.), *Organization and Pathology of Thought*. New York: Columbia University Press, 1951. Pp. 362–96. **15**

Havighurst, R. J. *Developmental Tasks and Education*. New York: David McKay Co., 1952. **110, 111**

————, and B. Orr, *Adult Education and Adult Needs*. Chicago: Center for the Study of Liberal Education for Adults, 1956. **111**

Hayes, O. W. *Your Memory—Speedway to Success*. New York: Exposition Press, 1958. **243**

Hebeisen, A. A. "The Performance of a Group of Schizophrenic Patients on a Test of Creative Thinking." In E. P. Torrance (Ed.), *Creativity: Second Minnesota Conference on Gifted Children*. Minneapolis: Center for Continuation Study, University of Minnesota, 1960. Pp. 125–29. **134, 319**

Heider, F. *The Psychology of Interpersonal Relations*. New York: John Wiley & Sons, 1958. **97**

Helson, H. "Adaptation-Level as a Basis for a Quantitative Theory of Frames of Reference." *Psychological Review*, 1948, *55*, 297–313. **119**

Heron, W. "Cognitive and Physiological Effects of Perceptual Isolation." In *Sensory Deprivation: A Symposium at Harvard Medical School*. Cambridge, Mass.: Harvard University Press, 1961. Pp. 6–33. **36**

Hiller, R. L. "Your Ideas Are Important: An Experiment in Creative Writing." In E. P. Torrance (Ed.), *New Educational Ideas: Third Minnesota Conference on Gifted Children*. Minneapolis: Center for Continuation Study, University of Minnesota, 1961. Pp. 168–75. **343**

Himler, L. E. "Human Relations and Accident Prevention." *Industrial Medicine*, 1951, *20*, 121–29. **174**

Hirsch, R. S. *The Effects of Knowledge of Test Results on Learning of Meaningful Material*. Port Washington, N. Y.: U. S. Naval Training Device Center, Office of Naval Research, 1952. **224**

Holzman, P. S., and G. S. Klein. "Motive and Style in Reality Contact." *Bulletin of the Menninger Clinic,* 1956, *20,* 181–91. **218, 220**

Hoppock, R. "Criteria of Adjustment." *American Psychologist,* 1957, *12,* 232. **11**

Hudson, B. B. "Anxiety in Response to the Unfamiliar." *Journal of Social Issues,* 1954, *10(3),* 53–60. **41, 223**

Hughes, J. M. *Human Relations in Educational Organization.* New York: Harper & Row, 1957. **95**

Hullfish, H. G., and P. G. Smith. *Reflective Thinking.* New York: Dodd, Mead & Co., 1961. **276**

Hutschnecker, A. A. *The Will to Live.* New York: Thomas Y. Crowell Co., 1951. **42**

Hyman, R. "On Prior Information and Creativity." *Psychological Reports,* 1961, *9,* 151–61. **344, 345**

Ilg, F. L., and L. B. Ames. *Child Behavior.* New York: Harper & Row, 1955. **104**

Jackson, J. M. "The Effect of Changing the Leadership of Small Work Groups." *Human Relations,* 1953, *6,* 25–44. **175**

Jahoda, M. *Current Concepts of Positive Mental Health.* New York: Basic Books, 1958. **13, 14, 15**

James, W. *The Principles of Psychology.* New York: Holt, Rinehart and Winston, 1890. **237**

Janis, I. L. *Psychological Stress.* New York: John Wiley & Sons, 1958. **259, 260**

Jennings, J. W., and D. M. Johnson. "Context Effects in Production and Judgment." *Journal of Psychology,* 1963, *56,* 53–9. **353, 354**

Jennings, H. H. *Sociometry in Group Relations—A Work Guide for Teachers.* Washington, D. C.: American Council on Education, 1948. **117**

Johnson, D. M. *The Psychology of Thought and Judgment.* New York: Harper & Row, 1955. **277, 350, 354, 355, 357, 360, 370, 371, 375**

―――――. "Reanalysis of Experimental Halo Effects." *Journal of Applied Psychology,* 1963, *47,* 46–7. **360**

―――――, and J. W. Jennings. "Serial Analysis of Three Problem-Solving Processes." *Journal of Psychology,* 1963, *56,* 43–52. **353, 360**

Joint Commission on Mental Illness and Health. *Action for Mental Health.* New York: Basic Books, 1961. **5, 303**

Jones, E. E., and J. W. Thibaut. "Interaction Goals as Bases of Inference in Interpersonal Perception." In R. Tagiuri and L. Petrullo (Eds.), *Person Perception and Interpersonal Behavior.* Stanford, Calif.: Stanford University, 1958. Pp. 151–78. **97**

Josephson, M. *Edison.* New York: McGraw-Hill Book Co., 1959. **110, 327**

Jourard, S. M. *Personal Adjustment.* New York: The Macmillan Co., 1958. **66**

Kagan, J., L. W. Sontag, C. T. Baker, and V. L. Nelson. "Personality and IQ Change." *Journal of Abnormal and Social Psychology,* 1958, *56,* 261–266. **115**

Kaluger, G., and R. Martin. "The Loneliness of the Gifted Child." *Elementary School Journal,* 1960, *61,* 127–32. **60**

Kardiner, A., and H. Spiegel. *War Stress and Neurotic Illness.* New York: Hoeber, 1947. **54**

Katona, G. *Organizing and Memorizing.* New York: Columbia University Press, 1940. **245**

Kelly, G. A. *The Psychology of Personal Constructs.* (Two volumes.) New York: W. W. Norton & Co., 1955. **267**

Killian, L. M. "Some Accomplishments and Some Needs in Disaster Study." *Journal of Social Issues,* 1954, *10(3)*, 66–72. **47**

Kinsey, A. C., W. B. Pomeroy, and C. E. Martin. *Sexual Behavior in the Human Male.* Philadelphia: W. B. Saunders Co., 1948. **73**

————, W. B. Pomeroy, C. E. Martin, and P. H. Gebhard. *Sexual Behavior in the Human Female.* Philadelphia: W. B. Saunders Co., 1953. **73**

Kirkpatrick, E. A. "Individual Tests of School Children." *Psychological Review,* 1900, *5(7)*, 274–80. **311**

Klausmeier, H. J. *Learning and Human Abilities.* New York: Harper & Row, 1961. **261**

Klein, G. S. "Need and Regulation." In M. R. Jones (Ed.), *Nebraska Symposium on Motivation.* Lincoln: University of Nebraska Press, 1954. Pp. 224–74. **220**

Koffka, K. *Principles of Gestalt Psychology.* New York: Harcourt, Brace & World, 1935. **248–249**

Kubie, L. S. *Neurotic Distortion of the Creative Process.* Lawrence: University of Kansas Press, 1958. **318**

Kubzansky, P. E. "The Effects of Reduced Environmental Stimulation on Human Behavior: A Review." In A. D. Biderman and H. Zimmer (Eds.), *The Manipulation of Behavior.* New York: John Wiley & Sons, 1961. **36**

Lacy, O. W., N. Lewinger, and J. F. Adamson. "Foreknowledge as a Factor Affecting Perceptual Defense and Alertness." *Journal of Experimental Psychology,* 1953, *45*, 169–74. **238**

LaForge, R., and R. Suczek. "The Interpersonal Dimensions of Personality: II. An Objective Study of Repression." *Journal of Personality,* 1954, *23*, 129–53. **83**

Lagemann, J. K. "What Monkeys Are Teaching Science About Children." *This Week Magazine,* March 3, 1963, 4–5f. **118, 119**

Langhof, W. *Rubber Truncheon.* New York: E. P. Dutton & Co., 1935. **55**

Lazarus, R. S. *Adjustment and Personality.* New York: McGraw-Hill Book Co., 1961. **133**

Leary, T. *Interpersonal Diagnosis of Personality.* New York: The Ronald Press Co., 1957. **83**

Leavitt, H. J., and R. A. H. Mueller. "Some Effects of Feedback on Communication." *Human Relations,* 1951, *4*, 401–10. **180**

Lee, D. *Freedom and Culture.* Englewood Cliffs, N. J.: Prentice-Hall, 1959. **228**

————. "Developing the Drive to Learn and the Questioning Mind." In A. Frazier (Ed.), *Freeing Capacity to Learn.* Washington, D. C.: Association for Supervision and Curriculum Development, 1960. Pp. 10–22. **228**

Lee, F. J., M. Horwitz, and M. Goldman. "Power Over Decision Making and the Response to Frustration in Group Members." Paper read at the annual convention of the American Psychological Association, September 1954. **149**

Lee, I. J. "Procedures for 'Coercing' Agreement." *Harvard Business Review,* 1954, *32*, 39–45. **370**

Lehman, H. C. *Age and Achievement.* Princeton N. J.: Princeton University Press, 1953. **109**

Levinger, L. "The Teacher's Role in Creativity: Discussion." *American Journal of Orthopsychiatry,* 1959, *29*, 291–97. **127**

Levy, C. "The Independent Mind." *California Monthly,* February 1962, *72*, 15–19. **385**

Lias, G. *I Survived*. London: Evans Brothers, 1954. **51**

Libo, L. M. *Measuring Group Cohesiveness*. Ann Arbor: University of Michigan, Research Center for Group Dynamics, 1953. **174, 175**

Lichter, S. O., E. B. Rapien, F. M. Seibert, and M. S. Sklansky. *The Drop-Outs*. New York: Free Press of Glencoe, 1962. **116, 117**

Liddell, H. S. "Conditioning and Emotions." *Scientific American*, 1954, *190*, 48–56. **31, 35**

————. *Emotional Hazards in Animals and Man*. Springfield, Ill.: Charles C Thomas, Publisher, 1956. **31, 37**

Lilly, J. C. "Mental Effects of Reduction of Ordinary Levels of Physical Stimuli on Intact, Healthy Persons." *Psychiatric Research Reports, American Psychiatric Association*, 1956, *5*, 1–28. **36**

Lindner, R. M. *Rebel Without a Cause*. New York: Grune & Stratton, 1944. **36**

Linkletter, A. *Kids Say the Darndest Things*. New York: Pocket Books, 1959. **90**

Lippitt, R., J. Watson, and B. Westley. *The Dynamics of Planned Change*. New York: Harcourt, Brace & World, 1958. **163**

Llano, G. A. *Airmen Against the Sea*. Maxwell Air Force Base, Ala.: Arctic, Desert, Tropic Information Center, Air University, 1955. **50, 53**

Lorge, I. "The Teacher's Task in the Development of Thinking." *Reading Teacher*, 1960, *13*, 170–75. **275**

Lowe, A. "Individual Differences in Reaction to Failure: Mode of Coping with Anxiety and Interference Proneness." *Journal of Abnormal and Social Psychology*, 1961, *62*, 303–8. **263**

Luchins, A. S. "Mechanization in Problem Solving: The Effect of *Einstellung*." *Psychological Monographs*, 1942, *54*, 1–4. **298**

McCarty, S. A. *Children's Drawings: A Study of Interest and Abilities*. Baltimore: The Williams & Wilkins Co., 1924. **310**

McConnell, T. R. "Discovery vs. Authoritative Identification in the Learning of Children." *University of Iowa Studies in Education*, 1934, *9(5)*, 13–62. **128**

McDonald, F. J. *Educational Psychology*, 2nd ed. Belmont, Calif.: Wadsworth Publishing Co., 1965. **125**

McKeachie, W. J., D. Pollie, and J. Speisman. "Relieving Anxiety in Classroom Examinations." *Journal of Abnormal and Social Psychology*, 1955, *50*, 93–98. **241**

MacKinnon, D. W. "The Highly Effective Individual." *Teachers College Record*, 1960, *61*, 367–78. **5, 306**

Macworth, N. H. *Cold Acclimatisation and Finger Numbness—Field and Laboratory Studies*. London: Medical Research Council, Royal Naval Personnel Research Committee, Climate Efficiency Sub-Committee, 1953. **54**

Maier, N. R. F., and A. R. Solem. "The Contributions of a Discussion Leader on the Quality of Group Thinking: The Effective Use of Minority Opinions." *Human Relations*, 1952, *5*, 277–88. **178**

Maltzman, I. "On the Training of Originality." *Psychological Review*, 1960, *67*, 229–42. **337**

————, J. Fox, and L. Morrisett, Jr. "Some Effects of Manifest Anxiety on Mental Set." *Journal of Experimental Psychology*, 1953, *46*, 50–54. **287**

Mann, F. C., and H. Baumgartel. "Absences and Employee Attitudes in an Electric Power Company." Ann Arbor: Institute for Social Research, University of Michigan, 1953. **174**

Mann, F. C., and J. E. Sparling. "Changing Absence Rates: An Application of Research Findings." *Personnel,* Jan. 1956, pp. 3–19. **174**

Markey, F. V. *Imaginative Behavior in Pre-School Children.* New York: Bureau of Publications, Teachers College, Columbia University, 1935. **311**

Marshall, S. L. A. *Men Against Fire.* New York: William Morrow & Co., 1947. **42, 157**

Maslow, A. H. *Motivation and Personality.* New York: Harper & Row, 1954. **15, 216, 229, 326**

Mayer, G., and M. Hoover. *When Children Need Special Help with Emotional Problems.* New York: Child Study Association of America, 1961. **120, 122**

Mead, M. *Sex and Temperament in Three Primitive Societies.* New York: William Morrow & Co., 1935. **8**

————. *The School in American Culture.* Cambridge, Mass.: Harvard University Press, 1951. **272**

Meadow, A., and S. J. Parnes. "Evaluation of Training in Creative Problem Solving." *Journal of Applied Psychology,* 1959, *43,* 189–94. **353**

Meerloo, J. A. M. *Patterns of Panic.* New York: International Universities Press, 1950. **40, 43, 48**

————. *The Rape of the Mind.* Cleveland: The World Publishing Co., 1956. **171**

Mellinger, G. D. "Communication, Consensus and Interpersonal Attraction." Doctoral dissertation. University of Michigan, 1955. **166**

————. "Interpersonal Trust as a Factor in Communication." *Journal of Abnormal and Social Psychology,* 1956, *52,* 304–9. **166**

Menninger, K. A. *Psychological Homeostasis and Organismic Integrity.* Topeka, Kan.: Publications Division, Menninger Clinic, 1956. **20, 47**

————. *The Vital Balance.* New York: The Viking Press, 1963. **47**

Merrifield, P. R., J. P. Guilford, P. R. Christensen, and J. W. Frick. *A Factor-Analytic Study of Problem-Solving Abilities.* Los Angeles: Psychological Laboratory, University of Southern California, 1960. **277**

Michael, D. N., and N. Maccoby. "Factors in Influencing Verbal Learning from Films Under Varying Conditions of Audience Participation." *Journal of Experimental Psychology,* 1953, *46,* 411–18. **224**

Milgram, S. "Behavioral Study of Obedience." *Journal of Abnormal and Social Psychology,* 1963, *67,* 371–378. **388**

Millar, G. *Horned Pigeon.* London: William Heinemann, 1953. **53**

Millar, W. M. *Valley of the Shadow.* New York: David McKay Co., 1955. **56**

Miller, E. B. *Bataan Uncensored.* Long Prairie, Minn.: Hart Publications, 1949. **236**

Miller, G. A. "Information and Memory." *Scientific American,* August 1956(a) *195,* 42–46. **266, 267**

————. The Magical Number Seven, Plus-or-Minus Two: Some Limits on Our Capacity for Processing Information." *Psychological Review,* 1956(b), *63,* 81–97. **266**

————. "Communication and Information as Limiting Factors in Group Formation." In *Symposium on Preventive and Social Psychiatry.* Washington, D. C.: Walter Reed Army Institute of Research, 1958. Pp. 1–13. **266**

Miller, J. G. *The Development of Experimental Stress-Sensitive Tests for Predicting Performance in Military Tasks.* Washington, D. C.: Adjutant General's Office, 1953. **24**

————. "Mental Health Implications of a General Behavior Theory." *American Journal of Psychiatry,* 1957, *113,* 776–82. **20, 46**

405

References and Index to Authors of Works Cited

Milton, G. A. "The Effects of Sex Role Identification Upon Problem-Solving Skill." *Journal of Abnormal and Social Psychology*, 1957, *55*, 208–12. **294**

Mintz, A. "Non-Adaptive Group Behavior." *Journal of Abnormal and Social Psychology*, 1951, *46*, 150–59. **44**

Moore, O. K. "Problem Solving and the Perception of Persons." In R. Tagiuri and L. Petrullo (Eds.), *Person Perception and Interpersonal Behavior.* Stanford, Calif.: Stanford University Press, 1958. Pp. 131–50. **97**

Moreno, J. L. *Who Shall Survive? A New Approach to the Problem of Human Interrelations.* Beacon, N. Y.: Beacon House, 1934. **11, 12, 85, 117, 173**

————. (ed.). *Sociometry and the Science of Man.* Beacon, N. Y.: Beacon House, 1956. **117, 173**

Moseley, H. G. "USAF Experience with Ejection Seat Escape." *Journal of Aviation Medicine.* 1957, *28*, 69–73. **50**

Mowrer, O. H. "An Experimental Analogue of 'Regression' with Incidental Observations on 'Reaction Formation.' " *Journal of Abnormal and Social Psychology*, 1940, *35*, 56–87. **265**

Murphy, G. *Personality: A Biosocial Approach to Origins and Structure.* New York: Harper & Row, 1947. **100**

————, and J. M. Levine. "The Learning and Forgetting of Controversial Material." In E. E. Maccoby, T. M. Newcomb, and E. L. Hartley (Eds.), *Readings in Social Psychology.* New York: Holt, Rinehart and Winston, 1958. Pp. 94–101. **262**

Murphy, L. B. "Learning How Children Cope With Problems." *Children*, July–August 1957(a), *4*. U. S. Department of Health, Education, and Welfare, Social Security Administration, Children's Bureau. **193, 194, 198**

————. "Psychoanalysis and Child Development, Part II." *Bulletin of the Menninger Clinic*, 1957(b), *21*, 248–58. **71**

————. *The Widening World of Childhood.* New York: Basic Books, 1962. **59, 193, 194, 195, 196, 200**

Myers, R. E. "Creative Writing and Training in Divergent Thinking." Master's thesis. Reed College, Portland, Ore., 1960. **341**

————, and E. P. Torrance. *Invitations to Thinking and Doing.* Eugene, Ore.: Perceptive Publishing Co., 1961. **341**

————, and E. P. Torrance. *Invitations to Speaking and Writing Creatively.* Eugene, Ore.: Perceptive Publishing Co., 1962. **341**

Myklebust, H. R. *The Psychology of Deafness: Sensory Deprivation, Learning and Adjustment.* New York: Grune and Stratton, 1960. **234**

Nansen, F. *Farthest North.* Vols. I and II. New York: Harper & Row, 1897. **54, 55, 56**

Nation's Business. *Make the Most of Your Time.* Washington, D. C.: Nation's Business, 1960. **382**

Newcomb, T. M. "The Prediction of Interpersonal Attraction." *American Psychologist*, 1956, *11*, 575–86. **97**

Nichols, R. G. "What Can Be Done About Listening?" *Supervisor's Notebook* (Scott, Foresman and Co.), 1960, *22(1)*, 1–4. **269**

Nicholson, P. J., III. "An Experimental Investigation of the Effects of Training Upon Creativity." Doctoral dissertation. University of Houston, Houston, Tex., 1959. **337**

Northway, M. L., and M. M. Rooks. "Creativity and Sociometric Status in Children." In J. L. Moreno (Ed.), *Sociometry and the Science of Man*. Beacon, N. Y.: Beacon House, 1955. Pp. 194–201. **173**

————, and L. Weld. *Sociometric Testing—A Guide for Teachers*. Toronto: University of Toronto Press, 1957. **117**

O'Kelly, L. I. "An Experimental Study of Regression. I. Behavioral Characteristics of the Regressive Response." *Journal of Comparative Psychology,* 1940, *30*, 41–53. **265**

Ornstein, J. "New Recruits for Science." *Parents' Magazine,* February 1961, *36(2)*, 42 ff. **128**

Osborn, A. F. *Developments in Creative Education*. Buffalo: Creative Education Foundation, 1960. **353**

————. *Applied Imagination,* 3rd ed. New York: Charles Scribner's Sons, 1963. **60, 308, 337, 343**

Panken, J. "Coercive Education—Menace." *Nervous Child,* 1946, *5*, 241–43. **303**

Parnes, S. J., and J. F. Harding (Eds.), *A Source Book for Creative Thinking*. New York: Charles Scribner's Sons, 1962. **337**

————, and A. Meadow. "Effects of 'Brainstorming' Instructions on Creative Problem Solving by Trained and Untrained Subjects." *Journal of Educational Psychology,* 1959, *50*, 171–76. **337**

————, and A. Meadow. "Evaluation of Persistence of Effects Produced by a Creative Problem-Solving Course." *Psychological Reports,* 1960, *7*, 357–61. **337, 353**

Patrick, C. *What is Creative Thinking?* New York: Philosophical Library, 1955. **131, 125, 317, 324**

Patterson, T. T., and E. J. Willett. "An Anthropological Experiment in a British Colliery." *Human Organization,* 1951, *10*, 19–23. **174**

Paul, I. H. *Studies in Remembering*. New York: International Universities Press, 1959. **244, 246–248**

Pavlov, I. P. *Lectures on Conditioned Reflexes*. (Translated by W. H. Gantt.) New York: International Publishers Co., 1928. **31, 35**

Peak, H. "Psychological Structure and Person Perception." In R. Tagiuri and L. Petrullo (Eds.), *Person Perception and Interpersonal Behavior*. Stanford, Calif.: Stanford University Press, 1958. Pp. 337–52. **97**

Pepitone, A. "Motivational Effects of Social Perception." *Human Relations,* 1950, *3*, 57–76. **166**

Petrullo, L., and B. M. Bass (Eds.). *Leadership and Interpersonal Behavior*. New York: Holt, Rinehart and Winston, 1961. **139**

Polya, G. *How to Solve It*. Princeton, N. J.: Princeton University Press, 1945. **277**

Powell, J. W., and J. Rayner. *Progress Notes: Disaster Investigation July 1, 1951–June 30, 1952*. Edgewood, Md.: Army Chemical Center, Medical Laboratories, 1952. **164**

Quarantelli, E. L. "The Nature and Conditions of Panic." *American Journal of Sociology,* 1954, *60*, 267–75. **39–40**

Rank, O. *Art and Artist*. New York: Alfred A. Knopf, 1932. **318**

Rapaport, D. *Emotions and Memory*. New York: International Universities Press, 1950. **255**

————, M. Gill, and R. Schafer. *Diagnostic Psychological Testing, Vol. I*. Chicago: Year Book Publishing Co., 1945. **218**

Rasmussen, G., and A. Zander. "Group Membership and Self Evaluation." *Human Relations*, 1954, *7*, 239–51. **167**

Raths, L. E. "Sociological Knowledge and Needed Curriculum Research." In J. B. MacDonald (Ed.), *Research Frontiers in the Study of Children's Learning*. Milwaukee: School of Education, University of Wisconsin, Milwaukee, 1960. Pp. 21–34. **285**

Raven, B. H., and J. Rietsema. "The Effects of Varied Clarity of Group Goal and Group Path Upon the Individual and His Relation to His Group." *Human Relations*, 1957, *10*, 29–45. **181**

Redl, F., and W. W. Wattenberg. *Mental Hygiene in Teaching*, 2nd ed. New York: Harcourt, Brace & World, 1959. **119, 120, 270, 274**

Reynolds, G. S. "The Effects of Stress Upon Problem-Solving." *Journal of General Psychology*, 1960, *62*, 83–8. **293**

Rich, C. J. "The Tradition of Force and Punishment." *Nervous Child*, 1946, *5*, 222–25. **303**

Rickenbacker, E. *Seven Came Through*. New York: Doubleday & Co., 1943. **260**

Ritholz, S. *Children's Behavior*. New York: Bookman Associates, 1959.

Roe, A. "Personal Problems and Science." In C. W. Taylor (Ed.), *The Third (1959) University of Utah Research Conference on the Identification of Creative Scientific Talent*. Salt Lake City: University of Utah Press, 1959. Pp. 202–12. **318, 335**

———. "Crucial Life Experiences in the Development of Scientists." In E. P. Torrance (Ed.), *Talent and Education*. Minneapolis: University of Minnesota Press, 1960. Pp. 66–77. **232**

Rogers, C. R. *Client-Centered Therapy*. Boston: Houghton Mifflin Co., 1951. **15**

———. "What It Means to Become a Person." In C. E. Moustokas (Ed.), *The Self*. New York: Harper & Row, 1956. Pp. 195–211. **224**

———. *On Becoming a Person*. Boston: Houghton Mifflin Co., 1961. **326**

Rokeach, M. "The Effect of Perception Time Upon Rigidity and Concreteness of Thinking." *Journal of Experimental Psychology*, 1950, *40*, 206–16. **370**

———. *The Open and Closed Mind*. New York: Basic Books, 1960.

Rosen, B. C. "Race, Ethnicity, and Achievement." *American Sociological Review*, 1959, *24*, 47–60. **231, 232**

Roucek, J. S. (Ed.). *The Difficult Child*. New York: Philosophical Library, 1964. **326**

Rouse, S. T. "Effects of a Training Program with Educable Mental Retardates on Selected Tests of Productive Thinking." Doctoral dissertation. George Peabody Teachers College, Nashville, Tenn., 1963. **338**

Ruch, F. L. *Psychology and Life*, 4th ed. Chicago: Scott, Foresman and Co., 1953. **264**

Russell, B. *Philosophy*. New York: W. W. Norton & Co., 1927. **292**

Russell, D. H. *Children's Thinking*. Boston: Ginn and Co., 1956. **295, 324, 325**

———, and P. J. Groff. "Personnel Factors Influencing Perception in Reading." *Education*, 1955, *75*, 600–603. **284**

Sarason, S. B., K. Davidson, F. Lighthall, R. Waite, and B. K. Ruebush. *Anxiety in Elementary School Children*. New York: John Wiley & Sons, 1960. **237**

Schachtel, E. G. "The Development of Focal Attention and the Emergence of Reality." *Psychiatry*, 1954, *17*, 309–24. **235**

Schachter, S. *The Psychology of Affiliation*. Stanford, Calif.: Stanford University Press, 1959. **75, 76, 77**

Schafer, R. *The Clinical Application of Psychological Tests.* New York: International Universities Press, 1948. **218**

Schilder, P. *Medical Psychology.* New York: International Universities Press, 1953. **261**

Schutz, W. C. "What Makes Groups Productive?" *Human Relations,* 1955, *8,* 429–65. **84, 85**

————. *FIRO: A Three-Dimensional Theory of Interpersonal Behavior.* New York: Holt, Rinehart and Winston, 1958. **178**

————. "Empirical Tests of the FIRO Theory of Interpersonal Behavior." Cambridge, Mass.: Laboratory of Social Relations, Harvard University, 1959. (Dittoed) **85–86**

Schwartz, S., and B. Winograd. "Preparation of Soldiers for Atomic Maneuvers." *Journal of Social Issues,* 1954, *10,* 42–52. **223**

Scott, W. A. "Research Definitions in Mental Health and Mental Illness." *Psychological Bulletin,* 1958, *55,* 29–45. **12**

Sears, R. R. "Experimental Analysis of Psychoanalytic Phenomena." In J. McV. Hunt (Ed.), *Personality and Behavior Disorders,* Vol. 1. New York: The Ronald Press Co., 1944. Pp. 306–32. **70, 77**

Secord, P. F. "Facial Features and Inference Processes in Interpersonal Perception." In R. Tagiuri and L. Petrullo (Eds.), *Person Perception and Interpersonal Behavior.* Stanford, Calif.: Stanford University Press, 1958. Pp. 300–315. **97**

Seidman, J. M. (Ed.). *Educating for Mental Health,* New York: Thomas Y. Crowell Co., 1963. **387**

Selye, H. *The Physiology and Pathology of Stress.* Montreal: Acta, 1950. **20, 46**

————. *The Stress of Life.* New York: McGraw-Hill Book Co., 1956. **20, 46, 196**

Shackle, G. L. S. "Final Comments." In C. F. Carter, G. P. Meredith, and G. L. S. Shackle (Eds.), *Uncertainty and Business Decisions.* Liverpool: University of Liverpool Press. 1954. Pp. 98–100. **367**

Shands, H. C. *Thinking and Psychotherapy.* Cambridge, Mass.: Harvard University Press, 1960. **298**

Sheviakov, G. V., and F. Redl. *Discipline for Today's Children and Youth.* (Revision by Sybil K. Richardson.) Washington, D. C.: Association for Supervision and Curriculum Development, 1956. **105**

Shils, E., and M. Janowitz. "Cohesion and Disintegration in the Wehrmacht in World War II." *Public Opinion Quarterly,* 1949, *12,* 281. **55**

Simpson, R. M. "Creative Imagination." *American Journal of Psychology,* 1922, *33,* 234–43. **311**

Small, W. E. "Bats, Porpoises Teach Electronics." *Science News Letter,* June 30, 1962, *81(26),* 410–11. **337**

Smith, E. E. "Individual versus Group Goal Conflict." *Journal of Abnormal and Social Psychology,* 1959, *58,* 134–37. **154–155, 157, 388**

Sontag, L. M., C. T. Baker, and V. Nelson. "Mental Growth and Personality Development: A Longitudinal Survey." *Society for Research on Child Development Monograph,* 1958, *86,* 23. **115**

Spearman, C. E. *Creative Mind.* London: Cambridge University Press, 1930. **280**

Spiegel, J. P. "Emotional Reactions to Catastrophe." In S. Liebman (Ed.), *Stress Situations.* Philadelphia: J. B. Lippincott Co., 1955. Pp. 37–66. **51**

References and Index to Authors of Works Cited

Spitz, R. A. "Hospitalism." In *Psychoanalytic Study of the Child*. Vol. 1. New York: International Universities Press, 1945. Pp. 53–74. **37**

Stecklein, J. E. "How to Measure More Than Facts with Multiple-Choice Items." (*Bulletin on Classroom Testing* No. 7.) Minneapolis: Bureau of Institutional Research, University of Minnesota, 1956. **241**

Stewart, G. R. *Ordeal by Hunger: The Story of the Donner Party*. New York: Holt, Rinehart and Winston, 1936. **171**

Stotland, E., S. Thorley, E. Thomas, A. R. Cohen, and A. Zander. "The Effects of Group Expectations and Self-Esteem upon Self-Evaluation." *Journal of Abnormal and Social Psychology*, 1957, *54*, 55–63. **167**

Suchman, J. R. "Inquiry Training: Building Skills for Autonomous Discovery." *Merrill-Palmer Quarterly*, 1961(a), *7*, 147–70. **351, 373**

————. "The University of Illinois Studies in Inquiry Training." In E. P. Torrance (Ed.), *New Educational Ideas: Third Minnesota Conference on Gifted Children*. Minneapolis: Center for Continuation Study, University of Minnesota, 1961(b). Pp. 67–84. **351, 374**

✗ ————. *The Elementary School Training Program in Scientific Inquiry*. Urbana: School of Education, University of Illinois, 1962. **334**

Sullivan, H. S. *The Interpersonal Theory of Psychiatry*. New York: W. W. Norton & Co., 1953. **15, 80, 81, 90, 91, 94, 95, 129**

————. *The Psychiatric Interview*. New York: W. W. Norton & Co., 1954. **80**

Super, D. E. *The Psychology of Careers*. New York: Harper & Row, 1957. **107, 109, 110**

Tagiuri, R. "Social Preference and Its Perception." In R. Tagiuri and L. Petrullo (Eds.), *Person Perception and Interpersonal Behavior*. Stanford, Calif.: Stanford University Press, 1958. Pp. 316–36. **97, 350**

————, and L. Petrullo (Eds.), *Person Perception and Interpersonal Behavior*. Stanford, Calif.: Stanford University Press, 1958. **97, 350**

Tannenbaum, A. J. *Adolescent Attitudes Toward Academic Brilliance*. New York: Bureau of Publications, Teachers College, Columbia University, 1962. **230**

Taylor, H. L., J. Brözek, A. Henschel, O. Mickelson, and A. Keys. "The Effects of Successive Fasts on the Ability of Men to Withstanding Fasting During Hard Work." *American Journal of Physiology*, 1945, *143*, 148–55. **123, 206**

Tchernavin, T. *Escape from the Soviets*. New York: E. P. Dutton & Co., 1934. **50**

Thorndike, E. L., et al. *The Measurement of Intelligence*. New York: Bureau of Publications, Teachers College, Columbia University, 1927. **189, 190**

Thrall, R. M., C. H. Coombs, and R. L. Davis (Eds.). *Decision Processes*. New York: John Wiley & Sons, 1954. **369**

Thurstone, L. L. "Primary Mental Abilities." *Psychometric Monograph No. 1*, 1938. **189, 347**

————. "A Factorial Study of Perception." *Psychometric Monograph No. 4*, 1944. **308, 347**

Tindall, R. H. "Relationships Among Measures of Adjustment." *Educational and Psychological Measurement*, 1955, *15*, 152–62. **12**

Titus, H. E., and E. P. Hollander. "The California F Scale in Psychological Research: 1950–1955." *Psychological Bulletin*, 1957, *54*, 47–64. **239**

Tolman, E. C. *Collected Papers in Psychology*. Berkeley: University of California Press, 1951. **262**

Torrance, E. P. "Self-Concepts and Their Significance in the Learning and Adjustment of College Freshmen." Doctoral dissertation, University of Michigan, 1951. **43**

————. "Methods of Conducting Critiques of Group Problem-Solving Performance." *Journal of Applied Psychology*, 1953, *37*, 394–98. **183, 357**

————. *Psychological Aspects of Survival: A Study of Survival Behavior.* Washington, D. C.: Human Factors Operations Research Laboratories, Bolling Air Force Base, 1954(a). **142, 223**

————. "The Behavior of Small Groups Under Stress Conditions of Survival." *American Sociological Review*, 1954(b), *19*, 751–55. **146**

————. "Some Consequences of Power Differences in Decision Making in Permanent and Temporary Three-Man Groups." *Research Studies of the State College of Washington*, 1954(c), *22*, 130–40. Also in A. P. Hare, E. F. Borgatta, and R. F. Bales (Eds.), *Small Groups*. New York: Alfred A. Knopf, 1955. Pp. 482–92. **157, 158, 176, 178, 300, 356**

————. "The Relationship of Attitudes and Changes in Attitudes Toward Survival Adequacy to the Achievement of Survival Knowledge." *Journal of Social Psychology*, 1954(d), *40*, 259–65. **223**

————. "Techniques for Studying Individual and Group Adaptation in Emergencies and Extreme Conditions." In G. Finch and F. Cameron (Eds.), *Symposium on Air Force Human Engineering, Personnel, and Training Research*. Washington, D. C.: National Academy of Sciences–Research Council, 1956(a). Pp. 286–97. **122**

————. "Sociometric Techniques for Diagnosing Group Ills." In J. L. Moreno (Ed.) *Sociometry and the Science of Man*. Beacon, N. Y.: Beacon House, 1956(b). Pp. 241–56. **85**

————. "Group Decision-Making and Disagreement." *Social Forces*, 1957(a), *35*, 314–18. **125, 157, 158, 159, 172, 300**

————. "What Happens to the Sociometric Structure of Small Groups in Emergencies and Extreme Conditions." *Group Psychotherapy*, 1957(b), *10*, 212–20. **147**

————. "Leadership in the Survival of Small Isolated Groups." In *Preventive and Social Psychiatry*. Washington, D. C.: Walter Reed Medical Research Center, 1958(a). Pp. 309–27. **141, 151, 152, 172, 302**

————. *Alone or in Groups?* Minneapolis: Bureau of Educational Research, University of Minnesota, 1958(b). **169**

————. "An Experimental Evaluation of 'No Pressure' Influence." *Journal of Applied Psychology*, 1959(a), *43*, 109–13. **8, 25**

————. "The Influence of Experienced Members of Small Groups on the Behavior of the Inexperienced." *Journal of Social Psychology*, 1959(b), *49* 249–57. **123**

————. "Sensitization versus Adaptability in Preparing for Emergencies." *Journal of Applied Psychology*, 1959(c), *43*, 109–13. **206**

————. "A Theory of Leadership and Interpersonal Behavior Under Stress." In L. Petrullo and B. M. Bass (Eds.), *Leadership and Interpersonal Behavior*. New York: Holt, Rinehart and Winston, 1961. Pp. 100–117. **139**

————. *Guiding Creative Talent.* Englewood Cliffs, N. J.: Prentice-Hall, 1962. **312, 331, 334, 336**

————. *Education and the Creative Potential.* Minneapolis: University of Minnesota Press, 1963. **91, 231, 337, 338, 339**

Torrance, E. P. *Role of Evaluation in Creative Thinking.* (Report on Project Number 725, Cooperative Research Branch, U. S. Office of Education.) Minneapolis Bureau of Educational Research, University of Minnesota, 1964. **126, 314, 340, 342, 344, 352**

————, and K. Arsan. "Experimental Studies of Homogeneous and Heterogeneous Groups for Creative Scientific Tasks." In W. W. Charters, Jr., and N. L. Gage (Eds.), *Readings in the Social Psychology of Education.* Boston: Allyn and Bacon, 1963. Pp. 133–40. **342**

————, and J. A. Harmon. "Effects of Memory, Evaluative, and Creative Reading Sets on Test Performance." *Journal of Educational Psychology,* 1961, *52,* 207–14. **224, 344, 352**

————, R. LaForge, and R. Mason. *Group Adaptation in Emergencies and Extreme Conditions.* Randolph Air Force Base, Tex.: Office for Social Science Programs, Air Force Personnel and Training Research Center, 1956. **142, 143, 151, 154, 157, 158, 159, 301**

————, and R. Mason. "The Indigenous Leader in Changing Attitudes and Behavior." *International Journal of Sociometry,* 1956, *1,* 23–38. **152**

————, and R. Mason. "Instructor Effort to Influence: An Experimental Evaluation of Six Approaches." *Journal of Educational Psychology,* 1958, *49,* 211–18. **25–27**

————, and R. E. Myers. *Teaching Gifted Elementary Children How to Do Research.* Eugene, Ore. Perceptive Publishing Co., 1962. **244**

————, and J. Ross. *Improving Social Studies Education in Minnesota.* Minneapolis: Bureau of Educational Research, University of Minnesota, 1961. **216**

————, and R. C. Ziller. *Risk and Life Experience: Development of a Scale for Measuring Risk-Taking Tendencies.* Lackland Air Force Base, Tex.: Air Force Personnel and Training Research Center, 1957. (*Research Report* AFPTRC–TN–57–23, ASTIA Document No. 09826.) **198, 299**

————, and R. C. Ziller. "Crew Conditions Under Conditions of Uncertainty." In G. Finch and F. Cameron (Eds.), *Symposium on Air Force Human Engineering, Personnel, and Training Research.* Washington, D. C.: National Academy of Sciences–National Research Council, 1958. Pp. 2–26. **299**

True, G. H. "Creativity as a Function of Idea Fluency, Practicability, and Specific Training." Doctoral dissertation. Iowa State University, 1956. **337**

Tyhurst, J. "Emergent Leadership." In *Preventive and Social Psychiatry.* Washington, D. C.: Walter Reed Medical Research Center, 1958. Pp. 329–35. **142**

Tyson, R. "Monograph Supplement: Current Mental Hygiene Practice." *Journal of Clinical Psychology,* 1951, *7,* 2–94. **9**

Van Doren, C. C. *Benjamin Franklin.* New York: The Viking Press, 1938. **110**

Von Neumann, J., and O. Morgenstern. *Theory of Games and Economic Behavior,* 2nd ed. Princeton, N. J.: Princeton University Press, 1947. **367**

Waite, R. R., S. B. Sarason, F. F. Lighthall, and K. S. Davidson. "A Study of Anxiety and Learning in Children." *Journal of Abnormal and Social Psychology,* 1958, *57,* 267–70. **263**

Weber, C. A. "Let's Teach Them How to Decide." *Phi Delta Kappan,* 1953, *34(4),* 119–124f. **346**

Weinland, J. D. *How to Improve Your Memory.* New York: Barnes & Noble, 1957. **253, 261, 264, 268**

Wellington, C. B., and J. Wellington. *Teaching for Critical Thinking.* New York: McGraw-Hill Book Co., 1960. **376**

Whyte, A. P. L. *Escape to Fight Again.* London: George C. Harrap, 1942. **51**

Whyte, W. H., Jr. *The Organization Man.* New York: Simon and Schuster, 1956. **5**

Wile, I. S. "What Constitutes Abnormality?" *American Journal of Orthopsychiatry,* 1940, *10,* 216–28. **13**

Will, Patricia P. "A Study of the Effects of Possible Emotional Disturbance on the Creative Behavior of a Group of Delinquent Girls." Master's research paper. University of Minnesota, 1964. **317**

Williams, S. B. "Transfer of Extinction Effects in the Rat as a Function of Habit Strength." *Journal of Comparative Psychology,* 1941, *31,* 263–80. **72**

Witkin, H. A., H. B. Lewis, M. Hertzman, K. Machover, P. B. Meissner, and S. Wapner. *Personality Through Perception.* New York: Harper & Row, 1954. **221**

Wolf, A. "The Dynamics of the Selective Inhibition of Specific Functions in Neurosis: A Preliminary Report." *Psychosomatic Medicine,* 1943, *5.* **35**

Wolfenstein, M. *Disaster.* New York: Free Press of Glencoe, 1957. **43, 44**

Yamamoto, K. "Development of Ability to Ask Questions Under Specific Testing Conditions." *Journal of Genetic Psychology,* 1962, *101,* 83–90. **351**

Zander, A., A. Cohen, and E. Stotland. *Role Relations in the Mental Health Professions.* Ann Arbor: Research Center for Group Dynamics, University of Michigan, 1957. **95, 96, 159, 167**

————, E. Thomas, and T. Natsoulas. *Determinants of Motivation and Performance Under Pressure.* Ann Arbor: Research Center for Group Dynamics, University of Michigan, 1957. **66, 67, 159, 167**

Zeigarnik, B. "Über das behalten von arlidigten handlungen." *Psychologische Forschung,* 1927, 9, 1–85. **265**

Ziller, R. C. "Leader Flexibility and Group Cohesiveness: Determinants of Group Problem-Solving Processes and Concomitant Affective Group Member Behavior." *American Psychologist,* 1953, *8,* 159. (Abstract) **154, 157, 158**

————. "Leader Acceptance of Responsibility for Group Action Under Conditions of Uncertainty and Risk." *American Psychologist,* 1955(a), *10,* 475–76. (Abstract) **301, 302**

————. "Scales of Group Judgment: A Determinant of the Accuracy of Group Decisions." *Human Relations,* 1955(b), *8,* 153–64. **301, 302, 308**

————. "Four Techniques of Group Decision-Making Under Uncertainty." *Journal of Applied Psychology,* 1957(a), *41,* 384–88. **157, 158, 299**

————. "Group Size: A Determinant of the Quality and Stability of Group Decisions." *Sociometry,* 1957(b), *20,* 165–73. **176, 302**

Subject
Index

A

Absenteeism, 174, 183
Absorption in thinking, 329
Abstracting, 248, 355
Acceptance:
  of assignments, 181
  of authority, 80–81, 88, 285
  of facts, 205
  of fear appeals, 263
  of food, 26
  by the group, 174
  of group decisions, 301, 383
  of guidance, 204
  of incorrect information, 272
  of inferior solutions, 177
  of limitations, 195, 321, 362
  of need to remember, 270
  of seriousness of situation, 22–23, 205
Accidents, 35, 174–175
Acclimatization, 54
Achievement:
  lack of, 143, 167, 194, 205
  standards of, 139
  tests, 205, 217, 224–225, 240, 344, 364, 373
Activity:
  as antidote, 53, 221
  based on best-supported hypotheses, 277
  creative, 318
  exploratory, 107–108, 200, 268, 325, 334, 351, 357
  intense, 265
  new, 285
  organized, 24
  ritualistic, 72
  sustained mental, 262
  unusual, 180
Adaptation:
  continued, 22–23, 53–54, 271, 383
  energy, 54, 128, 168, 196, 256
  level, 119
  over time, 50, 100, 143–145
  process of, 19–27, 47–48, 140, 207
  rejection of demands for, 124
  and state of organism, 29

Addiction, 71, 73, 122
Adolescence, 73, 81, 93–95, 105, 111, 121–122, 123, 229, 299
Affect, 146–147, 154–156, 169–175, 331
Affective psychoses, 135
Age and achievement, 109
Aggressiveness, 114, 130, 163, 193, 199, 201, 270, 343
Aimlessness, 108
Aircrews, 25–26, 38, 50, 55–56, 141, 172, 260, 356
Alarm, 42, 122
Alcohol, 235
Alcoholism, 70, 122
Allport-Vernon-Lindzey *Study of Values*, 5
Alternate Uses Test, 309
Altruism, 330
Ambiguous stimuli, 41, 223, 247, 331, 363
Amnesic state, 40, 254
Anaclitic love object, 77, 78
Anagrams, 213, 288
Anal:
  erotic, 71–72
  sadistic, 71–73
  stage, 71–72
Analysis, 277, 285, 297, 382
Anchors in reality, inadequate, 32, 39, 42, 45, 58–59, 62, 389
Anger, 89, 237
Aniseikonik Lenses Test, 219
Anticipatory panic, 40
Anxiety:
  arousal of, 41, 167, 193, 196, 229
  and convergent thinking, 287
  and learning, 237
  and memory, 259, 263
  reduction or relief of, 69–70, 73, 115, 116, 235, 237, 260, 268
  as a restricter of awareness, 94
  states, 131–132
  and thinking, 286
Apathy, 18, 47, 48, 109, 121, 122, 145, 163, 168, 195, 204, 207, 301, 343, 378
Apparent Movement Test, 219

415

172